The Poverty of Pr

CHANGING WAYS OF LIFE IN IN

Other Titles of Interest

Dammann, E.
The Future in Our Hands

Diwan, R. K. & Livingston, D.
Alternative Development Strategies and Appropriate
Technology

Forslin, J., Sarapata, A., & Whitehall, A.
Automation and Industrial Workers

Giarini, O. & Louberge, H.
The Diminishing Returns of Technology

Lozoya, J.
The Social and Cultural Issues of the New International
Economic Order

Peccei, A.
The Human Quality

Sauvant, K.
Changing Priorities on the International Economic Order

Tevoedjre, A.
Poverty: Wealth of Mankind

Tropman, J., Dluhy, M., & Lind, R.
New Strategic Perspectives on Social Policy

Related Journals*

WORLD DEVELOPMENT

The multi-disciplinary journal devoted to the study and
promotion of world development.
Chairman of the Editorial Board: Paul Streeten, Center for
Asian Development Studies, Boston University, USA

TECHNOLOGY IN SOCIETY

The international interdisciplinary journal which creates a single
forum for the discussion of the political, economic and
cultural roles of technology in society, social forces that
shape technological decisions, and choices open to society
in the use of technology.
Editors: Dr. George Bugliarello and Dr. A. George Schillinger,
Polytechnic Institute of New York, Brooklyn, USA

* Free specimen copy available on request

The Poverty of Progress

CHANGING WAYS OF LIFE IN INDUSTRIAL SOCIETIES

Selected proceedings of two international conferences
on 'Alternative Ways of Life', organized by the Goals,
Processes and Indicators of Development Project of the
United Nations University and by the Society for
International Development, held in Cartigny,
Switzerland, 1978, and Trappeto, Sicily, 1979

Edited by

Ian Miles and John Irvine

Science Policy Research Unit, University of Sussex, UK

with

Monica Wemegah and Dag Poleszynski

PERGAMON PRESS
OXFORD · NEW YORK · TORONTO · SYDNEY · PARIS · FRANKFURT

U.K.	Pergamon Press Ltd., Headington Hill Hall, Oxford OX3 OBW, England
U.S.A.	Pergamon Press Inc., Maxwell House, Fairview Park, Elmsford, New York 10523, U.S.A.
CANADA	Pergamon Press Canada Ltd., Suite 104, 150 Consumers Rd., Willowdale, Ontario M2J 1P9, Canada
AUSTRALIA	Pergamon Press (Aust.) Pty. Ltd., P.O. Box 544, Potts Point, N.S.W. 2011, Australia
FRANCE	Pergamon Press SARL, 24 rue des Ecoles, 75240 Paris, Cedex 05, France
FEDERAL REPUBLIC OF GERMANY	Pergamon Press GmbH, 6242 Kronberg-Taunus, Hammerweg 6, Federal Republic of Germany

First edition 1982

Library of Congress Cataloging in Publication Data
Main entry under title:
The Poverty of Progress.
"Selected proceedings of two international conferences on 'alternative ways of life', organised by the Goals, Processes, and Indicators of Development Project of the United Nations University and by the Society for International Development, held in Cartigny, Switzerland, 1978, and Trappeto, Sicily, 1979."
Contents: Introduction/John Irvine and Ian Miles – Why the concern with ways of life?/ Johan Galtung, Dag Poleszynski, and Monica Wemegah – The 'abundant society and world order/Steven Arnold and Denis Goulet – (etc.)
1. Social history–1970 – Congresses.
2. Quality of life–Congresses. 3. Social change– Congresses. I. Miles, Ian. II. Irvine, John, fl. 1979- III. United Nations University.
IV. Society for International Development.
HN3.P68   1982   303.4   81-17779

British Library Cataloguing in Publication Data
The Poverty of Progress.
1. Social change-Congresses
I. Miles, Ian II. Irvine, John
III. Goals, Processes and Indicators of Development Project IV. Society for International Development
303.4   HM101

ISBN 0-08-028906-1 (Hardcover)
     0-08-027935-X (Flexicover)

In order to make this volume available as economically and as rapidly as possible the authors' typescripts have been reproduced in their original forms. This method unfortunately has its typographical limitations but it is hoped that they in no way distract the reader.

Printed in Great Britain by A Wheaton & Co. Ltd., Exeter

Preface

SARTAJ AZIZ

One of the most significant 'discoveries' of the development
dialogue of the mid-1970s was the realization that the search
for alternative development strategies could not be confined
to low income developing countries, but was an equally relevant
and urgent priority for the industrialized countries.

Initially this realization was spurred by the energy crisis
of 1973-4 and by other reports that the physical resources of
this world were finite and the rate at which they were being
used was excessive and wasteful. But very soon the list of
ills and problems facing the industrialized countries became
longer and more formidable: these countries had conquered want,
and, in terms of material well-being, all their citizens were
able to meet their basic needs, but this had rapidly led to
overconsumption for a sizeable segment of the population. At
the same time, this overemphasis on material progress, through
ruthless competition, was slowly but surely destroying some of
the more basic social values, like respect for the family and
the community and the place of human compassion in our lives.
As a result, while economically and industrially these advanced
countries had made remarkable progress, and had also evolved
democratic political institutions, socially they were bursting
at the seams. This was clearly reflected in the rising incidence of senseless crime and violence and in the growing
sense of insecurity felt by people living in Europe and the USA.

This analysis inevitably led to the conclusion that the industrialized countries had not been able to achieve balanced
social and economic development, but in a certain sense were
'maldeveloped' — i.e. overdeveloped in economic and material
terms, but underdeveloped in non-material and social terms.

It was against this background that the Society for International Development (SID) began, under its new mandate, its
programme on Alternative Development Strategies in 1977. A

viii   Preface

study of the Alternative Ways of Life in high income countries
was an important part of this programme and was undertaken in
collaboration with the United Nations University project on
'Goals, Processes and Indicators of Development'. This volume
presents the results of this sub-programme.

The SID World Conference held in Colombo, Sri Lanka, in
August 1979, at which some of the papers in this volume were
presented, confirmed once more that there are no easy development choices for either rich or poor countries for the remaining
two decades of this century. Both groups have run out of soft
options. But the problems they face in these 20 years will be
more formidable than those they tackled in the preceding 20
years. As a result, the conflict between short-term political
expediency and longer-term objectives will probably be even
sharper.

These papers present a number of concrete ideas on how to
achieve a better balance between economic and social objectives.
They call for a major movement, through mutually reinforcing
programmes, to correct the main ills of the dominant ways of
life in industrialized societies and to prepare the ground for
alternative ways of life. It is hoped that this volume will
help to stimulate further debate on these questions and will
encourage more and more people to join the search for more
meaningful ways of life.

Rome, September 1980   S. Aziz
                        Society for International Development

<u>NOTE</u>
   Since the production of this book was completed, the Society
for International Development has continued its interest in
Alternative Development Strategies and changing ways of life.
This is reflected, for example, in its journal *Development,* and
in the work of its Grass Roots Information Service. SID's
International Headquarters are based at Palazzo Civiltà del
Lavoro, 00144 Roma, Italy.

March 1982   P. Wignaraja
                                          SID Secretary-General

Acknowledgements

The editors wish to express their gratitude to the Society for
International Development, and the United Nations University,
for encouraging and sponsoring the series of meetings on
'Alternative Ways of Life' on which this volume is largely
based. They are also grateful to the EEC for providing financial
support for subsequent editorial work. The hosts and participants in these meetings, of course, must take much of the credit
for the appearance of this volume. Particular thanks are due to
Johan Galtung, who co-ordinated the Goals, Processes and Indicators of Development Project of the United Nations University,
Monica Wcmcgah who co-ordinated the 'Alternative Ways of Life'
sub-project, and Catherine Pfister who provided central secre-
tarial assistance, over this period.
Our work as editors would have been impossible without the
congenial environment of the Science Policy Research Unit as
our intellectual base, even if our homes and friends have taken
most of the strain of our work here. Numerous secretaries have
struggled with our often illegible drafts, but particular
thanks are due to those who suffered most heavily: Anne Tyrrel,
Judi Wilks and Helen Williams. For their companionship, tolerance, and therapeutic powers, our appreciation to Liliana Acero,
Pat Aspinall, Matthew Forster, Dot Griffiths, Rose Lacey, Ben
Martin and Howard Rush.
Sources of data are given under each table and listed in the
bibliography at the end of each chapter. We are grateful to
Annuaire Statistique Suisse and to Z-Verlag for permission to
use material in Chapter 4. For the chapter on Great Britain,
our thanks are due to Her Majesty's Stationery Office for permission to use the many tables drawn from a wide range of their
publications; to Earth Resources Research Publications for
permission to use several tables from C. Wardle (1977) *Changing
Food Habits in the UK;* and to the author and the Clarendon

Press for allowing us to use data from J. Goldthorpe (1980) *Social Mobility and Class Structure in Modern Britain*. Table 10.1 originally appeared in OECD (1976) *Public Expenditure on Income Maintenance*. The Food and Agriculture Organization of the United Nations has given permission to reproduce Table 10.2 which originally appeared in *Population, Food Supply and Agricultural Development* in 1975.

While every attempt has been made to trace copyright owners, this has not been possible in all cases. Any owner of copyrighted material which has not been acknowledged is requested to contact the publisher.

Contents

List of Contributors

Steven H. Arnold is an Associate Professor at the School of
International Service of The American University in Washington
DC. His research has focused on 'North-South' relations,
including articles and monographs on the impact of the United
States, selected European nations, and international financial
institutions upon Third World development. He is also the
Director of the International Development Programme at the
University.

Peter Ester is a Research Fellow at the Institute of Environ-
mental Studies, Free University of Amsterdam. He is a socio-
logist, and his research has mainly concerned environmental
problems, energy conservation and certain aspects of theoretical
sociology. He is the editor of two books: *Social Aspects of
Environmental Problems* (Assen, 1979) and *Energy as a Social
Problem* (Assen, 1981). In 1981 he was Visiting Professor at
Claremont Graduate College, Pomona, California, and Virginia
Polytechnic Institute and State University, Blacksburg,
Virginia.

Jens Falkentorp is a translator. Since 1975 he has been active
in grassroots movements and groups like 'Support Christiania',
'The New Society', 'Community Action in Europe' and 'No to
Nuclear Arms', mainly in the communication field.

Johan Galtung is Professor of Development Studies at the
Institut Universitaire d'Études du Développement in Geneva and
until 1981 co-ordinated the Goals, Processes and Indicators of
Development project of the United Nations University. He is
the author of about 700 research articles and books in methodology, social science theory and empirical studies, and particularly in peace and conflict, development and futures studies

xiii

— among them *Theory and Methods of Social Research* (Allen and
Unwin, 1967), *Essays in Peace Research,* Vols. I-V (Ejlers,
Copenhagen, 1975-80) and *The True Worlds* (Free Press, New York,
1980).

Denis Goulet is O'Neill Professor in Education for Justice at
the University of Notre Dame and Associate Fellow of the Over-
seas Development Council. His research centres on value con-
flicts posed by development and the policy requirements of
pursuing alternative strategies in culturally diverse settings.
His major books include *The Cruel Choice, The Myth of Aid* (with
Michael Hudson), *A New Moral Order,* and *The Uncertain Promise.*
Of special interest are two recent studies: *Looking at Guinea-
Bissau: A New Nation's Development Strategy* and *Survival With
Integrity: Sarvodaya at the Crossroads.*

Dino Hansen is a sinologist. As well as lecturing at the Ros-
kilde University, Denmark, he works as an author and film
documentarist. He has written numerous articles on modern China
and books on Mao and the Chinese Revolution and Mao Documents,
1956-74. Since the beginning of 1980 he has been participating
in a research project concerning worker-owned enterprises and
producer co-operatives and collectives in Denmark.

John Irvine is a Fellow of the Science Policy Research Unit,
University of Sussex, where he works on a range of issues connected with science, technology and the future. He is the co-
editor of *Demystifying Social Statistics* (Pluto Press, 1979),
the author of a number of articles on the social assessment of
science and technology, and has been active within the Radical
Statistics Group and the British Society for Social Responsibility in Science.

Richard Jolly is Director of the Institute of Development
Studies, University of Sussex, where he works on issues of
national development strategy and international measures in
support of it. He has participated in ILO missions on employ-
ment and basic human needs in Kenya, Colombia, Sri Lanka and
Zambia. His recent publications include 'Restructuring out of
World Recession' in Khadija Haq (ed.) *Dialogue for a New Order*
(Pergamon,1980), editing *Disarmament and World Development*
(Pergamon, 1978), and co-editing with Paul Streeten *Recent
Issues in World Development* (Pergamon, 1981). He is a member
of the North-South Round Table and Governing Council of the
Society for International Development and rapporteur of the UN
Committee on Development Planning.

Steen Juhler works as an architect. He has been active in
Danish environmentalist movements throughout the 1970s, producing articles and radio programmes on various aspects of alternative ways of life, focussing on the experience of Christiania
and the commune movement. He has carried out research on consumer influence and organization.

Hidetoshi Kato is currently a Professor at Gakushuin University,
Tokyo, where he teaches sociology and anthropology. He is an
author and critic on a variety of subjects, and his selected
writings are compiled in twelve volumes and published by Chūo
Kōron Sha, Tokyo. He also serves as a member of several governmental committees.

Mogens Kløvedal is a freelance writer, working on both film
scripts and articles. After never finishing a study of literature at the University of Copenhagen, he became an organizer
in the Conscientious Objectors Association. He has been a
social worker concerned with detoxicating drug-addicts, later
working in a crisis-centre taking care of run-away children.
He lived in a commune for 8 years, and is now a single parent.

Per Løvetand, architect, teacher and researcher at the Royal
Academy of Fine Arts, Copenhagen, through the 1960s and 1970s
has been working with Industrialized Building, User-participation
and Ecology. He has been deeply engaged from the beginning in
the development of the Freetown of Christiania, has been author
and co-editor of articles and books about the Freetown and
alternative ways of life, and is now working on a thesis about
Christiania as a social experiment besides practising AWL in a
wider context.

Ian Miles has worked at the Science Policy Research Unit,
University of Sussex, since 1972, and apart from his own *The
Poverty of Prediction* (Saxon House/Lexington Books, 1975), has
contributed to SPRU forecasting studies such as *The Art of
Anticipation* (ed. S. Encel *et al.,* Martin Robertson, 1975),
World Futures: The Great Debate (ed. C. Freeman and M. Jahoda,
Martin Robinson, 1978) and *Uses and Abuses of Forecasting* (ed.
T. Whiston, MacMillan, 1979). He has also co-edited *Problems
and Progress in Social Forecasting* (ed. C. Freeman *et al.,*
Social Science Research Council, 1975) and *Demystifying Social
Statistics* (ed. J. Irvine *et al.,* Pluto, 1979). This has left
some time over for personal and political activities, and he is
currently active in the British Nuclear Disarmament Movement.

Dag Poleszynski has been associated with the Chair of Conflict
and Peace Research, University of Oslo. He has acted as a consultant to environmental and alternative ways of life groups in
Norway, has co-authored and edited seven books on atomic energy,
energy policies and alternative development strategies, besides
publishing a number of articles on issues relating to energy,
health, nutrition and development. He has helped establish an
alternative network of researchers in Norway, the Interdisciplinary Research Forum (TFF), having as its primary focus an
alternative development path for Norway and a holistic and en-
vironmentally-based development philosophy.

Anneke H. Schipper-Van Otterloo holds a part-time teaching and
research post in the Department of Sociology, University of
Amsterdam. She has published in the field of the sociology of
religion and has most recently been working on a research
project concerned with setting AWL in the Netherlands in a
historical perspective.

Andrzej Siciński is Assistant Professor of Sociology and head
of the Division for Lifestyles Studies at the Institute of
Philosophy and Sociology, Polish Academy of Sciences, Warsaw.
He is a member of both the Presidium of the Committee 'Poland
2000' of the Polish Academy of Sciences, and of the Executive
Committee of the World Future Studies Federation, and has published several books and about sixty articles on public opinion,
culture, styles of life, futures research, and social science
methodology.

Monica Wemegah works as a researcher at the Geneva-based co-
ordinating unit of the GPID Project of the United Nations
University, acting as co-ordinator for the Alternative Ways of
Life subproject. She has published articles on a range of contemporary social issues such as political corruption, trade
negotiations, land-planning politics, the problems of marginal
groups, alternative life-styles and human-centred development.
Being an active Christian, her special interests lie in the
effects of religious beliefs upon society. Her recent books
include *Aménagement du territoire et Administration fédérale*
(Georgi, 1979), *Fédéralisme en action* (Georgi, 1979) as well as
a forthcoming book *Alternative Ways of Life in Contemporary
Europe* (co-editor). She has been a consultant to the Society
for International Development in Rome and is a member of the
recently founded Geneva International Peace Research Institute
and a member of the executive committee of the Swiss Political
Science Association.

List of Figures

List of Tables

List of Tables

List of Tables

Introduction

JOHN IRVINE AND IAN MILES

Few people would deny that the world is in a grim state. Although many sparks of light are visible, much of the world appears to be deeply enmeshed in economic and political crisis. The rattling of nuclear sabres makes many of us wonder whether human civilization will even survive this century. Most observers would agree on many of the symptoms of malaise in the industrial countries of the world (both East and West), and agree that these have not appeared overnight, but rather have been accumulating for decades. Unemployment, alienation from work and politics alike, cruelty and violence to others, self-abuse of many varieties, environmental degradation and a technology that seems to be out of control — these form only the beginning of a possible list of symptoms, symptoms which lead many people to argue that a fundamental change in our ways of life is long overdue.

The ways of life to which we are accustomed are indeed liable to change drastically in coming years. In some cases, the problems associated with our current social and economic practices are building up to intolerable levels. In other cases, activists are promoting change in the belief that we can live more healthy and fulfilling lives. And new technologies seem to be reshaping our work and leisure alike. But these are only the pressures that are internal to industrial societies: there are also forces for change external to these societies. For Third World nations are seeking to change an international order which has fulfilled its promise of 'development' for so few of them.

That a new stage in 'North-South' relations has been reached has been evident at least since OPEC increased petroleum prices in the early 1970s, thus demonstrating that industrial countries could no longer rely on cheap resources from the rest of the world to sustain their ways of life. To the argument that

changing our ways of life is desirable in order to resolve
the problems internal to our 'developed' societies, then, are
added claims from the 'developing' societies that such changes
are necessary in order to establish a more equitable world.
With increasing global instability, this claim may become more
than a moral plea: it may be enforceable through political or
economic action.

It is clear, then, that a range of different forces are together exerting pressure on existing ways of life in industrial
societies. But, to what extent are the various changes that
these diverse pressures promote compatible? How far can such
changes be the product of deliberate choice; how much may we
find them forced upon us? These are questions that urgently
need to be debated, and which this volume aims to throw light
upon. The chapters that follow each contribute elements for
such a debate. Though several different viewpoints are represented among the contributors, continuing close dialogue
between us has enabled us to relate our work together in
numerous ways, even while addressing different aspects of the
problem of changing ways of life.

Despite their differing standpoints, the studies that follow
share common concerns. What is good and bad about our ways of
life? Are they changing for the better or the worse? How can
more positive changes be encouraged? A range of views are expressed. For some authors the problems cited are transitory
ones that a little tolerance and goodwill could overcome. For
others, fundamental flaws in our value-system are signalled,
with excessive materialism being at the heart of our problems.
Yet others argue that our existing political and economic
systems are simply inadequate to ensure survival in the face of
the awesome responsibilities of our highly technological way of
life.

With equal urgency, theoretical assessments of what is wrong
with our ways of life have to be accompanied by action to change
or preserve crucial features of our social world. And we find
here, too, divergences over the implications of the present
period of crisis for such action. Many people would argue that
revival of economic growth is required as the necessary basis
for restoring falling employment levels and satisfactory welfare
services. But most of the contributors to this volume would
argue, rather, that economic growth, at least of the variety we
have experienced in recent decades, is itself part of the crisis.
Simply rejuvenating past patterns of production and consumption
is not enough. The economic crisis provides an opportunity for
a wider public to be alerted to the complex of problems characterizing ways of life in industrial societies. With choices

posed more starkly than ever, alternative directions for our
societies may be seen as not only desirable but realistic, and
as capable of being realized.

Two concepts underpin two corresponding groups of chapters
that largely constitute this book. The first concept is that
of Dominant Ways of Life (DWL). This refers to the patterning
of our relationships with each other and with nature which
characterizes a given industrial society. Within such a society,
these relationships are given a structure which means that
social and environmental interactions typically vary systematically across class, sex and age group, and that their main
features are reproduced with few drastic changes. This brief
definition, which is amplified in the chapters that follow,
should be sufficient to indicate that by calling attention to
ways of life we are doing more than considering the lifestyles
of particular groups — whether they be swingers in San Francisco,
anarchists in Amsterdam, dropouts in Dublin or bohemians in
Berlin. We also want to go beyond thinking of ways of life as
the accidental outcome of millions of isolated individual
choices to understand how our choices are channelled within
political, economic and cultural institutions, and how this
social structuring of choices and opportunities affects our
quality of life and our possible futures.

The second concept we use extensively is that of Alternative
Ways of Life (AWL). Agreeing that all is not well with our DWL,
our authors are concerned with what alternatives might promote
more satisfactory human and environmental relationships within
countries, and a more just and peaceful international order.
We are thus hoping to provide some of the analysis necessary
to guide and support action to change the DWL in desirable ways.
AWL, then, involve countering the reproduction of social and
environmental relationships of the DWL referred to above. In
part, this is done by considering what alternatives to our ways
of life already exist within our societies, and in part by
taking up questions of the strategies which can effect different
sorts of change.

The first six chapters of this book, however, focus especially
on problems of the DWL in industrial societies. The scene is
set by Galtung, Poleszynski and Wemegah who provide an interpretative overview of these problems, arguing that they have to
be seen in terms of tendencies deeply rooted into Western culture. They present a view of the DWL which is shared by several
other contributors, according to which the malaise of the rich
countries can be understood as reflecting an overconsumption of
material goods at the cost of neglecting non-material satisfiers.
This chapter provides a sophisticated and forceful statement of
this viewpoint, and several subsequent chapters use this general

approach to assess DWL and AWL in more empirical detail. Nevertheless, not all contributors are convinced by this approach,
and a range of qualification, disagreements, and alternative
perspectives are presented throughout the book.
The remainder of this first set of chapters demonstrate this
amply. Five 'case-studies' are presented in which the DWL of
a number of industrial countries are assessed in terms of their
human costs and benefits. Each country is, furthermore, an
exemplar of one or other model to which the rest of the world
is urged to look for inspiration concerning the goals of
development and the good life. The United States represents
the 'American dream' of abundance; Norway is one of the paradigm cases of 'welfare capitalism'; Switzerland has allegedly
established such a placid DWL that it has only sought 'to invent
the cuckoo clock' in recent centuries; the United Kingdom may
be seen by some as a sadly declining industrial power, but to
others the homeland of parliamentary democracy is now pioneering
'post-industrial society'; while centrally-planned Poland presents an example of 'socialist development' (albeit of an ex-
ceptional kind within Eastern Europe), a development strategy,
which many countries have sought to emulate.
  With such a range of countries, it is valuable to consider
both common features and divergences. Each chapter features a
common core of statistical material to facilitate such comparison. In the British, Norwegian and Swiss cases, furthermore,
data are assembled so as to permit an assessment of the respec-
tive DWL in terms of how well they provide for the four 'human
needs' of welfare, security, identity, and freedom. (Readers
are invited to contrast the approaches taken to operationalize
these concepts.) The scope and implications of the statistics
presented are illuminating. As well as their common core, the
chapters are united by their clear indications that existing
DWL are developing in ways detrimental to vital aspects of our
well-being. Of course, there are different perspectives presented, and thus differences in emphasis. For instance, some
chapters feature ecological and health issues strongly, while
others emphasize questions of power and injustice. The contrast
of these different perspectives provides useful insights into
both their value and limitations as ways of assessing and understanding ways of life.
  Arnold and Goulet take up the question of the DWL in the most
powerful country in the world today, the United States. They
reveal that the 'good life' of the 'average American' is a
rather contradictory affair, characterized by inequalities and
discrimination, by crime and unhappiness with 'mass society'.
In order to understand how these contradictions are managed,
the authors point to three institutions and their associated

'myths': capitalist enterprise and the myth of social mobility;
industrial technology and the myth of technological progress;
and military security and the myth of national interest. For
every myth, however, a counter-myth may suggest new values and
meaning systems, new ways of life and social organization.
Change within the United States may be necessary for a more
equitable world order, but, the authors suggest, such change is
itself likely to be prompted by international events as much as
by a struggle for AWL within the American dream.

The chapters by Poleszynski and Wemegah on Norway and Switzerland, respectively, treat their countries as 'overdeveloped'.
Problems in welfare, security, identity and freedom are seen as
deriving from an economic system that insists on churning out
increasingly unnecessary material goods, while failing to address
a variety of non-material needs. People suffer, in consequence,
from overconsumption of commercial products (leading, for example, to obesity and poor health), and from a lack of adequate
interpersonal and cultural opportunities (which is reflected in
psychiatric and communal problems of various kinds). The environment, likewise, suffers from a resource- and energy-
intensive way of life, while people suffer from a paucity of
contact with natural things. Ecological movements, opposition
to nuclear power, and self-help groups are among the reactions
to the process of overdevelopment which these authors see as
bearing most promise of reversing the dangerous tendencies in
their countries.

It is not only the differing national contexts, but also
different political and theoretical standpoints that account
for the distinctive approaches of the next two chapters.
Irvine and Miles interpret many critical problems in Britain's
DWL as the immediate consequence of a world recession compounded
on a protracted national economic crisis, but see the fundamental causes of these phenomena as located in the class relations
of that country. Rather than diagnosing a condition of overdevelopment, they point to wide inequalities that mean that many
Britons still fail to reach a reasonable material living standard, and demonstrate the ways in which such inequalities correspond to the structure of political and economic power. The
question of power, then, is here introduced as a key feature of
identity and freedom and a key determinant of welfare and
security.

In assessing the DWL of Poland, Siciński, too, argues that
many areas of his society could benefit from more, rather than
less, material production. As a critical view, from inside,
of the implications of Eastern European development strategies
for the living conditions of the citizens of one country, his
chapter is of particular interest. Whilst far from the polem-

ical abuse with which daily life in 'socialist' countries is
often portrayed in the West, his account is certainly not apol-
ogetic, and demonstrates the similarities as well as some differences in the problems of the DWL across markedly different
types of industrial society. It is also of particular interest
in that a number of distinctive lifestyles, pursued by different
groups, within the DWL, are outlined.

This first set of chapters, then, provide 'cost-benefit analyses' of the DWL in a range of countries as a means of throw-
ing light on the paths we have travelled and the choices that
lie ahead. Without prescribing one single solution, these
chapters make it clear that the transformation of ways of life
in industrial societies must necessarily be a central feature
of programmes of social change in the coming decades. Indeed,
while we may debate how ways of life should and can be changed,
and hope that our contributions here can stimulate and inform
this debate, we would argue that analysis and action around
creating AWL is vital if a tolerable future is to be secured.[1*]

If the DWL is a source of many problems, what are we to do
about it? Many political activists proclaim that only sweeping
structural changes can meaningfully cope with the malaise of
modern societies. Others see this as irresponsible: they point
to significant reforms and improvements that can and have been
achieved, and argue that to abdicate from the pursuit of such
goals is to risk social stagnation or decline. Beyond these
polarities, we may point out that simply overhauling institutions is often not enough: to effect a lasting change in social
structures it is necessary to transform many of the features of
everyday life that have been shaped by them (and thus support
them); and that it is equally restrictive to assume that the
DWL can be reshaped without posing questions of institutional
change and thus of the interests that these institutions elicit
and the power they confer.

From this perspective, the group of five chapters that concludes this volume consider changes that are already underway
in the DWL, experiments in AWL that may provide guides to future
possibilities, and the strategies necessary to promote the
development of more satisfactory ways of life.

Falkentorp, Hansen, Juhler, Kløvedal and Løvetand provide an
admirable start to this task. These authors provide fascinating
case-studies and participants' views of alternative institutions
within Denmark. Among their examples are new educational forms
(the Tvind schools), 'leisure' activities (Island Camps, the
Thy Camp), household structures (communes) and communities
(Christiania). These flourishing activities are surprisingly
unfamiliar to English speakers,[2] and we are pleased to be able

(* Superscript numbers refer to notes at end of chapter).

to give them coverage. It will be apparent, too, that the
practices of AWL described in this chapter are not simply
individuals opting-out of Danish society: for many of those
involved, they are seen as part of a deliberate strategy aimed
at promoting wider social change.

Otterloo and Ester describe the search for alternative relations with other individuals and with the natural environment
as it has been manifested in Holland. They seek to combine an
historical and theoretical overview with their descriptions of
current AWL activities, demonstrating that such a search is no
new phenomenon. While particular clusters of values are seen
as motivating and structuring attempts to lead AWL, a wide
variety of different practices are graphically shown to be
possible outcomes here. It is noted that concerns around
ecological issues and attempts to resolve problems of individual
identity are often associated together, and case-studies of
work communities, a meditation centre, and a 'New Life-Style
Movement' are used to illustrate the convergences and divergences here, and the degree of impact that different AWL practices may have on the wider society.

Kato's chapter takes a rather different approach. He is concerned with changes in Japanese values that would seem to indicate a general social evolution complementary to the goals
being fought for by the AWL movements. His general argument
is that the market for material commodities is becoming increasingly saturated in Japan, that people are turning from
'things' to 'experiences' and seeking to develop their aesthetic
and cultural potentialities. Although the current economic
recession has rather overshadowed them, voices can still be
heard suggesting that the same trend is apparent in Western
societies, too.[3]

The two final chapters draw rather less directly on specific
national examples. Jolly takes a more global focus, reflecting
his participation in debates on these issues within the Society
for International Development. His theme is the extent to which
AWL will be demanded by, and to what extent they might contribute to, the making of a new, more viable, more equitable world
order. He rightly stresses the point that there is an intimate
connection between our ways of life and the organization of the
world political and economic system, and points out that rich and
poor countries are not necessarily locked into a zero-sum game in
which improvements in one region inevitably mean losses elsewhere.
Changing ways of life in the 'North', then, are of more interest
to development planners and people in the 'South' than would be
indicated simply by thinking of industrial countries as models
for the future of the whole world.

Finally, Miles and Irvine attempt to draw together many of
the threads spun in previous chapters by discussing different
strategies for effecting change in ways of life. An outline is
provided of how different perceptions of the nature of the DWL
are associated with different political standpoints, and in
turn related to different views of the forces in society capable
of, and potentially interested in, establishing AWL. This
chapter provides both a guide to the debates over these issues,
and an outline of when and how various strategies might be
effective.

This book, then, should amply testify to the importance of
the issues that we have been outlining above. It provides some
of the intellectual tools that can help us to understand and
intervene in the processes involved. Many researchers have
been working on such matters, and the preparation of this book
has only been possible because of the lived experience and
debate among members to the SID/UNU project on Alternative Ways
of Life. (An Appendix to this volume lists papers produced in
the course of this project.) The issues are ones for action
and argument as well as research, however, and concerned people
and policymakers everywhere hopefully will be provoked and
stimulated by this collection. Final answers are clearly not
possible at this point in time. Assessing AWL and the strategies to achieve them must depend upon practice, upon our learning from the changes that are underway in our way of life, and
from the results of our attempts to influence the social trans-
formations of which we are necessarily part. But it is increasingly urgent that questions about our way of life are
posed. If we have helped raise those questions, and to advance
in a small way the practical realization of their answers, we
will be well content.

NOTES

1. At this point we should make it clear that we do not believe
that *all* aspects of our societies are deteriorating, nor that
every ominous trend necessarily signifies worsening conditions
in the DWL. These positions are often ascribed to social critics
of all persuasions, but do not apply to the contributors to this
book. As for the first point, we accept that, even over recent
decades, many facets of life have improved, often as a result
of hard struggle. Much difficult and unpleasant work has been
abolished; many lives have been saved that would once have been
lost; we know more about conditions in other parts of the world;
and so on. The problem that we seek to confront is that of explaining how such benefits can be produced alongside new levels

of disillusion, despair and destruction; and of determining how
we can preserve such benefits while removing the causes of our
social ills.

As for the second point, perhaps an example will be helpful.
Hirayama (1979) has shown that an increase in oesophageal cancer is not, apparently, related to new food additives or pollution. Rather, general improvements in the level of health have
permitted the ill effects of a traditional foodstuff, bracken
fern (wild food enthusiasts beware!), to become visible. It is
likely that numerous phenomena of this sort exist, and of course
it is in everyone's interest that they should be located and
publicized. However, it is our assessment that many more of
the newly increasing problems of industrial society are to do
with new facets of our industrial ways of life, and in giving
general overviews of health issues these will naturally be
stressed. Nevertheless, it may be that the bracken fern example
can provide some insights into social affairs: the longstanding
oppression of women in the typical nuclear family, for instance,
may become more evident and more a source of concern as women
gain more equality in economic activity. More generally, we
may speculate that alleviating current crises may often reveal
that these are merely the immediate manifestation of problems
that are grounded deep in long-lived social structures (see,
especially, chapter 11).

2. One English-language account of Tvind schools is in Castles
and Wursterberg (1979).

3. Examples of such arguments are Inglehart (1977) and the
OECD (1979). On the other hand, there is some evidence that
material goods are substituting for services (e.g. Gershuny,
1978), and we should also stress the prospect of new technologies
forming the basis for new material goods and thus market demands.

BIBLIOGRAPHY

Castles, S. and Wursterberg, W. (1979) *The Education of the
    Future.* London, Pluto.
Gershuny, J. I. (1978) *After Industrial Society?* London,
    MacMillan.
Hirayama, T. (1979) Diet and Cancer, *Nutrition and Cancer,* 1
    (3), 67-81.
Inglehart, R. (1977) *The Silent Revolution.* Princeton, New
    Jersey, Princeton University Press.
OECD (1979) *Facing the Future* (Interfutures Project). Paris,
    OECD.

1
Why the Concern with Ways of Life?[1]*

JOHAN GALTUNG, DAG POLESZYNSKI AND MONICA WEMEGAH

INTRODUCTION: THE MALAISE OF THE 1970s IN RICH COUNTRIES

At the end of the 1960s a large scale comparative study was undertaken under the auspices of the European Coordination Centre for Research and Documentation in Social Science. This was to result in the report *Images of the World in the Year 2000*. Close to 9000 people were asked nearly 2000 questions, giving a total of 1,800,000 answers. The survey covered people from eight European countries, north and south, east and west, and in addition a large number from India and Japan. One particularly important set of findings emerging from this research concerned the relatively high degree of pessimism about the future among the younger generation of people aged 15-40 years old, though this was related quite strongly to the level of technical-economic development of the country of respondents:

> When it comes to domestic perspectives the organizing axis is the level of technical-economic development. Nations high on this dimension are pessimistic, bewildered and uncertain, probably (a) because they see the negative effects of this type of development, (b) because they feel they have exhausted the program of their societies and that the future is without challenging and clear goals. Nations low on that dimension do not have this vision and may even reject it. They follow in the same footpaths but with the optimism stemming partly from the ignorance of the adverse effects, partly from the feeling of having a program. And this seems to be the program defined and developed by countries that are already disillusioned by it. (Ornauer *et al.*, 1976, p. 118).

---

*Superscript numbers refer to notes at end of chapter.

11

A broad range of issues were seen to be involved here: a
certain scepticism toward science in the more 'developed'
countries; a general pessimism concerning social progress, with
heavy emphasis placed on the associated social costs; and what
was termed 'a feeling of development fatigue, with predictions
of retrogressive development, for one's country as well as for
oneself, towards the end of the century' (Ornauer et al., 1976,
p.116). The researchers point out that

> these are not data reflecting an innovating humanity
> exploring and facing a fascinating open-ended future.
> These seem rather to be data reflecting a humanity
> with its back to the future, looking at the past, and
> the present — and projecting from that experience into
> the future. In a sense these are the data one would
> expect at the end of a phase in human history, not at
> the beginning of a new one. (Ornauer et al., 1976,
> p.118).

The 1970s seem to have borne out this prediction based on data
from the late 1960s. The mood these data indicated apparently
crystallized around a set of concrete political issues, manifesting itself in growing public concern over nuclear power, energy,
resource wastage, ecology, lifestyles, local autonomy, urban
problems, and so on. Furthermore, a range of pathologies in
rich countries came to be widely recognized as important during
the 1970s. These are listed in Fig. 1.1. There seems to be an
increased consciousness about these issues, with wider awareness
of the extent of problems and a deepening development of theories
about their causes. More and more they seem to be seen as having
social origins — and avoidable ones — thereby giving rise to a
proliferation of social movements, some focussing on specific
issues, others of more general scope.

Taken together, the pathologies spelt out in Fig. 1.1 present
the image of a sick society[2]. This is a society whose population
has a high level of life expectancy, but does not necessarily
enjoy good health because it is suffering from cardiovascular
diseases, tumours, occupational diseases and accidents, and is
threatened by internal violence or terrorism and even by large-
scale wars. There are high levels of mental disorders, with
people not knowing the sense and meaning of their existence,
and often withdrawing into 'observerism', with active minorities
engaging in crimes of various sorts, and vandalism and aggression
increasingly threatening the survival of others. Such societies
may claim to be keeping the levels of social injustice and inequality (including inequality of opportunity, for instance
between the sexes) within bounds, but they are certainly failing

Human pathologies

Body: cardiovascular diseases; tumours; occupational diseases; accidents; injuries from internal/external war.

Mind: mental disorders (schizophrenia, psychoses, neuroses); addiction to drugs, alcohol, tobacco; suicide.

Spirit: a sense of meaninglessness, alienation.

Social pathologies

Behavioral: this includes passive pathologies such as withdrawal and 'observerism', as well as active ones (crime, violence, etc.).

Distributional: injustice; inequality; inequality of opportunity.

Structural: inequity; dependency; unemployment.

Environmental: resource depletion; pollution.

Cultural: the exaggerated acceptance of exogenous culture and rejection of endogenous culture.

Fig. 1.1   A tentative list of pathologies in rich countries

to reduce them significantly. They cannot even offer socially useful employment to all their citizens, while those who are employed are finding themselves subjected to greater levels of exploitation (inequity), with growing control of economic institutions by central governments and foreign countries. Often, too, there is a penetration and domination of local culture by national culture; and of both, in turn, by foreign culture. Finally, a wholesale degradation of the environment, in terms of both resource depletion and pollution, is taking place. The picture presented is an unsavoury one: it is not strange that movements have been organized to develop alternatives!

Among the many movements — and no effort will be made here to give a complete list — we can cite ecological movements, peace movements, women's movements, religious movements, the 'undogmatic' left, *Bürgerinitiativen* (citizen's movements), and a whole range of alternative ways of life (AWL) movements — focusing on, for example, alternative technologies, new food habits, self-sufficiency, simple living, and personal growth[3]. At the political level, various types of extraparliamentary politics

have flourished, with an increase in political activity at the
grassroots level. In short, what was no more than a mood at
the end of the 1960s exploded in a scatter of issue-oriented
campaigns and associated movements during the early 1970s — all
testifying to the inadequacy of the traditional political
machinery. As the 1970s wore on, governmental initiatives
attempted to come to grips with these issues, but achieved
little success. The problem was that these attempts were based
on the sectorially highly-segmented government machinery of the
industrially advanced nations, and thus typically sought to
deal with the issues in a piecemeal fashion.

To be sure, there is a general malaise in the economically
advanced, industrialized, high-income countries. In itself,
this already answers the question of why there is such concern
with ways of life (WOL), but we have to go beyond listing issues
and movements, for these are merely the surface of the phenomena.
We must ask whether there is some kind of common denominator,
something that links them together. Such a question is not only
an invitation to intellectual activity, to develop social theory;
it is also a precondition for meaningful political activity.
There are problems in asking and answering such questions: there
is a dangerous tendency to say that these phenomena are 'nothing
but' expressions of whatever the pet theory of the authors deems
as central. As well as the point that people in general, not
just experts, should formulate such theories, there is also the
problem that reducing variety, and possibly oversimplifying
complex matters, may give a dangerously simplistic basis for
political action.

Hence, we must proceed with care. What follows in this chapter is not an effort to construct a solid theoretical edifice,
but merely an attempt to explore what lies beyond the surface
of these phenomena. Firm understanding can only be built as we
better come to grips with the phenomena described in our everyday attempts to develop AWL. This chapter is an invitation to
the reader to become involved in this process by outlining what
is wrong with our WOL as they are currently constituted.

THE PERSPECTIVE OF BASIC NEEDS: UNDERDEVELOPMENT,
OVERDEVELOPMENT AND MALDEVELOPMENT

Most readers would probably agree that the pathologies listed
in Fig. 1.1 are not unrelated to each other. They concern WOL
at both the social and individual level, and affect our daily
life both directly and indirectly.

But many people might be surprised at such questioning of WOL:
the last few decades have brought a level of material affluence

unheard of in history, not only to the ruling elites of the
world, but also to large numbers of ordinary people in industrialized countries. They might ask why, given the increasing
affluence, there should be concern with WOL in this part of the
world? Why not sit down and enjoy the high living standard
which many of us have achieved, and look forward only to the
day when the whole population reaches the hoped-for abundance?
Pathologies or not, surely things are now better than they were
in the past?

Unfortunately, the development of modern industrial societies
has not been so even and successful as is often claimed. One
way of describing (rather than explaining) the process whereby
pathologies and material affluence have been produced at the
same time involves focussing on the idea of *basic human needs*.
Such needs are *basic* in the sense that they have to be satisfied
for us to continue existing as human beings[4]. They are *human*
in the sense that they are felt at the individual level, however
much the satisfaction manifests itself at the social level.
Thus, the need for food is expressed as hunger felt at the
individual level, while very few human beings would actually
be able to satisfy this need alone. Mass societies emerged
precisely because of the necessity for collective action to
satisfy such basic needs. The same obviously applies to the
need for togetherness; and however much some people might feel
that the need for a sense of meaning on life can be fulfilled
through a sufficiently high level of consciousness, in retreat
from the material world, many would probably discover as hermits
that, in the longer run, meaning is largely and ultimately
derived from social interaction.

As with many other social processes, important elements of
the structure of needs can be illustrated graphically. Figure
1.2 presents three possible perspectives on the long-run trend
of the relationship between the consumption of objects and experiences and the satisfaction of needs.

Taking these possible relations in turn, A is the well-known
exponential curve. This indicates a very high level of optimism:
the more consumption that takes place, the greater the satisfaction — indeed they are exponentially related. In contrast,
optimism is rather more guarded on the part of those who would
put forward B, the *logistic* curve, as better representing the
real state of affairs. Here the notion of a saturation level
is implicit: after a certain level of consumption has been
reached, there is no longer any appreciable gain in satisfaction.
Curve C carries this mode of thinking still further: now, not
only does utility decrease after a certain level of consumption,
but increasing disutility results from additional consumption.

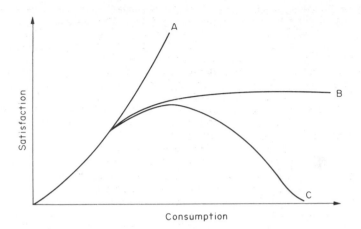

*Fig. 1.2   Three possible consumption-satisfaction
relations*

One example here is the consumption of food, which, at first
highly useful for hunger-abatement, becomes decreasingly useful,
and is then increasingly harmful.

This harmfulness does not mean that hunger starts increasing
again; rather, other needs become dissatisfied through increasing consumption. Thus, in curve C the needs referred to on the
vertical axis may not be the same as one ascends and descends
the curve. The same also holds true for more non-material
needs. Take the case of a person in search of meaning in life.
At the beginning of that search, discussion and togetherness
with others, reading books, pursuit of new experiences, may be
extremely productive, after some time decreasingly so, and after
more time even counter-productive. An upper limit has been
reached and for more of such 'inputs' to yield more in terms of
meaning of life some inner changes have to take place (matur-
ation, growth, spiritual renewal). Just as there is an upper
limit as to how much food a body can digest, there is also an
upper limit to how many impressions a mind can digest into something spiritually meaningful.

Thus, we would argue that curve C is the most typical of the
relationship between many human needs and the consumption of
'need-satisfiers'. The case can be made more strongly by
classifying human needs into four groups: those for *survival*
and for *welfare* (more 'material' needs), and those for *freedom*
and *identity* (more 'non-material' needs). A certain minimum of
material production is of course required for these needs to be

satisfied, and this is not at issue. What is in question is the
fact that industrial societies have concerned themselves less
with production for human development than with production for
its own sake, disregarding the fact that at some point the level
of material production may start becoming less useful: increments
in consumption may mean progressively less for human development,
and, eventually, become counterproductive. When material
increases impede, rather than promote, human development there
is a state of *overdevelopment* (Fig. 1.3). Thus we can distinguish development from *maldevelopment*, the latter consisting
of both underdevelopment and overdevelopment in coexistence.
It is only within a certain range of consumption, at a certain
sufficiency level (no doubt varying with different cultures and
historical conditions), that we may classify a society as developed.

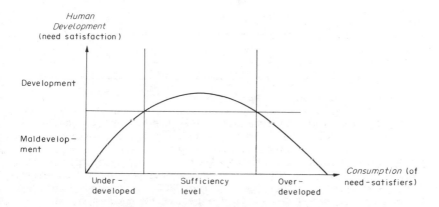

Fig. 1.3 Relationship between human develop-
ment and production level

We have put 'consumption', not 'production', on the horizontal
axes of Figs. 1.2 and 1.3 for the reason that the particular
needs-dialectic here takes place around individual consumption.
Production may go on for a very long time without leading to
overconsumption, providing the products (goods and services)
are well distributed. We can even define 'well-distributed' as
meaning that people have access to enough 'need satisfiers' to
avoid underconsumption, but not so many that they enter into
overconsumption. The problem, however, is that strong social
factors seem to counteract the adequate distribution of what is
produced, so that high levels of underdevelopment (patterned

underconsumption) and overdevelopment (patterned overconsumption)
are both produced in our societies at the same time. Thus we have
used the terms 'underdevelopment/overdevelopment' above, rather
than 'underconsumption/overconsumption'.

'Maldevelopment' can be introduced here as a more general
concept, covering both of these states. There are obviously
many types of maldevelopment, and Fig. 1.4 offers a simple
typology of them. The typical structure of maldevelopment in

		Non-material needs	
		under-developed	over-developed
Material needs	under-developed	A	C
	over-developed	B	D

Fig. 1.4 A maldevelopment typology

OECD countries might combine overdevelopment where the satisfaction of material needs is concerned with underdevelopment
in respect of the satisfaction of non-material needs. But
considerable underdevelopment in terms of some material needs
remains in these countries (and not only in pockets of poverty).
Thus, both types A and B apply to the OECD countries. There
may also be an element of type D — people surrounded by an
abundance of satisfiers of material needs, but also of all the
things needed for their non-material needs — people they know,
their living rooms stuffed with books, records, cassettes,
video tapes, with access to travel and all kinds of experiences.
In less affluent countries, too, extremely rich cultural surroundings may be provided to the point that they actually become counter-productive, even if they are not privatised into
living-rooms. Clearly a person does not become richer simply
by being surrounded by art treasures; in this case museum
guards and temple wardens would be among the richest people in
the world in terms of inner growth. Hence while type A exists,
type C maldevelopment may apply to several of the economically
less-advanced, low-income countries. The process here seems
evident in many of the capitals of Third World countries today.
Figure 1.5, concentrating only on material consumption/satis-

faction, indicates how people can be sucked through a 'tunnel' from material underdevelopment straight into material over-development with no intervening platform of development on which one could declare *j'y suis: j'y reste*. By the time they come out at the other end of the tunnel such people belong to the 'elite' because they have all the trappings of the elite. These trappings include those of Fig. 1.1: they will now die from cardiovascular diseases and cancer rather than from malaria or bilharzia, and so on down the list. The development of these pathologies will depend on the extent to which the transition from material underdevelopment to material overdevelopment is accompanied by increasing underdevelopment of non-material dimensions.

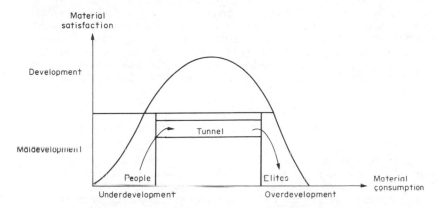

Fig. 1.5 Maldevelopment as a process

Returning to the problems of the rich countries, some — but not all— of the phenomena listed in the preceding section can be conceived of in terms of underconsumption. The phenomena best accounted for are those in which a high level of production of goods and services leads to a high level, and, in time, a sur-plus, of consumption. Natural resources are used in production, and some of the consequent impacts on nature are highly negative; the results are resource depletion and pollution, and this has led to the formation of movements dedicated to protecting nature. Similarly, movements to protect the human body, mind and spirit, have arisen, and these focus on those issues mentioned in Fig. 1.1 under human pathologies.

Those pathologies classified as 'distributional' or 'struc-tural' are, however, not adequately accounted for under this approach. That goods and bads are unjustly and unequally distributed, that the social system provides little work and much exploitation and dependency, are phenomena that go deeper than a needs-oriented analysis alone can uncover. At this important point, the needs approach shows its limitations; it rightly brings the individual into focus, but is weak on distributional and structural issues. As our focus here is on the type of maldevelopment found in rich countries, we may tend to emphasize material oversufficiency at the expense of undersufficiency, hence downplaying the maldevelopment afflicting materially poor groups, classes and countries. Thus those who try to escape from the malaise of material poverty into alternative ways of life (AWL) can be contrasted to those who try to escape from the malaise of spiritual poverty despite or because of excessive (material) progress. To pose such problems in terms of an analysis of social class relations is indispensable, as is an understanding of the role of social movements such as socialist/ workers' parties and trade unions in countering these problems with demonstrations and strikes. But these movements reflect a long tradition of classical conflict in the rich countries; our concern here is more with the new phenomena clustering around WOL.

ROOTS OF MALDEVELOPMENT: THE BOURGEOIS WAY OF LIFE AND THE EXPLOITATIVE STYLE OF DEVELOPMENT

Maldevelopment is, as we have seen, a convenient term for grouping together a number of related problematic characteristics of modern societies. In looking at the roots of maldevelopment, we shall try to see social life more from the inside, from the point of view of what people in general try to obtain from life, and from the point of view of how elites of various kinds try to structure options and possibilities. Thus, from general social philosophy, our focus now shifts more to individual patterns of behaviour, be they at the mass or elite levels.

The way of life most people are steered towards may be defined as the dominant way of life, DWL. But this includes several WOL. One might simplistically talk about an upper class WOL, a middle class WOL and a working class WOL. However, in OECD societies most of the population seem now to identify themselves with the middle classes, trying to deny both upper class and working class origins. And one factor behind this might be a certain shared ideal of the WOL that the overwhelming majority of the population would like to lead. In a sense, this DWL is a mixture of all three, developing out of the urban/ industrial sector of these societies. It is the lifestyle of the

burgher, the bourgeois, for which reason it will be referred to
here as the 'bourgeois way of life' (BWL), a WOL evolving out
of a certain pattern of production and a certain class in
society.

Four major characteristics can be shown as *together* defining
the BWL:[5] (1) non-manual work (avoidance of heavy and dirty
work); (2) material comfort (with increasing material consumption); (3)privatism/familism; (4) predictability/security. Thus,
the bourgeois is materially non-productive, at least when this
is taken in the sense of touching nature with one's hands in
order to work on it. Material comfort is likewise a way of
creating distance between nature and human beings, by controlling
the environment, and keeping it within an agreeable range where
temperature, humidity, movements, smells, noise, etc., are concerned. Privatism defines the nuclear family, and more particularly the home/house which supposedly is its castle (*Burg*), as
the primary unit of consumption and also of reproduction.[6] And
predictability/security adds a time-dimension to all of this:
the quest is for a predictable future at a high level of security, the latter meaning that the first three conditions will
obtain for oneself throughout one's lifespan, and also for one's
offspring, (familism, standing for nuclear family — mother,
father and offspring — limits the time perspective here).

The BWL is thus a distinct way of life, with coherence and
inner logic; it is readily recognizable in contemporary societies.
In North European societies it takes a relatively modest form,
involving the majority of the population in the 'one-two-three-
four syndrome': one spouse, two children, a three room apartment
and a four-wheel private car. (The same theme may be multiplied,
too, with divorces bringing new wives, husbands and children
into the picture, together with a division of accumulated assets
and a consequent rebuilding of the collection of material assets). There are also extreme versions of the BWL: the one
plane, two boats, three cars, four television set family (Mishan,
1969) — but it should also be noted that social norms have grown
against affluence spilling over into too much opulence. In short,
the BWL is not only a goal for the working classes, but also
possibly has a levelling-down function for the upper classes.

For this type of WOL to become the DWL, obtainable and obtained by the majority of people in society, a certain style of
development is needed. On the one hand, much is wanted by most
people in terms of material goods; on the other, the ideal for
them is not to participate in this material production directly.
How does one solve this contradiction? Reasoning from the BWL
the answers are obvious: by means of a pattern of production
that gets a maximum of material output from a minimum input of
manual working hours (in other words, high labour productivity);

by expropriating as much as possible of the material goods produced from those who manually produce them (in other words,
through exploitation, providing the producers with salaries so
low that they can only repossess a small fraction of what they
have produced, whether the producers are found in the 'internal
proletariat' — the OECD working classes — or the 'external proletariat' in the Third World countries); and by pressing nature
as hard as possible to squeeze out the material products (in
other words, through unecological practices). This particular
style of development is thus based on four pillars:[7] (i) high
productivity (exploitation of self); (ii) exploitation of the
internal proletariat; (iii) exploitation of the external proletariat; (iv) exploitation of nature.

Just as certain patterns of exploitation are needed in order
to implement the BWL programme for a high proportion of the
population, once put into motion this style of development produces an enormous amount of material goods in search of consumers without producing a corresponding amount of manual jobs.
Conceivably it might still produce enough jobs for everybody if
the non-manual sector were to expand as rapidly as the manual
sector contracts. But the term 'non-manual' conceals the rather
important distinction between alienated and non-alienated jobs.
The former are programmed by others (as contrasted to the latter
which are programmed by oneself), and, as routine jobs, can
have continual productivity increases worked into their routines,
thereby reducing employment here too. The nature of non-manual
work is thus changing rapidly: one result is the growing unemployment of non-manual workers as productivity effects come to
bite; another is the greater 'self-exploitation' of those who
remain employed, whose pace of 'non-alienated' work increases
so much that they never have time to relax in routine activities.
In short, the BWL and the exploitative style of development go
hand in hand!

We are now in a position to shed some light on the maldevelopment pathologies discussed earlier. The quest for BWL, with an
exploitative style of development as the instrument for achieving
change, results in a process by which non-material factors are
systematically sacrificed for material growth. The gradual
erosion of human beings, somatically, mentally, and spiritually —
particularly the working classes who are given little chance to
enjoy some of the more positive sides of the BWL (escape from
unnecessarily heavy and dirty work and from the hazards of
nature) — as well as the erosion of nature, clearly emerge from
this picture of contemporary WOL. One can also sense the sheer
monotony of the BWL, a monotony apparently alleviated sometimes
through CWL, the chemical/circus way of life: the use of drugs,

tobacco and alcohol; the dependence on spectator entertainments, with most people passively watching sports or events on television. Class perspectives emerge in the malaise derived from too much BWL. But, in addition, we should see exploitation as a *social* relation which sooner or later will lead to reactions — that is, to struggles against exploitation. This is true whether one sees the problem in terms of unequal exchange, or purely in terms of excessive exploitation, beyond the carrying capacity that permits regeneration (the German *ausbeuten* as opposed to merely *ausnützen*). A remarkable point about the 1970s was that reactions against all types of exploitation became very crystallized. Through the formation of trade unions and workers' parties a relatively high level of wages had been won over a long period of time for manual workers in many of the high-income countries; since these gains would not easily be given up, the inevitable result was that exploitation had to take new forms — in particular, the utilization of new groups of labour such as women or imported foreign workers, or the relocation of industries to other countries.[8] The designation of OECD countries as a high labour-cost area became part of the official explanation for the 'crisis' of the 1970s. In addition, the 'external proletariat' — the Third World countries — protested very effectively against delivering so many resources, particularly energy resources, without receiving in return an acceptable purchasing power for other material goods. This provided the basis for debate over changing the terms of trade between rich and poor countries, as expressed in the call for a New International Economic Order, and symbolized dramatically by the OPEC action of 1973/4. Another landmark of the 1970s was the clear understanding that was developed concerning the limits to which nature can be pushed, giving rise to a proliferation of national and international ecological movements. Yet to come, however, is the widespread recognition of a linkage between increasingly higher levels of productivity — defined above as exploitation of self — and the various symptoms of fatigue in the human body, mind and spirit.

There is a reason why this recognition has not (yet) been achieved. Turning back to the four 'pillars' used to define the exploitative style of development above, the last three are becoming resistant to being squeezed further — if exploitation of self also has to be given up, not only will this style of development crumble, but also the BWL that is materially based on it. In other words, to challenge increasing productivity is today to challenge the very basis of the social formation of OECD countries — a formation that is, with ever increasing production,

and ever increasing consumption, showing the ever more negative
consequences of too much BWL. This is precisely what makes the
1980s so important: will the point be reached where the doctrine
of high productivity becomes a political issue, with movements
organized to fight against it — thereby making for more jobs at
constant levels of production, and possibly with a richer job
content? Or, will the present pathological trends carry on into
the future unchallenged?

THE STRUCTURAL ARGUMENT: THE UNDERLYING SOCIAL FORMATION

   Again, this leads to a new question: Exactly why do we have a
bourgeois way of life, and an exploitative style of development?
In the preceding section we characterized the BWL as more or
less a pattern of values and attitudes, translated into behaviour. The exploitative style of development is thus seen
merely as something chosen to fit the BWL. If this were the
case, one could simply change the WOL and change the style of
development, assuming that there is nothing deeper, more solid,
that would constrain our choices. But there certainly is scope
for asking whether there is not something more solid, more
permanent, that generates both phenomena. And indeed there is
such a thing — an entire social formation, sometimes known as
the 'modern' or 'capitalist' system.
   There are many ways of describing this social formation. One
useful approach is as follows: the 'modern system' emerged out
of the Middle Ages when a 'modern period' was built on the
waning feudal system. Characteristic of this system is a con-
cordat between state and capital, bureaucracy and corporation,
increasingly supported by a growing intelligentsia whose role
was to produce general formulae useful in developing understanding and policies for control.[9] Bureaucrats, capitalists and
intelligentsia — a triangle of those most clearly engaged in non-
manual labour — constituted, and still constitute, the elites of
the social formation. The technologies they developed for
material (and non-material) production would tend to be bureau-
cracy-, capital- and intelligentsia-intensive; such development
reinforces their position in society by making them indispensable, and also provides similar elite positions for their male
offspring (females being relegated to reproductive functions in
the privacy of the family). Capital provides financial support
for the state in the form of direct and indirect taxes, while
the state provides a unified national market for capital, possibilities for overseas expansion, infrastructural support and
so on. Meanwhile, the rest of the population became clients of
bureaucracy and consumers for the corporations, paying for what

they received as clients with conformity, and for what they received as consumers with labour.

At this point, it is worth focusing on a peculiar characteristic of the social formations found in most OECD nations. Certainly all 'civilized' societies have elites that combine non-manual work with material comfort; but not all of them have such rapidly expanding elites with a seemingly relatively high level of willingness to share the essential characteristics of their way of life with, if not everybody, at least many members of their societies. In this respect, we should note once again that the BWL is not monopolized any longer by a small group; it has become the dominant way of life. This should perhaps lead us to wonder whether the elites are preserving something else as a monopoly while letting people in general enjoy the BWL — much as the upper classes went flying when the railroads became relatively classless, went to the Caribbean when more people were able to have holidays in the Mediterranean area (and then to small islands in the Indian and Pacific Oceans when people started 'flooding' the Caribbean).

One such possibility would be the monopolization of access to non-alienated work; the jobs of bureaucrats, capitalists and intelligentsia would become the only non-programmed and non-programmable jobs in society, as these are the jobs held by the programmers themselves.[10] Yet another possibility lies in the elites latching on to the possibilities for alternative ways of life as an escape from the meaninglessness and emptiness of the BWL, in the same way that the CWL offers a retreat from its more oppressive aspects. But for AWL to remain exclusive, as an elite activity, they will have to be patterned in an exclusive way. If AWL are to be the negation of BWL then four leading characteristics are implied: more manual work (which the elites have always been able to include in the form of gardening and hobby activities); less comfort (which the elites have always been able to include in the form of hazardous styles of vacationing such as British aristocratic pursuits); efforts to escape the confines of the nuclear family (by extra-marital activities and exclusive elite clubs); and a lower level of predictability and security (accessible to the elites through political, economic and intellectual risk-taking, given that they have the advantage of still retaining a material base on which to land after the risks have been indulged in).

No doubt this facet of the AWL phenomena is one of the reasons why elites have become interested in such movements in recent years. But there is much more to AWL than the provision of an outlet for the elites from the BWL. This is clear from recent developments in the OECD countries, and particularly in North America and Europe today.

The outline above should be seen as a way in which the elites
may detach themselves from the structure which they serve and
which serves them well in return. We should treat AWL as a much
wider social phenomenon, involving far more people — across age,
sex and class structures — and, above all, involving rather
deeper changes in the content of their WOL. In this respect,
practitioners of AWL actually tend to put a great deal of stress
on becoming more independent of the elites in the present social
formation. Thus they substitute self-management (autogestion)
for the bureaucrat-intensive practices of the present social
order; economic self-sufficiency and greater emphasis on the
informal economic sector for the corporate-intensive aspect;
and the drive for self-definition, the capacity to come to grips
with one's own existence, using one's own means, for the intelligentsia-intensive aspect.[11] To the extent that these ideas
are implemented, there will be little or no comfort for the
elites, who will become redundant, superfluous — as is precisely
the intention.

Moreover, many of the practices constituting AWL point in the
direction of another development style — one that is more arti-
sanal, less productivity-oriented, co-operative domestically
and globally (rather than being exploitative of the internal and
external proletariat), and which seeks to live in partnership
with nature, to be integrative rather than exploitative here
too. What has been said above is still at the level of slogans
and indications, but there is no difficulty today in substanti-
ating the notion that AWL seek to develop, and are being developed, in this direction by those actively engaged in them.[12]

This is not to say that all practitioners of AWL are agreed
over what is wrong with the DWL and therefore over what needs
to be done to effect change. There are those who, seeking to
understand the phenomena of DWL and AWL, pick up one corner
only of the bureaucrat-capitalist-intelligentsia triangle
referred to above. Thus some would base their analysis on the
role of the state and develop a more anarchist ideology, others
on the capitalist system and develop a more socialist ideology,
while still others would focus on the intelligentsia and develop
a more populist ideology. The present analysis, however, aims
to encompass all three trends, since in social reality the
corners of the triangle blend together as patterns of the dominant social formation, constituting the factors which generate
the issues and structure the ideologies which inspire the concrete activity of social movements. Of course, the relative
weight of these three factors differs from issue to issue, from
movement to movement, from country to country, and over historical time. What is clear, then, is that a rich form of under-

standing is needed to accommodate much of what seems to be underlying the general malaise with which we are concerned. In making
this case for AWL, we are implicitly mounting a challenge to the
ideologies of the last century that still remain strong today
due to lack of any alternative. Liberalism promised happiness
with continued economic growth, but was blind to the problems of
inequality and inequity, and also to the problems of too much
affluence. Socialism introduced class analysis to come to
grips, through redistribution and revolution, with problems of
inequality and inequity, but was equally blind to the problems
of affluence. (Socialism, when practised as the right to a BWL
for all, seems to lead to some of the same problems as liberalism, although in Eastern Europe these have evolved more slowly
because the countries involved were materially less developed
and have taken the problems of underdevelopment more seriously.)
Nor do anarchism and populism seem to have been any more successful at asking the crucial questions suggested by analysis of the
trends evident in Fig. 1.3. In particular, what are the upper
limits to the types of remedy suggested: certainly, small is
beautiful, and to do without experts is fine, but how far can
we go here? How to combine small and big, 'red' and 'expert',
are the key problems in China today, and perhaps they will be
in the rich countries tomorrow.

THE CULTURAL ARGUMENT: THE UNDERLYING COSMOLOGY

Again, we may pose the question: Why do we have such a social
formation as exists today? And, again, we may venture down one
more level, this time to what we consider as the rock-bottom
foundation. This is the deep culture, the cosmology of the
Western civilization within which these social formations have
taken root. Of course, these social formations in turn reinforce the cosmology, and become embedded in it as a part of the
deep culture. The cosmology is not a cause with a structure as
one of its effects; rather, we see the structure as a manifestation of that deep cosmology, a way in which the cosmology un-
folds itself.[13]
More concretely, a few central aspects of the Western cosmology currently seems to be important in this connection. First,
there is the general idea of a *dichotomy between the spiritual
and the material,* between god and the world, with human beings
somewhere in-between, being partly of god, partly of the world,
but endowed with a capacity to choose.[14] Suspended between the
two, yes, but with no doubt as to which is better, the superior-
ity of the non-manual over the manual and the non-natural over
the natural are easily arrived at. The empirical counterpart

of this (in turn reinforcing the logical distinction) would be
precisely the quest for the first two components of the bourgeois way of life: non-manual work and material comfort.
Another aspect of Western cosmology is equally important in
this respect — the idea of progress. If the non-manual is better
than the manual, and material comfort is better than discomfort,
then increasing proportions of people engaged in increasingly
non-manual work, and living in increasing personal comfort,
should be important elements of progress.[15] That the BWL should
be a major goal for the majority of members of Western civilization (or of people anywhere where Westernization is established) is entirely in agreement with fundamental principles of
that civilization. So is the exploitative style of development.

The exploitation of nature is totally in line with a principle
that puts distance between human beings and their natural environment. The same applies to increased productivity, in so
far as it is based on a technology founded upon a system of
natural sciences (and to some extent also a system of social and
human sciences) that objectifies and looks at nature from the
outside. But what about the internal and external exploitation?
The former can also be regarded as one more manifestation of the
distances set up between spirit and world, person and nature,
manual and non-manual activity. Thus, those who work with their
hands, close to nature, are treated as if they belonged to a
lower kind of social order; hence, they are not only exploitable,
but legitimately exploited. For the latter, a third aspect of
the deep culture of Western civilization is typically drawn upon
for legitimization: the conceptualization of socio-geographical
space in which the West is seen on the centre, and the non-West
as a periphery waiting to be Westernized. Implicit in this
scheme of things is the idea of a waiting room, with the most
recent 'arrivals' accorded the most menial tasks from which they
may graduate through 'development'. External exploitation,
then, is not only seen as natural and normal according to this
cosmology; it also presents an invitation for those in the periphery to join, as if some kind of favour was being bestowed
upon them.[16]

The growing centrality of such a cosmology in the social
structure will lead to an elite engaged not only in non-manual
work, but also in programming others at the centre; an elite
continuing the work of god the creator. Efforts to change the
social structure, making it less exploitative, will therefore
have a tendency to regenerate this particular characteristic,
and perhaps also the centre-periphery formation when seen on a
world scale. Certainly, AWL movements often try to go beyond
this in their efforts to establish partnership with nature, with

the Third World, and with the internal proletariat (which would
then no longer be an internal proletariat), and achieve independence from the elite through self-management, self-sufficiency
and self-definition. In so far as this is true, AWL movements
are not only directed against a particular social structure as
we know it, but also against the cosmology of which this structure might be said to be a manifestation. In short, what is
contested is Western civilization itself.

CONCLUSION

    Why the concern with ways of life? There are, as we have
seen, many answers to this important question, each focusing
on different levels of analysis.
    At the *first* level, that of issues and movements, there are
a number of highly concrete and very nagging issues, which form
the raw material for mass media reports, countless books and
articles, and so on. The basic point here is that these issues
are now parts of our way of life. They can no longer be seen
as 'unfortunate consequences' of our DWL; they are simply
descriptions of our social environment. Our many material possessions have not led to unmitigated happiness and satisfaction,
and the many social pathologies mentioned increasingly seem to
dominate people's lives, making life on Earth increasingly un-
attractive for all but a small minority who have somehow managed
to escape the structural and cultural bounds to needs satisfaction. Some of those able to escape are elites with the means
to do so; others are non-elites engaging in alternative ways of
life. These AWL groups are often fragmented and poorly linked,
reacting in different ways to environmental problems, domestic
and global poverty and hunger, to alienating structures in their
own society, and so on. Practised for different reasons, the
various AWL nevertheless constitute a movement, a force which
is threatening the DWL in industrialized societies. As we see
it these movements have the potential of establishing new DWL-
ways of life possibly more harmonious, less exploitative, and
more in line with the environmental and social constraints that
are now known to exist. In short, the movement for AWL can be
seen as a family of movements addressing themselves to a family
of issues which are highly complex, highly diversified — and
certainly not as clear in empirical reality as we have tried to
portray in this chapter.
    At the *second* level, that of needs, one may see the concern
with ways of life as a question of individuals reaching out to
each other to protect themselves, as a form of self-defence.
Our societies have saved many people from the terrible pains of

underconsumption, hunger, malnutrition, nature-inflicted
diseases, and other environmental hazards, yet in turn have
exposed them to society-inflicted diseases and non-material
malnourishment of various kinds. In their acts of self-defence,
people try to construct social niches, islands, even ghettoes,
more or less effectively protected from the social pathologies
dominating the outside. In short, they try to generate development rather than various types of maldevelopment.

At the *third* level, the concern with WOL can be seen more
concretely as a reaction against a bourgeois way of life that
is becoming the DWL in industrialized societies, and as a reaction against its exploitative underpinnings. At this point
the struggle over ways of life becomes overtly political, because it affects power and privilege, potentially undermining
some of the bases on which the elitist power structures in the
world of today, both domestically and globally, are founded.

At the *fourth* level, this becomes a challenge not only to
concrete policies, but to the entire social structure, with
visions of a much more decentralized society of small self-
regulating units (which would have to be tied together in ways
not yet specified by the AWL movement in theory or in practice).
And at the *fifth* level the concern with ways of life challenges
underlying cultural assumptions, the cosmology of Western
civilization as a whole. This is evidenced most clearly in the
tendency of AWL movements to invoke non-Western cultural perspectives and symbols, indicating that they cannot find sufficient building blocks in the Western culture as such to construct the ethos needed by a movement challenging the status
quo.

So to the question, 'Why the concern with ways of life?', we
have five different sets of answers, deriving from five different levels of analysis, here weakly woven together in some kind
of theoretical framework. This framework is very much work in
progress, and like all theories open to challenge. In conclusion, then, it is naive today to believe that this concern
should be limited to the industrially advanced countries. As
indicated in Fig. 1.5, contemporary development practices, with
economists and other 'development specialists' acting as tunnel-
diggers, make possible, and actually produce, maldevelopment
such as we have been analysing here. Consequently, in all probability, the AWL phenomenon will soon be as widespread as the
maldevelopment phenomenon all around the world — with more or
less the same issues and movements.

NOTES

1. This paper was first presented at the meeting organized by
the World Future Studies Federation in connection with the
Fourth Meeting of the Alternative Ways of Life subproject of
the Goals, Processes and Indicators of Development Project, the
UN University — in Grzegorzewice, Poland, 2 June 1980; it was
also presented at the Fifth Network Meeting of the GPID Project,
Montreal, 27 July to 4 August 1980. The paper is the outcome
of countless discussions among the authors, within the AWL sub-
project, the GPID project and in many other settings — gratitude
is hereby expressed to all discussants.

2. It should be pointed out that this is a list for rich countries. For poor countries the social pathologies may perhaps
not be too different, but the human pathologies pertaining to
the body would be different — malaria rather than cardio-vascular
diseases, to take the famous example used by the President of
Singapore.

3. This list is based on those suggested by Huber (1979) and
Arnold and Goulet (this volume).

4. For an exploration of this, see the articles by Kreye,
Mallmann and Galtung in part I of Lederer (1980).

5. This theme is explored in some detail in Galtung (1980).

6. In saying this, we are not denying that the nuclear family
is today in crisis, breaking up both vertically (parents and
children becoming increasingly alienated from each other) and
horizontally (the divorce of parents and the separation of
children). All of this does not constitute an AWL as such, but
rather a disruption, indeed a destruction, of the effort to
attain a BWL.

7. This is explored in some detail in J. Galtung, 'Global Processes and the World in the 1980s', in Marcus et al. (forthcoming).

8. This concept, developed by André Gunder Frank, is used by
Kreye et al. (1979).

9. For an elaboration of this point, see Galtung et al. (1980a).

10. The tendency towards routinization of productive activity,
the conversion of all work into jobs, creeps higher and higher
into the upper echelons of society: computerization of legal

decisions could eliminate a number of 'highly qualified' lawyers,
standardization of entrepreneurial practices could eliminate a
number of 'highly-qualified' managers. One might perhaps say
that the only ones who are not so easy to eliminate would be
those who are genuinely creative, inventing new paradigms, new
'algorithms' all the time — but maybe they/we should not feel
too safe?

11. Whatever their particular goal and form of action, AWL, as
a general social phenomenon in the West, are indeed a deeply
rooted protest movement against the increasing concentration of
power, authority, and privelege embodied in ever larger state
bureaucracies, private corporations and academic brain trusts
at the top of society. At all levels of human action, AWL stand
for *self*-realization, *self*-regulation, *self*-determination, *self*-
reliance, *self*-management, etc., as opposed to *Fremdsteuerung*
of social life by anonymous, technocratic mechanisms. For a
general overview of the AWL movement, see, for example, Galtung
and Wemegah (1978), Galtung and Wemegah (1979), and Galtung *et
al.* (1979). One of the most comprehensive alternative movements
in the Western world to date is perhaps the movement for self-
management (Selbstverwaltungsbewegung, mouvement autogestion-
nair), to the extent that it addresses itself to the psychological, economic, social, ecological as well as political problems involved in breaking away from mainstream society. For
empirical assessments, see, for example, Holenweger and Mader
(1979); Netzwerk Selbsthilfe (1979); Hollstein and Penth (1980);
and Huber (1979). It should be noted that AWL movements are
currently in a process of overcoming the initial social, economic and political isolation which they encountered at first.
For an appraisal of the situation facing AWL movements today
see, for instance, Wemegah (1980) and Poleszynski and Wemegah
(1980).

12. It is important to realize that AWL is not a 'navel-gazing'
movement interested solely in personal emancipation of the
people engaged in it, but is equally concerned with problems of
maldevelopment showing up in the wider social and natural environment, both at home and abroad. The great merit of AWL is
to show that a development style compatible with global solidarity and ecological equilibrium implies a dramatic change in
the West's consumer habits, which are directly or indirectly
responsible for the unrelenting exploitation of both people and
natural resources throughout the world. One of the first movements to have pointed to the dialectical relationship between
underdevelopment in the Third World and overdevelopment at home
is the Norwegian movement, 'The Future in Our Hands', created in

1974, and now having branches in Sweden, Denmark, and Finland, and possibly soon in the United States. For further reference, see Rivers (1977); Allaby (1977); Holenstein (1977); Strahm (1977); and Gowan et al. (1976).

13. For more on the concept of cosmology as we use it here, see Galtung et al. (1980b).

14. As a professing Christian, Monica Wemegah would like to indicate that the Western cosmology described here has no similarity with the cosmology contained in the Bible; indeed it is arguable whether the West ever had a Biblical cosmology, given its history of conquest, exploitation, force and sub- jugation. Fromm (1979), though not a Christian himself, simi- larly argues that the West's conversion to Christianity was — apart from many genuinely Christian movements — largely a sham, because it did not mean a change of heart. In Wemegah's view, the BWL as conceived of here, with its scorn of manual work, preference of human-made over natural things, striving for ever more material possessions and ever higher material comfort, exclusive interest in one's own (family) life at the expense of concern for people living outside one's narrow private sphere, and the assumption that such attitudes towards fellow-men and nature are not only desirable but perpetuable over generations is just one of the consequences of man/woman's unregenerated, hence egocentric, nature.

15. Nowhere can this be seen so clearly, and so intelligently expressed, as in the promise held out for posterity by Keynes in his famous *Economic Possibilities for our Grandchildren* (1930).

16. Wemegah would like to stress that in her view the distance between man and nature is by no means God-given, but is the result of human arrogance and lovelessness *vis-a-vis* both the human and natural environment. When God gave us dominion over the earth and every living creature thereupon (Gen. 1:28), the subjugation should have been that of a caring husbandman, which the first Adam was made (Gen. 2:15), not that of a rap- acious ruler. We were to respect the regenerative capacity of the land (Lev. 25:4; Ex. 23:10-11), regard the life of animals (Prov. 12:10, Deut. 25:4, Deut. 22:6-7), not strip the land bare, but leave the gleanings of the field for the poor (Deut. 24:21); and even under the pressing need of harvest, the labourer and the beast were to enjoy their rest (Ex. 23:10). The prophet's warning 'Woe unto them that join house to house, that lay field to field till there be no place left' (Isaiah

34	The Poverty of Progress

5:8) sounds curiously contemporary when we think of the current problems of high density housing and of intensive farming techniques producing pest infestation, requiring large pesticide and fertilizer inputs, causing in their turn pollution from leaching, genetic loss of old strong strains, etc. Very briefly, the underlying theme of Biblical Christianity is that God made the world for people to use but use does not equal exploitation. People, in the avarice of their estrangement, exploit not only nature, but their fellow humans also. Little wonder that the Bible says that God will come 'to destroy those that destroy the earth' (Rev. 11:18).

BIBLIOGRAPHY

Allaby, M. (1977) *The Survival Handbook*. London, Pan.
Fromm, E. (1979) *To Have or To Be*. London, Sphere.
Galtung, J. (1980) Global Goals, Global Processes and the Prospects for Human and Social Development, United Nations University/GPID prepublication paper.
Galtung, J., Heiestand, T. and Rudeng, E. (1980a) *Macro-History and Western Civilization*. Oslo.
Galtung, J., Heiestad, T. and Rudeng, E. (1980b) On the Last 2500 Years in Western History, and Some Remarks on the Coming 500, Chapter 12 of companion volume to *The New Cambridge Modern History*. London, Cambridge University Press.
Galtung, J. and Wemegah, M. (1978) Overdevelopment and Alternative Ways of Life in High Income Countries, *Internationale Entwicklung,* Oesterreichische Forschungsstiftung für Entwicklung, 4, 5-12.
Galtung, J. and Wemegah, M. (1979) *The Struggle Against Maldevelopment*. Report prepared for the European Economic Commission and the United Nations Environment Programme, Geneva.
Galtung, J., Wemegah, M. and Poleszynski, D. (1979) Overdevelopment and Alternative Ways of Life in High Income Countries, in Society for International Development, *Alternative Ways of Life*. Rome, SID.
Gowan, S. *et al.* (1976) *Moving Toward a New Society*. Philadelphia, New Society Press.
Holenstein, A.-M. (1977) *Zerstörung Durch Ueberfluss (Destruction Through Abundance)*. Basel, Z-Verlag.
Holenweger, T. and Mäder, W. (eds) (1979) *Inseln der Zukunft? (Islands of the Future?)*. Zurich, Limmat Verlag.
Hollstein, W. and Penth, B. (1980) *Alternativprojekte: Berspiele Gegen Die Resignation (Alternative Projects: Examples*

Against Resignation). Reinbeck bei Hamburg, Rowohlt Taschen-
buch Verlag.
Huber, J. (ed) (1979) *Anders Arbeiten - Anders Wirtschaften,*
Frankfurt a.m., Fischer Taschenbuch Verlag.
Keynes, J.M. (1972) Economic Possibilities for our Grandchildren,
in *Essays in Persuasion.* London, MacMillan (first published
1930).
Kreye, O., Froebel, F. and Heinrichs, J. (1979) *Die Neue Inter-
nationale Arbeitsteilung (English Edition: The New Inter-
national Division of Labour.* London, Cambridge University
Press)
Lederer, K. (ed.) (1980) *Human Needs: A Contribution to the
Current Debate.* Köngstein, Anton Hain.
Marcus, S. (ed.) (forthcoming) *Visions of Desirable Worlds.*
Bucharest.
Mishan, E. (1969) *The Costs of Economic Growth.* Harmondsworth,
Penguin.
Netzwerk Selbsthilfe (1979) *Ein Jahr Netzwerk (One Year's Net-
work).* Berlin, Netzwerke Selbsthilfe.
Ornauer, H., Wiberg, H., Sicinski, A. and Galtung, J. (eds)
(1976) *Images of the World in the Year 2000.* The Hague and
Paris, Mouton.
Poleszynski, D. and Wemegah, M. (1980) The Green Wave — The Rise
of the Green Pole as a Political Actor. (Paper presented at
UNU/GPID Meeting, Montreal, 25 July to 5 August.)
Rivers, P. (1977) *Living Better on Less.* London, Turnstone
Books.
Strahm, R. (1977) *Pourquoi Sont-lls Si Pauvres? (Why Are They
So Poor?).* Neuchâtel, Ed. de la Bâçonnière.
Wemegah, M. (1980) Alternative Networks. (Paper presented at
UNU/GPID Meeting on Alternative Ways of Life, Warsaw,
30 May to 1 June.)

2

The 'Abundant Society' and World Order: Dominant Ways of Life in the United States

STEVEN ARNOLD AND DENIS GOULET

No strategy to reach a more humane world order can ignore the
interests, values, and institutions of the principal actors in
the present global system. Chief among these is the United
States. Richard Falk points to the crucial role of the United
States in world order questions in these words:

> In this sense, the domestic political arena of the Un-
> ited States is also a critical world order arena, perhaps
> even the single most critical one. Without fundamental
> changes in the US world role, no substantial progress
> toward world order goals can be realistically envisioned,
> except possibly in a post-catastrophe setting . . . .
> (Falk, 1975, p. 49)

The United States is important not only because of its military and economic strength, but also because of its widespread
'demonstration effects'. How it views its approach to global
issues like war, poverty, social justice, and environment has
a great impact on discussion of these issues at the international
level. Hence the utility of examining the interplay of myths,
values and institutions within American society; it is this
interplay which can resolve contradictions and offer a framework for meaning. 'Counter-myths', in turn, supply alternative
meaning systems. Were these to displace dominant values and
approaches within the nation, the US would necessarily adopt a
different international stance. Yet it is extremely difficult
to 'take the pulse' of values and life-styles in the United
States.
Numerous impressions strike even casual visitors to the United
States: speed, power, complexity, and diversity. The most
salient impression, however, is one of exuberant material abundance. And one central institution stands out everywhere in
this pluralistic society: the shopping centre, comprising dozens

of stores of every type laden with every imaginable commodity, girded by acres of parking lots for the ubiquitous symbol of American life, the automobile. As one probes more deeply, one discovers that proliferation is not confined to material objects alone; it also extends to ideas and values. At the physical level the shopping centre presents a jumble of things; at the symbolic level it reflects the plurality of meanings which assault the consciousness of Americans, portraying a rich but bewildering array of dreams, values and, ultimately, philosophies of life. Mere abundance, however, has not led to generalized happiness. Indeed the American mood has become reflective of late, and social commentators weary not of analyzing the relationship between abundant goods, deeper meanings, and the inner quality of life.[1]*

To assess the goods and evils present in a large and complex society like the United States is an overwhelming task requiring a critical analysis of the interplay between the values Americans cherish and the institutions they support. Clearly this brief chapter cannot do justice to this ambitious undertaking. Its more modest role is to highlight some of the most important features of present American society, and to speculate upon their merit, significance, and implications.

The first section of this chapter offers an impressionistic view of US society, based on a series of statistical 'still pictures' which attempt to capture, albeit inadequately, certain key characteristics and contradictions in American society. Statistical portraits, however, must be set in the context of broader social institutions and the values which give them meaning. Accordingly, we move in the second section to describe three of the most salient institutions of US society, together with the underlying 'myths' usually invoked to legitimize them. This combination provides a frame of reference for evaluating the social costs and benefits of life in the United States. Finally, we speculate upon the strength of these myths, and the challenge presented by 'counter-myths' which also proliferate in the country's abundant 'meaning market'.

CONTRADICTIONS IN THE ABUNDANT SOCIETY

To judge by statistical indicators, the abundant society has achieved an enviable record; it provides the 'good life' to that mythical abstraction, the 'average' American (Table 2.1). The statistically average American begins life in a hospital with an excellent chance of surviving birth itself and the first year of life. This individual can expect to live 69 years (if male) and 76 years (if female). The society's most serious

---

*Superscript numbers refer to notes at end of chapter.

health problems are associated with stress and old age, with
the major causes of death being heart disease, followed by
cancer and strokes.

Table 2.1
US 'Quality of Life': Selected Indicators, 1950-77

	1950	1960	1970	1977
Income-Employment				
Per capita GNP (current dollars)	1887	2801	4795	8713
Per capita GNP (1972 dollars)	3517	4078	5248	6167
Unemployment rate (%)	5.3	5.5	4.9	7.0
White-collar jobs (% of total jobs)	37.5	43.4	48.3	49.9
Education				
Median school years completed (persons 25 years of age and older)	9.3	10.6	12.2	12.4
Illiteracy (as % of those 14 years of age and older)	3.3	2.4	1.2	*
Health				
Life expectancy at birth:	68.2	69.7	70.9	72.8[a]
Life expectancy at birth (whites)	69.1	70.6	71.7	73.5[a]
Life expectancy at birth (non-whites)	60.8	63.6	65.3	68.3[a]
Infant mortality rate (per 100,000 under one year of age)	2920	2600	2000	1520[a]
Principal causes of death:				
Heart disease (per 100,000)	*	515.1	496.0	454.0[a]
Cancer (per 100,000)	*	149.2	162.8	175.8[a]
Stroke (per 100,000)	*	108.0	101.9	87.9[a]
Other				
Crime rate (per 100,000):				
Violent	*	161[b]	364	467
Property	*	1726[b]	3621	4588
Homicide (per 100,000, 15 years of age and older)	7.2	6.9	11.6	12.1[a]

(cont.)

Table 2.1 (cont.)

	1950	1960	1970	1977
Other (cont.)				
Suicide (deaths per 100,000, 15 years of age and older)	15.6	15.4	16.2	16.5[a]
Divorce (rate per 100,000)	260	220	350	500[c]
Persons in nursing homes (1000s)	*	491[d]	850[e]	1286[a,c]
Death by cirrhosis of the liver (per 100,000)	9.2	11.3	15.5	14.7[a]
Estimated rate of alcoholism (per 100,000, 20 years of age and older)	*	*	4200	4200[f]

Source: Statistical Abstract of the United States (1978), except where noted.

Notes: * Data not available.
       [a] Data are for 1976.
       [b] Data from *Statistical Abstract of the United States* (1976).
       [c] Preliminary data.
       [d] Data are for 1963.
       [e] Data are for 1969.
       [f] Data are for 1975.

This 'typical' American appears to be well-off economically, enjoying an average per-capita income of almost $9000 in 1977. More than 90 per cent of Americans who actively seek work are employed, almost half of them holding white-collar jobs. In addition, 'typical' individuals are literate; they have completed secondary schooling and possibly some higher education. They also own their own home, which possesses, on the average, five rooms and is equipped with all modern plumbing fixtures. This residence is well stocked with sundry appliances: a television set, a refrigerator, a washing machine, one or more telephones, electric kitchen equipment (such as a mixer, frying pan, coffee maker, and blender), a clothes dryer, and at least one air conditioner. In the garage can be found one or more automobiles. The typical person's diet is plentiful and varied; it includes large quantities of meat, fresh fruits, vegetables, milk, cream, and sugar (Table 2.2).

Not all aspects of reality as portrayed by these indicators of abundance are reassuring, however. From scattered evidence

Table 2.2
US 'Quality of Life': Housing and Nutrition, 1976

	1976
Housing and Domestic Equipment	
Home ownership (% of persons who own their place of residence)	64.7
Median number of rooms in US dwellings	5.1
Percentage of households with various appliances and other amenities:	
Telephone	90.3
Air conditioning	51.0
One or more automobiles	83.8
Full plumbing	96.6
Electric blender	50.0*
Clothes dryer	59.3*
Clothes washer	73.3*
Dishwasher	40.9*
Electric mixer	92.4*
Refrigerator	99.9*
Radio	99.9*
Television	99.9*
Colour television	81.3*
Electric frying pan	64.4*
Electric can opener	57.9*
Home freezer	44.8*
Electric iron	99.9*
Electric toaster	99.9*
Nutrition	
Nutrients available for civilian consumption per capita per day:	
Protein (grams)	103
Protein (index, 1967=100)	104
Fat (grams)	159
Fat (index, 1967=100)	106
Carbohydrates (grams)	390
Carbohydrates (index, 1967=100)	104
Calories	3380

(cont.)

Table 2.2 (cont.)

	1976
Per capita annual consumption of major food commodities (lbs):	
Meat	194.8
Milk	245.0
Fresh fruit	86.6
Processed fruit	49.4
Fresh vegetables	102.5
Canned vegetables (except potatoes)	52.8
Frozen vegetables (except potatoes)	10.2
Potatoes	135.7
Refined sugar	94.7
Corn syrup and sugar	37.5
Wheat flour	111.0

Source: Statistical Abstract of the United States (1978)
Note: *Data for 1977.

available, one is led to entertain doubts about the true benefits of the 'good' life. To illustrate, the suspicion is growing that Americans suffer from over-consumption or distorted consumption in their diet, given their predilection for meals which are over-rich in meats, animal fat, sugar and eggs. This says nothing of their addiction to so-called 'junk foods'. Not surprisingly, therefore, obesity and poor nutrition are becoming very serious health problems in the United States (US Senate, 1978). Indeed, health planners in Montgomery County, a suburb of Washington, D.C. and one of the richest counties in the country, have found that poor eating habits and alcoholism are the two major health problems of residents (*Washington Post,* 1978).

Aggregate statistics which describe abundance for 'average Americans' also necessarily obscure the unequal distribution of the benefits. As one analyst notes, the concept of 'average' is itself misleading, as 'Mississippi sharecroppers and Marin County, California commuters do not 'average' out to Toledo factory workers' (Wattenberg, 1965). Looking beyond this statistical 'average' and into the real world, however, even first-time visitors to typical large American cities note striking contrasts in the satisfaction of such basic needs as health and

education. A dramatic example of such unevenness in the nation's
capital appears in data prepared by the Overseas Development
Council which compared infant mortality rates in the richest
and poorest sections of Washington, D.C. It was found not only
that the gap between rich and poor was wide, but that the gap
has been widening, as virtually all of the improvement in infant mortality rates since 1960 has been confined to the rich
section (Table 2.3). The fact that the rich section is predominantly white, while the poor section is predominantly black,
also suggests a continuing discrimination against black Americans, a conclusion reinforced by nation-wide statistics which
show that illiteracy for blacks is 7 per cent, while for whites
it is less than 2 per cent. Moreover, almost two-thirds of
white Americans own their own homes, a benefit enjoyed by less
than half of the black population (*Statistical Abstract*, 1975,
p. 717).

Table 2.3
Infant Mortality, Washington, DC, 1960-75
(per 1000 live births)

	Total Washington D.C.	Service Area 6[a]	Service Area 8[b]
1960	30.4	43.4	23.7
1970	28.9	38.1	13.6
1975	29.0	38.0	9.0

Source: Calculated by Overseas Development Council, Washington,
D.C. from figures supplied by the Department of Human
Resources, District of Columbia.

Notes: [a] Service area 6 is the poorest of the 9 Washington,
D.C. sections (1970 median income: $6612). It also
has the highest percentage of black persons (96% of
births in 1973 were black).

[b] Service area 8 is the richest of the 9 Washington,
D.C. sections (1970 median income: $18970). It also
has the lowest percentage of black persons (17% of
births in 1973 were black).

   In addition to the inequalities between black and white, one
can see discrimination against the elderly, who are placed with
increasing frequency in nursing homes (Table 2.1), and against

women, who, notwithstanding recent efforts, still lag considerably behind men in employment, education, earnings, property
ownership, social status, and political power.

Although these scattered statistics on over-consumption and
maldistribution of abundance are unsettling, even more disquieting are certain intangible side-effects which many critics associate with the society of abundance. Complaints generally
take the form of sweeping critiques of the society as a whole,
which is branded as unjust, exploitative, and alienating. The
US is called superficial, 'plastic', overbureaucratized, over-
individualistic, commercialized, racist, incapable of promoting
confidence, fulfillment, or the joy of living. To cite two
critical observers:

> Disorientation, apathy, and often despair, haunting Am-
> ericans in all walks of life, have assumed in our time
> the dimensions of a profound crisis. . . . A heavy,
> strangulating sense of emptiness and futility of life
> permeates the country's moral and intellectual climate.
> . . . The malaise deprives work of meaning and purpose;
> turns leisure into joyless, debilitating laziness;
> fatally impairs the educational system and the condi-
> tions for healthy growth in the young; transforms re-
> ligion and church into commercialized vehicles of 'to-
> getherness'; and destroys the very foundation of bour-
> geois society, the family. (Baran and Sweezy, 1964,
> p. 281)

Any attempt to judge the claims on behalf of, and criticism
against, US society faces an obvious difficulty in determining
the precise meaning conveyed by the statistics themselves. The
statistics on divorce illustrate clearly the problem of interpretation. Everyone agrees that the divorce rate has been
climbing sharply since the Second World War. But does this
rise provide ammunition for the critics of the society of abundance, who see it as evidence of increasing alienation — or to
its supporters, who argue that more divorces signify increasing
choice and opportunity, enabling persons trapped in unhappy
marriages to explore more fulfilling avenues in life? Similarly,
critics of American society point to increasing crime rates as
evidence of gross inadequacies, whereas its supporters argue
that the increase is traceable to the fact that since the post
Second World War 'baby boom', an increasing percentage of the
society is currently in the 14-24 age bracket which tends to
commit most crimes.

Although the difficulty of interpreting statistical evidence
is inherent in the nature of data, it also reflects the pro-

liferation of meaning systems within American society. To some
observers, the US appears to be groping uncertainly in 'a moral
and aesthetic free-for-all', experiencing frequent and confusing
shifts in moral and philosophical fashions. With some hyper-
bole, one commentator has described this as appearing to be
characterized by

> rapid switches from Leninism to vegetarianism, from
> thought-less wastefulness to obsessive conservation,
> from preoccupation with issues of foreign policy to
> fixation on the domestic, from singing the praise of
> monogamy to acclaiming open marriage. . . . (Hollander,
> 1978, p. 51)

Even if one dismissed these changes as superficial or as an
example of 'media-hype', one must nonetheless acknowledge
the conflicting nature of the underlying American values which
give them weight. Certain troubling dichotomies emerge repeatedly. Among these are: the practical deification of 'winners'
(and the parallel denigration of losers) balanced by a concern
for egalitarianism; a sense of individualism and the cult of
the 'superstar' countered by the perceived desirability of co-
operation and team work; the stirrings of moralistic enthusiasm
in foreign affairs constantly reined by a more pragmatic view
of global policies; a legalistic 'quid pro quo' mentality
(which works against the maintenance of networks of continuing
obligations), set against the felt need for a nurturing sense
of community; and a sense of thrift and self-denial countered
by a desire for immediate gratification. It is never clear
which of the polar values is the dominant one, or which principles can best integrate conflicting demands issuing from the
same interest groups.

MANAGING CONTRADICTIONS IN THE ABUNDANT SOCIETY:
INSTITUTIONS, MYTHS, AND ORGANIZING PRINCIPLES

   The mere existence of contradictions in a society does not
necessarily point to a fatal flaw. On the contrary, it is
doubtful whether any society can be free of serious inconsist-
encies. Moreover, the iron test of the strength of institutions
and social orders is not their internal consistency but rather
their ability to explain and justify the behaviours demanded by
the existing social system, thereby providing legitimacy to some
values held in the society while relegating other values to the
realm of privatized existence. To state the matter differently,
institutions can establish incentives and sanctions which order
society's values, allowing some values to set the tone for the

society at large while other, perhaps even contradictory,
values play a subordinate role.
It is not fully clear how this legitimizing process works,
but a crucial role is the capacity of an institution to structure beliefs and symbols. Sociologist Peter Berger argues that
any all-embracing institution tries to supply its followers
with a comprehensive 'meaning system' (Berger, 1963, pp.
51-2; Berger and Luckmann, 1966) which claims to explain the past and
the present and predicts a bright future if its precepts are
followed. This meaning system, in Berger's view, is supported
by key 'myths' which, in effect, strive to explain away contradictions within the social institutions. Given the complexities
of social relations in a large, varied society like the US,
such myths are difficult to prove or refute. There is no doubt,
however, that they are firmly held. Political scientist Murray
Edelman thinks that

> large numbers of people continue for long periods of
> time to cling to myth, to justify it in formulae that
> are repeated in their cultures, and to reject falsify-
> ing information when prevailing myths justify their
> interests, roles, and past actions, or assuage their
> fears. (Edelman, 1977, p. 3)

The presence of explanatory myths provides society with a two-
edged sword. Thus, although the integrative power of the myth
may usefully mobilize the society, conferring upon it a vision
of the future and the collective will to achieve this vision,
the myth also obscures the patterns of costs and benefits inherent in the institutions it legitimizes. According to Berger,
myth impedes careful and critical analysis because, by its
nature, 'myth fosters total commitment, and people who are so
committed tend to be blind to mythologically inconvenient facts
and indifferent to the costs of their mythologically legitimized
programs' (Berger, 1974, p. 30). Long ago Karl Mannheim (1951,
p. 191) concluded that the presence of myth helps change institutionalized behaviours from being purely instrumental 'social
mechanisms' into 'organizing principles' of the social structure.
And, by implication, organizing principles are beyond criticism
or dispute.
The principles indicated by Berger and Mannheim centrally
affect how the calculus of costs and benefits attaching to the
American way of life is established. The reason is that the
myths which support the organizing principles of the social
structure tend to exaggerate the benefits and minimize the
costs. The authors of this chapter have accordingly taken as
their main task to list and analyse three major 'organizing

principles' and their supporting myths in the American society of abundance. These are: the institution of capitalism (with its myth of mobility); the technological society (with its myth of progress); and the national security state (with its myth of the national interest). Costs and benefits are examined in each case, first within the context of the prevailing myths, and then from an alternative perspective.

CAPITALISM AND THE MYTH OF MOBILITY

Capitalism is clearly one of the dominant institutions in the United States, where it is usually referred to as 'private enterprise'. Capitalism makes competition and profit-seeking not mere instrumental techniques to control against waste and duplication, but the organizing principles of economic activity. The basis for doing so is the belief that the most effective social system is one characterized by the private ownership of the means of production and the legal separation of institutions of economic and political power.

According to the historian David Potter (1954), in the abundant society, the myth that legitimizes capitalism as a morally sound organizing principle is the belief in the existence and virtue of almost unlimited social mobility. (He further argues that mobility has replaced status as the key structural feature of American society.) The power of this myth is revealed in this: that it can allow one to proclaim the value of equality, while accepting a society which is manifestly unequal. Or, to use a notion employed by Charles Elliott in his research on Third World societies, the myth of mobility serves as a 'confidence mechanism' which promotes the legitimacy of a system by allowing those in the lower strata of society to retain the belief that they have an 'acceptable chance' of winning the rewards of competition (Elliott, 1975, pp. 10-11).

In essence, this argument states that opportunity for each member of the abundant society is unlimited. Moreover, since mobility means that all have an acceptable (if not entirely equal) chance of benefiting from these opportunities, rewards tend to go to those who, through their skill, intelligence, and hard work, prove themselves to be the most capable (Potter, 1954, chapter 4). Moreover, the resulting inequality can be justified not only on moral grounds (rewarding the deserving), but also on social grounds much in the vein of the 'social Darwinism' preached by Herbert Spencer and others a century ago. Differential rewards, it is assumed, are necessary to encourage the most capable to display industriousness, prudence, discipline and ingenuity to get the most out of the available

resources, thereby increasing total production and benefitting
the society at large. As Charles Maynes observes, the myth of
mobility basically means that those possessing wealth and power
are presumed to deserve their good fortune. And conversely,
'If the rich deserve what they receive, equally merited is the
unfortunate fate of those who fall by the wayside' (Maynes,
1974). More importantly, those individuals who are presumably
less capable than others also benefit from the inequality, in-
asmuch as the society at large will grow faster with the more
competent individuals at its helm. Within the bounds of this
mode of reasoning, mobility which does actually exist is used,
not to provide opportunity for all, but to preserve the illusion
that those who do not succeed fail as a result of their own
shortcomings and not because of defects intrinsic to the system
itself (Elliott, 1975, p. 11).

Nevertheless, the counter-myth of exploitation is also difficult to demonstrate conclusively in our complex and ambiguous
society. To state that inequities exist does not by itself
prove that marginalization has reached intolerable limits or is
getting worse. Hence the ultimate conclusions one draws from
examining the evidence appear to turn on whether one chooses to
regard a glass as half empty or as half full.

To illustrate, the opinion pollster Louis Harris finds that
some two-thirds of black Americans (who comprise about 12 per
cent of the population) feel discriminated against in housing
and white-collar jobs and a majority feel discriminated against
in education. A majority also feel that they are not 'even
treated as human beings' by the white society (Harris, 1975,
pp. 3-4). And speaking of the 26 million Americans whom he
judges to be living 'in poverty', Harris calls them the 'living
sick' who, lacking proper nutrition and health care, live in a
permanently weakened and pathological state on the fringes of
society. Many of these people, he adds, are probably worse
off than previous generations. He adduces as evidence the fact
that about half the ghetto blacks and 60 per cent of the Appal-
achian whites judge their own health to be worse than that of
their parents (Harris, 1975, pp. 110, 122). On the other hand,
Ben Wattenberg uses census data to demonstrate that tremendous
progress has been made. In a chapter subtitled 'The rich get
richer, and so do the poor', he alleges that the proportion of
the population considered to be 'in poverty' has been over-
estimated. Besides, those who are poor have improved their
incomes at least as much as the rich, while others who were
formerly poor have escaped their lot thanks to social mobility
(Wattenberg, 1965, chapter 8). On similar grounds, Wattenberg
demonstrates that black Americans are improving their position.

The American black, he writes 'is winning his fight — certainly
not as fast as he wishes to win it — but winning it nonetheless'
(Wattenberg, 1965, p. 297).
What is important to note about the United States, however,
is not that myths and counter-myths both exist in the meaning-
market, but that one of these myths is dominant. The poor and
disadvantaged in the United States display a 'quiescent acceptance of chronic inequality, deprivation, and daily indignities'
(Edelman, 1977, p. 14), thereby manifesting the potency of the
myth of mobility according to which the poor are largely responsible for their poverty. This belief, Edelman continues,
persists not only because it justifies the status, power, and
roles of the middle class, public officials, and a variety of
'helping professions'(educators, social workers, etc.) but also
because it is accepted by large sectors of the working and poor
classes, who 'have little ground for self-esteem except their
identification with the state and the elite' (Edelman, 1977,
p. 8).
Even if we discount the social costs of marginalization, however, the alleged benefits flowing from a generalized system of
social mobility may also be fewer than the myth suggests.
Potter believes that the psychological sense of security provided by status disappears in a society that is perceived to be
highly mobile (Potter, 1954, p. 103). Pursuing this theme,
Baran and Sweezy consider that in the perceived absence of fixed
status roles, individual self-esteem must be based on continu
ally 'proving' oneself. At work, one must engage in an endless
series of efforts to 'get ahead' at the expense of others.
Material goods are purchased not only for their utility but also
for their status-bearing qualities: they serve as 'a means of
climbing up a rung on the social ladder' (Baran and Sweezy,
1964, p. 345). If work and consumption are truly like this for
millions of Americans, they can obviously become very alienating
experiences. 'Work and consumption thus share the same ambiguity:
while fulfilling the basic needs of survival, they increasingly
lose their inner content and meaning' (Baran and Sweezy, 1964,
p. 346). Thus as one increasingly relies on work and consumption
to build one's status, their central functions and their ability
to bring satisfaction tend to disappear.[2]
Moreover, if psychological and economic rewards are no longer
based on status but on the demonstration that one is 'directly
productive' to the society, many individuals who are deprived
of status and not directly involved in the economy in a statistically measurable way may suffer unduly. Such a system, for
example, can easily legitimize what by other criteria appear

to be an unjustifiably small portion of the fruits of abundance going to 'marginal' sectors of the population like the retired, the unemployed, children and women (or men) who work in the home or at other unsalaried but essential tasks.

To reward mobility instead of status can also lead to less efficient production, as more and more time is spent in deciding who is on top, rather than in deciding what to produce. An examination of the 'how to succeed in corporate life' literature suggests that strategies for planning one's career route to the top have little to do with increased corporate efficiency (Korda, 1975, 1977). A system based on competitive mobility can also stifle innovations from below, as bosses become fearful of recognizing the competence of subordinates lest they lose their own jobs.

To step outside a society wherein the myth of mobility legitimizes inequality leads one to a very different view of capitalism as an organizing principle. It becomes evident that the alleged benefits of productivity can easily be exaggerated and that social costs like inequality, exploitation, and alienation at work are very high. Whatever the merits of this alternative vantage-point of evaluation may be, however, the myth of mobility displays a striking ability to rationalize persistent poverty within the United States. The source of the myth's power is not altogether obvious, although Edelman (1977) suggests that the self-esteem of the poor is based on their vicarious identification with the elite, while Elliott's (1975) 'confidence mechanism' holds out the tantalizing possibility that some individual members of the poorer classes will actually join their 'superiors' thanks to successful striving. Any alternative vision of a desired social system must therefore address these two problems if it is to be effective.

TECHNOLOGY AND THE MYTH OF PROGRESS

Capitalism is not the sole organizing principal at work in the abundant society of the United States. A second principle, distinct although related, is that of industrial technology. Like capitalism, it is elevated from the position of a mere social regulatory mechanism to that of a 'meaning system' or organizing principle of social structure. One early attempt to assess the costs and benefits of a contemporary society organized around the principle of technology is that of the British economist E. J. Mishan (1970, 1972, 1976). He concluded that advanced industrial societies now face a situation in which an exploding technology is out of control, shapes the world and produces so many 'disamenities' that 'within the span

of a few years the unlimited marketing of new technological
products can result in a cumulative reduction of the pleasure
once freely enjoyed by the citizen' (Mishan, 1970).

Unfortunately, argues Mishan, most people are blinded to these
costs because technology as a 'meaning system' is also dominated
by a myth. This myth is the inevitability of 'progress', and
it emphasizes the alleged benefits of technology (most particularly the provision of a widely expanding array of choices)
while ignoring possible costs by stressing man's infinite
capacity for 'adaptation'.

Typically, it contrasts the comforts and range of choices
offered by present-day life against the 'harshness' and limited
options of older life styles, all the while ignoring the natural
and spiritual satisfactions of the 'old ways' (Mishan, 1970).
This distorted calculation of costs and benefits is further
exaggerated, says Mishan, by our 'future-oriented' mentality,
which allows us to be willing to accept as real benefits the
promise of future opportunities. Yet, as Berger asserts, future
benefits are often nothing more than 'pie in the sky' promises
(Berger, 1974). Jacques Ellul (1967) and others maintain that
the very concept of costs and benefits is stripped of meaning
by the technological perspective, which views the world in
terms of 'problems' amenable to technical 'solutions', rather
than of social contradictions requiring equitable settlement.
The technological perspective further trivializes calculations
by promoting the notion that the 'scientific' approach can embrace all forms of human knowledge — a view described by one
observer as 'essentially a false image of science which . . .
many of the important philosophers have regarded as 'the fundamental false consciousness of our age'.'3

Mishan tries to go beyond the meaning system of technology to
list possible costs more comprehensively and to re-examine
technology's alleged benefits. In examining costs Mishan introduces the concept of 'spillover' effects which are rarely
included in social calculations. Thus, in order to ascertain
the true social benefit of a vacuum cleaner plant, one must
calculate not only the value of the intended product (vacuum
cleaners) but also the possibly negative value of other 'products' of the factory, such as smoke (Mishan, 1970, p. 30).
The fact that spillovers are often difficult to measure because
they fall upon the public at large, Mishan adds, should not
obscure the reality of their impact.

As examples of negative spillover effects Mishan cites a now-
familiar list including the destruction of natural beauty and
the transformation of air, rivers and sea into vast sewers and
cesspools. He insists that these problems are directly related
to the abundant society. In times past, industrial plants were

small enough and few enough that their negative side products
could be absorbed into the cycle of nature, but the current
technological explosion has now exceeded sound ecological
limits.

Following a similar perspective, Lewis Mumford, the foremost
early observer of technology in the United States, examined the
impact of the automobile, considering it to be one of the most
significant technological inventions. It has led to the dominant American industry, and although it promised freedom it
brought instead increased congestion, suburban dullness and high
commuting costs. Mumford concluded that:

> The American has sacrificed his life as a whole to the
> motorcar, like someone who, demented with passion,
> wrecks his home in order to lavish his income on the
> capricious mistress who promises delights he can only
> occasionally enjoy. (Mumford, 1958)

Moreover, the cumulative impact of technological change seems
destined, according to Mishan, not only to increase such disamenities as pollution and economic distortions, but also to
lead to a profound spiritual crisis, in which God is dethroned
and the intrinsic value of the human being is called into
question. Thanks to technology, Mishan notes, 'We have no
choice but to realize that in one attribute after another, we
are being outdone by contraptions of wire and chemicals' (Mishan,
1970, p. 132), an idea hammered home to the American television
public exposed to a new set of 'bionic' superheroes whose
special powers are dependent upon artificial arms, legs, ears,
and eyes. As Mishan argues, in such a state goals now become
set not by people, but by the flow of technology. As he views
it, one will

> live by the grace of the scientist, destined to become
> a drone, protected for a time by social institutions
> and the persisting remnants of a moral tradition, but
> transparently expendable like some thousand million
> others heaped like ants over the earth. (Mishan, 1970,
> pp. 132-3)

But does not the technological society offer an ever-widening
array of choice? Mishan (1970, p. 52) insists that 'as the
carpet of 'increased choice' is being unrolled before us by the
foot, it is simultaneously being rolled up behind us by the
yard'. The new 'choices', loudly trumpeted by commercial advertising, are often trivial ones such as new car models and
plastic toothbrushes. In exchange for offering these petty
choices, however, technology takes away choices fundamental to

one's enjoyment of life, such as the right to be protected from
assaults by noise, poisons in the air and water, and the
destruction of natural beauty. But consumers have never agreed
to 'trade off' new cars for bad air; this trade off has never
been offered to them, clearly refuting the claim that modernization brings increasing choice at any meaningful level
(Mishan, 1970, pp. 52-3).

The solution to this problem is to 'internalize the externalities', (Goulet, 1977, pp. 24-30) by structuring the productive
system in such a way that the spillover effects do enter into
the initial social calculus of benefits and costs. Once all
the true costs are known, people might then opt for a society
less tied to the production of technological surpluses. But
Marcuse (1964, p. 170) sees this as a naive hope, since the lack
of such a comprehensive cost-benefit calculus is not merely an
oversight; this absence reflects the essence of contemporary
industrial society guided by 'one-dimensional' thinking which
redefines thought to 'coordinate mental operations with those
in the social reality'. In the American system based on managerial manipulation, the emphasis is upon the 'therapeutic'
function of thought, leading to affirmation and positive thinking rather than to a critical examination of larger structural
issues. The result, says Marcuse, is a new form of conformism
resulting from technological rationality which is 'the happy
consciousness — the belief that the real is rational and that
the system delivers the goods' (Marcuse, 1964, p. 84).

Studying social reality from a slightly different perspective,
Potter stresses the structural difficulties inherent in creating
a cost-benefit calculus for the technological society. Such a
course, he observes, would require not only a change in the
meaning system but perhaps a change in the system of government
as well. American democracy, explains Potter, works well because the assumption of abundance has meant that one can focus
on wealth creation rather than the more painful issue of wealth
redistribution. He writes:

> The American mind . . . often assumes implicitly that
> the volume of wealth is dynamic, that much potential
> wealth still remains to be converted; and that diverse
> groups — for instance, capital and labor — can take
> more wealth out of the environment by working together
> than they can take out of one another by class warfare.
> (Potter, 1954, p. 118)

If the myth of technological progress is successfully dethroned
the promise of dynamic wealth creation may also disappear, with
unfathomable implications for the existing political system.

NATIONAL SECURITY AND THE MYTH OF NATIONAL INTEREST

A third important organizing principle in the United States, along with capitalism and technology, is national security. Two recent analysts, Gerald and Patricia Mische (1977) portray the United States as trapped in a balance-of-power system driven compulsively to maintain a favourable balance of payments, a positive balance of weapons, and a competitive edge in the struggle for the world's scarce resources. The underlying assumption about international relations is the need to preserve a balance of power, and the meaning system that rationalizes the costs and benefits of the national security state is the myth of 'national interest' which holds that the preservation of credible state power in the international arena is the only way to protect one's national values. The late President Lyndon B. Johnson once put it succinctly: 'We are the number one nation, and we are going to stay the number one nation'.[4] Much as the technological perspective can skirt moral questions thanks to its reliance on 'scientific' procedures, so too the national security perspective encourages policy-makers to set moral scruples aside, on the grounds that they must deal with an anarchic and amoral system of nation-states. Yet, this 'realist' view of the world grows increasingly unrealistic: it leads to increasing costs while the nation-state becomes increasingly unable to maintain genuine national sovereignty.

One highly visible cost of the national security state is reflected in the national budget. Huge defence budgets reduce the amounts available for the development of human resources or ecological protection of the environment, or, as Barnet (1971, p. 8) puts it: 'The Economy of Life in America has been starved to feed the Economy of Death'. Although during the 1970s the military budget as a percentage of the gross national product was reduced, current trends, as indicated by the most recent Defense Department budget, (Department of Defense, 1980) lead many observers to agree with Emma Rothschild:

> This country is in the early years — not, despite the new shine of the Carter doctrine, at the very beginning — of the most expensive military boom in history. In the process, the distinction between the military and the nonmilitary modes of the American economy is being suppressed. (Rothschild, 1980, p. 31)

Motivated by the fears of increased Russian military spending, increased international turbulence, and a need to maintain through defence spending not only the current actual balance of power but the perceptions of that balance, military spending is

growing rapidly, while social sectors of the budget are being
cut in the domestic battle against inflation.
  In this increasingly tense national-security climate, it is
quite likely that in addition to these cuts in domestic programmes, crucial domestic needs and values will be denounced
as 'subversive' of the national interest. As the Misches (1977,
p. 56) argue, the national security state supports 'machismo'
virtues like secrecy, power, ethnocentrism, and competitiveness,
while downgrading such values as truth, love, community, and
free conscience. (The same thesis is amply documented in David
Halberstam's *The Best and the Brightest,* 1969.) Human and
religious values are often branded as disloyal because they
work against the security of the state and, consequently, the
state's alleged ability to guarantee national welfare. Similarly, say the Misches, values such as those concerning proper
food, shelter and environment are ignored in favour of international economic competition. Moreover, the focus of the
security ideologies is on protecting the nation, not its individual citizens. Not surprisingly, therefore, religion is
privatized to focus on personal salvation rather than on public
social issues that might threaten the existing system (Mische
and Mische, 1977, pp. 213, 230). This general tendency has,
however, always been combatted by certain intellectuals and
institutions whose chosen mission has been to marry ethical
reflection with policy formulation. One thinks, for instance,
of the enormous influence exercised by the theologian Reinhold
Niebuhr with his theory of 'realistic ethics' or of institutional
contributions such as those made by the CRIA (Council on Religion
and International Affairs) 'Ethics in Foreign Policy' publications, or research promoted by the recently-created Churches'
Center for Theology and Public Policy. Notwithstanding these
and other worthy efforts, it remains true that *most* policy
actors view ethical and theological considerations as subordinate
to pragmatic approaches founded on an amoral vision of power and
interest conflicts.
  The justification for accepting high social costs is that they
are unavoidable or that they must be borne in order to obtain
greater benefits, in this case increased security. But the
alleged benefits deriving from the national security myth may
prove to be hollow. Paradoxically, the more a nation spends on
arms in quest of security, the less secure that nation becomes.
And widening economic and ecological interdependence has transformed many issues (such as food, inflation, pollution) into
global problems, thereby rendering the 'fortress America' concept no longer tenable.[5]
  History's lessons suggest that a nation's search for security
is misdirected when it focuses on international arenas. Toynbee

and Barnet both conclude that most great empires of the past
'have gone down not by invasion from without, but because of
social dissolution within. . . . The greatest security problems for a nation are the hostility and frustration of its own
citizens' (Barnet, 1971, pp. 6-7). For Barnet, the massive
American spending on national defence is ironic: The result of
this gigantic investment in security has been to make the
American people among the most insecure on the planet (1971,
p. 6). He cites the President's Commission on Violence, whose
report found that an American is four times more likely to be a
victim of violence than a European. Finally, Barnet offers the
view that 'Americans are more afraid to walk the streets of
Washington than the streets of (wartime) Saigon' (Barnet, 1971,
p. 6). In a most literal sense, then, the American public has
been unable to buy its own security.

Does the national security mentality have a future? Has the
Vietnam tragedy successfully exposed the unrealities of the
national interest myth and opened the door to alternative images?
Foreign policy analysts pride themselves on their ability to
stretch their minds and engage in what Herman Kahn calls 'thinking about the unthinkable'. Nevertheless, even these adventures
of the spirit rarely find new premises upon which to base the
foreign policy of the United States. What remains unthinkable
even for the boldest of these intellectual gamesmen is that
this country give up its national myths, its obsession with
security, its reliance on warfare, its faith in competition,
and its uncritical world imagery.

The inability of United States policy-makers to break away
from sterile balance of power imagery, even when existing
policies were clearly inadequate, is revealed in a 1970 interview of Eugene Rostow, an adviser to Lyndon Johnson on the
Vietnam war, by reporter William Whitworth of the *New Yorker*.
In a long exchange with Whitworth, Rostow admits failure in
these words:

> Nobody had a greater stake than Nixon in finding an al-
> ternative policy in Vietnam. Nothing would have done
> him more good at home politically, nothing could have
> helped the future of the Republican Party more. I think
> the fact that he and Kissinger and everybody else
> couldn't do it, that they came up with exactly the same
> balance-of-power analysis, and the same conclusions, is
> very significant. (Whitworth, 1970, p. 56)

A likely explanation of the failure of the security managers
to devise alternatives is that they confined their questioning
to purely instrumental matters; they never engaged in what

Brzezinski (1970, p. 160) (in his previous academic role) has
called 'fundamental dissent'. Falk also points this out, ob-
serving that in calculating defence 'reforms', the existing
world order system is assumed to exist (Falk, 1975, p. 430).
Whereas fundamental dissent would contest the meaning system
on which the social order is founded, instrumental dissent aims
at making relationships between a given political system and
society more compatible. Apparently without being aware of the
contradiction between these two forms, security managers in the
United States habitually attempt to dilute fundamental dissent
into a more instrumental mode, hoping thereby to show that the
social order they defend is tolerant enough to learn, even from
its enemies. Given the incompatibilities of the two forms of
analysis, however, most of their efforts to reach new priorities
are condemned to failure; the very framework within which their
probes are made precludes asking the right questions. This
unwillingness to challenge the organizing framework is reinforced by the institutional structures which, in the words of
Barrington Moore, Jr., have made of the United States a 'predatory democracy' (Moore, 1970, p. 72). Moore questions the
common radical assertion that the United States economy would
collapse without the injection of spending for defence. Nonetheless, he concludes that the current distribution of benefits
derived from military spending makes it unlikely that any 'widespread and effective' demand for change can succeed. More
specifically, he judges that abandonment of the national security system would have a profound negative impact on a few major
firms, and some minor damage to numerous others. Thus, since
the likely benefits, although considerable, would be widely
spread throughout the society, it is easy to see that, in
political terms, the greatest incentives to exert political
pressures rest with the potential big losers rather than the
many marginal winners. In this situation

> there will be no material incentive to alter the social
> order. In more theological language, for some specific
> groups the prospective rewards for political virtue are
> peanuts, while for other groups the wages of sin are ex-
> cellent, even if the *overall* social gains from virtue
> would be greater. (Moore, 1970, p. 144)

Not, of course, that the 'predatory' approach is inevitable,
but simply that this **'solution'** is merely the most obvious one,
and in the short run the pleasantest, easiest, and cheapest
for a very large number of American citizens'. (Moore, 1970,
pp. 144-5)

CONCLUSIONS

To describe and assess American life-styles is a complex, albeit pertinent, undertaking. Available indicators and conceptual frameworks only imperfectly reflect the existing life-styles and their many contradictions. Moreover, any effort to determine what is 'important' in the dominant life-style is inevitably influenced by myths and meaning systems whose implied purpose is to justify society's existing institutions and organizing principles. Each of the three myths and meaning systems described in this essay as characterizing the American society of abundance has found within itself a means of avoiding the need to make 'moral' choices. Capitalism, for example, uses its myth of mobility to allow the 'invisible hand' to reward the most deserving. For technology, all inquiry into values is reduced to the status of 'scientific' questions. And, for national security, the view of the world as anarchic and amoral renders moral actions 'unthinkable' unless they can also be justified on the basis of a calculus of interest or power. Significantly, all three forms of social organization reward 'instrumental' but not 'fundamental' dissent, thereby ensuring that the basic structure of the social system remains substantially unchanged.

Viewed from the perspective of social critics, political dissidents, and certain adepts of alternative living styles, however, the organizing principles of the American system are open to the charge of exaggerating the alleged benefits and understating the costs of present social arrangements. Indeed competitive capitalism, as Galbraith and others have suggested, may well be less productive and more alienating than the myth of mobility allows. And technology may provide only trivial choices, while it exercises profound determinizing of its own in exchange for excessive costs. Finally, national security officials may paradoxically insist on policies which destroy their nation's security while seeking to protect it.

Such critiques of the United States may be regarded by many as overly pessimistic, but the very proliferation of critical views does testify to the potential weaknesses inherent in the dominant meaning systems as well as the institutional systems they support. In the vast meaning-market which is American society, counter-myths are potential challengers to dominant myths and meaning systems. Moreover, in recent years the dominant institutions have faced serious shocks; the productivity of capitalism is now being fought by environmentalist coalitions, with the spectacular failure at Three Mile Island giving particular strength to anti-nuclear groups; and conventional images of national security are being challenged and possibly redefined

in the wake of the trauma of the Vietnam War and the increasing
awareness that world interdependence may require increased, if
grudging, international perspectives and cooperation. An obvious question must here be raised. Are alternative myths
strong enough to weld together a new blend of American values
around a different meaning system, one which presents fundamental, and not mere instrumental, dissent, challenging existing
institutions at their core?

Even those who acknowledge weaknesses in the organizing principles of American society do not necessarily think, however,
that the society is falling apart. On the contrary, many people
have grown accustomed to digesting even radical critiques of
their institutions and still end up favouring the status quo.
The trajectory followed by Patricia Hearst and Eldridge Cleaver
is not untypical: dutiful mainstream citizen, revolutionary,
and return to the mainstream. Within United States capitalism
the poor identify vicariously with the elite, and although their
hope of a larger share in benefits is largely illusory, they
have accepted social inequality as a legitimate or necessary
fact of life. As for technology, the possibility of getting a
truer assessment of the costs and benefits by 'internalizing
the externalities' appears remote, thanks to the persuasiveness
of 'one-dimensional thinking' and to the redistributive difficulties inherent in any reassessment of comprehensive social
costs. As for institutions of national security, major change
appears most difficult, if not impossible. The reason is that
the gains, although great, would be widely and thinly distributed, whereas the costs, although relatively small, hit hardest
on a few powerful groups. Incentives for political action lie
with the few big losers rather than with the many potential
small winners.

Existing institutions remain strong in spite of problems and
contradictions. Therefore, a formidable challenge confronts
those who would create alternative myths and meaning systems
able to transform society at large.

This challenge is compounded by the uncertainty regarding the
levers that lead to social change. Some of the most longstanding analysts of the American political scene (Campbell et
al., 1976) warn that we really know very little about the precise relationship between values and institutions. To explain
such fundamental shifts as the 1954 Supreme Court decision
reversing racial discrimination, for example, one can merely
speculate that the idea of integration had 'reached its time'.
These authors conclude that:

> we know very little about the way a new idea is germin-
> ated in some segment of society, how it is influenced

The Poverty of Progress

by passing events, how it diffuses through the population generally, or how it moves from a public idea to
an institutional act. We are equally ill-informed as
to the impact on public thinking and behavior of such
an institutional act once it is taken. (Campbell *et al.*,
1976, p. 4)

In conclusion, the future shape of American society is most
uncertain. Alternative myths may hold certain values that
resonate well with the American public at large, but commercial
and other interests can easily tap these values to produce conventional results, thereby leaving alternative ways of living
at the fringes of an unchanged society. One must never rule
out, however, the possibility that alternative ways of living
might successfully integrate key American values into a new
coalition capable of changing society's institutions and myths.
Meanwhile, of course, they stand in witness to other ways of
living.

Upon final reckoning, events in international arenas may well
exercise a greater influence upon American society than domestic
groups trying to create alternatives. Who can imagine what
changes in mass consumption would result from a lengthy new oil
embargo by OPEC countries, or the adoption by the rest of the
world of Special Drawing Rights or some other cluster of cur-
rencies as the basis of international trade, or the advent of a
worldwide economic depression similar to that of the 1930s? In
these global arenas, change processes at work in less developed
countries in quest of alternative development strategies meet
up with the multiple experiments carried out in developed countries in the name of more meaningful, and alternative life-
styles. However, it is difficult to assume that this will produce the global political consciousness in the United States
which would provide what Falk (1975, pp. 287-92) calls the
essential beginning towards an international structural transformation. The old myths and meaning systems continue to pose
a formidable challenge to rethinking the major international
issues of war, poverty, social justice and ecological balance
required by a new world order.

NOTES

1. Literature on the 'quality of life' is large and rapidly
growing. One stream of research has been generated by the
social indicators 'movement' in the United States, including
such works as Bauer (1966), Duncan (1969), and Sheldon and Moore
(1968), as well as government-sponsored works (*Toward a Social
Report*, 1970). More recent works in social indicators include

Campbell *et al.*, (1976), Andrews and Withey (1976) and Taeuber (1978). A newer, but growing stream of research has focused on 'basic human needs', and includes such works as ILO (1976), and ILO (1977).

2. On this subject, see also R. Sennett and J. Cobb (1972).

3. Gerald Radnitzky (1973, p. 417), as quoted in Jon Wisman (mimeograph).

4. Quoted in Richard Barnet (1972, p. 3).

5. See, for example, John Sewell, 'Can the Rich Prosper Without Progress by the Poor?', Overseas Development Council, *Agenda for Action* (1978).

BIBLIOGRAPHY

Andrews, F. M. and Withey, S. B. (1976) *Social Indicators of Well-Being: Americans' Perception of Life Quality*. New York, Plenum Press.
Baran, P. and Sweezy, P. (1964) *Monopoly Capital*. New York, Monthly Review Press.
Barnet, R. (1971) *The Economy of Death*. New York, Atheneum.
Barnet, R. (1972) *Roots of War*. New York, Atheneum.
Bauer, R. A. (1966) *Social Indicators*. Cambridge, Mass., MIT Press.
Berger, P. (1963) *Invitation to Sociology*. New York, Anchor.
Berger, P. (1974) *Pyramids of Sacrifice*. New York, Basic Books.
Berger, P. and Luckmann, T. (1966) *The Social Construction of Reality*. New York, Doubleday.
Brzezinski, Z. (1970) *Between Two Ages, America's Role in the Technetronic Era*. New York, Viking.
Campbell, A., Converse, P. and Rogers, W. (1976) *The Quality of American Life*. New York, Russel Sage.
Department of Defense Annual Report, Fiscal Year 1981. Washington D.C., Department of Defense, 1980.
Duncan, O. D. (1969) *Toward Social Reporting: Next Steps*. New York, Russel Sage.
Edelman, M. (1977) *Political Languages: Words that Succeed and Policies that Fail*. New York, Academic Press.
Elliott, C. (1975) *Patterns of Poverty in the Third World*. New York, Praeger.
Ellul, J. (1967) *The Political Illusion*. New York, Alfred A. Knopf.

Falk, R. (1975) *The Study of Future Worlds*. New York, Free
    Press.
Goulet, D. (1977) *The Uncertain Promise: Value Conflicts in
    Technology Transfer*. New York, IDOC/North America.
Halberstam, D. (1969) *The Best and the Brightest*. New
    York, Random House.
Harris, L. (1975) *The Anguish of Change*. New York, Norton.
Hollander, P. (1978) 'Reflection on Anti-Americanism in Our
    Times', *Worldview*, June.
ILO (1976) *Employment, Growth, and Basic Needs: A One World
    Problem*. New York, Praeger.
ILO (1977) *The Basic Needs Approach to Development: Some Issues
    Regarding Concepts and Methodology*. Geneva, ILO.
Korda, M. (1975) *Power: How to Get it: How to Use it*. New York,
    Random House.
Korda, M. (1977) *Success*. New York, Random House.
Mannheim, K. (1951) *Freedom, Power, and Democratic Planning*.
    London, Routledge & Kegan Paul.
Marcuse, H. (1964) *One-Dimensional Man: Studies in the Ideology
    of Advanced Industrial Society*. Boston, Beacon Press.
Maynes, C. (1974) 'The Hungry New World and the American Ethic.
    Washington Post, December 1.
Mische, G. and Mische, P. (1977) *Toward a Human World Order:
    Beyond the National Security Straightjacket*. New York,
    Paulist Press.
Mishan, E. J. (1970) *Technology and Growth: The Price We Pay*.
    New York, Praeger.
Mishan, E. J. (1972) *Economics for Social Decisions*. New York,
    Praeger.
Mishan, E. J. (1976) *Cost Benefit Analysis* (new and expanded
    edition). New York, Praeger.
Moore, B. Jr., (1970) *Reflections on the Causes of Human Misery*.
    Boston, Beacon Press.
Mumford, L. (1958) *The Highway and the City*. New York,
    Harcourt Brace & World
Overseas Development Council. *Agenda for Action*. Washington,
    Overseas Development Council (annual publication).
Potter, D. M. (1954) *People of Plenty: Economic Abundance and
    the American Character*. Chicago, University of Chicago
    Press.
Radnitzky, G. (1973) *Contemporary Schools of Metascience*.
    Chicago, Henry Regenery Co.
Rothschild, E. (1980) 'Boom and Bust' (Review of the Department
    of Defense Annual Report, Fiscal Year 1981). *The New York
    Review of Books*, April 3, 1980, 31-34.
Sennett, R. and Cobb, J. (1972) *The Hidden Injuries of Class*.
    New York, Knopf.

Sheldon, E. B. and Moore, W. E. (1968) *Indicators of Social Change*. New York, Russel Sage.
Statistical Abstract of the United States (annual publication).
Taeuber, C. (ed.) (1978) *America in the Seventies: Some Social Indicators* (*Annals of the American Academy of Political and Social Science*), Vol. 435, January.
Toward a Social Report (1970) Ann Arbor, Arbor Science Publishers.
United States Senate (1978) *Report: Dietary Goals for the United States*. Washington, D.C., January.
The Washington Post, June 15.
Wattenberg, B. (1965) *This USA*. New York, Doubleday.
Whitworth, W. (1970) 'A Reporter at Large, Some Questions about the War'. *The New Yorker,* July 4.
Wisman, J. *Legitimation, Ideology-Critique, and Economics* (mimeograph). The American University, Washington, D.C.

3

The Dominant Way of Life in Norway: Positive and Negative Aspects

DAG POLESZYNSKI

INTRODUCTION

This chapter[1]* presents a view of the dominant way of life
(DWL) in Norway. Many people in other parts of the world have
held Norway to be some kind of 'ideal' in realizing key development goals. Certainly, in comparison with many other industrialized nations, Norway seems to have succeeded reasonably well in
securing for the average citizen a high level of material welfare, and in achieving relative equality between the elites and
the people-at-large. Infant mortality rates are among the
lowest in the world, life expectancies among the highest; crime
rates are relatively low, and Norwegians are portrayed as living
healthy, well-exercised lives surrounded by the serene beauty of
the Norwegian countryside. But things are changing even in
provincial Norway as she seems to be approaching the post-
industrial age. Are we indeed about to become people living in
an overdeveloped country, which, in spite of its non-colonial
past, exploits the poor masses of this world?

OVERDEVELOPMENT AND INDUSTRIAL SOCIETY

A central thesis in the theory of overdevelopment (outlined
in Chapter 1) is that most so-called 'developed' countries are
really on their way towards higher degrees of overdevelopment.
A central aspect of this process, manifested in numerous ways,
is that the means chosen to satisfy certain needs either become
counterproductive to the need itself, or to other needs, in
ourselves or in others.
The two cells of the first row of Fig. 3.1 are related to our
own needs satisfaction, and represent the idea that overdevelopment is bad for the overdeveloped. Thus, needs could have
been better satisfied with fewer means (for instance, less

---

*Superscript numbers refer to notes at end of chapter.

Overdevelopment relative to:	Preventing satisfaction of: same need	other needs
(1) Ourselves	Counterproductive	Trade-off/asymmetry
(2) Others now	Conflict (Imperialism)	
(3) Others later	Latent conflict (Future imperialism)	
(4) Nature	?	

Fig. 3.1 Overdevelopment and Human Needs

medication for better health)[2] relative to the need itself, or
the fulfilment of one need hampers the fulfilment of another
(the need for mobility, for example, is satisfied by cars which
threaten our survival, cause inequality and upset the ecological
balance) (Illich, 1975a). Further, other people's needs are
constantly frustrated in consequence of our overdevelopment,
creating conflict and struggles against imperialism in underdeveloped countries. The third row refers to the latent conflict between present-day beneficiaries (the middle-aged and
the old) and those young or not yet born, who will reap the
fruits (or lack of them) of past generations' environmental mal-
practice. Finally, it is clear that the natural environment,
represented by the final row, is affected by overdevelopment,
even if it cannot express deprivation of needs (unless ecological imbalance is precisely nature's own need-deprivation).
   This chapter will focus on the first row in Fig. 3.1, overdevelopment relative to 'ourselves', taking as its starting
point the list of needs presented in Fig. 3.2. We will concentrate on 'welfare' and 'identity' needs, which pose fewer
measurement problems. These two groups of needs are no more
important than the needs for 'survival' and 'freedom', both of
which will also be discussed below, although the empirical
material for these groups of indicators is less substantial.
But, first, we discuss briefly some of the features of a
'statistical Norwegian' as a general indicator of the DWL.

SOME CHARACTERISTICS OF THE NORWEGIAN WAY OF LIFE

   Norwegians enter this world with a good chance of longevity:
infant mortality rates are among the lowest in the world, with
below 10 deaths per 1000 live births in the late 1970s. A
baby boy born in 1976/7 could expect to live slightly longer

GROUP OF NEEDS (types of needs specified under sub-headings)	SATISFIERS OR INSTITUTIONS held to be relevant in industrial societies

SECURITY NEEDS (Survival needs, to avoid violence)
  Against individual violence
    (assault, torture)
  Against collective violence
    (internal/external wars)
	
	Police
	
	Military

WELFARE NEEDS (Sufficiency needs, to avoid misery)
  For air, water, nutrition,
    rest
  For movement, exercise
  For avoidance of excessive
    strain
  For protection against nature
  For protection against disease
  For self-expression, dialogue,
    education
	
	Air, water, food
	Space
	
	Technology
	Clothing, shelter
	Medicines, doctors
	
	Schools

IDENTITY NEEDS (Needs for closeness, to avoid alienation)
  For self-expression, creativity,
    praxis, work
  For self-actualization,
    realizing potentials
  For being active and subject
    and not being passive, client
    or object
  For challenge and new
    experiences
  For affection, love, sex,
    friends, spouse, offspring
  For roots, belongingness,
    support, esteem, association
    with similar people
  For understanding social
    forces; for social
    transparency
  For partnership with nature
  For sense of purpose, of
    meaning in life; closeness
    to the transcendental,
    transpersonal
	
	Jobs, tools
	
	Jobs, leisure
	
	Recreation, family
	
	Jobs, recreation,
	transport system
	
	Primary groups
	
	Secondary groups, ancestors
	
	Political activity
	Parks, countryside
	
	Religion, ideology

FREEDOM NEEDS (Freedom to choose, options; to avoid repression)	
Choice in receiving/expressing information/opinion	Communication
Choice of people/places to visit/be visited by	Transportation
Choice in consciousness-formation	Meetings, media
Choice in mobilization	Organization, party
Choice in confrontation	Elections, action groups
Choice of occupation	School system, labour market
Choice of place to live	Housing market
Choice of spouse or life partner	Contact market
Choice of consumer goods	Marketplace
Choice of way of life	Tolerance
Choice of death	?

Fig. 3.2 A typology of human needs

Source: This is a modified version of Johan Galtung's typology
of basic human needs developed in connection with the
World Indicators Programme initiated by the Chair in
Conflict and Peace Research, University of Oslo,
Norway.

than 72 years, a baby girl more than 78 years. Although times
may change, the prospects are that the high material consumption
of today's generation will continue well into the future. Norway is a resource-rich country, being able to use ample resources
of hydro-power and petroleum for domestic production or to
raise revenue for imports.

Per capita calorie consumption is below 3000 kcal per day.
However, counting the primary calories in the fodder needed to
sustain a milk- and meat-rich diet, the total calorific consumption surpasses 10,000 — about four times the daily need.
Considering the relative scarcity of good agricultural land,
it is worth noting that our present eating habits mean that
land in other countries, equivalent to some 20 per cent of the
total Norwegian land area devoted to grain production, is used
to secure our consumption of tobacco, coffee, tea, sugar, wine
and liquor, cocoa and tropical fruits. So much protein cake,
carbohydrate-rich fodder, etc., is imported that Norwegian self-
sufficiency in foodstuffs on a calorific basis during 1974-8

was as low as 35-36 per cent.[3] *Per capita* consumption of sugar
in 1978 was above 40 kg, with meat about 51 kg, milk 167 kg,
cheese about 11.5 kg and butter and margarine around 21 kg.
Norwegians also consumed slightly more than 36 kg of fish *per
capita* in 1978, reflecting the fact that Norway is one of the
world's major fishing nations.

Norwegians enter school at the age of 7, having already spent
1 year in kindergarten, and perhaps several years in nurseries.
Nine years schooling is mandatory, and university studies may
start after 18. At the age of 19 years or more, many men begin
a year of compulsory military service or start a working career.
Registered unemployment in Norway has traditionally been low,
seldom above 1 per cent except during the last few years, when
it has exceeded 2 per cent. However, the *real* unemployment
figure is considerably higher, because many unemployed are
classified as disabled and receive social security payments instead of unemployment compensation.

Working conditions in Norway are well regulated and work hours
shorter than in most countries; a 40-hour week, weekends off,
four weeks paid vacation (5 weeks for those over 60), and
retirement at 67, is standard fare for most people.

Norwegians spend most of their holidays in close contact with
nature, skiing in the winter and hiking in the mountains or
boating around the coastline in the summer. But with the advent
of cheap charter trips to warmer climates, vacations are becoming
more energy-intensive. Despite a well-developed public transportation system, cars have become more important, even since
the OPEC price rises. In 1975, 72 per cent of total urban
passenger travel was by automobile (OECD, 1976). This figure
may now be even higher, as record sales of automobiles in recent
years have brought the number of inhabitants per private car
down to almost three by the end of 1979.[4] Norway is a major
world producer of such energy-intensive products as aluminium,
magnesium, ferro-alloys, paper and pulp, which results in energy
use being among the highest in the world: some 8 tonnes of oil
equivalent per person at the end of the 1970s. Annual electric
power production per inhabitant surpassed 22,000 kwh in 1979,
higher than for any other nation.[5]

Life in Norway may be good or bad — and as Norwegians usually
compare themselves to other overdeveloped countries, we feel
that we are doing fairly well. Through the whole idea of
technical assistance we also have become accustomed to comparing
ourselves with underdeveloped countries, making ourselves feel
even better! But a closer look reveals some discomforting trends.

SURVIVAL NEEDS

In Fig. 3.2 we defined survival needs to include the need to
avoid both individual and collective violence. One major type
of violence is caused by accidents, where people are killed
because of inadequate job design or traffic structures favouring
speed rather than people's security. Table 3.1 below, shows
the record of violent deaths by accidents in Norway over the
past century.

Table 3.1
Violent Deaths by Accident, 1876-1978 (Norway)

Year	Average number of [a] deaths per year	Deaths per million [b] population
1876-90	888	458
1891-1900	1207	575
1901-5	1168	511
1906-10	1108	472
1911-20	1147	457
1921-5	1041	384
1926-30	1109	398
1931-5	1001	350
1936-40	1622	551
1941-5	2945	968
1946-50	1477	459
1951-60	1567	453
1961-5	1792	487
1966-70	1909	497
1971-5	2022	509
1976-8	1896	469

Source: Historical Statistics (1968, 1978) and annual
data from Central Bureau of Statistics, Oslo.

Notes: [a] Five-year periods for the original data have
been converted to decades for almost identical
figures.

[b] Number of deaths per million population in the
median year of the period.

Table 3.1 shows no single trend during the total period.
Death rates from accidents seem to have jumped rather suddenly
around the turn of the century. Subsequently, they declined to

a low point in the 1931-5 period, but rose dramatically during
the Second World War and plunged again during 1946-60. A steady
upwards trend follows until the last 3 years, when accident
rates again fell to more moderate levels. If you die from an
accident, the probability of dying counts to you, not the way in
which you die. But the disaggregated figures reveal dramatic
decreases in accidents from fishing and water transportation
during the period, as well as from drowning. Since 1911 motor
vehicle accidents have risen dramatically, but the figures have
actually been declining in the last few years. Child deaths in
traffic accidents have been very high by international standards
during recent decades. However, from 1969 to 1979 the number of
children killed dropped from a total of 105 to 53, while birth
rates only fell by 22 per cent.[6] Although the figures are still
unacceptably high, this is an encouraging trend. Aviation
accidents have only risen moderately since they were first
reported in 1921. Judging from Table 3.1, there have been two
good periods from the point of view of accidents in Norway during
the last 100 years, namely during 1921-35 and 1946-60. It is
still too early to tell whether we are now entering a third such
period.

Another form of violent death involves homicide, trends
which seem easier to ascertain than accidents. Table 3.2 shows
a relatively stable picture before the Second World War, with
the lowest homicide levels during 1916-25 and 1931-40. The
abnormal war years were followed by relative tranquility during
1946-55, when homicide rates reached historically low levels.
However, there has been a marked and steady increase since,
with more than three times as many homicides in 1979 as during
1951-5 (thirty five compared to eleven), a sign that Norway may
have passed some optimum level and entered into a phase of overdevelopment.

Another threat to our sense of security is posed by violence
against people. Table 3.3 shows the situation during the last
two decades. To the extent that these statistics are reliable,
they show that after a fairly stable period, the personal violence rate had, by the end of the 1960s, almost doubled from
that of 1956. Since then, it has remained at the same **high**
level.

Expenditure on the military is supposed to provide national
security against wars. In an overdeveloped society, however,
such expenditure often becomes an end in itself, or, rather, a
means to further the growth of the military-industrial establishment. With excessive resources spent on the military, the
search for so-called national security may take resources from
the satisfaction of other needs. Furthermore, in the event of
the war, the destructive power of a modern defence system may

The Poverty of Progress

Table 3.2
Homicides in Norway, 1876-1979

Year	Average number of deaths per year	Homicides per million population
1876-1900	19	9.1
1901-10	20	8.4
1911-15	23	9.4
1916-25	19	7.0
1926-30	25	9.0
1931-5	22	7.7
1936-40	14	5.1
1941-5	313	103.0
1946-50	14	4.3
1951-5	11	3.3
1956-60	17	4.8
1961-5	19	5.2
1966-70	22	5.7
1971-5	27	6.8
1976-9	32	7.9

Source: Figures for 1979 published in *Dagbladet,* 29 May, 1980; otherwise, Central Bureau of Statistics, Oslo.

Table 3.3
Offences of Violence Recorded Between 1956 and 1977 (Norway)

Year	Number of cases:	
	Annual total	Per million population
1956	1666	482
1957-8	1950	556
1959-60	1910	536
1961-2	1960	540
1963-4	1976	537
1965-6	2120	567
1967-8	2470	597
1969-70	2973	769
1971-2	3226	824

(cont.)

Table 3.3 (cont.)

Year	Number of cases:	
	Annual total	Per million population
1973-4	3520	886
1975-6	3606	898
1977	3283	911

Source: As for Table 3.1.

be so large that it destroys the very values it claims to protect. But this cannot be conclusively shown unless Norway goes
to war at some time in the future, which does not seem at present realistic, and, of course, we all hope to avoid. It is now
impossible to assess whether the relatively moderate death tolls
experienced in the Second World War would have been different
with a stronger defence system.

Could the resources used by the military have been put to
other uses which, in the long run, would save more lives than
military preparedness could ever hope to? Since Norway now has
about 4.1 million inhabitants (in 1980), could for instance the
military budget have been used to buy food for this many people?
A brief look at the data for the Norwegian military budgets
during 1875 to 1975, converted to potato equivalents, tells us
that since 1960 the military budget could have bought more food
than the whole population could eat. Norwegians are already
well-fed, of course, but we could have provided food for more
than 5 million people elsewhere in 1975 had we spent the money
as food aid (Table 3.4).

In our calculations, we have assumed that 1 tonne of potatoes
is sufficient to keep one person alive for 1 year (3 kilos per
day), which means that we are incurring structural violence to
the tune of 5.4 million lives per year. In place of our military expenditures a large number of people in the Third World
could be provided with the basic foodstuffs they are at present
so lacking. As structural violence is a form of conflict made
possible through imperialism (see Fig. 3.1), attempts by underdeveloped countries to liberate themselves from such dependency
may eventually threaten our own security. So, indirectly, our
high military budgets should give us reasons for worrying about
our long-run security.

If we look at survival needs in a wider perspective, a measure
of the extent of social development is the probability of remaining alive at different ages. The lower the probability of

74   The Poverty of Progress

Table 3.4
Military Expenditures Converted to Potato
Equivalents 1875-1975 (Norway)

Year	Military budget [a] in current million Nkr	1000s tonnes of potatoes [b] the budget could be used for
1875	8	100
1880	8	100
1890	10	250
1900	20	405
1910	20	345
1920	60	345
1930	40	520
1939	110	810
1950	355	1585
1960	1060	3530
1970	2770	4700
1975	4610	5420

Source: Based on data from Central Bureau of Statistics, *Historical Statistics* (1978).

Notes: [a]Rounded off to the nearest 5 million after 1890.
[b]Rounded off to the nearest 5000 tons (the idea to convert the military budget into potato equivalents came from Anders Helge Wirak).

death, the more developed the country. A levelling out, or, particularly, an increase in death probabilities, while the material welfare of the population is still rising, could be interpreted as a sign of overdevelopment. We shall not reproduce all the data on this subject given by the Central Bureau of Statistics, but summarize some of the more important figures in *Historical Statistics,* 1871-1977. For males the death probability declines throughout the whole period for ages up to around 40 (although the decline is minimal for men over 20 after 1951-5). For the age group 50-90, the death probability is lowest in the 1950-60 period and slightly higher more recently. The age-group 60-90 had their lowest chances of dying in 1951-5, with a significant increase in the death probability during the two subsequent periods. (An exception must be made for 90-year-olds, who in 1974-5 had a very low death rate). For men aged 94 or above, the 1871-80 period was actually the best: probabilities of dying increased to a peak in 1951-5, and declined since then, but not to the previous low level.

Females have lower death probabilities in all periods, and
for all ages, than males. In general, their death rates have
continued declining, though only marginally so since 1951-5.
Rates are lowest in the most recent years with one exception:
a 20-year-old woman had the lowest death probability in 1961-5.
For very old women, the rates are still going down, though 94-
year-olds had worsening chances in all years after 1871-80 except for very recently (1976-7).

In general, then, chances of survival at almost all ages have
not improved much since the 1950s. Infant mortality rates have
declined to a much larger extent than adult survival rates.
Indeed, men who are above 50 may even expect an increasing probability of dying, while people who are really old today may be
in worse shape than the old of 100 years ago.

WELFARE NEEDS

It is quite clear that the overall level of material welfare
has been increasing in Norway over recent decades. The market
for most common consumer goods is now saturated, and increased
sales can only be achieved through intensive marketing efforts,
shortened product life and/or new product design. But costs
are also incurred in this process, which has involved large
changes in infrastructure, industrialization, increased
international trade and conversion to an industrial form of
agriculture. In particular, such developments have only been
possible because of vast energy subsidies, bringing with them
environmental destruction, pollution and scarring of the landscape. Since 1900, energy usage in Norway has increased more
than ten times, with our large resources of hydro-electricity
giving an almost ten-fold rise in the consumption of electricity
alone during the last 50 years. In 1979, total inland energy
use was equivalent to about 30 million tonnes of oil equivalent
(toe), ie almost 8 *per capita*, topping the world list of the
most energy-consuming nations.[7] In addition, the Norwegian
merchant fleet consumed in 1977 almost 10 million toe (down from
13-14 mtoe when prospects were brighter), thus performing its
duty within the international division of labour, the imperial-
istic practices of overdeveloped countries.

An indication of how much energy we really need to satisfy
welfare needs can be gained by studying energy availability in
other countries which have managed to secure basic welfare
needs coverage for their population. Countries like China,
Cuba and Albania have eradicated absolute poverty, yet have a
per capita energy consumption some 10 per cent of that of Norway (and these countries can in no way be regarded as utilizing

their energy resources with maximum efficiency) (Poleszynski,
1977b). It should be added, though, that almost half of Norway's energy consumption is accounted for by industry, where
energy-intensive production disposed in 1977 of more than 80
per cent of total electricity output (whilst providing only 15
per cent of industrial employment). These industries also used
about 40 per cent of all heating fuels, meaning that firms
employing 85 per cent of the industrial work force were responsible for the remaining 60 per cent of fuel consumption and
only 20 per cent of electricity usage.[8]

Although hydro-power and North Sea oil enable Norway to maintain high levels of imports of agricultural products, machinery,
and a vast array of consumer goods, there are also large, often
non-quantifiable costs involved in pursuing such energy-intensive industrial policies. Hydroelectric power is a renewable
energy source, but not without environmental costs: large
reservoirs of water destroy agricultural and grazing lands,
change the natural flows of water, alter local climatic conditions and decrease the fertility of river banks and surrounding
areas; moreover, recipient capacity of rivers is reduced, and
there are adverse effects on both inland and sea fisheries.[9]
The consequences of burning fossil fuels are well known: acidic
rain with consequent negative effects on human health and plant
growth, the emission of carbon monoxide and dioxide (contributing
to global heating of the atmosphere), as well as the production
of noxious fluoride particles and gases, hydrocarbons and
nitrous gases.[10] Moreover, North Sea oil exploitation has meant
that oil spillages have become routine, and has increased the
chance of possibly catastrophic blow-outs close to perhaps the
richest fishing grounds in the world. Finally, our continued
reliance on fossil fuels makes future conversion to renewable,
non-polluting sources of energy structurally more difficult; at
the same time it reduces the energy options for others, today
and tomorrow.

We have dwelt so much on energy up to now because our ability
to convert energy from one form to another sets limits on how well
we can live. However, what counts is not how much energy we
can use or how many products we can dispose of; our concern is
more with ends (such as good health) than with means (material
production, provision of housing, medical services, means of
transportation and communication, etc.). Accordingly, let us
consider some data which shed light on our possibilities for
achieving personal growth, or human and social development.

As can be seen from Table 3.5, the overall infant mortality
rate declined continuously during the period 1921 to 1977, when
it reached 9.2 deaths per 1000 live births. Interestingly
enough, the period of most rapid decline was 1951-5, though

Table 3.5
Infant Mortality Rates, 1921-77 (Norway)

Year	Deaths under 1 year of age per 1000 live births [a]				
	Total	Under 4 weeks[b]	4 weeks- 11 months[c]	Legitimate	Illegitimate
1921-5	51.7	22.1	29.6	49.4	82.8
1926-30	49.5	24.5	25.0	47.2	80.5
1931-5	44.9	22.5	22.4	42.5	76.8
1936-40	39.4	21.3	18.1	37.4	68.8
1941-5	37.3	18.4	18.8	34.5	71.2
1946-50	31.1	16.0	15.0	29.4	63.7
1951-5	22.6	13.1	9.6	21.7	46.9
1956-60	19.9	12.4	7.4	19.2	37.2
1961-5	17.1	12.0	5.1	16.7	26.8
1966-70	13.9	10.3	3.6	13.5	20.3
1971-5	11.6	8.4	3.2	11.0	17.5
1976	10.5	6.8	3.7	10.0	14.8
1977	9.2	6.5	2.7	8.8	12.5

Source: Central Bureau of Statistics, Statistical Yearbook,
(1976-9).

Notes: [a]All figures are the annual average for each 5-year
period (except for 1976 and 1977).
[b]Prior to 1951 this was for deaths under 1 month.
[c]Prior to 1951 this was for deaths between 1-11 months.

1966-70 and 1971-5 also showed markedly greater improvement
than did other periods. The death rate for babies 4 weeks to
11 months old shows a much more marked decline than that for
babies under 4 weeks, and differences between death rates for
legitimate and illegitimate births decrease over the period
(the latter being about two-thirds higher than the former in
1921-5, but only 42 per cent higher in 1977), indicating that
'illegitimate' births are now gaining legitimacy.
  The declining infant mortality rate during the last century
has given rise to a drastically heightened life expectancy at
birth, with a 44 per cent increase for males and females during
the period 1891-1900 to 1976-7. However, most of the gain was
achieved during the first half of this period, and the gain for
older age-groups has been progressively less important. This
can be seen from Table 3.6.
  For males, no significant increase in life expectancy at birth

The Poverty of Progress

Table 3.6
Life Expectancy in Norway, 1891-1977 [a]

Age:	0		10		30		50		70	
Period:	M	F	M	F	M	F	M	F	M	F
1891-1900	50.41	54.14	51.05	54.11	37.69	39.43	23.34	24.86	10.29	10.97
1901-10	54.82	57.70	52.92	55.08	38.85	40.24	23.95	25.30	10.59	11.24
1911-20	55.62	58.71	52.65	54.98	38.83	40.35	24.10	25.28	10.40	11.15
1921-30	60.98	63.84	56.27	58.35	40.39	42.14	24.41	25.87	10.63	11.40
1931-40	64.08	67.55	58.56	61.25	41.48	43.55	24.90	26.35	10.71	11.38
1946-50	69.25	72.65	62.63	65.24	44.22	46.29	26.43	27.95	11.43	12.03
1951-5	71.11	74.70	63.65	66.72	44.81	47.31	26.60	28.57	11.60	12.30
1956-60	71.32	75.57	63.50	67.30	44.57	47.74	25.21	28.84	11.38	12.36
1961-5	71.03	75.97	62.94	67.49	43.93	47.87	25.62	28.88	11.04	12.29
1966-70	71.09	76.83	62.69	68.10	43.61	48.49	25.32	29.47	10.87	12.83
1971-5	71.41	77.68	62.80	68.71	43.76	49.10	25.41	30.04	10.88	13.19
1975-6	71.85	78.12	63.05	69.12	43.98	49.53	25.55	30.39	11.00	13.57
1976-7	72.12	78.42	63.23	69.35	44.10	49.73	25.68	30.60	11.10	13.76

Source: Central Bureau of Statistics, *Statistical Yearbook*
(1979).

Note: [a] M = Males; F = Females

has taken place since 1951-5. In fact, males in all other age
groups could expect to live longer in 1951-5 than during any
later period. For females the picture is rather more positive,
with increases for all ages throughout the entire period. The
relative gain in life expectancy up to age 10 during the entire
period was nearly identical for the two sexes. However, females
over 30 years of age have gained significantly more in life
expectancy than males, a difference magnified with increasing
age. It remains to be seen whether recent changes in the way
of life of women (especially their wider integration into the
labour market, and increased propensity to smoke)[11] will make
the life expectancy curves for male and females converge to a
greater extent.

In Table 3.7, we show another positive result of the development of the Norwegian welfare state. This is the rapidly
declining death rate during the last four decades for women
giving birth. Before 1946, more than 100 women died each year
during childbirth; today, deaths can be counted on one hand.

Even after 1966-70 there is a marked drop in the maternal
mortality rate. Indeed the rate had dropped by over half up to

Table 3.7
Maternal Mortality in Norway, 1936-77

Year	Maternal Deaths	
	Per 1000 births	Per 100,000 females at ages 15-49 years
1936-40	2.35	13.2
1941-5	2.32	15.5
1946-50	1.16	9.2
1951-5	0.74	5.8
1956-60	0.50	4.0
1961-5	0.22	1.7
1966-70	0.18	1.7
1971-5	0.08	0.6
1976	0.13	0.8
1977	0.10	0.6

Source: Central Bureau of Statistics, Health Statistics
(1975, 1977).

the period 1971-5. However, since the low point of 1975, the
mortality rate has actually increased slightly, indicating that
further improvement may prove extremely difficult.

During recent decades, many diseases which were once more or
less endemic have almost totally disappeared. Among the more
well-known diseases we have experienced the following improvements:[12]

(a) Mortality from tuberculosis declined drastically from 1896
to the present. While many people previously died each
year from this disease, the number today is almost negligible. From about 300 deaths per 10,000 inhabitants in the
late 1890s the death rate has fallen to just over 2 per
100,000 in 1974. This figure is probably greatly exaggerated, with older tuberculosis patients dying from heart
disease later in life still being recorded as dying from
tuberculosis. New cases of the disease today are seldom a
cause of death.[13]
(b) Leprosy was endemic in Norway in the nineteenth century.
In 1856, 2858 known cases were reported, but its decline
was rapid — less than 1000 cases were reported in 1890, 500
in 1905, 100 in 1925, and in 1948 only 16 cases were known.
Today, leprosy is not even recorded in the statistics.
(c) Notified cases of typhoid fever, acute poliomyelitis and
diphtheria have more or less vanished over the period 1915-

The Poverty of Progress

66. General vaccination against polio started in Norway in
1956, and reported cases are now down to about two per year
from a widely varying number (almost 1000 cases in 1936) a
few decades ago. Vaccination against diphtheria was introduced in 1943-4, after reported cases had surged up from a
few hundred per year before 1940 to 22,700 in 1943.[14] The
last 15 years have not produced any new cases.
(d) *Whooping cough,* traditionally afflicting large numbers of
children, previously caused about fifty infant deaths per
year. Today, the death toll is practically nil.

In general, improved nutrition and hygiene, and better housing
and clothing are the major factors behind the considerable
reduction in death from contagious diseases. Medical science
seems to have played a minor role in the prevention of such
diseases, with the exception of vaccination against smallpox
and poliomyelitis.[15] Most of the gains involving infectious
diseases occurred before 1960; improvements after this time
have been almost negligible.
We have illustrated, then, some of the positive aspects of
present development patterns in Norway in the field of health.
Are there any indications of costs associated with the material
boom of recent decades? Among the more common medical complaints related to overconsumption we may cite heart disease,
cancer, tooth decay, obesity and diabetes. Being largely
preventable, such diseases give rise to unnecessary deaths, as
well as to a high level of morbidity in the population at large.
Table 3.8 depicts the upwards trend of the most important killer
in our society, cardiovascular disease. This is especially
marked for men, whose mortality rate was below that of women
until 1956-60. Today, males have a 20 per cent higher death
rate than women, though the upward trend seems broken for both
sexes after 1975.
The statistics for cancer mortality rates presented in Table
3.9 show a similar development to that for cardiovascular
disease, but with one important exception. The death rate is
not slowing down, either for men or for women. Mortality rates
for males caught up with those for women after 1955 and are now
about 20 per cent higher (comparable to the situation for
cardiovascular disease).
Of the 1978 cancer death rate of 226 per 100,000 population
for males and 190 for females, approximately a quarter of all
cases could be attributed to cancer of the stomach, intestine,
mouth and oral cavity. For males, another 16 per cent of cases
were connected with the wind pipe, the bronchial tubes and
another 15 per cent with the prostate glands; women frequently

Table 3.8
Mortality from Cardiovascular Disease, 1931-78 (Norway)

| Year | Deaths per 10,000 population | |
	Males	Females
1931-5	269	288
1936-40	280	311
1941-5	236	267
1946-50	279	316
1951-5	358	383
1956-60	432	424
1961-5	503	459
1966-70	539	450
1971-5	554	462
1976	538	449
1977	533	440
1978	539	451

Source: Central Bureau of Statistics, Oslo.

Table 3.9
Mortality from Malignant Neoplasms, 1931-78 (Norway)

| Year | Deaths per 100,000 population | |
	Males	Females
1931-5	128	136
1936-40	135	141
1941-5	133	142
1946-50	147	153
1951-5	157	159
1956-60	166	158
1961-5	179	159
1966-70	193	171
1971-5	204	172
1976	220	184
1977	221	188
1978	226	190

Source: Central Bureau of Statistics, Oslo.

experienced cancer of the breast (about one-sixth of all cancers) and the sexual organs (some 10 per cent), but only about 5 per cent of all cases related to the lungs.

PP- D*

It is sometimes said that people today do not die *of* cancer, but rather die *with* cancer. This argument does not hold up very well to close scrutiny, however. In Norway, a recent study on cancer care predicts an average yearly increase in cancer incidence rates of 3 per cent per year, rising from 307 per 100,000 in 1975 to 404 in 1985 and 484 in 1990.[16] Only half the predicted increase is attributed to the population ageing. If there is no major breakthrough in cancer cure within the next decade, the prospects are that the associated death rates from cancer for men and women will increase by 60 per cent from the 1978 level of 200 per 100,000 to around 320. In that case, cancer death rates will have reached the level attained by heart disease during the 1950s.

It is beyond the scope of this chapter to go deeply into the etiology of the different diseases. However, we cannot overlook today's medical orthodoxy that the major causes of heart disease, cancer and many other ailments are related to the DWL in industrialized countries. In particular, dietary habits, the large intake of sugar and fats, and the lack of fibre in the daily food intake, seem to be major factors in heart ailments and some forms of cancer.[17] Industrial pollution and occupational exposure to carcinogenic substances also play a central role in the development of many types of cancer[18] while cigarette smoking remains one of the major health hazards which individuals can actually do something about.[19] The role of dietary factors in relation to heart disease was clearly established during the Second World War, when the consumption of both sugar and fats (especially margarine) fell drastically, as did the death rate from heart disease.[20] And, of course, the rather obvious connection between a higher sugar intake and poor dental health was established a long time ago.[21]

A number of chronic diseases, as well as acute conditions, are related to nutrition. According to West German estimates,[22] diseases related to nutritional factors (mostly overeating) cost 2 per cent of Germany's total Gross National Product in 1976. In the U.S., potential annual savings in nutrition-related costs were conservatively estimated in 1977 at $40 billion,[23] amounting to at least $180 for every man, woman and child in just 1 year! Some of the nutritionally related diseases are listed in Fig. 3.3.

Unfortunately, while we have good data on causes of death, Norway lacks reliable statistics on chronic diseases. Deaths from diabetes occur with a frequency of approximately 7 per 100,000 population, but the number of people mildly or severely affected by this disease is probably of the order of a few percentage points. According to the above-mentioned West German

---

Diabetes

Gout

Myocardial infarction

Stroke, cerebral apoplexy

Hypertension

Hyperlipidaemia

Gall-stone

Arthritis of the hip and knee joints

Disc disorders

Hernia

Varicose vein, thrombophlebitis

Menstrual disorders, sterility

Post-operative complications

Pulmonary emphysema

---

*Fig. 3.3 Diseases triggered or favoured by
              overweight*

report, diabetes affected only a few individuals per 1000 of the
German population around 1900 while in 1976 at least 3 per cent
were severely affected and probably as many as 9 per cent were
mildly affected. Although comparable data do not exist for
Norway, the differences in food habits and calorific intake
(above 3000 kcal per person in West Germany, but slightly under
3000 in Norway) and activity levels (the Norwegians are notorious for skiing and hiking etc.), lead us to suspect that the
real Norwegian diabetes incidence rates are likely to be at the
lower end of those reported in the industrialized West (according to *Der Spiegel*,[24] this range spans between 2 and 5 per cent).
In a health survey performed in 1975, 11,014 Norwegians answered
questions concerning their health, and of these, only 0.75 per
cent reported themselves to be diabetic, a figure which seems
somewhat low.[25] However, the reported frequency of various
chronic diseases was very high (Table 3.10).

It is interesting to note that women reported a higher incidence of chronic conditions than men. This may possibly be due
to the fact that women live on average 6 years longer than men,
and that many chronic conditions only develop late in life.
For both sexes, however, one might well argue that the health

Table 3.10
Chronic Conditions at the Beginning of the Survey
Period^a by Diagnosis (Norway)
(per 1000 persons in 1975)

Condition reported	Both sexes	Males	Females
All causes^b	688.6	630.7	744.8
Nervous conditions	72.8	49.4	95.6
Diseases of nervous system	47.2	39.2	55.0
Diseases of eye and ear	47.6	49.0	46.2
Heart diseases	104.0	87.0	120.4
Diseases of respiratory system	58.0	66.3	49.9
Ulcer, etc.	30.1	39.6	21.0
Other disease of the digestive system	21.3	19.5	23.1
Disease of genito-urinary system	32.3	19.7	44.6
Diseases of the skin	59.0	55.5	62.5
Diseases of the musculo-skeletal system	147.6	142.3	152.8
All other diseases and symptoms	49.6	37.0	61.9
Injuries	18.9	26.2	11.8
Number of respondents	11,014	5,427	5,587

Source: Central Bureau of Statistics Health Survey (1975),
pp. 122-3.

Notes: ^{a}Survey period lasted 14 days.
^{b}Not including congenital conditions.

situation leaves a lot to be desired. As many as 41.3 per cent
of the sampled population reported some kind of chronic disease.
Adding the 5 per cent with congenital conditions (not included
here) one gets very close to half the population suffering from
some chronic condition or other. Similar data from 1968 indicate, furthermore, that people's health may actually be deteriorating. Table 3.11 compares the 1975 data with a previous 1968
survey in respect of all cases of illness (chronic and acute).

Table 3.11
Cases of Illness at the Beginning of the Survey
Period[a] by Diagnosis (Norway)
(per 1000 persons, in 1968 and 1975)

Diagnosis	Total		Males		Females	
	1968	1975	1968	1975	1968	1975
Causes, total	758	804	729	745	785	861
Nervous conditions	62	78	48	54	75	102
Diseases of nervous system	34	51	30	43	78	58
Diseases of the eye	59	39	50	38	69	40
Diseases of the ear	51	27	57	30	44	23
Cardiovascular diseases	64	106	57	89	71	122
Diseases of the respiratory system	97	76	98	86	96	67
Diseases of the digestive system	60	54	63	62	57	46
Diseases of the genital organs	8	15	6	10	10	20
Diseases of the urinary system	16	23	10	14	20	32
Diseases of skin and sub-cutaneous tissue	45	62	41	59	48	66
Diseases of the musculo-skeletal system[b]	128	174[b]	114	169	140	179
All other diseases and conditions	74	72	71	56	79	87
Injuries[c]	60	27[c]	84	35	38	19

Source: Central Bureau of Statistics, Health Survey (1975),
p. 20.

Notes: [a]Survey period lasted 14 days.
[b]Directly comparable figure with 1968 is 149 per 1000.
In 1975 a number of secondary effects and injuries are
included under the morbidity conditions reported here.
[c]Directly comparable figure with 1968 is 60 per 1000
population. See note b.

The 1975 data indicate that around 85 per cent of reported illnesses are chronic conditions. If this were also the case in 1968 (there are no comparable data), then the annual growth of chronic illness among the population has been somewhat below 1 per cent. We should stress, however, that this figure should be used with caution.

Comparing the data in Table 3.10 and Table 3.11, we can pick out those diseases which seem to be chronic for some people and those which afflict people more at random; i.e. those diseases which have similar frequencies of occurrence in both tables. The most obvious cases are those affecting the heart, digestive system, and skin, which occur practically only as chronic diseases. Diseases of the eye, the ear and the musculo-skeletal system seem to have the least chronic nature, and injuries must also be included in this category. If we are to draw any overall conclusion here, it is that about 55 per cent of the Norwegian population feel themselves to be at less than full health, again an indication that Norway is not a well-developed country, but is in many ways maldeveloped in this respect.

IDENTITY NEEDS

Identity needs have to do with belongingness, closeness to other people, partnership with nature, and the feeling of meaning to life. In Norway, it is probably fair to say that most people score high on their contact with nature, although urbanization, increased industrialization, and hydro-power construction are gradually taking this very essential aspect of life away from many Norwegians. One reaction to alienation and lack of purpose in our society is to resign into complete passivity, or at the extreme end, to terminate one's life. Table 3.12 indicates the trend in suicide rates in Norway during the last five decades.

We have no breakdown of these data by sex after 1961-5, but up to this point the frequency of suicide for men was three to four times that of women. Although suicide data may not be entirely reliable (some suicides may be recorded as death because of illness), Table 3.12 indicates a consistent increase in the suicide rate after the Second World War. The increase is so large (nearly a doubling in 35 years) that there are grounds for believing that overall mental health is deteriorating, although the evaluation of trends in the population's mental health is clearly a difficult task. Not only are comparable data often lacking, but society's perception of what constitutes poor mental health may also vary. In some countries, for instance, the number of people held in mental hospitals may

The Dominant Way of Life in Norway 87

Table 3.12
Deaths by Suicide in Norway, 1931-78

Year	Number of cases reported	Suicides per million population[a]
1931-5	187	65
1936-40	198	67
1941-5	182	60
1946-50	215	67
1951-5	241	71
1956-60	255	72
1961-5	274	75
1966-70	295	76
1971-5	365	92
1976	433	108
1977	460	114
1978	473	117

Source: Central Bureau of Statistics, Historial Statistics
(1978) and Statistical Weekly Report, 49, (1979).

Note: [a] Calculated by author, using mean population for each
period.

indicate more about the regime's way of dealing with dissidents
than about the population's mental state. Recent public debates
in Norway on the mental health care system suggest that some
people are detained in such institutions without actually being
mentally ill. Many psychiatric patients who could have been
given help in their own environment, with the assistance of
friends and relatives, are instead placed in central institutions. Nevertheless, we will maintain that the numbers of
patients in mental hospitals do tell us something about the
extent to which identity needs are taken care of in our society.
    Data on the numbers of mental patients in hospital, nursing
homes and family care at the end of each year from 1935 to
1970[26] are of little use here. The number of patients per
100,000 population actually declined by 10 per cent during the
period, something which could be due to more liberal discharge
practices or to a more rapid turnover of patients. Figures on
movement of patient population in mental hospitals, presented
in Table 3.13, give a rather different impression of the
development of mental disease since 1950. Mental hospitals had
an average patient population of around 8000 during the 1950-75
period, with numbers gradually decreasing after 1965.

The Poverty of Progress

Table 3.13
Movement of Patient Population in Norwegian Mental Hospitals
1950-75

Year	Admissions			Per 100,000 population[a]			Discharged patients
	First Admissions	Readmissions	Total	First	Readmissions	Total	
1950	1571	1253	2824	48	38	86	2445
1955	1518	1515	3033	44	44	88	2731
1960	2173	2544	4717	61	71	132	4406
1965	2889	3804	6693	78	102	180	5991
1970	2948	4418	7366	76	114	190	6829
1975	3310	5909	9219	83	147	230	8568

Source: Central Bureau of Statistics, NOS Mental Hospitals (1975).
Note: a Calculated by the author.

However, the important trend involves the number of patients
per 100,000 population that were first admissions. This actually increased by 75 per cent, while the readmission figures
nearly quadrupled in the 25-year period. The number of patients
discharged during the period increased three and a half times.
In other words, more mental patients seem to have relapses during
later years, while hospital beds have a larger turnover. One
explanation for this situation is the increased use of psychotropic drugs, both inside and outside of hospitals, permitting
more people to 'function' in society, even if they have mental
problems.[27] Table 3.11 showed that more people in 1975 considered themselves to have nervous problems than in 1968, with
an increase from 62 to 78 per 1000 persons reporting 'nervous conditions'. From the figures in Table 3.10, we estimate that
about 93 per cent of the nervous conditions were chronic: when
people have developed mental problems they tend to last a long
time.
    In the Health Survey, 1975 some 14 per cent of respondents
reported having been told by a doctor, at some point in their
life, that they suffered from nervous or psychological problems
(almost 11 per cent of males and 18 per cent of females).
Slightly less than 7 per cent of respondents reported nervous
or psychological problems during the 2-week survey period,
while almost a quarter of all people over 16 had taken medicine
or drugs for the nerves at some point.
    Several studies on mental health in Norway confirm this sad
state of affairs. One study widely publicized in 1973 reported

a comparative analysis of the mental health of 352 junior high
school students in Oslo and 101 similar students from a small
district in the countryside. (Lavik, 1976, p. 34). This study
concluded that almost 20 per cent of the Oslo youth and nearly
8 per cent of the Skodgal youth had 'poor mental health'. A
similar study contrasting people's mental health in Oslo with
that in a small rural municipality (Dalgard and Sørensen, 1977),
found that 8.6 per cent of the interviewees in Oslo had psychiatric problems at the time of interview, while the frequency in
the rural sample was 3.8 per cent. Respectively, almost 15 per
cent and 6 per cent reported symptoms of a psychiatric character
at some point in their lives.

A well-known psychiatrist described the Norwegian population's
mental health as implying that approximately 1 per cent of the
population will develop schizophrenia during their life-time,
6-7 per cent will suffer from psychoses, 10-12 per cent will
become neurotic, and about one-third of the population will be
in need of psychiatric attention. Another indicator of poor
mental health is that about 36 per cent of all patients in
Norwegian hospitals during the mid-seventies were in psychiatric
institutions (Rettersdøl, 1975).

According to Dr Assen Jablenski,[28] of the Mental Health Division
of the World Health Organization, research shows a marked increase in the frequency of neuroses in Scandinavian countries.
Barely a few per cent of the population suffered from neuroses
at the turn of the century, but today's figure is estimated at
up to 20 per cent. Our guess, however, is that the recorded
incidence of poor mental health only represents the tip of the
iceberg. Probably, most people are at some time or other
depressed, are feeling insecure and lonely; some toy with the
idea of suicide while many others experience a lack of a sense
of purpose in life. Many such cases will clearly never be recorded as mental disturbance, and today it may even be that
such feelings can be considered a normal part of everyday life.
This in itself indicates that Norwegians do not score very high
on the satisfaction of identity needs, that we are becoming an
alienated people with increasingly serious mental problems.

FREEDOM NEEDS

The subject of freedom is probably the most complicated in
our list of needs categories, largely because it is hard to
quantify with relevant indicators. Some choices we wish to
make are much more important than others (choice of way of life,
choice of occupation, of place to live, and of life partner(s),
being more important than choice between essentially identical
consumer goods), but they are rarely made explicit. Such choices
are understood, are part of the structural and cultural make-up
of society. Furthermore, available choices may be too numerous
for us to make rational decisions, or we may not be fully aware
of all possible options, so it is easy to choose according to
interests other than our own.

Compared to many other countries, Norwegians enjoy a great
many freedoms. We may choose among a number of different media
for receiving and expressing information and opinion. Newspapers, periodicals, books, lay and professional magazines of
nearly all kinds are freely available in public libraries
throughout the country. In 1978 there were 1394 public libraries
spread throughout the country, or less than 3000 people per
library.[29] Money allowing, one may buy almost any book or other
publication in any language. The only exceptions are hard-core
pornography, literature encouraging illegal practices (such as
how to grow marijuana), and on matters related to 'national
security'. It should be mentioned here that the information
available to the public on military issues is rather limited
and that regulations on the release of 'sensitive information'
are far stricter in Norway than, for instance, in the United
States. But as such issues are not a central public concern,
except for a small, politically active minority, most Norwegians
consider our freedom in this area to be rather complete.

People's freedom to communicate with each other has also been
greatly expanded by the spread of the telephone. However, the
telephone service in Norway is expensive, and only about 57 per
cent of all private households had access to a private telephone
in 1977. In contrast, 67 per cent of all households owned a
car, reflecting rather well the sort of choices encouraged by
the Norwegian leadership in a resource-scarce world. It should
be added that the capacity to install new telephones in 1977
was as low as 56,000, while car sales the same year reached an
all-time high of 145,000, thus further restricting the freedom
of the young to play in the streets or for all of us to breathe
fresh air.

Few restrictions exist on travel either within Norway or
abroad — freedom is only limited when it comes to visiting military installations, and, of course, by economics. In principle,

Norwegians may engage in whatever political or religious activities they choose, live where they want to, marry a partner they like, and buy almost any imaginable consumer good. Nevertheless, some limitations to choice do exist. Most of the population are registered members of the Lutheran State Church,[30] and all schools have mandatory Christian education. Accordingly, considerable conformity pressure exists regarding what faith people choose. Religious influences impose strict limitations on the way of life in some West Coast communities, where the sale of alcohol is forbidden, and public dancing arrangements for young people are regarded as 'sinful'. However, the Church did not manage to stop the recent liberalization of the abortion laws, now leaving the choice of whether or not one should give birth to the mother, instead of to the previous commission of doctors. Also, there is a rising trend towards non-membership of the State Church, giving hopes for more pluralism in choice of religion or other systems of thought in the future. At school, there is now the possibility of opting for human ethics instead of Christianity, although parental passivity and formal obstacles have so far prevented many students from opting out of traditional forms of religious education. It should be added too that the Norwegian broadcasting system is a state monopoly, where the official religion is given significant broadcasting time. Our choice is restricted to only one TV channel and two radio stations, national television in particular being rather careful when presenting controversial issues to the public.

Norway also has a censorship board for entertainment films. A long-dormant blasphemy law was recently invoked, banning the rather innocuous British comedy, *The Life of Brian*, and the Swedish anti-narcotic movie, *A Decent Life*. The former was banned because it indirectly attacked the Church, the latter because the censorship board considered it too instructive for potential drug addicts.[31]

On the surface, then, people's freedom needs are relatively well met in Norway, compared with most other countries. An important aspect of the possibility to make free choices has been the significant rise in people's real incomes, coupled with a relatively high level of education, which, incidentally, is based on a public, tuition-free system. But in practice, it takes more than money and education to break out of the relatively conformist Norwegian way of life, especially since industrial growth and technological imperatives limit people's choice of such essential goods as clean air and water, and recreation areas. Likewise, the Norwegian membership of such organizations as NATO, the International Energy Agency and the OECD is not based on people's choice, as for instance expressed in referenda, but on technocratic rule. It remains to be seen

whether the Norwegian people will remain content with the sorts
of freedom that currently exist, or if they will stand up and
fight for another structure which will allow a more pluralistic
and diverse nation to develop in the future.

CONCLUSION

This chapter has in many ways only scratched the surface when
it comes to evaluating positive and negative aspects of the DWL
in Norway. However, we feel sufficient aspects have been considered to paint a picture of a country which has surpassed an
optimum level of development. Norway can be said to have reached
a state of overdevelopment where on the one hand material things
are overabundant, while on the other many non-material aspects
of life are totally lacking. We would place Norway on the right-
hand side of the graph relating level of development and material
production, put forward by Galtung *et al.* in Chapter 1 of this
book (Fig. 1.2). It is maldeveloped in the sense of being overdeveloped. To put approximate dates onto this curve, 1930-5 can
be identified as the beginning of the sufficiency level and 1965-
70 as the end of the development period. Thus we would date the
beginning of overdevelopment around the beginning of the 1970s,
while our relatively most developed period could be said to
have been around 1950-60. However, the trend towards overdevelopment is not inexorable: it is quite within possibility
that enlightened action can lead our society towards a new high
point above the present curve at some time in the future.

What are the chances of escaping continued overdevelopment?
Many of the trends examined in our discussion of human needs
satisfaction are rather discouraging. However, there are some
bright spots, for instance reflected in stagnating death rates
for heart disease and decreasing cigarette smoking among men.
And one significant force behind the reversal of these disconcerting trends are the many alternative ways of life movements.
These are important in Norway, coinciding with what seems to be
a loss of vision by the ruling elites. Even if groups of
people in Norway are still lacking in material-needs satisfaction, the general picture is one of increasing feelings of
saturation, of people choosing to reject the dangerous climb
up the ladder of material consumption. With the quest for a
simpler life-style, the alternative movements give us some hope
that one day it will be possible to bridge the gap between
those having too little and those having too much, in a unified
search for human and social development for all.

NOTES

1. This chapter was first presented as a paper at the Second
Planning Meeting of the Goals, Processes and Indicators of
Development Project of the United Nations University, held in
Geneva, 10-14 January 1978. A revised version was published by
the UNU as a Working Paper 'Negative and Positive Sides of
Norwegian Life Style: An Empirical Assessment of Overdevelopment', publication HSDRGPID-26/UNUP-137, January 1980. For
this final version I am much indebted to comments made by Johan
Galtung, Monica Wemegah, John Irvine and Ian Milco, all members
of the GPID Project, and also to Hans Th. Waaler of the Norwegian Council for the Humanities and Science's Group for Health
Service Research in Oslo. The author is, however, solely
responsible for the opinions expressed, and any mistakes in
the analysis or in the data base presented.

2. Illich (1975b) was the first to develop a comprehensive
critique of health in modern industrial society, showing the
negative aspects of overmedication.

3. The figures presented here are taken from Statens Ernaerings-
rad (Norwegian Nutrition Board) (1979).

4. The problems following market saturation from the producer's
point of view are discussed by Poleszynski (1977c).

5. Figures are taken from The Ministry of Oil and Energy (1980).

6. Figures are calculated on the basis of statistics given in
Dagbladet, 1 February, 1980.

7. Official estimates of *per capita* energy use are about 30
per cent lower, since the high-quality Norwegian electricity
production is converted to oil according to its calorific heat
value. Taking account of the 65-70 per cent losses incurred
in thermal power plants, I have used 1 TWh (billion kilowatt
hour) = 0.28 million toe, instead of the heat value of 0.086
mtoe per TWh.

8. These figures are calculated by the author on the basis of
statistics published by the Central Bureau of Statistics in
Oslo.

9. See Norges Naturvernforbund (1979) for a discussion of the
environmental effects of hydro-power production and of other
energy uses.

10. Waldbott (1978) is a key source in understanding the
health effects of energy conversion in industrialized societies.

11. Norwegian surveys show that from 1976-78 the proportion
of women who were regular smokers increased from 35 to 37 per
cent, while the figures for men declined from 53 to 43 per cent
(National Association Against Cancer, 1979).

12. If not otherwise indicated, the figures presented in (a)-
(d) have been taken from *Historical Statistics*, 1978, or from
Statistical Yearbook, Central Bureau of Statistics.

13. According to Dr Hans Th. Waaler in a personal communication.

14. A historical perspective on medical advances in Norway
during the recent 50 years is given by Anton Jervell in Norsk
Medisinaldepot (1976).

15. This point was stressed by Waaler (see note 13, above) and
is further elaborated in Illich (1977).

16. Ministry of Social Affairs (1978).

17. According to the U.S. Surgeon General (1979a), 'most
serious illnesses — such as heart disease and cancer — are related to several factors . . . among them, cigarette smoking, poor
dietary habits, severe emotional stress — increased probabilities
for severe illnesses'. The connection between a fibre-deficient,
sugar-laden diet and many kinds of illnesses is extensively
documented by Cleave (1975), Dufty (1975) and Bruker (1978).

18. Epstein (1978) is a key source in this respect, but see
also Waldbott (1978).

19. The most comprehensive documentation of the negative
health effects of cigarette smoking is found in the gigantic
report, *Smoking and Health*, by the U.S. Surgeon General (1979b).

20. *New Scientist*, 6 May 1976.

21. See Cleave (1975), Dufty (1975), Bruker (1978) and U.S.
Senate (December 1977).

22. Deutsche Gesellschaft für Ernährung (1976), p. 105.

23. U.S. Senate (December, 1977; p. 2) gives a breakdown of

the estimated costs of dental disease, diabetes, cardiovascular disease, alcohol and digestive diseases. In addition should be counted costs related to cancer and kidney disease, hypertension, and long-term costs associated with low-birthweight babies due to maternal malnutrition, etc.

24. *Der Spiegel* (1976; p. 74).

25. Central Bureau of Statistics (1976).

26. Central Bureau of Statistics (1975).

27. Norsk Medisinaldepot (1980).

28. Personal communication to the author, April 1980.

29. Central Bureau of Statistics (October 1979).

30. According to Central Bureau of Statistics (October 1979; p. 17), 94 per cent of the Norwegian population were members of the State Church in 1970. Census results from 1980 are not yet available, but the recent trend towards non-membership will probably have reduced the figure by a few per cent.

31. *The Life of Brian* was eventually accepted for release in autumn 1980, although an introductory text was added, some parts not translated, and only 18 year olds and over allowed to view it.

BIBLIOGRAPHY

Bruker, M. O. (1978) *Krank durch Zucker. Der Zucker als Patho-genetischer Faktor*. Bad Homberg v.d.H, Helfer Verlag, E. Schwabe, 7th edition.
Central Bureau of Statistics (1975) *Social Survey, 1974*. Oslo.
Central Bureau of Statistics (1976) *Health Survey, 1975*. Oslo.
Central Bureau of Statistics (1979) *Statistical Yearbook, 1979*. Oslo.
Cleave, T. L. (1975) *The Saccharine Disease*. Connecticut, New Canaan.
Dalgard, O. S. and Sørensen, T. (1977) Mimeo from Institute of Psychiatry, University of Oslo.
Der Spiegel (No. 44, 1976) 'Diabetes: Grösste Epidemie der Menscheit'.
Deutsche Gesellschaft für Ernährung (1976) *Ernährungsbericht 1976*. Frankfurt a.M.

Dufty, W. (1975) *Sugar Blues*. New York, Warner Books.
Epstein, S. (1978) *The Politics of Cancer*. San Francisco,
Sierra Club Books.
Galtung, J., Poleszynski, D. and Wemegah, M. (1979) *Alternative
Ways of Life*. Society for International Development (Rome)
and UNU/GPID, Geneva.
Galtung, J. *et al*. (1980) *Norge i 1980 - årene* (Norway in
the 80s). Gyldendal Norsk Forlag, Oslo.
Illich, I. (1975a) *Energy and Equity*. London, Caldor and Boyars.
Illich, I. (1975b) *The Limits to Medicine*. London, Pelican
Books.
Landsforeningen mot Kreft (The National Association against
Cancer), (1979) *Mot Kreft (Against Cancer)*, No 1.
Lavik, N. J. (1976) *Ungdoms Mentale Helse* (Youth and Mental
Health). Oslo, Oslo University Press.
Ministry of Oil and Energy (1980) *St.meld. nr.54 (1979-80)
Norges Framtidige Energibruk - og Produksjon* (Future
Energy Use and Consumption in Norway). Oslo.
Ministry of Social Affairs (1978) *NOU 1978:38 Kreftomsorgen i
Norge, (Cancer Care in Norway)*. Oslo.
Norges Naturvernforbund (1979) *Energi, Miljø og Samfunn,
(Energy, Environment and Society)*. Oslo, H. Aschehoug & Co.
Norsk Medisinaldepot (1976) *Yearly Report*. Oslo.
Norsk Medisinaldepot (1980) *Legemiddelforbruket, 1976-79* (Drug
Consumption in Norway). Oslo.
OECD (1976) *Energy Conservation in the IEA, 1976 Review*. Paris,
OECD.
Poleszynski, D. (1977a) 'The Concept of Overdevelopment:
Theories, Causalities and Indicators'. *Papers* No. 53, Chair
in Conflict and Peace Research, University of Oslo.
Poleszynski, D. (1977b) 'Waste Production and Overdevelopment,
An Approach to Ecological Indicators'. *Journal of Peace
Research*, Vol. XIV.
Poleszynski, D. (1977c) 'Utskiftninger i Markedet og Tendenser
i Produktutviklingen', (Changes in the Market and Tendencies
in the Development of Products). *Melding* No. 52, Bekkestua,
Norway, The State Institute for Consumer Research.
Rettersdøl, N. (1975) *Menneskesinnet* (The Human Mind) and *Kriser
i Menneskesinnet* (Crisis in the Human Mind). Oslo, Cappelen
Forlag.
Statens Ernaeringsråd (1979) *Årsmelding 1978 og Rapport om Mat-
forsyning i Norge* (Yearly Report 1978 and Report on Food
Supply in Norway). Oslo.
U.S. Surgeon General (1979a) *Healthy People: The Surgeon General's
Report on Health Promotion and Disease Prevention*. U.S.
Department of Health, Education and Welfare, Washington
D.C., U.S. Government Printing Office.

U.S. Surgeon General (1979b) *Smoking and Health*. Washington
    D.C., U.S. Government Printing Office.
U.S. Senate (1977) *Dietary Goals for the United States*, (2nd
    Edition), Select Committee on Nutrition and Human Needs.
    Washington D.C., U.S. Government Printing Office.
Waldbott, G. L. (1978) *Health Effects of Environmental Pollut-
    ants*, (2nd Edition). St. Louis, Missouri, The C.V. Mosby
    Company.

4

The Dominant Way of Life in Switzerland: A Case Study of Symptoms of Overdevelopment

MONICA WEMEGAH, WITH JEAN-PAUL BÄRFUSS

INTRODUCTION

Using the conceptual framework presented in Chapter 1 of this volume, we will identify a whole range of symptoms of over-development in Switzerland. The Dominant Way of Life (DWL) can be shown to frustrate people's needs for security, welfare, identity and freedom in many ways, and in presenting a statistical picture of life in contemporary Switzerland we shall draw upon unofficial as well as official data.

Before we start out in this task, though, a brief general description of the country and its people is needed. Switzerland covers a total surface area of 41,293 square kilometres, 25 per cent of which is unproductive land. In 1978, the country had a total population of 6,337,000, of which one-sixth were foreigners,[1]* and a population density of 153 inhabitants per sq. km. Its legendary riches are reflected in the high average annual income per capita, which has grown rapidly in the postwar period, to U.S.$11,606 in 1978.[2] The increasing wealth of the Swiss is also shown by the fact that they spend less and less of their income on food, and more and more on 'non-essentials' such as education, leisure, transport and communication. On the other hand, in parallel with the ever rising standard of living, the Swiss are increasingly worried about protecting their possessions from theft, fire or loss, and their lives from accidents, sickness or death. An enquiry carried out in 1971 revealed that the 'average Swiss is afraid of the future — she thinks even more about insuring herself than about enjoying and educating herself'.[3]

These figures, as averages, do not indicate the social, economic and cultural differences among Swiss people. It is important to point out that Switzerland is a federal state

* Superscript numbers refer to notes at end of chapter.

consisting of twenty-three sovereign cantons, with four national languages (German, French, Italian and Rhaeto-Romanic), two main religious denominations (Protestant and Catholic) and two fundamentally different regions (the plain and the mountains). Despite generally growing affluence, regional differences have been accentuated over the years (Reich, 1977). Thus, beside a highly urbanized and extremely rich canton, like Basle-Town, with an annual per capita income of SFr. 32,831, we find very poor agricultural cantons like Appenzell-Innerroden with a per capita income of only SFr. 11,398 in 1975. Thirty-three per cent of all inhabitants of Switzerland live in the two cantons of Bern and Zürich, whereas a mere 2.3 per cent live in the five rural cantons of Glarus, Uri, Nidwalden, Obwalden and Appenzell put together. The highly unequal development of the various regions within Switzerland fully justifies the label 'maldeveloped', for the country as a whole, and 'overdeveloped' for those areas, both geographically and socially speaking, where too many material goods have begun to impede the well-being of the very people who are supposed to profit from them.

SECURITY NEEDS

Given the overall affluence of Switzerland, it is interesting to begin an evaluation of the DWL by considering the level of security experienced by the average Swiss person. In this respect, the available figures on violent death caused by either accident or homicide (given in Table 4.1) show no clear trend, although the overall picture seems to be improving. It is note-worthy that almost half the accidental deaths involve road accidents. Fatal traffic accidents quadrupled between 1900 and 1970, whereas the homicide rate decreased by more than half over the same period. In parallel, convictions for road traffic offences have increased dramatically, although a slowdown has become noticeable since 1973.

As for crime in general, Switzerland compares favourably with countries like the United States, the German Federal Republic, and Sweden. It is true that certain crimes such as bank robbery have increased over the years as Switzerland's wealth has become more (intolerably?) conspicuous. However, a comparison between Zürich (the largest Swiss city) and other similar-sized cities such as Stuttgart, Denver, and Portland shows that the Swiss still live in relative safety from murder and robbery, even in their cosmopolitan centres. This is demonstrated quite clearly in Table 4.2.

To judge from the available data, then, Switzerland seems to satisfy people's need for protection against physical assault or accidents fairly well. The increasing number of attacks on

Table 4.1
Violent Deaths (Switzerland)
(per 100,000 inhabitants)

	1900	1910	1920	1930	1940	1950	1960	1970	1976
Traffic Accidents	7.8	7.3	9.3	18.1	12.8	18.9	26.9	27.8	20.6
Other Accidents [a]	54.3	48.4	40.1	39.2	35.9	33.0	30.1	32.6	26.5
Total Accidents	62.1	55.7	49.4	57.3	48.7	51.9	57.0	60.4	47.1
Homicide	4.2	4.2	7.2	5.2	4.2	2.8	1.9	2.5	1.3
Total Deaths	66.3	59.9	56.6	62.5	52.9	54.7	58.9	62.9	48.4

Source: Annuaire Statistique Suisse (1961), p. 75; (1977), p. 68.

Note: [a] For example, accidents at work or playing sports.

Table 4.2
Robbery and Homicide Offences in Zürich
and Comparable Foreign Cities
(1973)

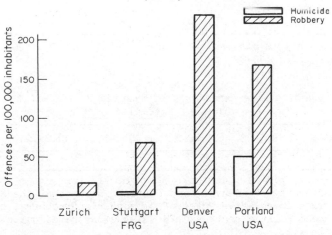

Source: Sociologisches Institut der Universität Zürich, *Almanach der Schweiz* (1978), p. 231.

The Poverty of Progress

insurance companies, and private and public banks does seem to
indicate, however, that material wealth in our country has
reached a point beyond which it may become a curse rather than
a blessing.

WELFARE NEEDS

Demography and Welfare

   If demographic trends are to be believed, the Swiss, it seems,
not only live increasingly well but also longer. As Tables
4.3 and 4.4 demonstrate, a progressive decrease in infant mortality and increase in life expectancy have both taken place
over the past century.

Table 4.3
Infant Mortality (Switzerland, 1900-76)
(Deaths during the first year of life, per 1000
live-born children)

	1900	1910	1920	1930	1940	1950	1960	1970	1976
Boys	156	127	92	57	52	35	24	17	12
Girls	129	103	73	45	40	27	18	13	9
Proportional Average	143	115	82	51	46	31	21	15	11

Source: Annuaire Statistique Suisse (1940), p. 90; (1961),
         p. 70; (1977), p. 61.

Table 4.4
Average Life Expectancy (Switzerland, 1880-1973)
(m=male; f=female)

Age	1880-99		1900-19		1920-39		1940-59		1960-70		1968-73	
	m	f	m	f	m	f	m	f	m	f	m	f
0	44.5	47.1	50.0	54.8	57.8	63.1	65.9	70.4	69.3	75.0	70.3	76.2
10	48.4	49.6	51.9	53.2	54.9	57.7	59.2	63.2	61.2	66.7	62.0	67.6
30	32.5	34.2	34.7	36.9	37.4	40.2	40.8	44.2	42.3	47.1	43.1	48.0
50	18.5	19.6	19.4	21.2	20.9	23.1	23.1	26.0	24.1	28.3	24.7	29.1
70	7.5	7.6	7.9	8.3	8.5	9.2	9.4	10.7	10.1	12.0	10.3	12.6

Source: Annuaire Statistique Suisse (1977), p. 72.

As can be seen, the average life expectancy has risen steadily
for all age groups. Women enjoy a greater longevity than men
throughout the period under consideration. Thus, boys born
between 1880 and 1899 could expect to live to 44.5 and girls to
44.7 years of age, while today newborns have a life expectancy
of over 70 years, with girls better off than boys by some 6
years. The increase in life expectancy over the past century
has been greater for girls than for boys.

At the other end of the age pyramid, old people have gained
relatively few additional years of life when compared to other
age groups; women, however, again improved their position relative to men over time. The increased life expectancy of the
Swiss is due less to any spectacular 'prolongation' of life
than to the lowering of child mortality by, among other things,
the successful elimination of infectious diseases. It should
also be noted that the higher life expectancy of women as compared to that of men is a recent phenomenon: a century ago, the
life expectancy for both sexes was practically the same. The
gap between the two developed as a result of industrialization
since the end of the last century, with the dramatic change of
professional and family roles it occasioned.

These statistical data are, of course, crude averages, and do
not take into account the physical and social differences
between individuals and groups. Stressful work or unbalanced
nutrition, in particular, can drastically reduce the life expectancy of both men and women, and may be responsible in part
for a slower increase in life expectancy than might be expected
since the middle of this century. Table 4.5 demonstrates this
slowdown in the increase in life expectancy over time.

On the basis of these trends, estimates for the future now
suggest that life expectancy will in all likelihood be augmented
by fractions of years only.[4] Apparently, scientific progress
in the field of medicine and hygiene has reached a limit beyond
which life cannot be prolonged. On the other hand, the dominant
economic and social structures in our country seem to lead
people into a way of life that might actually reduce longevity,
or affect its quality, so that a long life need not necessarily
be a good life. One might expect, therefore, that increasing
the life expectancy of the Swiss population will stop being a
primary objective of investments in the health sector. Rather
than adding years to life, the Swiss may have to start thinking
about adding life to the years.

So far we have said something about the quality of life, but
nothing as yet about numbers of Swiss living particular ways of
life. According to Ginsbourg (1973) the Swiss population is
likely to grow little, or maybe even diminish, over the coming

Table 4.5
Gains in Life Expectancy over 20-year Periods (Switzerland)

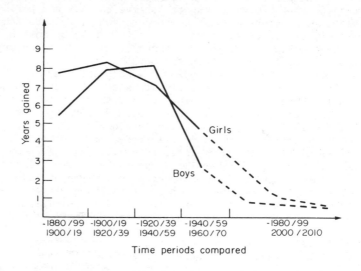

Source: Calculated by the author from Table 4.4.

decades, due to a falling birth rate. This fall has been taking
place throughout the present century, with the exception of the
immediate postwar period and its associated baby boom. As is
shown in Table 4.6, the fall has been particularly sharp in the
1970s, with the death rate during this period staying practically constant.

Table 4.6
Population Movement in Switzerland
(per 1000 inhabitants)

	1880	1900	1920	1940	1950	1960	1970	1975
Birth rate (live births)	29.6	28.6	20.9	15.2	18.1	17.6	15.8	11.7
Death rate	21.9	19.3	14.4	12.0	10.1	9.7	9.1	9.0
Excess of birth rate to death rate	7.7	9.3	6.5	3.2	8.0	7.9	6.7	2.7

Source: *Annuaire Statistique Suisse* (1977), p. 35.

Several factors can be held responsible for this apparently
unabating trend to decreasing births. The development and
spread of modern contraceptive methods, the pill in particular,
have undoubtedly had a considerable influence. It is, however,
not the pill as such, but the motives for taking it which are
revealing. The small size of flats in the urban areas, the
desire of women to work outside the home, and the cost of 'unproductive' children are among the reasons that account for
the lessening enthusiasm of potential parents. It also seems
that an increasing proportion of the younger generation look
at the future with mistrust, if not fear, and are unwilling to
burden their innocent offspring with the possible catastrophic
consequences of present development patterns.[5] Further, there
is growing dissatisfaction with an urbanization process that
fails to provide living and playing space for children, let
alone a generally convivial environment for all those who live
in the cities. Recently, the federal authorities responsible
for land planning recognized that 'it is not enough to guarantee
material comfort if conviviality in a higher sense of the word
is not provided at the same time' in our cities.[6] Today, at
least thirty residents' associations are fighting for qualitative improvement in the urban areas, for the benefit of the
town dwellers in general, and children and the elderly in
particular.[7]

One important consequence of the lower birth rate will be an
increase in the proportion of the population that is economically
inactive. As shown in Table 4.7, Switzerland presents the
typical image of an industrial nation whose ageing population
is becoming proportionally more numerous.

Table 4.7
Age Cohorts of Population (Switzerland)
(distribution per 1000 inhabitants)

Age	1860	1900	1920	1940	1960	1970	1976
0-4	110	114	85	72	81	78	61
5-19	282	301	295	230	233	228	231
20-34	248	246	239	238	231	237	232
35-49	183	171	195	221	192	190	191
50-64	126	120	128	154	171	153	154
65-79	56	53	52	48	86	96	108
86+	5	5	6	9	16	18	22

Source: Annuaire Statistique Suisse (1977), p.2.

Whereas 100 years ago the Swiss population structure resembled
a pyramid, with a sparsely populated top (relatively few old
people) and a broad base (relatively many young), today the
pyramidal form has given way to an 'onion' shape. The proportion of children and youth has decreased considerably, with an
'ageing' of the total population. This 'ageing' is purely
relative, however, since the age group 20-65 has remained more
or less stable in size over the past 100 years. It is the
changes at the top and bottom of the structure that cause
concern, particularly since some regions of Switzerland are
more affected than others. Analysis of demographic trends for
rural communes (of which there are about 3000) reveals that in
certain regions, especially those situated near or in the mountains, 'the spectre of a Swiss population on its way to ex-
tinction' is more than a mere fantasy. Today about one-sixth
of all Swiss communes report fewer births than deaths, particularly among the native Swiss population.[8] Quite clearly, this
cannot be solely attributed to socially or personally motivated
unwillingness to have children; urbanization is systematically
shifting the rural population away to the towns. Deserted
rural areas are, of course, the other side of the coin of crowded
cities and an increasingly inhospitable urban environment.

A slow down in population growth need not in itself be a bad
thing, since it provides a welcome opportunity to think about
improving the living conditions of both urban and rural inhabitants in the face of a future social environment where excessive
demographic pressure will be a thing of the past. The Swiss
federal authorities now insist that zero population growth is
no reason to stop planning, but on the contrary provides opportunities for qualitative improvement of both the physical and
human environment in our country.[9] Whether such improvement is
actualized will remain to be seen.

Urbanization and Welfare

The unchecked growth of towns is intimately related to demographic maldistribution and exploitative land use in Switzerland. Over the past 30 years, the urbanized area has more than
doubled, producing a greater than 50 per cent increase in urban
space per inhabitant (Table 4.8).

While Switzerland does not yet possess gigantic metropoles
crammed with several million inhabitants, the overall urbanization of the population is well underway. This can be seen
in Table 4.9. The process is unlikely to be halted unless the
central authorities succeed in pushing through new legislation
on land use, intended to provide an effective check on the rural

Table 4.8
Evolution of Urbanized Areas[a] in Switzerland

Urbanized surface (hectares)		Total population		Urbanized surface per inhabitant (square metres per person)	
1942	1967	1941	1970	early 1940s	late 1960s
77,888	177,795	4,265,703	6,269,783	183	284

Source: Delegierter für Raumplanung, *Raumplanung Schweiz* (1975), no. 2, p. 17.
Note: [a] 'Urbanized area' is defined here as the sum of terri-tories used for construction, industrial complexes, and communications infrastructure.

exodus and to achieve a generally more balanced distribution of the population in the country as a whole.

Table 4.9
Urban Population (Switzerland, 1850-1975)

	1850	1880	1900	1910	1920	1930	1940	1950	1960	1970	1975
Total population (in millions)	2.39	2.83	3.31	3.75	3.88	4.07	4.27	4.71	5.43	6.27	6.37
Density per sq. km.	58	69	80	91	94	98	103	114	131	152	154
Urban population (% of total population)	6.4	13.3	22.0	25.4	27.6	30.5	32.9	36.5	41.9	45.3	52.0

Source: Annuaire Statistique Suisse (1977), p. 13.

Urbanization in Switzerland appears to have involved two dis-tinct processes. To begin with, rural areas have been progres-sively transformed into urban sites. Thus, between 1850 and 1975 the number of communes with 5000-10,000 inhabitants in-creased from 21 to 121. While about 45 per cent of all Swiss communes have fewer inhabitants today than at the beginning of this century, the number of towns of more than 10,000 inhabitants has grown from eight to ninety-two over the same period. On

The Poverty of Progress

the other hand, there has been a movement away from the towns
to the so-called agglomerations or suburbs, from where an increasing number of people commute daily to work in the city.
A more and more marked division of activities thus appears: the
resident population in the town decreases at the same time as
new work places are created in the town centres themselves.[10]
Whereas in 1950 only one in six Swiss people worked outside
their place of residence, twice as many now do so.

Our dying city centres perfectly illustrate the negative
consequences of urban development beyond a certain point, a
point that has clearly been reached when people start to com-
plain about, or actively fight against, what have been called
visual pollution, the imperialism of the rectangle, and the
empire of the tertiary sector.[11] Since 1960, the latter has
increased by leaps and bounds — the corollary of industrial mass
production. In 1975, about half the active population worked
in such branches of the service sector as banks, transport,
commerce, education or administration, so that Switzerland
appears to well deserve the label 'post-industrial'.

Table 4.10
Employment in the Three Economic Sectors
(Switzerland, 1850-1975)
(as % of active population)

	1850	1880	1900	1910	1920	1930	1940	1950	1960	1970	1975
Primary sector	57	42	31	27	26	21	21	16	12	8	6
Secondary sector	33	42	45	46	44	44	44	47	50	48	45
Tertiary sector	10	16	24	27	30	35	35	37	38	44	49
Total	100	100	100	100	100	100	100	100	100	100	100

Source: Annuaire Statistique Suisse (1976), p. 16; (1977), p. 13.

A stroll through the centre of Geneva, or of any of the big
Swiss cities, reveals that the infrastructural needs of the
service sector have systematically been given priority over
'softer', individual needs for street life, hospitality and
atmosphere. No wonder, then, that an increasing number of
people choose to move out of the cities to the suburbs. A
recent opinion poll revealed that around a half of all Swiss
people desire to live in the countryside, and virtually all
those who already live there would refuse to move to a town.[12]

Not surprisingly, 59 per cent of those who want to quit urban areas belong to the working class, who are most severely hit by the negative aspects of city life such as noise, pollution, and lack of green space. Along with the elderly, workers and small employers tend to form the bulk of the population in the bigger towns and their nearby 'cité-dortoirs', whereas the middle and upper classes have settled in the most desirable places such as by the lakeside, in the hills, near the forest or in sunny and quiet areas.[13] The current politics of 'zoning' practised at all levels of the Swiss Confederation will most probably speed up this regrettable process of social segregation with regard to living space.

Another striking feature of urbanization in our country concerns the enormous expansion of roads, and the combined impact of urban growth and communication lines on agricultural land. Whereas in the nineteenth century about 20 per cent of the total surface of towns was taken up by roads, today they cover over 40 per cent of the total urban area, the main reason for this tremendous increase being the ever growing number of car parks. Recent calculations (Table 4.11) show that more than half of the occupied surface in Switzerland is used for driving and parking.

Table 4.11
Surface Area Occupied by Various Activities (Switzerland)

For living	50 m^2 per inhabitant
For working	30 m^2 per inhabitant
For leisure/education	40 m^2 per inhabitant
For driving	140 m^2 per inhabitant

Source: *Panda* (Review of the World Wildlife Fund), Switzerland (1978), No. 1, p. 22.

Since the enactment in 1960 of a federal law on the construction of national roads, motor highways in particular have become terrific 'devourers of landscape' (Krippendorf, 1977). About half of the 2000 km. of road planned by the law has been built at the cost of over 100 square kilometres of agricultural land. Since only at great expense could roads be converted back into agricultural land, each new road causes irreparable damage to the environment in general and to agriculture in particular.

Agriculture and Welfare

The never-ending need for land for non-agricultural purposes,
such as for communication lines, buildings and industrial
plants, lies at the heart of the current political debate on
land utilization. The price paid for the present day urbanized
areas (see Table 4.8) amounts to the loss of roughly 100,000
hectares of agricultural soil since the last war alone; this
corresponds to an average loss of 3500 hectares per year; that
is, about 1 square metre per second! For such a small and
densely populated country this development is truly alarming,
especially taking into account the fact that 80 per cent of the
sacrificed land comes from the regions of the plain containing
the most fertile agricultural soil. In 1975, the Federal
Office for Land Planning argued that the inexorable progression
of built-up areas would set Switzerland an 'existential problem'
in regard to its future indigenous food supply.[14]
    In the light of the current agricultural productivity figures,
talking about an 'existential problem' may at first sight
appear to be a gross exaggeration. For as Table 4.12 shows, the
loss of agricultural soil has been more than compensated by a
tremendous increase in farming efficiency.

Table 4.12
Production of Various Crops in Hundredweights[a] per Hectare
(Switzerland)

Years	Winter wheat	Summer barley	Corn	Potatoes	Sugar-beet
1931-40	22.7	18.6	27.4	155[b]	365
1941-50	25.1	21.8	29.7	186	367
1951-60	30.6	27.9	35.3	245	420
1961-5	32.9	32.2	46.6	302	410
1966-70	36.1	33.3	55.6	343	457
1971-5	42.0	38.9	61.3	399	479

Source: Hohlenstein (1977).

Notes: [a] Equivalent to 50 kg.
        [b] Average for 1936-8.

Between 1930 and 1970, the production of winter wheat, summer-
barley and corn per hectare roughly doubled, while that of
potatoes increased by 157 per cent. Obviously, such achievements involved heavy mechanization and industrialization of
agriculture, and a gradual replacement of animal power by
mechanical traction (Table 4.13).

Table 4.13
Technical Equipment in Agriculture (Switzerland)

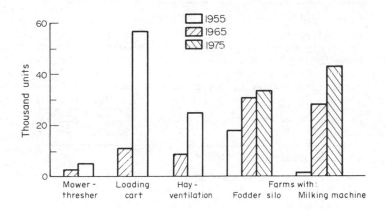

Source: Hohlenstein (1977), p. 32.

Mechanization alone, however, would not have led to such
astonishingly high yields without recourse to chemical fertilizers and pesticides on a large scale. In fact, the use of
chemical fertilizers has increased not only in absolute terms,
but also relative to the input per hectare (Table 4.14). But
those who pride themselves on the admirable performance of the
Swiss farmers rarely stop to think, it seems, of the price
paid for the present high productivity in social, energy,
ecological and, ultimately, political terms.
     The increasing cost of production involved in acquiring arti-
ficial manure, machines and gasoline has led to a continuous
reduction of small-scale farming in favour of larger, financially
more profitable farms, particularly since 1955 (Table 4.15).
Those most severely hit by this change have been the farmers in
the mountainous regions, where land is more difficult to cultivate and considerably less suitable for capital-intensive
food production. The unequal economic opportunities afforded
to peasants in the mountain areas have led many of them to give
up farming and join either the industrial or service sector
workforce.

Table 4.14
Chemical Fertilizer Usage (Switzerland)

	1964	1972
Acquired fertilizer in kg/hectare		
Pure nitrogen	18.7	34.6
Phosphoric acid	44.5	47.5
Pure potassium	50.9	70.4
Total consumption in Switzerland in cwt[a]		
Pure nitrogen	205,800	380,900
Phosphoric acid	489,770	522,930
Pure potassium	560,000	774,000

Source: Hohlenstein (1977).

Note: [a] Equivalent to 50 kg.

Table 4.15
Change in Size of Farms (Switzerland)
(as percentage of total productive agricultural land)

Area in Hectares	1929	1939	1955	1965	1975
0-5	59.7	57.6	53.1	46.1	43.2
5.01-10	24.0	24.8	25.9	24.6	18.5
10.01-30	14.7	16.5	19.8	27.3	34.9
+30	1.6	1.1	1.2	2.0	3.4
Total	100	100	100	100	100

Source: Statistiques et Évaluations (1964), p. 10;
(1976), p. 12.

The gradual abandonment of alpine pastures and traditional
farmhouses is now readily visible in the Swiss mountains. In
1973, 80,000 hectares of previously cultivated land lay fallow
in the mountainous regions; it is forecast that by the end of
the century this area may have more than tripled unless drastic
measures are taken to redress the situation (Hohlenstein, 1977,
p. 61). One problem is that Swiss farmers as a whole have not
profited from increased levels of productivity as much as they
might have hoped, given the steep levels of capital investment
needed; this is in part because rising productivity has not

The Dominant Way of Life in Switzerland 113

been matched by a parallel increase in demand for domestic
agricultural produce, so real prices of farm products have
declined. At the same time, the peasant farmers, in particular,
have experienced the rising cost of living like the rest of the
population — perhaps even more so — in that the cost of modern
agricultural machinery has risen much more sharply than the
prices of agricultural products (Table 4.16).

Table 4.16
Evolution of the General Price Index of
Agricultural Produce and Means of Production (Switzerland)
(1961/65 = 100)

Years	Agricultural products[a]			Agricultural means of production
	Vegetable cultivation	Animal production	Total	
1966	109	109	109	115
1967	107	112	110	120
1968	109	110	110	124
1969	112	111	111	129
1970	116	116	116	139
1971	121	125	124	149
1972	143	131	134	159
1973	155	138	142	176
1974	179	147	154	200
1975	172[b]	153[b]	157[b]	214

Source: *Fünfter Landwirtschaftsbericht* (1976), p. 100.

Notes: [a] According to the Annual Index of the Swiss Farmers'
Secretariat of Producer Prices of Agricultural Produce.
[b] Provisional data.

In order to compensate for their diminishing returns per unit
of output, farmers have tended to resort to increased production,
which in the milk sector periodically leads to the notorious
'milk flood' with all its political intricacies. Many small
farmers also take on a second job outside the farm, which means
additional stress, especially for their wives and children.
Others find it necessary to sell part of their land for construction purposes in order to pay off debts or to enable
further investment on the farm. As we have seen, this gnaws
at the very basis of Switzerland's alimentary self-sufficiency —
the soil.

PP - E*

The negative consequences of an agriculture oriented to increasing yields show up in both our social and physical environment. The use of insecticides, herbicides and pesticides is
not only costly in financial but also in ecological terms.
International studies have shown that biocides poison both
animals and humans, and, furthermore, lead to both water and air
pollution.[15]

Between 1969 and 1972 alone, the total number of thornhedge
sparrows in Switzerland had decreased by 78 per cent, while
that of garden redstarts dropped by 72 per cent in only 1 year
during 1968/9.[16] The consumer's wish for aesthetically impec-
cable merchandize further pushes up the extent to which crops
are sprayed, despite the fact that some 80 per cent of all
cancers are now believed to be caused by environmental poisons
of one kind or another.[17]

Perhaps most worrying of all, and in spite of massive investments in higher productivity, Swiss agriculture is less and less
able to cover the alimentary needs — or greeds — of the population. In 1975, each Swiss person ate an average of 170 eggs
and 46 kg of sugar, not to mention meat (*per capita* consumption
of which went up from 40 kg in 1930 to 79 kg in 1976). Only
about 75 per cent of the demand for meat is now met by indigenous
production, while the degree of self-sufficiency is even lower
for eggs (65 per cent) and sugar (33 per cent). Officially,
overall Swiss self-sufficiency in foodstuffs on a calorific
basis for the years 1969/70 was estimated at 52.6 per cent,
meaning that the country succeeded in producing little more
than half of the daily 3126 calorie intake per person during
that period. However, Hohlenstein (1977) shows that the figure
is actually much lower than this (41.5 per cent) when imports
of fodder for meat production are taken into account. In fact,
the larger part of imported cereal consumption goes to animal
feed (Strahm, 1977). In Switzerland, animals eat about twice
as much cereal as do humans — a truly absurd situation given
that millions of people in the Third World lack food. Annual
Swiss imports of cereals destined for fatstock could nourish up
to 5 million people in the poor countries (Hohlenstein, 1977,
p. 26).

There could be no better illustration than this of the intimate link between our DWL and maldevelopment — both at home and
in the world at large. For, beside the highly immoral aspect
of our present eating habits from a global perspective, these
farming practices are also a central cause of Switzerland's
precarious self-sufficiency in foodstuffs. If we further consider that our modern agricultural system is heavily dependent
on energy, particularly oil, for the production of artificial
manure and the fuelling of machines, self-sufficiency sinks to

a mere 8.3 per cent (Hohlenstein, 1977, p. 55).
In view of the heavy dependence of our agriculture on energy
and food imports, every additional loss of fertile soil will
therefore quite clearly aggravate the 'existential problem' so
vividly evoked by our authorities. Preserving agricultural
land will, however, not be enough to guarantee self-reliance in
food without radical change in our eating habits and agricultural
production methods. Awareness of this latent food crisis,
solidarity with the hungry, and concern with health are among
the reasons prompting growing numbers of Swiss into simpler
eating habits, domestic food production and less energy-intensive, ecologically sounder ways of farming.

Energy and Welfare

According to Poleszynski (1978) the highly energy-intensive
lifestyle of the industrial countries is largely responsible
for many of our societies' social pathologies and for much of
the world-at-large's maldevelopment. Switzerland is no exception to this rule: our increasingly urbanized, electrified and
mechanized WOL corresponds with an ever higher consumption of
energy. As is shown in Table 4.17, energy consumption *per
capita* more than trebled between 1950 and 1973. After a
temporary slow-down in the wake of the oil crisis, energy
consumption has again risen since 1975.[18]

Table 4.17
Energy Consumption in Switzerland

	1920	1940	1950	1960	1970	1973	1975
Total con-sumption in Tcal [a]	23,000	33,000	42,000	74,000	150,000	173,000	155,000
Per capita consumption in million kcal/year	5.9	7.6	8.9	13.7	23.8	27.5	24.2

Sources: Tages-Anzeiger, no. 4, 27 January 1973; and *Panda*
          (1977), no. 5; (1977), no. 9, p.11.
Note: [a] 1 Tcal = 10^8 kcal.

Increasing energy use has meant that from the Second World
War on, solid fuels such as wood and coal have been rapidly

Table 4.18
National Supply of Primary Energy 1910-75 and
Consumption of Secondary Energy in 1975 (Switzerland)

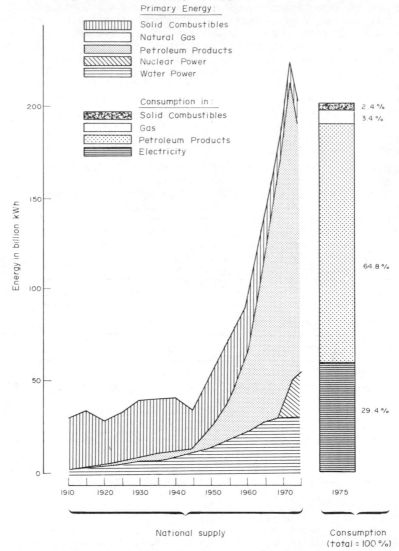

Source: Almanach der Schweiz (1977), p. 53.

replaced by oil, as can be seen in Table 4.18. Coal, which in
1950 furnished 41 per cent of our energy, today accounts for
only 21 per cent. In the past, Switzerland was also highly
dependent on hydro-electricity — the only currently available
domestic energy source. However, all feasible hydro-power sites
were tapped by 1970, making the country henceforth heavily
dependent on foreign energy supply. Thus, oil products, which
in 1950 constituted only 25 per cent of total energy consumption,
met 75 per cent of our energy needs in 1977. By the end of the
1960s, nuclear power had also entered the Swiss energy scene,
and now makes a significant contribution to our energy needs —
in 1976 Switzerland received 22 per cent of its electrical power
from nuclear stations (as can be seen in Table 4.18). The recourse to nuclear power has, however, triggered off a series of
protest movements which not only fight against nuclear plants
for environmental, social and political reasons, but also
question the wisdom of our energy-intensive DWL. Over the past
few years, various research groups have put forward proposals
to cut down wasteful energy usage.[19] As can be seen in Table
4.19, energy used for heating is a prime candidate for conservation measures.

Table 4.19
Social Distribution of Energy Consumption, 1974 (Switzerland)

	With heating (%)	Without heating (%)
Household	40	3
Handicrafts/ Agriculture	7	2
Industry	29	24
Transport	24	24
Total	100	53

Source: T. Ginsbourg, cited in Arbeitsgemeinschaft Umwelt,
(1975), p. 148.

Following a number of sharp rises in petrol prices and growing
local opposition to nuclear power, the Federal Minister for
Transport and Communication launched, in 1977, a campaign to
conserve energy. Focusing on the large amount used in heating,
he stressed: 'We must change our way of life and appreciate
energy for what it is worth. . . .'[20] Likewise, the mass media
have sought to raise popular consciousness as to the necessity

of, and possibilities for, more economical use of energy in the
kitchen, the household, and in industry and transport. Little
attention, however, has yet been paid to the question of garbage
and refuse, although they constitute a prime example of wasteful practices in general and of energy squandering in particular.
In 1970, Swiss industry and households together produced 3
million tonnes of refuse.[21] Every Swiss resident thus throws
away some 200 kg of household refuse every year, while industrial
waste amounts to 170 kg per head. In urban agglomerations,
where half the population resides, every city dweller produced
an average of almost 1 kg of waste each day! Reflecting an
overcomsuming society, kitchen garbage constitutes the lion's
share of the refuse (Table 4.20). But the tertiary sector is
no better: Swiss public and private offices throw away vast
quantities of paper.

Table 4.20
Composition of Household Garbage and Waste (Switzerland)
(as a proportion of weight of dry material)

Kind of material	Household refuse (%)	Solid municipal waste (household refuse and industrial waste) (%)
Kitchen and garden garbage	57	26
Paper	20	36
Cinders, slags	10	10
Rubber, synthetics	4	10
Glass, pottery, stone (including iron and non-ferrous metals)	3	14
Textiles	2	4

Source: See note 22.

The problems of dealing with such garbage are equally enormous: 1975 saw Swiss purification plants (and to date only 50
per cent of all planned plants are operational) producing 3
million cubic metres of sewage sludge, containing 46,000 tonnes
of organic material, 6000 tonnes of calcium, 3400 tonnes of
nitrogen, 400 tonnes of potassium, as well as various trace
elements (magnesium, etc.).[22] The re-use of these wastes and
the problem of detoxifying them are being studied, for it ap-

pears that solid municipal refuse constitutes a potentially
important energy source. The calorific value of just 1 year's
refuse corresponds to about 350,000 tonnes of petroleum, which
is equivalent to 7 per cent of the total petroleum imports in
1971.[23] Thus, without seeking to justify our present practices,
it is becoming technologically feasible to temper in part the
tremendous wastage of packaging materials and other products
by converting these to energy.

Health and Welfare

   Numerous medical commentators have pointed to marked increases
in diseases of civilization in Switzerland since the Second
World War. Our high living standard and emphasis on all forms
of material comfort, with the concomitant waste of energy,
gives rise to disagreeable side effects: the lack of physical
exercise with ensuing malfunctioning of the circulatory and
musculo-skeletal systems; high rates of road accidents; over
nutrition as well as 'softening' from fear of pain, cold, heat
and physical effort.[24] A wide range of statistical data can be
marshalled to illustrate the health aspects of overdevelopment
in Swiss society. Table 4.21 outlines some of the major causes
of death today. The main point here is that the big problems
no longer lie in containing infectious diseases such as typhoid,
diphtheria and tuberculosis. Chronic illnesses are now more
significant: cardiovascular diseases and cancer together accounted for more than two-thirds of all deaths by illness in
1976.
   As can be seen, *circulatory afflictions* are now the major
cause of natural death. The growth in arteriosclerosis, in
particular, illustrates dramatically the close interdependence
of the DWL and our physical well-being. Among the factors responsible for this disease we find stress, tobacco and alcohol,
as well as metabolic problems. Other factors include such
sometimes surprising ones as cobalt in beer (used for stabili-
zation of the foam), soft water (in which metal containers or
pipes are more prone to dissolve), air pollutants like sulphides
and carbons, and certain heavy metals (e.g. lead and cadmium,
which favour hypertension and therefore arteriosclerosis).[25]
Several factors are evidently linked — e.g. obesity and physical
inactivity. Similarly, among the main reasons for hypertension
are excessive psycho-social stimulation (stress) and excessive
food intake (obesity). In this connection, we should note that
Switzerland, like many other rich countries, has continuously
modified the composition, and sometimes the quality, of its
food intake. The consumption of more animal products means an

The Poverty of Progress

Table 4.21
Natural Causes of Death by Type of Illness (Switzerland)
(per 1000 deaths)

	1920	1930	1940	1950	1960	1970	1976
Infectious and parasitic diseases	334	184	140	64	60	38	40
Nervous system disorders	67	86	65	53	47	56	53
Circulatory system disorders	206	286	370	474	504	472	484
Digestive system disorders	69	74	63	62	55	56	45
Respiratory system disorders	146	122	106	60	60	60	65
Disorders of urinary system genital organs	45	54	52	46	36	34	24
Malignant tumours	109	159	174	210	210	234	251
Blood and metabolic disorders	24	35	30	32	32	49	38
Deaths per 100,000 inhabitants	149	93	100	85	83	79	81

Source: Annuaire Statistique Suisse (1961), pp. 71-76; (1977), pp. 65-69.

increasing intake of saturated fats and cholesterol, mainly found in animal fats — in meat, sausages, and milk products, especially cheese, cream, chocolate, etc. Arteriosclerosis thus has many causes, but the combination of factors cited are those characteristic of an overdeveloped society.

Cancer is currently the second most important cause of death in Switzerland, the number of such deaths having approximately doubled between 1921-35 and 1966-9 (from 5558 to 10,548 deaths per year). The increase has been more marked among men, who now account for 58.6 per cent of the total as opposed to 50.9 per cent previously.[26] It is now believed that most cancers are related, directly or indirectly, to such environmental factors as food consumption, alcohol, smoking and life- and working-style. In Switzerland, about 4 per cent of 2063 lung-cancer cases treated in 1974 were said to have been due to

occupational causes and 91 per cent due to the use of tobacco.[27]
It has now been realized, too, that chemical substances —
medicines, solvents, preservatives, lubricants, pesticides,
asbestos, etc. — are rather more carcinogenic than was previously
thought. A study of the influence of road traffic on a small
industrialized region of 3000 inhabitants, carried out between
1959 and 1970, showed that among seventy-five people whose death
was due to cancer, three had lived in rural areas, twenty-five
on the outskirts of the town and forty-seven in the centre of
the town.[28] Whatever the main causes behind the upsurge in
cancer deaths, it is clear that the disease is another example
of the social 'costs' associated with the DWL.

As for *respiratory problems*, a clear correlation has been
demonstrated between obesity and the development of angina
pectoris or pulmonary embolism.[29] It is also an accepted fact
that smokers and overweight people tend to have more respiratory
system problems than do others.[30] Since about half of all
Swiss are estimated to be overweight, the rise in respiratory
problems is clearly no accident. Hollenstein (1977, p. 7)
reports that the excess fat the Swiss carry around on their
bodies would add up to an amazing figure of 26,000 tonnes of
accumulated grease. The embarrassment should be more than
cosmetic — at the same time, vast numbers of humanity are
struggling for sheer survival! In fact, Hollenstein also notes
that obesity has a direct bearing on life expectancy: life
insurance companies have calculated that life expectancy is
highest among people who are 10 per cent *under*weight. For those
who are 10 per cent overweight, life expectancy decreases by
15 per cent, while people who are 20 per cent overweight can
reckon on a 40 per cent reduction.

Tobacco is another powerful factor in respiratory diseases.
Air pollution and the cigarette are together held as mainly
responsible for chronic bronchitis, the incidence of which has
assumed truly alarming proportions. In Switzerland, this increase accounts for approximately 1000 deaths per year — in
other words, around one-third of all deaths due to diseases of
the respiratory system in 1975 derived from chronic bronchitis.
Switzerland has the fourth highest percentage of deaths from
chronic bronchitis in the world in the 55-64 age group, while
5 per cent of the active population aged between 20-25 in
Geneva already suffers from the disease.[31]

Though disorders of the *digestive system* represent only 10-15
per cent of all diseases in Switzerland, one-third of the
population over 50 years are sufferers.[32] One of the most
common of these diseases is cirrhosis of the liver, which is
believed to be related to alcohol consumption. Table 4.22
shows that consumption of alcohol has risen again since 1945

after having dropped earlier in the century. Overconsumption
of alcohol and medicaments also appears to be at least partially
responsible for the increase in stomach ulcers, while the main
cause of gall-bladder problems seems to involve excessive and
unbalanced nutrition.

Table 4.22
Annual Per Capita Alcohol Consumption (Switzerland)
(litres)

	1893-1902	1923-32	1933-8	1945-55	1961-5	1971-5
Wine	88.0	50.0	44.0	36.7	37.0	44.5
Cider	28.1	37.7	36.1	35.3	11.0	6.5
Beer	61.6	50.0	54.6	34.1	73.5	74.8
40% spirits	7.17	6.73	2.88	3.02	4.46	5.30

*Source: Statistiques et Évaluations Concernant l'Agriculture et
l'Alimentation* (1954), p. 29; (1977), p. 123.

The DWL can also be held responsible for certain deficiencies
in our sight and hearing, as well as in the locomotory system.
As to the latter, one-eighth of all children in Zurich and Basle
already suffer from malformation of the spinal column at the
beginning of school age and one-third at the end. The situation
seems to be worsening, among men at least: whereas in 1962 around
1 per cent of potential recruits for the military were not in-
ducted because of malformation of the back, the proportion had
risen to 1.9 per cent in 1969.[33] Seventy per cent of such malformations are estimated to arise from poor posture. As far
as hearing is concerned, statistics show 40 per cent of Swiss
workers to have deficient hearing, around 6 per cent of whom
have severely impaired hearing indeed.[34] We can only hope that
Switzerland will soon follow the lead set by other countries in
legislating lower noise limits — particularly in industry.
There is much that might be achieved, too, in regard to the
sight of Swiss people: it has been estimated that 52.2 per cent
of the population over 15 years old have deficient sight.[35]
These deficiencies seem to stem from diseases which indirectly
impair sight (diabetes, hypertension), or from the physical
aggression implicit in modern life (mental and physical strain,
concentration, illumination). Increasing incidences of blind-
ness in Switzerland are produced by road accidents (glass
splinters) and by accidents at work (especially with caustic

liquids and solid particles).

One final and particularly revealing indicator concerning health in the era of overdevelopment relates to the state of people's teeth. In Switzerland today, virtually everyone has defective teeth, and practically the whole population suffers from the loss of one or more teeth (Müller, 1977, p. 70). Research work on dental caries show that industrially processed food in general, and white sugar in particular, are the main causes of dental deterioration. It is not just the old who suffer. Müller quotes the case of a military recruit's school in the Valais where, in 1968, 97.5 per cent of all recruits had dental caries, and 4.5 per cent of the 18 year olds already wore false teeth! He also notes that, in four districts of Lausanne, 88 per cent of children aged between 5 and 6 were found in 1968 to suffer from caries. This amply illustrates the destructive action of sweets, with which we 'spoil' our children much more than we can imagine.

Among the many factors which contribute to the diseases discussed above, our nutrition appears to be a primary pathogenic factor. Certainly many infectious diseases have been overcome, but increasing ill-health caused by excessive and unbalanced nutrition, together with environmental pollution, noise and stress, is symptomatic of the fact that the costs of our abundant society have begun to outweigh the benefits.

Further, health care itself is a striking example of overdevelopment: too many medicaments and too much technology in medical care threaten our physical and mental well-being rather than increase it. Developments in the health sector, however, entail costs not only of a social, but also of a financial, nature. Whereas in 1950 the total cost of medico-pharmaceutical care represented 3 per cent of Swiss GNP, it rose to 8 per cent in 1975, and may well reach 12 per cent in 1985 and 15 per cent in the year 2000.[36] Between 1960 and 1975 the cost of medical treatment quadrupled, that of medicaments quintupled, while expenses for hospital treatment have multiplied twelve-fold.[37] The principal factors responsible for this disconcerting trend are the increasing sophistication of medical technology, with commensurate increases in 'professional' staff, as well as a burgeoning consumption of medicaments substituting for the dialogue between doctor and patient. Although the Swiss may, from the technical point of view, experience better care, their psycho-social care has diminished in quality. Evidence for this comes in particular from the elderly sick, whose number will certainly grow over the coming decades. Surveys have shown that old, infirm people dislike being nursed in hospitals, waiting to die uprooted from their social and family circles, their household environment, and their memories.[38]   People

The Poverty of Progress

nursed at home feel more at ease, display less anxiety and are
more disposed to fight actively for recovery. Impersonal and
technical care, and a lonely death, are the price we pay for
modern medical treatment: it may be more efficient, but how
much less human!

IDENTITY NEEDS

   The picture we have painted of the physical health of the
'average Swiss' would be incomplete if we neglected to consider
the psychological impact of the DWL. According to Jean-Denis
Schweblin (speaking in an interview), approximately one-third
of all illnesses in Switzerland have a psychosomatic basis, and
60 per cent of patients visiting their family doctor do so to
be treated for depression. Some sources speak of 230,000
depressives in 1977,[39] while almost 600,000 people were affected
by mental disorders in the same year. This is reflected in the
number of first-time patients confined in psychiatric hospitals,
which, as Table 4.23 shows, has exhibited a marked increase over
recent years. Whereas in 1940 only 2504 first-time patients
were confined on average at any one time, the number had swelled
to 5239 by 1970. The age structure of this population has also
changed: there has been a noticeable trend to greater confinement of the very old and the very young.
   Another aspect of psychiatric confinement, apart from the
average daily number of inpatients, is the number of admissions

Table 4.23
Psychiatric Confinement: Proportion of First-time
Patients in Psychiatric Hospitals by Age Group (Switzerland)

Age	1940 (%)	1950 (%)	1960 (%)	1970 (%)
0-19 M:	9.9	9.7	12.3	12.3
F:	7.4	8.1	9.2	9.2
20-39 M:	41.2	36.2	32.8	35.7
F:	40.4	33.6	31.4	33.8
40-59 M:	30.7	33.2	30.7	27.8
F:	31.9	33.7	26.9	26.1
60 + M:	18.2	20.9	24.2	24.2
F:	20.3	24.6	32.5	30.9
Total M:	100	100	100	100
F:	100	100	100	100
Total number of patients	2504	3297	4518	5239

Source: Annuaire Statistique Suisse (1956), p. 491; (1973), p. 521.

to hospitals, and the proportion of new admissions as opposed
to re-admissions. As can be seen in Table 4.24, the number of
confinements has risen from 10,652 in 1943 to 23,265 in 1970.
While the proportion of new admissions decreased during this
period, that of patients re-admitted for the fourth or more
time has more than doubled — up from 13.8 per cent to 26.9 per
cent.

Table 4.24
Psychiatric Confinement: Percentage of New
Admissions and Re-admissions (Switzerland)

Number of previous confinements	1943 (%)	1956 (%)	1970 (%)
0	56.2	48.4	44.9
1	20.4	19.7	18.0
2	9.6	10.9	10.2
3	4.7	6.4	6.7
4	2.6	4.4	4.6
5 or more	6.4	10.2	15.6
Total number of admissions	10, 652	17,227	23,265

Source: Annuaire Statistique Suisse (1946),
p. 492; (1961), p. 483; (1973), p. 519.

As with other areas of health care, modern technology has
made a marked impact. With the advent and increasing use of
psychotropic drugs, shorter stays have become more common in
psychiatric clinics and longer stays less so, since 'treatment'
can be continued more readily at home (Table 4.25).

Table 4.25
Discharges from Psychiatric Hospitals by Average
Length of Confinement (Switzerland)

Length of confinement	1943(%)	1956(%)	1970(%)
1-29 days	27.5	29.1	36.2
30-89 days	31.6	36.6	37.0
3-5 months	16.1	15.8	12.4
6-11 months	9.1	7.4	6.4
12-23 months	4.9	4.0	2.8
24+ months	10.8	7.6	5.2
Total discharges	10,461	17,053	23,249

Source: Annuaire Statistique Suisse (1946),
p. 495; (1961), p. 484; (1973), p. 520.

The Poverty of Progress

It is instructive, too, to examine the nature of mental illness. Table 4.26 presents a breakdown of discharges from mental
hospitals according to the category of illness diagnosed.

Table 4.26
Discharges from Mental Hospitals by Nature of
Illness (Switzerland) (percentages)

Illness	1933	1940	1950	1960	1970
Oligophrenia	6.3	4.4	4.5	4.6	4.0
Depression	8.1	7.4	7.2	10.1	8.1
Schizophrenia	36.9	37.6	33.9	28.5	24.1
Psychosis	12.2	15.0	13.9	15.9	13.7
Abnormal psychic states	15.5	17.4	21.1	22.9	30.5
Epilepsy	4.7	5.1	4.1	4.2	2.9
Alcoholism	13.2	10.4	12.0	8.8	11.8
Other drug addictions	1.0	0.8	1.2	1.6	2.6
Other conditions	2.1	2.1	2.1	3.4	2.3
Total discharges	8074	9138	13,314	19,131	23,249

Source: Annuaire Statistique Suisse (1946), p. 495; (1963),
p. 500; (1973), p. 520.

The trends in mental illness seem to manifest a latent psychological unease, with its roots in a society no longer able to
provide the necessary emotional security to its members. The
case can be made that many of these so-called mentally ill
people are in reality only unhappy, insecure, lonely individuals
who have lost their sense of belonging — the fruit of a society
oriented solely to ill-considered economic growth. Drug addiction is increasing, as people try to find chemical ways of
coping with the DWL, though as can be seen in Table 4.26,
alcoholism still constitutes a much greater social and medical
problem. It is estimated that Switzerland has a total of
130,000 alcoholics, and that a third of all hospitalizations
are related, directly or indirectly, to alcohol.[40] Calculations
show that 28,000 years of life are lost each year because of
the consumption of alcohol, and that likewise there is an annual
loss of 11,880 person-years of work, with alcohol being a factor

in 10,000 criminal offences and 83,000 traffic accidents.[41]
   Considered for a long time as a purely medical problem,
alcoholism is now being regarded as very much a social question.
This is particularly so in that it has become evident that in
recent years women and children have increasingly joined the
ranks of the alcoholics.[42] Both young people and women suffer
lack of affection, of comprehension and even of time from their
families. This can create not only a desire to escape into
alcohol or into drugs, but also a desire to die. As Table 4.27
demonstrates, suicide has once again been on the increase in
recent years.

Table 4.27
Suicide in Switzerland
(per 100,000 inhabitants)

1900	1910	1920	1930	1940	1950	1960	1970	1976
23.7	21.7	22.8	26.0	23.3	23.4	18.7	18.3	22.0

Source: Annuaire Statistique Suisse (1961), p. 75; (1977),
     p. 68.

   Out of 57,000 deaths in 1976, 1400 were officially recorded
as suicides. Given that the actual number may be up to four
times higher than this (due to social pressures on coroners to
identify causes of death as accidental, when possible), suicide
today figures among the most frequent causes of death in Switzerland.[43] As with alcoholism — often the last stage before
suicide — women are more affected than ever before. While in
1900 there were seven male to every one female suicide, this
ratio had fallen to 2.5 to one in 1976.[44] Undoubtedly this is
in part the fruit of increasing societal alienation: the young
experience frustration and family rupture, women face feelings
of 'uselessness', and men fear 'social failure'.
   Particularly disquieting is the fact that more and more
children seem to be attempting suicide. To cope with these
problems, Heinz Peyer set up the telephone service, 'SOS
Children', and found that during the first 6 months of 1978
more than 6000 children called for help. Most of the callers
were aged between 12 and 15 — but even younger children phoned,
the youngest being a mere 7 years old. After the first wave,
when children phoned out of curiosity, the calls became more
and more serious. Many children called complaining of batterings by parents and mistreatment by teachers. Other areas of
concern were problems hinging on sex and relationships (including worries over homosexuality). Peyer concluded that the

pressures towards youth suicide were so acute as to warrant his
setting up a mutual aid association between both children and
adults with a tendency to suicide, aimed at helping children
who have attempted suicide redevelop a taste for life. Also
symptomatic of our ever busier society is that many children
call the 'SOS Children' service because they are alone at home,
are bored, and have no parent to tell them a story. To meet
this problem, Peyer established a telephone service featuring
recorded fairy tales which became an immediate success: in just
one fortnight 4000 children called the service.[45]
Lack of human contact, isolation and loneliness are problems
that cut across all social classes and all age groups. It is
paradoxical that in the midst of today's freedom from material
want, the freedom to use overabundant resources has resulted
only in people feeling lonely, misunderstood and useless. For
how much longer can our society afford to wait before the material achievements in which we have so much pride will have
killed all human warmth and togetherness?

FREEDOM NEEDS

The irony of increasing alienation in our society appears all
the more stark when one considers that people today enjoy practically unlimited freedom of choice among things and activities
intended to make our lives more enjoyable, intellectually richer
and materially easier. As far as the latter is concerned, a
vast array of material amenities such as household appliances
and leisure devices have become readily accessible, even to
lower income groups, over the past 10 years. Table 4.28 shows
that patterns of ownership of such goods have changed markedly
over the past decade.
As yet, there can be no clear-cut answer as to whether today's
myriad of appliances are things that count or are merely things
that are countable. It is revealing, however, that when
questioned about the utility of their various possessions, one-
third of the people represented in Table 4.28 admitted that
they could easily do without such things as cameras, cine-
cameras or slide-projectors. High pressure marketing fosters
the acquisition of rather unnecessary goods that contribute
only marginally, if at all, to the well-being of the purchaser.
The most controversial object in this respect is probably the
private automobile. For many, the car offers the best, often
the only, means to commute from home to work, to escape to the
countryside or to reach a shopping centre. The mobility it
provides has meant that from the early 1950s the motor car has
become far and away the most important means of personal transportation (Table 4.29).

Table 4.28
Ownership of Leisure and Household Appliances
Among Salaried Households (Switzerland)
(%)

Item	1967	1977
Refrigerator	87	94
Hair dryer	74	92
Foodmixer	50	74
Sewing machine	63	73
Washing machine	39	45
Electric grill or infra-red	28	44
Dishwashing machine	2	22
Television	57	91
Camera	32	87
Stereo system	63	82
Tape recorder	15	57
Movie camera	9	27
Slide projector	12	24
Film projector	8	21

Source: Mouvement Populaire des Familles (1978),
       pp. 53-54.

Behind this trend towards private road traffic has been the heavy support that the Federal Government has given to highway construction, which for a long time has absorbed a major part of expenditure on transport infrastructure.[46] Thus, whereas in 1950 only one in twenty-five Swiss possessed his own car, there is now one car for every three people (Table 4.30).

Over the past few years, the usefulness of the car, however, has been thrown increasingly into question, while its negative individual, social and ecological impact has become evident. To begin with, traffic congestion has now become so acute that even the most enthusiastic driver can no longer escape long delays, particularly during the rush-hour period. Traffic congestion in its turn results from the social and functional

The Poverty of Progress

Table 4.29
Changing Patterns of Personal Transportation,
(Switzerland, 1950-70).

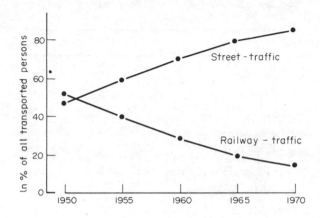

Source: Soziologisches Institut der Universität Zürich (1978),
p. 49.

Table 4.30
Number of Private Motor Vehicles (Switzerland)
(per 1000 inhabitants)

	1925	1935	1945	1950	1960	1970	1976
Cars	9	22	9	40	106	243	320
Motorbikes	5	8	1	16	54	106	120

Source: Annuaire Statistique Suisse (1961), pp. 226-7; (1977),
pp. 230-1.

segregation of the environment discussed earlier.
    Noise also affects increasing numbers of people. The auto-
mobile is today the most important source of noise in our
country: a quarter of all Swiss are now estimated to suffer

from traffic noise pollution, even when at home.[47]
Apart from being an obnoxious noise-maker and an important
energy waster, the private car is also a terrible air polluter.
Between 1950 and 1970, automobile carbon monoxide emissions
increased eight-fold, with total production of carbon monoxide
fumes reaching around 8.5 million tonnes in 1970. And these
are not the only social costs: about half of all accidental
deaths are caused by cars — the main victims being children and
elderly pedestrians, rather than drivers. Besides people, the
automobile also 'kills' the countryside; roughly 40 per cent of
the total constructed surface area in Switzerland is now taken
up by roads. It has been estimated that, in 1970, the total
social cost of the car amounted to approximately 3 billion
Swiss francs, while, in comparison, total public benefit barely
reached 2 billions (Soziologisches Institut der Universität
Zürich, 1978, p. 51). And these figures do not include such
unquantifiable costs as the destruction of natural beauty,
nervous stress, or the health effects of lack of physical exercise.
    The car thus provides an example, par excellence, of the
nefarious consequences of material development beyond a certain
point. It is not so much the car as such that restricts people's
overall freedom of movement as too many cars relative
to a given physical and social environment. What is true for
freedom holds equally for the other 'needs' discussed in this
paper. It is not the presence of food or energy, the existence
of roads or towns, the availability of hospitals or medicaments
as such that impair our well-being, security or identity, but
their overabundance or excess.

CONCLUSION

    Even if this chapter has only scratched the surface of things,
we have uncovered some rather disquieting trends in the Swiss
DWL. These changes, as we have seen, have become particularly
noticeable from the 1950s onwards, and, since then, the limits
within which urban, rural, working and family life are, on the
whole, conducive to general physical and psychological well-
being were systematically transgressed. From an international
perspective, Switzerland may still appear a haven of peace,
wealth and happiness. Within this country, however, people
have slowly and painfully become aware of their dying city
centres, disfigured landscapes, shrivelling agricultural soil,
polluted environment, resource wastage, loneliness, ill-feeling,
frustration and alienation. All these aspects of modern Swiss
society can be seen as an overdevelopment of the things that

once were supposed to make people very happy. Now, at various
places, and with increasing frequency, alternative movements
are coming into existence whose mere names — Anti-Waste Working
Group, Committee Against Nuclear Energy, Geneva Pedestrians'
Union, Association Against Technological Abuses — go a long way
towards showing both people's dissatisfaction with the DWL, and
their determination to transform Switzerland into a humanly
warmer and ecologically more sustainable society.

NOTES

1. The greater part of these (60 per cent) are Italian and
Spanish workers, many of whom enter Switzerland with a seasonal
or annual working permit.

2. Population and income data are taken from the Union Bank of
Switzerland (1979).

3. Inquiry carried out by the Office Fédéral de l'Industrie
des Arts et Métiers et du Travail, reported in *Feuille d'Avis
de Laussane* of 3 May 1973. The Swiss Association of Insurance
Companies has calculated that the Swiss spend more than 21
million francs per day in order to protect themselves against
the various risks of modern life: accidents, sickness, death,
theft, etc. This amounts to an average of SFr. 3 per person
per day. In comparison, the average Italian spends only SFr.
1.50. The record figure is still held by the American's
average of SFr. 3.50 a day.

4. 'On devient vieux, mais . . . ' in *Tribune de Genève*, 26
January 1978.

5. This is a general impression one gets when talking to the
young in Switzerland, particularly those involved in alternative
movements.

6. 'Ist raumplanung beim bevölkerungswachstum null überhaupt
notwendig?', in *Raumplanung Schweiz*, Bern (1976), nos. 1 and 2,
p. 6.

7. See, for instance, 'Les associations d'habitants poursuivent
leur lutte', in *Tribune de Genève* of 23/24 September 1978.

8. In fact, around 30 per cent of all births are now accounted
for by foreigners residing in Switzerland.

9. See Wemegah (1978) and *Raumplanung Schweiz* (1976), nos. 1
and 2.

10. In Zürich, for instance, 17,500 inhabitants left the city
between 1960 and 1970 in order to live in the surrounding
countryside. During the same period, about 30,000 work-places
were created in the town of Zürich itself.

11. See 'Lugano, une ville rongée par l'univers bancaire',
Tribune de Genève, 4 November 1977; and 'Massacre dans la cité',
Tribune de Genève, 2 May 1977.

12. 'Un Suisse sur deux veut habiter la campagne', *Tribune de
Genève*, 6/7 September 1978.

13. The towns particularly hit by this development are Geneva,
Zürich, Bern, and Basel. However, the social segregation in
big cities is much worse in countries like Great Britain or the
United States.

14. See *Raumplanung Schweiz* (1975), no. 2, p. 14.

15. See, for instance, 'Krebs durch Schädlingsbekämpfungs-
mittel?' in *Tages-Anzeiger*, 13 July 1976.

16. See *Tages-Anzeiger*, 4 May 1977. Of course, traffic and
industrial pollution must also be taken into account.

17. See *Tages-Anzeiger*, 13 July 1976.

18. See 'Le Suisse consomme toujours plus d'énergie' in *La
Suisse,* 27 June 1978.

19. See, for instance, *Alternativ Katalog* (1976), nos. 1, 2
and 3.

20. 'Ritchard: avant qu'une loi ne nous y contraigne . . .',
Tribune de Genève, 15/16 October 1977.

21. The following data sources have been used here: *Touring,*
no. 26, 4 July 1974; Arbeitsgemeinschaft Umwelt (1975); ORL/
Vademecum, Zürich, ORL Institüt (1971); and various documents
provided by Eidg. Anstalt für Wasserversorgung, Abwasserreini-
gung und Gewässerschutz, Annexanstalt der ETH, Dübendorf (1978).

22. See the journal *24-Heures*, 9 September 1975.

134   The Poverty of Progress

23.   See the journal *Touring*, 4 September 1974.

24.   See *Panda* (1977), no. 9, p. 9.

25.   See *24-Heures*, 15-17 September 1973, and 21-22 May 1977.

26.   Male and female cancer rates are from *Annuaire Statistique Suisse* (1961), p. 77; (1977), p. 70.

27.   See *24-Heures*, 15-16 November 1975.

28.   *Schweizerische Rundschau für Medizin* (1972), no. 16.

29.   See *24-Heures*, 3-4 July 1976, and 22-23 April 1972.

30.   According to a survey carried out on 20,000 people during the Basle Trade Fair in 1973.

31.   According to an estimate reported in *24-Heures*, 28-29 January 1978.

32.   See *24-Heures*, 22-23 March 1975.

33.   See *24-Heures*, 19 May 1972.

34.   Cited in *24-Heures*, 28-29 January 1978.

35.   According to *24-Heures*, 26-27 April 1975.

36.   According to a Swiss French television programme at 9.20 p.m. on 19 October 1977. See also 'Coûts de la santé: evolution catastrophique, quels sont les remèdes possibles en Suisse?', in *La Suisse*, 3 August 1978.

37.   See *24-Heures*, 14-15 May 1977.

38.   Cited in the TV programme referred to in note 36.

39.   See *24-Heures*, 25 November 1977.

40.   Cited in Swiss French television programme on alcoholism in Switzerland, 14 September 1978. See also Soziologisches Institut der Universität Zürich (1978), p. 82.

41.   See *La Suisse*, 23 September 1978.

42. 'Les jeunes boivent de plus en plus d'alcool: pourquoi?',
Tribune de Genève, 22 November 1977.

43. See 'Rapport federal: 51 Suicides en 3 ans dans nos
prisons', *La Suisse*, 15 September 1978.

44. According to M. Hartman, Director of the Institute for
Legal Medicine, Zürich University; quoted in *24-Heures*, 1
November 1977.

45. The source for this paragraph is *Construire*, no. 37, 13
September 1978.

46. In 1974, the Swiss Confederation spent 14.1 per cent of
its total budget on traffic and energy, out of which 9.4 per
cent was on roads and highways and a mere 3.5 per cent on railways. See Soziologisches Institut der Universität Zürich (1978),
p. 48 and p. 208.

47. Soziologisches Institut der Universität Zürich (1978),
p. 50.

BIBLIOGRAPHY

Annuaire Statistique Suisse (various years from 1940). Bern,
    Eidgenössisches Statistisches Amt.
Arbeitsgemeinschaft Umwelt (1975) *Umdenken-Umschwenken*. Zürich,
    AGU.
Delegierter für Raumplanung (1975) *Raumplanung Schweiz*. Bern.
Dezentrale (ed.), *Alternativ Katalog* (1975), Vol. 1; (1976),
    Vol. 2; (1977), Vol. 3; Köniz/Porrentruy, Dezentrale.
Fünfter Landwirtschaftsbericht (1976). Bern, Bundeskanzlei.
Ginsbourg, T. 'Mehr Schweizer, weniger Schweizer?', *Tages-
    Anzeiger Magazin*, 21 September 1973.
Hohlenstein, A.-M. (1977) *Zerstörung durch Überfluss*. Basel,
    Z-Verlag.
Krippendorf, J. (1977) *Les Dévoreurs de Paysages*. Lausanne,
    Ed. *24-Heures*.
Mouvement Populaire des Familles (1978) *Enquête sur les con-
    ditions et habitudes de vie des ménages salariés de Suisse
    romande*. Geneva, MPF.
Poleszynski, D. (1978) 'Social Pathologies and Energy Use in
    Overdeveloped Societies'. Mimeo, GPID project, UN Univer-
    sity.
Reich, R. (ed.) (1977) *Die Kluft Zwischen Armen und Reichen
    Kantonen in der Schweiz*. Bern, Paul Haupt Verlag.

136   The Poverty of Progress

Soziologisches Institut der Universität Zürich (1978) *Almanach der Schweiz*. Bern, Peter Lang Verlag.

Statistiques et Évaluations (various years from 1945). Brugg, Secrétariat des Paysans Suisses.

Strahm, R. (1977) *Pourquoi sont-ils si pauvres?*. Neuchâtel, Ed. *de la Baconnière*.

Union Bank of Switzerland (1980) *Switzerland in Figures, 1979*. Zürich, Union Bank of Switzerland.

Wemegah, M. (1978) *L'Aménagement du territoire et L'administration fédérale*. St. Saphorin, Ed. *Georgi*.

5

The Dominant Way of Life in Britain: A Case Study of Maldevelopment

JOHN IRVINE AND IAN MILES

INTRODUCTION: THE PECULIARITIES OF THE BRITISH[1]*

The 'British disease' has been much discussed by a wide range
of commentators from international organizations such as the
European Economic Community and the Organization for Economic
Cooperation and Development. The chief symptom of the disease
these pundits have been preoccupied with has been Britain's
unusually low rate of economic growth as compared to other
major industrial countries. In recent years, however, a number
of authors have begun to contest this diagnosis: themselves rejecting the continued frenetic pursuit of material wealth in
countries that are affluent when compared to most of the rest
of the world, they see Britain's low growth as indicating that
British people on the whole share this attitude, and are no
longer willing to sacrifice their time and energy to create
material wealth that is already overabundant. These writers,
usually foreign-born Anglophiles (e.g. Caesar, 1978; Nossiter,
1978), argue that Britain is leading the way in the Western
world, that it is the first truly post-industrial society. In
the words of Nossiter, Britain presents 'a future that works'.

Unfortunately, contemporary Britain does seem to show more
signs of social malaise than of content. The social and political impact of the world economic crisis has been particularly
severe in this country, exacerbating a range of social problems
that belie the picture of a nation 'taking it easy'. Action
groups, charities, political organizations, concerned academics — all have charted many of these problems in detail, as
we shall see below. Most of these activists would couple their
pleas for immediate attention to be paid to the issues that
particularly involve them (including material deprivation among
large sections of the population) with an acknowledgement that
more sweeping change in our dominant way of life (DWL) may be

---

* Superscript numbers refer to notes at end of chapter.

137

necessary for longer-term improvement. Few of those working to
secure better living conditions for the disadvantaged would
agree that the 'British disease' is alone responsible for the
problems they have to deal with, or that increased material produc
tion is the whole answer. Perhaps even fewer would agree that
Britain has already solved its problems by leading the world
towards new patterns of responsible consumption. Most would see
material production and consumption as being in some way at the
heart of the problems that the world must solve over the coming
decades.

The way to people's hearts is often said to be through their
stomachs: perhaps we can usefully illustrate the different
facets to the debate about the DWL in gastronomic terms! A
common representation of the world's wealth is in the form of
a cake, which is divided up among the peoples of the world,
although by no means equitably.[2] The richer countries receive
vastly disproportionate quantities of cake, consuming staggering
amounts of raw materials, energy and food, whilst most people
in the poorer countries have to struggle simply to stay alive.
The international maldistribution of resources is thus seen as
the link between underconsumption, and the deprivations associated with it, and overconsumption, with its different but
nevertheless pressing problems.

Two trends are thus typically seen as converging to make for
change in the DWL of the richer countries. On the one hand,
the industrialized nations are beginning to suffer from severe
'indigestion', perhaps even 'constipation', related to consuming
too much cake. On the other hand, Third World nations have
been pressing, often rather unsuccessfully, for larger portions
of the cake. The process of redividing the world cake would be
made a much smoother and peaceable business were the people of
the industrialized nations to undertake voluntarily to change
their DWL, adopting a more frugal 'diet' which could alleviate
their problems too. Such a transfer of resources is at the
heart of the policy recommendations implicit in the 'overdevelopment' perspective, advanced in this volume by Galtung,
Poleszynski and Wemegah (Chapter 1).

There are, however, reasons to question the effectiveness of
strategies for change based on the 'cake theory'. Certainly
such a theory does highlight many of the problems facing the
rich countries and puts the need for change on the agenda, but
its focus on the size and distribution of the cake, on the
issue of how much different people should consume, tends to
lead to a neglect of other important questions. What about the
composition of the cake? Who decides on its ingredients, and
who controls the bakery? These are germane questions, and are
not unrelated to the matter of how the cake comes to be dis-

tributed in a given way.
The point that concern with only the size and distribution of
the cake typically diverts attention from these, and other,
possibilities is an important one. It is worth noting, in this
respect, that further economic growth in the rich countries has
been seen for many years as a foolproof means of improving
equality within these countries without reducing anyone's share
of the cake. A bigger cake was thought to mean bigger portions
for everyone. The cake theory has likewise been used to advocate
giving larger portions of the world's wealth to the poorer
countries — either by exhorting the ordinary people of the industrial world to change their DWL (i.e. reduce their consumption) in order to free resources (but this may mean no more than
an increase in elite consumption in the poorer countries with
few benefits for the masses in dire poverty) — or by raising
overall production levels in the industrialized countries (in
which case it is by no means certain that the extra goods produced will find their way to those most in need). In neither
case do we possess the key to a more equitable world order. It
is necessary, we will argue, to undertake a more widely-based
evaluation of the DWL. We need to focus on more than the national
and international distribution of resources. We must consider the
pattern of control over *production* as well as the level and distribution of *consumption*. These broader perspectives aid our interpretation of the statistics presented later, which, as we will see,
hardly document a land of abundance, harmony and equal opportunity;
they provide reasons to be suspicious that the cake theory is used
to obscure or actually defend the massive maldistribution of power
which underlies what we would term Britain's 'maldevelopment'.

There are, too, more immediate reasons for such suspicion; in
the present world economic recession the cake theory is often
brought into play to urge people to accomodate to declining
living standards. The rhetoric of 'Alternative Ways of Life'
(AWL) has been taken over to justify, for example, reduced
welfare services and public utilities. In Britain the crisis
of the 1970s has led to attempts being made to 'rationalize'
the National Health Service, with such consequences as increased
waiting times before hospital treatment or the arrival of
emergency services. The argument that health services should
be more concerned with prevention than with cure was a refrain
that almost drowned the chorus of protests of those suffering
from the withdrawal of these services. It would certainly be
an advance for health workers to become more concerned with
preventive medicine, but in the context of major cuts in welfare expenditure, 'prevention' is presented as a matter of
individual responsibility. In the official booklet, *Prevention*

and Health: Everybody's Business (DHSS, 1976), where 'the connection between our way of life and some . . . causes of death'
is studied (p. 34), we are told that 'to larger extent . . . it
is clear that the weight of responsibility for his own state of
health lies on the shoulders of the individual himself' (p. 38).
While it might well be the case that adequately funded community
care would provide better answers to Britain's health problems
than continued expansion of high-technology medicine, we are currently presented with the destruction of existing health services with no equivalent increase in resources for communities.

Placing the onus on individuals to shoulder responsibility
for changing the DWL may in such cases be seen as a strategy
to legitimize a reduced share of the cake being allocated to
social expenditures, rather than an honest policy to facilitate
progressive changes in the DWL for the majority of the people.
'Tightening one's belt' may sometimes be good for you, as is
claimed in this health example. We certainly do not want to
argue that health problems are not related to cigarette smoking,
alcoholism, lack of exercise and the like. But in the example
cited, as in many others, the cake theory is used to argue for
people to take up 'AWL' that mainly involve a reduction in their
share of a cake whose ingredients remain the same. In the case
of health, for example, women relatives, rather than paid,
trained workers, are expected to take the burden. Instead of
tackling the barriers to the development of AWL, such policies
largely redistribute the costs of the DWL to the more disadvantaged.

In the rest of this chapter, we assess the costs and benefits
of Britain's DWL. Any such empirical assessment of the DWL
must admit some of the undisputed benefits of modern living.
For example, in common with the inhabitants of other industrial
societies, British people now live longer than they used to
(new-born infants can now expect, on average, to live about 30
years longer than they could a century ago); they are a good
deal taller and healthier than they used to be (although the
pattern of diseases has markedly changed); they have access to
a vastly expanded range of educational facilities and opportunities; and their consumption of energy and consumer durables
is now at levels that would have been inconceivable only a few
decades ago.

The assessment must not, however, end here. It is indeed
easy to demonstrate with statistics that the *quantity* of various
facets of life has increased. It is not so easy to talk about
the *quality* of life, however. But we must, nevertheless, attempt
not just to evaluate how much 'cake' Britain is consuming, but
also to consider how this cake is composed and distributed with-

in the country. For contrary to a simple reading of the 'cake
theory', the benefits of our DWL accrue to different sections of
society than do the costs. It is as if one group of people
consume the larger share of the cake, while the rest suffer the
indigestion. Despite the increase in material living standards
in Britain, major social inequalities persist, and have in some
cases widened. Some groups are particularly vulnerable to the
effects of economic fluctuations and the current round of price
rises and welfare cuts. Furthermore, some aspects of the
quality of life in Britain are clearly declining: the DWL has
costs as well as benefits and both are distributed unequally.

To relate these factors to each other, we shall employ the
four categories of human needs — security, welfare, identity
and freedom — used elsewhere in this volume. Under the heading
of security we will take not only a low degree of vulnerability
to accidental or violent death, for example, but also the likelihood of people not falling into unemployment, poverty or homelessness. By welfare we mean primarily physical health, and
access to the material conditions (good nutrition and housing,
safe work places, etc.) which can make this possible. By
identity we refer to positive alternatives to estrangement in
people's conceptions of themselves and relations with their
fellows. And, under the rubric of freedom, we will consider
people's ability to engage in various activities — as related
to their financial resources and class position, for example —
as well as their freedom from being detained or spied upon.

SECURITY

Two aspects of security — those relating to physical and
economic well-being — immediately come to mind. Taking physical
security first, it can be shown that while life expectancies
have in general been increasing, there are also considerable
inequalities here — along sexual, class, racial and regional
lines.[3] Table 5.1 below illustrates just how different are the
life-expectancies of males and females.

The differences here are also large between social classes —
the Department of Health and Social Security has estimated that
if all men of working age were able to have the same mortality
record as those in professional employment, some 22,000 lives
would be saved each year (DHSS, 1976). And while there is an
overall downward trend in death rates, Healy (1978) reports
that the number of deaths among immigrants from the New Common-
wealth is rising, despite the comparative youth of this group.

Defining physical security rather more narrowly — for example,

Table 5.1
Trends in Life-Expectancy by Age and Sex in
Great Britain, 1901-74

	Males				Females			
	1901	1931	1951	1974	1901	1931	1951	1974
Further number of years which a person can expect to live:								
At birth	48.1	58.4	66.2	69.3	51.8	62.5	71.2	75.6
At age 1 year	55.1	62.1	67.5	69.6	57.6	65.2	72.1	75.7
5 years	55.5	60.0	63.9	65.8	58.0	63.0	68.5	71.8
30 years	34.5	38.1	40.2	41.7	37.1	41.0	44.5	47.3
45 years	23.1	25.5	26.4	27.6	25.4	28.2	30.6	33.1
60 years	13.4	14.4	14.7	15.6	14.9	16.4	18.0	20.2
70 years	8.4	8.6	9.0	9.6	9.2	10.0	10.9	12.8
80 years	4.9	4.7	4.9	5.7	5.3	5.5	5.8	7.3

Source: Social Trends (1977), table 8.2. Reproduced with the
permission of the Controller of Her Majesty's Stationery Office.

in terms of the likelihood of avoiding serious accidents or
violence — we find a more mixed set of trends. Those for
accidental deaths in England and Wales are presented in Table
5.2 below, and for homicide in Table 5.3. A breakdown of accidental death rates in terms of sex, age and social class is
presented in Table 5.4: as can be seen, the physical insecurity
related to these risks is very unequally distributed.

It is clear, then, that certain groups of people face much
more physical insecurity in their daily lives than do others.
Those who have most resources to deal with mishaps, when they
occur, tend to be most secure from physical risk: it is the
very old and the unskilled workforce who are most likely to
suffer an accidental death, for example.

In addition, but related to issues of physical security, are
those of economic security. As we have seen, richer people are
not just less prone to suffer serious accidents; on the whole
they also have more resources to cope with them (for example,
private health insurance). Ill-health is an important con-
tributor to the economic problems of many British people: it
affects their employment and thus their access to a secure
level of income.

Table 5.2
Trends in Accidental Deaths in England and
Wales, 1955-75

Cause	1955	1965	1975[a]
All accidents[b]	16,015	18,632	15,069[c]
Transport accidents	5770	8021	6223
Home accidents	6651	7330	5325
Other accidents	3594	3281	3521

Source: DHSS (1977), table 14.1. Reproduced
with the permission of the Controller
of Her Majesty's Stationery Office.

Notes: [a] 1975 figures provisional.

[b] Certain adjustments need to be made
for the population increase in interpreting these figures. It is useful
to know, for example, that 'other accidents' killed 8.1 people per 100,000
population in 1955, and 7.2 per 100,000
in 1975.

[c] Accidental deaths accounted for over
2 per cent of all deaths in 1975.

Table 5.3
Trends in Murder, Manslaughter and Infanticide
in England and Wales, 1967-77

1967	1968	1969	1970	1971	1972	1973	1974	1975	1976	1977
354	360	332	342	407	410	391	527	445	489	432

Source: Home Office (1978), *Criminal Statistics*, table 9.3.
Reproduced with the permission of the Controller of
Her Majesty's Stationery Office.
Note: Even allowing for population increase, this still rep-
resents an upward trend in our homicide rates — up to
around 8 per million population in recent years.

Whatever its immediate cause, the likelihood of being unemployed is perhaps the most important indicator of economic insecurity. Unemployment in Britain by mid-1980 reached levels
higher than at any time since the Second World War. Table 5.5
below shows that more than 5 per cent of those in the labour market

144   The Poverty of Progress

Table 5.4
Accidental Deaths in England and Wales:
Social Structure

(a) *By sex* (1974)

Cause	Numbers killed	
	Males	Females
All accidents	8595	7113
Transport accidents	4638	2095
Home accidents	2086	3661
Other accidents	1871	1357

(b) *By age* (rate per 100,000) (1974)

Cause	Age (years)				
	0-4	5-9	10-14	15-64	65 +
All accidents	18.9	10.9	8.9	22.6	105.8
Transport accidents	4.3	7.2	5.6	14.0	25.8
Home accidents	10.6		1.2	4.4	57.0
Other accidents	4.0		2.3	4.3	23.0

(c) *By social class* (males aged 15-64) (1961)

	Social Class				
	1 (Professional)	2 (Intermediate)	3 (Skilled)	4 (Partly skilled)	5 (Unskilled)
Non-road accidents, standardized mortality ratios	43	56	87	128	193

Sources: (a) and (b) DHSS (1977), tables 14.1 and 14.2. (c)
DHSS (1976), table 4.2. Reproduced with the permission
of the Controller of Her Majesty's Stationery Office.

were jobless in early 1980 (and these data *underestimate* the total
unemployed by excluding certain groups, such as school leavers and
many housewives who are seeking work — see Miles and Irvine, 1979;
Hyman and Price, 1979). We shall see later that this one in twenty
chance of being unemployed very often leads to marked material and
social deprivation. (By 1982, the chance was one in ten - eds.)

Table 5.5
Unemployment Levels in Great Britain, 1966-80

	Jan. 1966	Jan. 1970	Jan. 1976	Jan. 1970	Jan. 1980
Thousands unemployed	335	609	1252	1485	1471

Source: Various issues of *Department of Employment Gazette.*

The chance of obtaining work is very unequally distributed:
the North and West of Britain (with regional unemployment rates
often well over 10 per cent) together contribute about half of
the nation's unemployed. In many declining industrial towns
more than one in ten workers are unemployed, with there being
little prospect of the situation improving in the immediate
future (CIS, 1977). Certain groups of workers are also particularly insecure: the young, the aged, women, minority group
members, and manual and less-skilled workers. Table 5.6 relates
unemployment to occupational status, age, sex, ethnic group,
and disability.

Table 5.6
Distribution of Unemployment (Great Britain)

(a) *Unemployment: by occupation*
    (Men under 65, Great Britain)

Occupation	Percentage of labour force in each occupation who are unemployed		Percentage of unem- ployed who are in each occupation	
	1972	1975	1972	1975
Professional and managerial	1.4	1.2	8	4
Other non-manual	1.8	2.6	11	12
Skilled manual	2.8	4.0	38	36
Semi-skilled manual	4.3	7.2	25	27
Unskilled manual	14.7	16.0	18	21

PP - F*

(b) *Unemployment: by age and sex, 1977*
(Percentage of unemployed men and women in each age group,
Great Britain)

	Under 18	18-19	20-29	30-49	50-59	60 +	Total
Men	6.3	7.0	29.3	31.2	13.3	12.9	100
Women	16.4	15.6	36.4	20.4	11.0	0.3	100

(c) *Unemployment among minority groups*
(Relative changes, 1974-7, by group and sex, of unemployed
in Great Britain; approximate)

	Minority	Other
Men	210%	100%
Women	420%	140%

(d) *Unemployment among school leavers (July)*

United Kingdom	1974	1977	1978	1979
Thousands	53	253	243	215

(e) *Unemployment: trends in proportion of disabled unable to
find work* (Great Britain)

Year	Numbers of unemployed registered disabled people (Thousands)	Unemployed registered disabled people as a percentage of all registered people
1948	78.07	8.9
1953	58.47	6.8
1958	52.06	7.0
1963	62.42	8.6
1968	65.35	10.0
1973	77.36	13.0
1974	63.37	11.0

Sources: (a) Layard *et al.* (1978), table 6.2; (b) RCDIW (1978),
table M.12; (c) *Social Trends* (1977), chart 5.17; (d)
Social Trends (1980), chart 5.17; (e) *Hansard*, 25
November 1974. Reproduced with the permission of the
Controller of Her Majesty's Stationery Office.

These trends and distributions of unemployment have not prevented the media and politicians from portraying joblessness as
a form of voluntary AWL whereby 'work-shy scroungers' exploit
the rest of the population. But rather than being a viable
AWL for most people, unemployment — and the threat of future
unemployment — is a form of economic insecurity. While many
people may not like their work, most regard it as necessary if
they are to live above a meagre subsistence level. Long-term
unemployment, in particular, invariably leads to economic hardship. Life 'on the dole' is thus not an option that many people
would take as a matter of choice. Figure 5.1, below, depicts
the 'poverty tree' as mapped out recently by a government-
commissioned research group. Practically three-quarters of all
families where the wife does not work and the husband has been
unemployed for most of the year are classified as living near
or below the poverty line.

Poverty is, of course, a form of economic insecurity whether
or not one is employed. Even in families with income from employment, poverty is still widespread. Figure 5.1 shows that
29 per cent of all British families (and this means more than
one-third of all children) are living in or perilously near
poverty. Many of these families report that they cannot manage
on their current incomes (Table 5.7): they are accumulating
debts, risking ill health, etc. More than half of these households can at best only just about cope in these conditions. In
terms of security, as well, these families are vulnerable to
all sorts of threats: illness, inflation, crime, etc. Perhaps
a quarter of all British families, then, were economically
insecure in this sense, even before unemployment rose to its
recent high levels.

Of course, individuals can attempt to make their future more
financially secure: loss of income does not necessarily lead
to hardship. Banks, insurance companies and the state all
point to the security of a 'nest egg' guaranteeing future income in case of unforseen problems. But, again, it tends to
be those who are already relatively secure who can afford the
outlay for such provisions. As can be seen from Table 5.8
below, wealth is distributed extremely unequally within the
United Kingdom — with the poorest four-fifths of the population
owning somewhat less than one-fifth of the total wealth.

It is important to distinguish between different forms of
wealth, for the assets owned by different sections of the
population vary significantly in both nature and extent. Table
5.9 demonstrates that the rich hold their wealth in rather
different assets than do the poor. This has quite important
implications for security since the land, industrial investments,
and merchant capital typically owned by the rich appreciate in

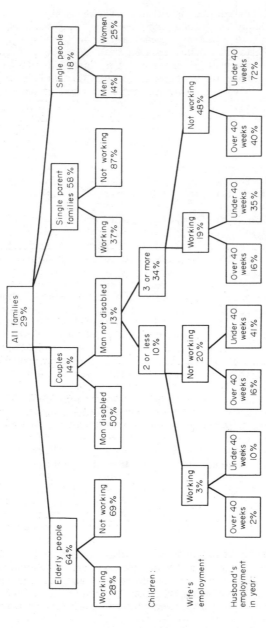

Fig. 5.1. The Poverty Tree (Great Britain).

Source: Layard *et al.* (1978), fig. 3.2, p. 29.

Note: This 'tree' depicts the proportion of families of various types whose household income is less than 40 per cent above the 'poverty line': the official level of supplementary benefits. The sexism inherent in the classification system used here probably reflects fairly accurately the contribution of sexually structured factors in income determination. The largest single group of the poor are elderly people (57 per cent); couples constitute 24 per cent; single people 13 per cent and single parent families 6 per cent.

Table 5.7
Branches of the Poverty Tree in Danger, 1977
(Great Britain)

Household type	Percentage of respondents in lower income households stating that on current income:	
	Cannot manage	Just about manage
Single elderly person	7	64
Elderly couple	4	72
Single non-pensioner	21	71
One parent family	39	59
Non-pensioner couple	18	68
Couple with one child	25	60
Couple with two children	20	78
Couple with three children	36	52
Couple with four or more children	39	57

Source: RCDIW (1978) table V.5 (based on a survey taken for the unpublished *Attitudes to Employment and Finances Survey,* 1977). Reproduced with the permission of the Controller of Her Majesty's Stationery Office.

Table 5.8
Distribution of Personal Wealth in the United Kingdom, 1977

Population group	Percentage share of estimated total personal wealth of adult population
Top 1 per cent own	24.0
Top 2 per cent own	32.2
Top 5 per cent own	46.4
Top 25 per cent own	83.9
Bottom 50 per cent own	5.0

Source: Social Trends (1980), table 6.30. Reproduced with the permission of the Controller of Her Majesty's Stationery Office.

Note: This estimate is based upon data from the Inland Revenue concerning tax returns of dead people, and is therefore, subject to a number of problems. Most importantly, the shares of wealth owned by the top 1 per cent and bottom 20 per cent both require revising upwards. For a further discussion of British wealth statistics, see Hird and Irvine (1979).

value and provide regular income, as well as afford an important
measure of control over social affairs. Medium wealth owners
have much of their wealth in dwellings (typically owner-occupied
housing), which have grown rapidly in value over recent years
while having remained readily marketable. But the wealth of
the poorest 51.5 per cent of the population, who own merely
10.9 per cent of the total wealth, consists mainly of national
savings (which attract a level of interest usually below that of
inflation), cash (which although easily convertible to other
forms of wealth, quickly depreciates), household goods (which
usually depreciate rapidly and are not readily marketable) and
life insurance (whose value is difficult to realize, and gives
future security of income only to the named benefactors). More
importantly, this wealth carries little or no economic power
with it.

It is this dual nature of wealth holding — not only does
the majority of the population own negligible amounts of wealth,
but that which it does own is of a qualitatively different
nature than that held by the rich majority — that underlies the
apprehension many people feel about the possibility of becoming
unemployed, or the prospect of retirement supported only by an
old age pension.

For those with access to neither a store of wealth nor adequate income, then, the DWL seems to involve continual accommodation to short-term survival — of often having to make do
with the crumbs or the stale left-overs of the 'cake'. And
official statistics rarely capture the full extent of such day-
to-day insecurities, typically because they have been produced
to monitor the operation of administrative agencies rather than
to map out areas of social concern (Irvine et al., 1979). This
is also true for another category of insecurity: homelessness.
British official data on homelessness are not based on a study
of people's accommodation situation, but on applications made
to local government for housing provision. According to these
data, some 33,680 households were classified in 1976 as homeless — equivalent to almost two out of every 1000 households
(Social Trends, 1977, tables 9.15 and 2.1). About one-third
of such applications are believed to involve one-parent
families. Other studies suggest that levels of homelessness
are actually much higher. Bailey (1977), in particular, has
reworked the official figures to show the number homeless as
over 50,000 in 1975 — a doubling from 1971 to 1975. (This
figure is unlikely to have dropped since then.) Unofficial
surveys carried out in selected towns have often suggested even
more homelessness — one carried out in London in 1972 indicated
that about 8000 young people were sleeping 'rough' in London
alone (Waugh, 1977). The number of people 'squatting' in

Table 5.5

Ownership of Selected Assets by Extent of Personal Wealth, United Kingdom, 1975

Nature of asset	Range of net wealth (lower limit)							Total
	Nil (%)	£5000 (%)	£10,000 (%)	£20,000 (%)	£50,000 (%)	£100,000 (%)	£200,000 (%)	(%)
Capital								
Land	0.8	2.2	6.0	20.4	29.4	19.4	27.4	100.0
Listed ordinary company shares	2.4	2.7	6.6	21.4	21.0	16.7	29.3	100.0
Other company securities	1.2	1.3	2.3	20.2	23.2	20.9	30.3	100.0
Listed U.K. govt. securities	2.0	6.1	-1.3	22.1	18.3	17.0	23.1	100.0
Cash								
National savings	35.2	22.3	23.5	13.0	3.1	1.4	1.1	100.0
Cash and bank deposits	17.4	15.7	9.4	19.8	4.5	7.5	8.7	100.0
Building society deposits	14.4	17.3	26.1	23.0	9.4	3.4	1.4	100.0
Other								
Dwellings	5.2	23.4	37.0	22.8	6.8	3.1	1.8	100.0
Life policies	17.2	23.0	31.3	21.7	4.6	1.5	0.7	100.0
Household goods	17.0	20.5	25.7	15.9	7.5	5.0	7.4	100.0
Net wealth	10.9	18.2	27.0	22.0	9.6	5.8	6.4	100.0
Numbers of people in range as a percentage of estimated total number of wealth owners	51.5	22.4	17.7	6.6	1.2	0.3	0.1	100.0

Source: RCDIW (1977), table 29. Reproduced with the permission of the Controller of Her Majesty's Stationery Office.

Note: The limitations of these data are similar to those mentioned in the note to table 5.8.

London, often in condemned properties, now runs into tens of
thousands. (Recent legislation has rendered the situation of
squatters little more secure than that of the homeless.)

Homelessness can have any number of immediate causes — eviction for non-payment of rent, family breakdown, and the like.
But at heart it is one extreme manifestation of economic insecurity, and one which compounds the difficulty of obtaining
employment or healthy living conditions. With a strong likelihood of reduced levels of economic security in Britain as a
whole, it will not be surprising if the incidence of homelessness, particularly among already disadvantaged groups, mushrooms in the near future.

Perhaps the most distressing forms of insecurity are those
relating to children. We have already seen that many British
children live in or near poverty, and that young children are
often accident victims (especially where domestic accidents are
involved). The National Society for the Prevention of Cruelty
to Children has estimated that an average of two babies are
battered to death each week by their parents in England and
Wales (Healy, 1977). An official inquiry reached a rather lower
estimate as to deaths, but nevertheless claimed that some 3000
children sustained serious, and 40,000 less serious, non-
accidental injuries per year — arguing that provision of better
housing was the priority here (*Select Committee on Violence in
the Family*, 1977).

A more insidious form of insecurity faced by children is the
lack of a secure home. In England and Wales, the total number
of children in local authority care increased from 62,000 in
1961 to over 100,000 in 1976; the greatest proportion of this
number, and the group with the largest increase, were children
of school age (*Social Trends*, 1977, table 3.6). While official
sources tend to relate this increase to family break-up and
changing moral values, it would be ridiculous not to see the
insecurity of these children as reflecting a more general
climate of economic insecurity.

WELFARE

Compared to most other nations, Britain is still regarded as
materially affluent. Even between 1972 and 1976, years of
economic gloom, the proportion of households renting telephones
increased from 42 per cent to 54 per cent; of those owning
washing machines and refrigerators from 66 per cent to 71 per
cent, and 73 per cent to 88 per cent respectively; and owning
vacuum cleaners and TV sets from 87 per cent to 92 per cent,
and 93 per cent to 96 per cent respectively (*General Household*

Survey, 1976). Televisions are such an established part of the
DWL that, for example, even households without televisions
receive letters demanding that they account for not purchasing
TV licenses.

But these signs of an increase in welfare — which do not seem
to have been substantially checked by the economic crisis — by
no means tell the whole story. Again, inequalities and deprivation persist, for while personal consumption may be increasing,
deteriorating social and physical environments often give reason
for much concern.

Let us begin with environmental welfare issues. In many respects the history of pollution control in Britain is rightly
hailed as a success story. Airborne smoke has been more than
halved, and sulphur dioxide nearly halved, since the early
1960s (*Social Trends*, 1975, chart 10.5). On the other hand,
regional differences in pollution are large, with Wales experiencing half the smoke concentration of Yorkshire, and London
experiencing a sulphur dioxide concentration almost twice as
high as some other areas (*Social Trends*, 1977, table 10.19).
Even so, London is no longer afflicted by regular outbreaks of
'the smog' (some 4000 people died in the smog of December 1952),
and its river, the Thames, is now cleaner than at any time since
the early period of the industrial revolution.

Pollution from road vehicles has been less well-controlled,
with only the oil crisis in 1974 breaking the upward trend of
carbon monoxide emissions (which rose by 56 per cent between
1964 and 1973, according to *Social Trends*, 1977, p. 172). Road
traffic is also a major source of noise pollution, disturbing
over one-third of inner London inhabitants at home in 1961, and
undoubtedly contributing to more than one in ten people surveyed
in 1972 citing noise as one of Britain's top four problems
(Independent Commission on Transport, 1974, pp. 73-4). For
those people living on or near the major throughways used by
road haulage traffic, the noise situation is being made progressively worse as the size of lorries continues to rise.
Alarm has also been generated recently over reports of lead
pollution posing a threat to the brain development of children
living or going to school near heavily-used roads. But changing
the orientation of the DWL away from the motor car (whose
victims in road accidents, incidentally, are more likely to be
pedestrians than drivers or passengers — see Table 5.10), is a
health issue that requires more than exhorting individual
motorists to change their ways when, often, no adequate alternative transport service or safer private vehicle is available.

The picture of pollution and hazards at work is far more grim.
While the dangers of being a coal miner or handling materials

Table 5.10
Transport Accident Victims in England and
Wales, 1975

User group	Deaths per year
Occupants of vehicles	770
Motor cyclists	2402
Pedestrians	2134
Total	6223

Source: DHSS (1977), table 14.3. Reproduced
with the permission of the Controller
of Her Majesty's Stationery Office.

Note: There were more than 77,000 people
seriously injured in road traffic
accidents in 1975, and more than
241,000 slightly injured.

like asbestos have in recent years become well known, many
other jobs involve working in conditions which pose long-term
health hazards (though this is only touched upon in passing in
the previously cited Prevention and Health: Everybody's Business).
A government inquiry into safety and health at work reported in
1972 the grim facts that over 1000 people die at their workplace each year in Britain, with around 500,000 suffering severe accidents. At current accident rates, nearly 1 per cent of
coal miners, for example, can expect to die at work during a
working life of 40 years, and around 40 per cent to sustain
severe injury. The full toll of occupational accidents and disease can be gathered from estimates made for the inquiry that
over 20,000,000 working days a year are lost as a direct result, the cost to Britain's economy amounting to some 0.87 per
cent of GNP in 1972 (Appendix to Robens, 1972). It is worth
noting that working days lost through work-related illness are
typically three or four times those lost through strikes —
which throws a completely new light on the so-called 'British
disease'.
    On an even darker note, Kinnersley (1973) has argued that
official statistics drastically understate the full extent of
occupational deaths and accidents. He estimates that in the
early 1970s there were each year some 2000 workers fatally injured at work, 1000 dying from recognizable industrial diseases,
and 1,000,000 off work for 3 days or more as a result of indust-

rial disease or injury. In addition, many commonplace conditions of work — such as noise, vibration, stress, and shift-
work — have debilitating effects. Concerning noise, for example,
Kinnersley estimated that around 1,000,000 workers were under
risk of losing their hearing in Britain through long-term exposure to noise at work; he notes that in the industrialized
north of England the big cinema chains set their amplifiers at
a higher level than they do in the south — for many people have
had their hearing capabilities drastically impaired.

Stress at work is certainly an important indicator of welfare — not least of all because around one-third of most people's
time is spent working. Direct indicators of stress at work are
not readily available — but a comparison of the types of reasons
given for workers' absence from work over the past decade suggests a sharp rise in stress-related illnesses as against a
striking, but more modest, decline in other diagnoses (Table
5.11). The growing incidence of headaches, migraines and the
like may well be indicative of growing stress at work.

Table 5.11
*Reported Reasons for Male Absenteeism in Great
Britain: Increasing and Decreasing Diagnoses,
1953-4 and 1971-2*

(Days of illness in 1971-2 as a percentage of
those in 1953-4)

Decrease %		Increase %	
Kidney infection and cystitis	77	Sprains and strains	368
Eczema and dermatitis	66	Nerves, debility, headaches	362
Gastritis	65	Displaced vertebral disc	288
Asthma	50	Diabetes	223
Septic skin disease	49	Diarrhoea and enteritis	213
Appendicitis	49	Arteriosclerotic heart disease	187
Pneumonia	38	Psychoneuroses	167
Ulcers	34	Migraine	153
Respiratory tuberculosis	14	Bronchitis	136

Source: Taylor (1974), tables 2 and 3.

Kinnersley (1973) relates these changing patterns of occupational illness to changing patterns of work. Increasing automation and speed-up in industry have increased the requirement

for shift work — between 1954 and 1973 the proportion of industrial workers on shifts grew from 12 per cent to over one-
third of the work force. Shift work, he argues, was responsible
for a sharp rise in working days lost due to the effects of
severe mental stress — of 152 per cent for men and 302 per cent
for women — over the 15 years up to 1970. Together these
accounted for 37 million working days lost in the year ending
June 1970. As usual, minorities and the lower paid tend to
suffer most from conditions that are likely to produce stress
at work, and Table 5.12 bears this out. Shift work (and over-
time) enables manual workers to earn a little more pay, of
course, and shift work is mostly a male activity (except in
some jobs like nursing). But it does have extremely negative
welfare consequences — as do other factors in the changing
nature of work.

Table 5.12
Percentage of Men Working Shifts in Britain,
by Ethnic Group, 1971

	Professional/ managerial (%)	White- collar (%)	Skilled manual (%)	Semi-skilled manual (%)	Unskilled manual (%)
Whites	3	12	15	40	12
Minorities	11	7	29	46	31

Source: Smith, cited by Community Relations Commission (1977),
table 1.

Other health — or illness — aspects of the DWL can also usefully be discussed here. Environmental pollution and iatro-
genesis (damage induced by medicines and medical treatment)
are often cited as sources of malformations among babies — most
notoriously in the case of thalidomide — and Table 5.13 indicates an increasing rate of malformations among infants in
England in recent years. (The similar degree of increase in
'all births' as compared with 'live births' bears out that this
is not just the result of an increasing ability of modern
medicine to keep endangered infants alive.)
    Malformation rates also vary regionally — with Suffolk and
other rural areas being at the low end of the scale. The high
rates of occupational and environmental disease that can be
mapped around urban conurbations, especially those associated
with heavy industrial development, are also reflected in rates
of malformation.
    Causes of death and disease also vary considerably across

Table 5.13
Malformation Rates Among Babies in England

Malformation rate (per 1000 births)	1971	1972	1973	1974	1975	1976
Live births	16.2	17.8	17.7	16.3	18.4	19.5
All births	18.3	19.7	19.7	19.9	20.4	21.2

Source: DHSS (1977), table 1.11. Reproduced with the permission
of the Controller of Her Majesty's Stationery Office.

life-cycle — more than half the deaths of 15-20 year olds are
due to accident and violence, for example (Table 5.14). Over
the entire age-range of 15-64, the most important killer for
men is coronary illness (ischaemic heart disease), while cancers
(especially breast cancer) are most important for women. Trends
in the tolls taken by these major causes of death — whose incidence is related to environmental pollution, smoking, consumption of certain foodstuffs, and the like — indicate that
ischaemic heart disease is on the increase, while the pattern
with respect to cancers is a mixed one; lung cancer, for example,
is increasing for men aged 45-64 (DHSS, 1977, p. 32).
   The relative incidence of accidental deaths across different
occupational groups was outlined while discussing security.
Equally striking variations are discernible when we consider
deaths due to disease (summarized in Table 5.15). It is worth
noting that the so-called 'diseases of civilization' strike
most heavily those who consume least of the British 'cake' — it
is clearly mistaken to conceive of the typical sufferer from
heart ailments as the over-worked executive. The largest differences across occupational groups relate to respiratory disease —
suggesting the impact of unhealthy conditions at home and at
work, although differences in smoking habits are also an important contributory factor here.
   Mortality is, of course, only one aspect of health welfare;
morbidity, in contrast, has more to do with the quality of one's
life than with its quantity. As one would expect, age is an
important factor here, but occupational status and sex are also
associated with major differences in rates of sickness (Table
5.16). Some 15 per cent of all British people report chronic
illness — they are restricted in activity for an average of 17
days per year. Occupational differences are again particularly
striking: being an unskilled manual worker, as compared to a
professional, is comparable to the difference between middle-
age and youth in terms of the number of days one is unwell.

The Poverty of Progress

Table 5.14
Main Causes of Death in England and Wales by
Age Group, 1977

Age	Death rate	Main cause of death	Second major cause	Third major cause
		Per million population		
1-4	349	Accidents 123	Congenital abnormalities 119	Respiratory diseases 83
5-14	253	Accidents 84	Cancer 36	Congenital abnormalities 30
15-34	687	Accidents 247	Cancer 123	Suicide 67
35-44	1720	Cancer 544	Heart disease 431	Accidents 156
45-54	5443	Cancer 1934	Heart disease 1847	Cerebrovascular disease 358
55-64	14,115	Heart disease 5082	Cancer 4870	Respiratory disease 1184
65-74	35,421	Heart disease 12,877	Cancer 9553	Respiratory disease 4240
75+	105,372	Heart disease 35,636	Respiratory disease 20,163	Cerebrovascular disease 17,458

Source: OPCS Monitor, DH2 78/5, 11 July 1978. Reproduced with
the permission of Her Majesty's Stationery Office.

Table 5.15

Standardized Mortality Ratios[a] for Major Causes
of Death, by Occupational Status (Husband's
Status for Women) and Sex, People Aged 15-64,
England and Wales, 1970-2

Cause of death		Profes-sional	Inter-mediate	Skilled non-manual	Skilled manual	Partly skilled	Un-skilled
Ischaemic heart disease	m	88	91	114	107	108	111
	mw[b]	58	77	81	125	123	146
Cancer: trachea, bronchus, lung	m	53	68	84	118	123	143
	mw	73	78	89	118	125	134
Other heart disease	m	69	75	94	100	121	157
	mw	45	75	83	114	137	173
Cerebrovascular disease	m	80	86	98	106	111	136
	mw	76	84	93	116	124	139
Pneumonia	m	41	53	78	92	115	193
	mw	63	66	80	130	129	171
Bronchitis, emphy-sema and asthma	m	36	51	82	113	128	188
	mw	41	60	74	125	130	189
Suicide	m	110	89	113	77	117	184
	mw	124	110	118	83	87	194

Source: Social Trends (1977), table 8.6. Reproduced with the permission
of the Controller of Her Majesty's Stationery Office.

Notes: [a] The use of standardized mortality ratios minimizes any differences between groups brought about through different age
structures.

[b] m = men; mw = married women.

The general, but uneven, long-term improvement in public
health (recorded in these statistics at least) is not, however,
matched by an improvement in health facilities in recent years.
We have already mentioned the way AWL rhetoric has been used to
justify cuts in National Health Service expenditure. But perhaps the most graphic consequence of such cuts was the 3 per
cent decline in hospital beds available in England for surgical
cases between 1971 and 1976, and the consequent rise in waiting
lists for surgery over this period from 539,000 to 665,000
(Health and Personal Social Services Statistics for England,
1977). For those requiring surgery, hints on changing one's

Table 5.16

Reported Sickness in Great Britain, 1974–5

(a) *By age and sex*

Indicator of sickness	Sex	Age range				
		0–14	15–44	45–65	65+	All
Average number of days per year where activity restricted, per person	Male	12	13	21	26	16
	Female	11	16	21	31	18
Number of people per thousand reporting long-standing sickness	Male	46	83	234	366	140
	Female	29	84	209	424	155

(b) *By occupation and sex*

Indicator of sickness	Sex	Occupation						
		Professional	Employers and managers	Intermediate and junior non-manual	Skilled manual and self-employed	Semi-skilled manual and service	Un-skilled manual	All
Average number of days per year when activity restricted, per person	Male	12	14	15	17	18	20	16
	Female	15	16	18	17	21	21	18
Number of people per thousand reporting long-standing sickness	Male	88	122	148	138	155	226	140
	Female	84	119	148	132	197	246	155

Source: Social Trends (1977), tables 8.7, 8.8. Reproduced with the permission of the Controller of Her Majesty's Stationery Office.

life-style are no substitute for hospital provision. This is
especially true in certain parts of Britain: in mid-1978, for
example, the waiting list for urgent heart operations in
Birmingham was around 2 months, and that for so-called 'non-
urgent' cases was up to 7 years — compared to a list for urgent
cases in Wessex of 2-3 days, and for non-urgent of 3 months.
The 2,300,000 richer people who, in 1976, had subscribed to
private medical schemes do not have to take their turn in what
the news reports described as a 'Regional heart operation
lottery'   (*The Guardian*, 17 August 1978).

Long waiting lists penalize other people, too: to take only
one example, it has been argued that the reason for Britain
having a higher rate of premature births (one in every fifteen
babies) than other European countries is due, in part at least,
to the waiting lists for medical care in early pregnancy (Wynn
and Wynn, 1977). *Prevention and Health*, predictably, sees problems at birth as resulting from irresponsibility on the part of
mothers — especially working class mothers who make least use of
such services. It does draw attention to other factors like
the role of cigarette smoking in infant mortality — estimating
that 1500 babies a year might be saved if no pregnant women in
Britain smoked.

People's health is intimately related to their consumption of
food. While the British diet has certainly improved in many
respects, over the long-run, it is also highly likely that
rising levels of heart disease and certain cancers relate to
increased consumption of fats and sugar, as well as to lack of
roughage. Dental problems are nowadays most commonly accepted
by the medical establishment as diet-related; the remarkable
statistic that over one-third of Britons have no teeth (Table
5.17) suggests that something is very wrong here.

Table 5.17
*Sufferers from Total Tooth Loss by Sex and
Social Class in England and Wales, 1968 (as
percentage of all ages)*

Sex	Socio-economic group			
	I, II and III non-manual	III manual	IV and V	All groups
Male	24	34.8	43.3	32.9
Female	29	33.0	49.0	40.2
All	27.1	33.9	46.3	36.8

Source: DHSS (1976), table 4.4. Reproduced with the permission
of the Controller of Her Majesty's Stationery Office.

Other diseases, such as rickets, have in contrast been practically eliminated by better diets — although Asian communities
in Britain have still been prone in recent years to this serious
bone disease. Rickets has been claimed to lead to the hospital-
ization of one in every twenty-five Asian children in Glasgow
(Buck, 1977). More generally, though, improved diets are no
doubt largely responsible for the increased longevity and height
of British people. Life expectancy has risen for people in
England and Wales from just over 40 years in 1841 to nearly 70
in the early 1970s, and the average height of the adult population has risen by around 3 inches since the Second World War
alone, to 5 feet 10 inches. Since the war, as Table 5.18 shows,
main items of increasing consumption are dairy products (associat
with heart disease), sugar (associated with a range of diseases)
'beverages' (one in eight drinks in Britain is now alcoholic, with
tea consumption diminishing relative to other beverages).

Table 5.18
Changes in Average Household Consumption of
Major Foodstuffs, 1950-73 (Britain)

Increases		Decreases	
Cheese	47.6%	Bread	39.8%
Fruit	38.8%	Fish	30.2%
Sugar	25.0%	Margarine	23.1%
Meat and meat products	24.3%	Potatoes	9.6%
Eggs	20.8%	Milk	1.6%
Butter	14.9%		
Beverages	13.6%		
Vegetables	12.0%		

Source: Wardle (1977), appendix 2, table 6.

Higher protein consumption may reflect the increasing efficiency of the British dairy industry, but is itself reflected
in high levels of obesity within the British population. In
this respect, it may be no bad thing that the energy value of
food consumed in Britain has decreased slightly in recent years,
after rising for most of this century. Average energy consumption per capita is currently around 2400 Kcals per day, which

is still above the recommended intake. In fact, as Table 5.19
illustrates, British people on average consume far more of every
nutritional requirement than is necessary, excepting Vitamin D.
(However, vitamin D is produced spontaneously by the body in
sunlight. There is controversy among experts about the optimal
levels of nutrients with some recommending, for example, large
vitamin C inputs. Also nutrient requirements vary by age, sex
and activity level).

Again, averages can be shown to hide large differences in food
consumption across different social groups. Certain people do
not get very much of the 'cake' — Wardle (1977) estimates from
official data that perhaps 1,000,000 people fall below recommended levels of energy consumption. Poorer people also consume
different types of 'cake' than rich people: they eat more sugar,
potatoes and bread, and less meat, fruit and vegetables, than
do the rich (Table 5.20). Overconsumption in Britain seems
curiously maldistributed. The result is that it is working
class, married women who form the highest proportion of acutely
obese people in Britain; unlike their middle-class counterparts
they cannot afford to purchase healthier foodstuffs, to attend
health clinics, etc.

Table 5.19
Nutritional Adequacy of Household Food:
British Averages, 1951-73

(Figures given as percentage of official DHSS
recommended intake)

Requirement	1951	1960	1970	1973
Energy value	100	106	111	104
Protein	104	101	128	124
Calcium	111	108	194	193
Iron	104	115	124	118
Thiamin	126	130	124	134
Riboflavin	106	114	130	132
Nicotinic acid	128	142	194	193
Vitamin C	235	240	184	189
Vitamin A	144	186	200	190
Vitamin D	—	—	84	89

Source: Wardle (1977), table 7, p. 75.
Note: Recommended levels were amended slightly in 1968.

Table 5.20
Consumption of Major Foodstuffs in Britain, 1973:
Percentage Difference Between Extreme Income Groups
(Those earning £85+ per week and under £19.50 per week)

Poor people consume more		Rich people consume more:	
Sugar and preserves	(74.0%)	Fruit	(132.0%)
Beverages	(71.2%)	Milk	(53.5%)
Potatoes	(60.4%)	Vegetables	(45.5%)
Cereal	(27.0%)	Fish	(29.9%)
		Meat and meat products	(24.6%)

Source: Wardle (1977), table 10, p. 78.

The data cited so far tell us little about whether food consumed is fresh, frozen, tinned, or whatever. An increasing
proportion of all foodstuffs have been of a 'convenience'
nature — which, in 1966-7 (the only period for which data are
available), accounted for 22.9 per cent of the average British
household's food budget, but contributed only 16.8 per cent
of its calorific, and 16.6 per cent of its protein, intake
(data cited by Wardle, 1977, p. 18). Sales of frozen foods have
been increasing particularly rapidly in recent years — by 13.4
per cent in 1977 (Financial Times, 17 June 1978). Processed
foods contain additives (stabilizers, sweeteners, colouring
agents, etc.) which further diminish their nutritional value
relative to fresh food — so the increased variety of foods and
brands offered to the consumer on the supermarket shelf (there
has been practically a ten-fold increase in the range of processed foods in the post-war period) has been obtained at some
cost, especially for those with monotonous diets.
    Another major determinant of welfare is housing conditions.
Together with the early improvements in sanitation and diet,
these are generally held to be in part responsible for diminishing mortality and morbidity. Housing conditions have been
improving in many ways in recent years, but there is still a
long way to go (Table 5.21).
    By now the differences between social groups in housing con-
ditions (Table 5.22) will come as no surprise. However, the most
striking data concerning poor housing conditions relate to the
elderly people of Britain. Some 35 per cent of pensioners living

Table 5.21
Housing Conditions in England, 1976

Percentage of all dwellings which are classified as:	All houses (%)	Other 'tenures' (mostly privately owned) (%)	Terraced houses (%)
Unfit for habitation	4.6	14.6	—
Without inside toilet	6.3	—	13.7
Without fixed bath in bathroom	4.7	—	10.0
Without wash basin	5.8	—	12.5
Without sink	0.3	—	0.4
Without hot and cold water at three points	8.7	—	14.3

Source: Social Trends (1977), tables 9.9, 9.1. Reproduced with the permission of the Controller of Her Majesty's Stationery Office.

Table 5.22
Housing Conditions by Ethnic Group and
Occupational Status of Head of Household,
for Great Britain, 1975-6

Housing conditions	Ethnic group		Occupational group				
	White	Non-white	Professional etc.	Intermediate etc.	Skilled etc.	Semi-skilled etc.	Un-skilled
Percentage of households lacking:							
Bath or shower	5	8	1	3	5	8	11
Inside toilet	8	18	2	6	8	12	14
Central heating	52	61	28	47	57	66	72

Source: Social Trends (1977), table 9.10. Reproduced with the permission of the Controller of Her Majesty's Stationery Office.

The Poverty of Progress

private rented accommodation lack inside toilets in their houses -
despite clearly needing them most (DHSS Welsh Office, 1978). Eigh
nine per cent of pensioners in 1972 were found to have living room
colder than the temperature recommended by the Department of Healt
and Social Security. Two million old people live in temperatures
would be illegal in factories and offices — and as a result it rea
is little surprise that in recent years between 45,000 and 80,000
old people have died in winter than at other times of year (Help t
Aged, 1977). These are startling figures, but it would be even mo
remarkable if the appropriate political will could not produce a
society in which improvements in the general welfare of the popula
were not accompanied by such appalling disparity and disadvantage.

IDENTITY

    It is difficult to agree upon the most important facets of
individual 'identity', let alone to evaluate statistically the
problems that the DWL raise in this respect. Relevant here is
the esteem with which individuals regard themselves and others,
as well as the degree to which their relations with other human
beings and the natural world are mutually satisfying and facilitate the development of creativity, solidarity and self-awareness.
Such ideas are often related together in terms of the notion of
alienation; we often hear, for example, of proposals to put an
end to alienating work, typified, usually, by reference to
ameliorating the monotony and drudgery of the assembly line.
However, we would regard alienation as a wider process whereby
people's activities and the things they produce are made alien
to themselves. At work it is an inevitable consequence of most
labour being controlled by firms and organizations whose purpose
is primarily to produce commodities for the market-place. This
structural feature of modern Britain is not removed by minor
reforms like providing better canteen facilities at work or slowin
down the assembly line. De-alienation would involve people being
able to orient their work and other activities to satisfying socia
needs which they have themselves played a conscious role in determining.[4] Our statistics, then, should not be interpreted as
referring to varying levels of alienation in Britain, but rather
as indicating the different ways in which an alienated social
structure affects the identity of the people to whom it assigns
different roles. A process worker might respond to the routine
and meaninglessness of his job by industrial sabotage, a bank
clerk escape from the continual pressure of day-to-day problems by
becoming alcoholic, or vice versa — we have no wish to argue that
one is more alienated than the other.

Self-destruction would appear to be a particularly important indicator of problems people have with their identity in modern Britain — few of our current suicides are deliberate political protests. In Table 5.14 suicide was shown to be the third most common cause of death among people aged 15-34. There is, however, some degree of uncertainty about whether suicide rates are increasing or declining in Britain; in discussing the relatively low figures for suicide in 1976 (almost 20 per cent down on 1968, and accounting for 0.64 per cent of all deaths), the Chief Medical Officer of England and Wales pointed out that there was 'a marked increase in deaths from poisoning with an 'open' verdict (DHSS, 1977, p. 14). Idiosyncratic judgements are involved in classifying deaths as suicide, accidental death, and the like. But the trend in Britain was widely regarded as diverging from the increasing suicide rates of most industrial countries. (Recorded suicides began to rise again in the 1980s, however.) Two factors are usually seen as responsible for this: first, decreased access to 'easy' means of self-destruction — for example, more caution by doctors in prescribing barbiturate drugs and the replacement of highly toxic coal gas by North Sea gas; and, second, the activities of groups like the Samaritans, who offer telephone counselling services for depressed and despairing people.

Less disputed is the fact that attempted suicides have risen at a high rate in recent years. The Samaritans estimate that some 200,000 suicide attempts are currently made in Britain each year. Mills (1974) presents data showing that the attempted suicide rate rose by 400 per cent in Cambridge during the 1960s, despite an increase of only 25 per cent in the actual suicide rate (itself running counter to national trends and perhaps reflecting the student population). Increases in suicide have tended to take place in towns where the Samaritans do not have branches. It may also be coincidental that the suicide rate last peaked in 1963, when the Samaritans first became a national organization, but the data they provide on the growth of their activities is certainly revealing.

A three-fold growth in the Samaritans' organization (in terms of branches) over the past 15 years has been accompanied by an almost twenty-fold increase in the new people contacting them for assistance (Table 5.23). In fact, the Samaritans estimate that one in forty households has recently been in contact with them. Young people are increasingly phoning in: the Central London Branch of the Samaritans recorded eleven clients as being under 13 years of age, and a further 333 between 13 and 16, in 1976 (Samaritans Central London Branch, 1977). These are grim figures in view of recent reports that suicide rates for young people are increasing: around three people under 16 years of

age kill themselves each month. The tendency for suicide is
stronger among males than females, among old than young, and
among those of lower rather than higher occupational status
(viz. Table 5.15), and these trends in suicide need to be ex-
plained in terms of social factors. Here, the Samaritans
regard loneliness as the factor common to most suicides and
attempted suicides. That an individual has few opportunities
to share anxieties with others, especially concerning family
problems and alcoholism, is, they argue, often a fatal condition
in British society.

Table 5.23
Suicide and the Samaritans

	1964	1970	1974	1976	1977
Number of suicides in England and Wales	5566	3939	3891	3813	—
Suicide rate per 100,000 population	11.7	8.0	7.9	7.7	—
Number of Samaritan branches (UK and Eire)	56	95	154	—	170
Number of new clients	12,355	68,531	192,284	—	229,970

Source: Stengel (1973); and The Samaritans (1978).

The social incidence of loneliness itself in Britain is difficult to establish without specially designed surveys. (Even
then, straight-forward and brusque questions are likely to provoke evasion in respondents afraid to admit their social isolation to themselves, let alone to others.) The growing promin-
ence of computerized marriage and friendship bureaux in Britain
is certainly indicative of the needs people have to make contact,
as is the 'lonely hearts' column now found in most newspapers.
Old people are particularly isolated: Help the Aged (1978) has
put together data demonstrating clearly just how deprived many
old people are of human contact. The old are frequently im-
mobile, and 24 per cent of them (accounting for one in six
British households) live alone; surveys in various towns
suggest that a large proportion of old people have hardly had
any contact with anyone else, not even that of the most minimal
kind. In Newcastle, 63 per cent of old people were found to
have had less than an hour's contact with neighbours per month
(Help the Aged, 1978). Nearly one-tenth of all suicides are,
not unexpectedly, accounted for by people aged over 75 (*OPCS*

Monitor, 1976), an age group that constitutes about one-
twentieth of the population.
    Other forms of self-destructive activity include self-
starvation (the incidence of anorexia nervosa and related
conditions is believed to have increased rapidly over the past
decade; Mills *et al*., 1973) as well as its corollary of compulsive over-eating (Orbach, 1978, argues that many drastically
over-weight married women compensate for their powerlessness
over their lives by continuous eating). Addiction to 'hard'
drugs is perhaps more publicized in terms of the extent of
damage caused. Here, official statistics generally seen
as indicating a decline in drug addiction, following a steep
rise in the early 1970s — with methadone and heroin being the
drugs most commonly used by an addict population which is predominantly in the age group 20-35, and around three-quarters
male. However, Tendler (1977c) has reported that when the
overall number of addicts registered throughout the year is
considered, rather than the number of people registered on one
day only, a steady rise is evident in both the total number of
addicts and the number of newly registered addicts. In 1976,
these figures indicated something like 1000 new addicts, and
well over 3000 addicts in total. These figures are well below
those of some other countries, which probably reflects Britain's
relatively humane drug dependence programmes. But, also like
other countries, the drugs addicts obtain through the black
market are not recorded in the official statistics — although
some indication of the growing problems here can be gained from
the continuing increase in criminal convictions for hard drug
offences. (See Table 5.24 for official data on mental hospital-
ization for drug addiction.)
    While heroin addiction is generally accepted as a self-
destructive activity, cigarette smoking is less likely to be
regarded in this light — few people actually overdose on
nicotine, although the long-term consequences of inhaling
tobacco fumes (including those created by other people smoking)
are well known. Campaigns to publicize these dangers have had
some success, and less than half the adult population in Britain
now smokes manufactured cigarettes — which is largely accounted
for by a drop in the number of non-manual workers smoking.
However, those who do smoke are in the 1970s smoking more (DHSS,
1976). Manual workers not only smoke more cigarettes, but
continue to use those brands with high tar and nicotine contents,
which probably reflects the importance to them of smoking as a
means of coping with their life and work, rather than a wilful
failure to protect their health.
    Alcohol is another controversial drug, and its mass consumption
in a whole range of social situations gives rise to an increas-

ingly widespread form of addiction — alcoholism. The 500,000
or so people in England and Wales who are estimated to suffer
from serious problems in this respect (DHSS, 1976) have gone
far beyond the uncompulsive consumption of alcohol for pleasure.
In the U.K., wine consumption rose between 1962 and 1974 from
0.7 gallons per capita to 1.9 gallons, with beer consumption
also increasing in this period from 17 gallons to around 22
gallons per capita. It is, however, the slowly increasing rise
in consumption of spirits that is generally seen as responsible
for the growth in hospitalizations associated with the overconsumption of alcohol (Table 5.24).

Table 5.24
Admission to Mental Hospitals and Units for
Illness Related to Alcohol and Drug Use for
England, 1964-74

Nature and rate of admission	1964		1970		1974	
	Men	Women	Men	Women	Men	Women
Number of admissions for:						
Alcoholic psychosis	303	119	646	211	1117	552
Alcoholism	3727	924	4586	1383	6932	2241
Drug dependence	449	383	993	530	999	476
Rate per 100,000 population:						
Alcoholic psychosis	1	1	3	1	5	2
Alcoholism	17	4	20	6	31	9
Drug dependence	2	2	4	2	4	2

Source: DHSS (1977) *Inpatient Statistics from the Mental Health
Enquiry for England, 1974*, table A2.1. Reproduced with
the permission of the Controller of Her Majesty's
Stationery Office.

Note: These data refer only to England: some 18,000 people in
the United Kingdom were admitted to hospitals for alcoholism and alcoholic psychosis in 1973.

Commensurate with these problems of alcoholism has been a
growth in offences of 'criminal drunkenness'. Such data, of

course, pose problems of interpretation, reflecting as they do
changing policy practices and social attitudes. Nevertheless,
a remarkable increase in successful prosecutions for drunkenness
has been marked up in recent years, so that currently more than
1 in every 200 men is found guilty for this offence every year.
(Table 5.25 shows trends in prosecution rates for England and
Wales.) There is currently a better than 1 per cent chance for
young men between 18 and 21 to be convicted of criminal drunkenness in a year.

Table 5.25
Findings of Guilt in Prosecutions for
Drunkenness for England and Wales, 1966-79

Rate of conviction	1966	1970	1975	1979
Number of cases:				
Men	66,468	77,072	96,880	108,377
Women	4031	5302	7572	9436
Rate per 100,000 population:				
Men	368	423	523	571
Women	21	27	38	46

Source: Home Office (1976), table 1; Home Office (1980),
tables 1 and 3.

Other drug problems, such as dependence on barbiturates, are
intimately related to the nature of medical provision in Britain,
and though deleterious to individual health cannot necessarily
be seen as self-destruction — although they are surely related
to problems of identity. What passes for psychiatry, in particular, largely relies upon chemotherapy: some 20,000,000
prescriptions for hypnotics, and 8,000,000 for anti-depressants,
were handed out in England in 1975 — at a cost of £25,000,000
in basic ingredients alone (MIND, 1977). Particularly relevant
to issues of identity is the treatment of 'hyperactive' school
children with stimulants in order to bring their behaviour into
conformity with classroom standards. Such practices are perhaps
as relevant to concerns about freedom as they are to identity,
but the growth in use of drugs to facilitate social control is
clearly an important issue — while less than 600 school children
were classified as maladjusted in 1960, nearly 14,000 were in
1975 (Box, cited by Vaughan, 1977).
   The use of psychotropic drugs is generally regarded as having

The Poverty of Progress

played an important role in curtailing the length of people's
stay in psychiatric hospitals, but their increased use in out-
patient treatment does not seem to have reduced the overall
rates of admission to these hospitals. Trends, however, are
difficult to identify with any degree of certainty (Table 5.26).

Table 5.26
Trends in Mental Hospital Admissions for
England, 1964-75

Category of admissions	1964	1971	1975
All admissions:			
Men	62,359	70,763	71,008
Women	92,943	102,467	104,103
First admissions:			
Men	—	25,587	23,680
Women	—	36,317	33,696

Source: DHSS (1978) *Health and Personal Social
Services Statistics for England, 1977,*
table 9. Reproduced with the permission
of the Controller of Her Majesty's
Stationery Office.

   Data on mental hospital admissions by no means fully reflect
the changing incidence of acute personal problems. MIND (1977)
reports a survey of doctors in England and Wales, which estimates that around 5,000,000 people consult their doctors annually
concerning one or other form of mental illness, with 12 per
cent of such cases being referred to specialist psychiatric
services. Particularly significant is the fact that women are
twice as likely to be involved here as men — one in seven consult their doctors on such grounds. As much of the literature
produced by the Women's Liberation Movement in Britain has argued, it is no accident that many of these cases are of women
trapped in marriage, without a career of their own, and bringing
up children on an extremely restricted budget. The dependence
of many married women on their husbands for both economic support can make for a security and identity which are distinctly
hollow. Just as some husbands turn to compulsive evening
drinking to drown the memories of a day's alienated labour in
the factory, some housewives turn to the doctor and pills as
a source of support. (For a discussion of these

problems faced by women, see Oakley 1974a,b, who reports
a good deal of survey data on the situation of the British housewife.) Recent hospital admission figures suggest that one in
six women and one in nine men will be hospitalized for mental
illness at some point in their lives. Particular pressures confront gay people (homosexuals and bisexuals) who are often
trapped in a social world that systematically denies their
sexual identity. They are subject to immense stress and victim-
ization and not infrequently treated as if it were their sexuality, rather than social attitudes, that is the problem.

The continuing high level of 'mental disorders' and the increasing medical use of drugs suggests that our DWL is not conducive to mental health. Recent studies by Brenner (1973, 1976)
have pointed to the association of high levels of incidence of
psychiatric problems with economic slumps. If such structural factors are central in the causation of these problems,
this provides ominous perspectives on the long-run costs of the
current economic crisis.

It is clearly important, then, to see psychiatric problems in
wider terms than as being just a psychological estrangement from
oneself. Human identity is essentially social in nature, and
psychiatric problems such as depression and anxiety are certainly
often closely bound up with difficulties in establishing or maintaining satisfactory interpersonal relationships, whatever the cause of
failure may be. We have already discussed the question of loneliness
in Britain, but as well as the lack of human contact we need also to
take into account the quality of available human relationships within
the DWL. Among the relevant indicators here are the data on
children assaulted by parents, presented in the discussion of
security issues. During the period 1976-7, the National Society
for the Prevention of Cruelty to Children was involved in cases
involving some 58,000 children, most of those who were found
to be most deprived or at risk being under 11 years of age.

Attention was also paid to murder as an issue in security, but
the pattern of killings has further implications for our discussion of identity. As is clear from Table 5.27, relatively
few killings involve total strangers: in fact, around half of
the victims of homicide live near, are related to, or are lovers
(sic) of their killers. With the family so important to many
people's identity in our DWL, the concentration of murder and
manslaughter within families seems highly significant: it suggests a high degree of pathology in this central social institution.

Child and wife batterings both also seem to be occurring much
more frequently. That it is wives who lose out so clearly in

The Poverty of Progress

Table 5.27
Victims of Murder and Manslaughter in England
and Wales, 1967-71

(a) *Victims Under 16*

	Relationship to suspect				
	Son or daughter	Other relative	Other associate	Stranger	Tota
Number of victims	307	7	40	25	379
Percentage of victims	81.0	1.8	10.6	6.6	100

(b) *Victims Over 16*

	Relationship to suspect				
	Wife, husband or lover	Other relative	Other associate	Police or prison officer	Stranger
Number of female victims	345	55	118	0	79
Percentage of female victims	57.8	9.2	19.8	0.0	13.2
Number of male victims	79	64	317	5	127
Percentage of male victims	13.3	10.8	53.6	0.8	21.5

Source: Gibson (1975), tables 11, 12 and 13, and appendix G.

the marriage violence stakes — by more than a factor of four over their spouses — also shows much about the nature of the

family in British society. Faced with the alternative of having
to look after their children with diminished economic support,
many women will choose to remain in the violence and insecurity
of their marriages. And both parents may vent their frustration
on their children. The official categories used to report the
causes of murder and manslaughter fail to grasp these structured
social processes, citing the main motives as rage and quarrels —
with many infant manslaughters classified as 'apparently motive-
less'. Other criminal offences may also be related to problems
with identity, although, again, rarely without some degree of
ambiguity — in terms of both the statistics and the motives involved. Table 5.28 indicates that there has been more than a
ten-fold increase in crimes classified as 'violence against the
person' over the last quarter of a century, with a smaller
increase in sexual offences (which is significant if one takes
into account the fact that some homosexual practices are no
longer classified as criminal offences for most adults, while
many acts of sexual violence like rape are believed to go un-
reported).

Table 5.28
Trends in Recorded Violence and Sexual Crimes,
England and Wales, 1951-77
(Thousands of offences)

Category of crime	1951	1961	1971	1977
Violence against the person	7	18	47	82
Sexual offences	15	20	24	21

Source: Social Trends (1977), tables 13.2 and
2.6. Reproduced with the permission
of the Controller of Her Majesty's
Stationery Office.

These data suggest that about 1 in 500 **people** are currently
the victims of reported criminal violence or sexual offences
each year (although some of these sexual 'crimes' are victim-
less — like the consenting adult partner in a gay relationship
who is under 21). A relatively small, but growing, number of
sexual offences are rapes: some 1000 were reported in 1976.
Though rape offences are under-reported, it is perhaps violence
within the family that is least reliably reported — with police
officers not wishing to get involved in marital fights in which
the technically criminal offences that may be committed are
perceived as none of their business.
    Despite the reputation of Britons to be great pet lovers,

cruelty to animals is also unlikely to be assiduously reported.
Yet the Royal Society for Prevention of Cruelty to Animals
still found itself in the position of investigating 22,891
complaints of cruelty in 1977. Of these, 1036 cases resulted
in successful prosecutions for offences against animals. Almost
half of these convictions involved cruelty to dogs; another
third involved birds and other pet animals.

The situation of animals reared for food and clothing is, of
course, different from that of pets. Systematic data are not
available, but it seems realistic to assume that the increase
in 'factory farming' has greatly increased the discomfort of
farm animals in Britain (see, for example, the articles on this
issue in *New Scientist*, 18 October, 1973). With farm animals
regarded as no more than particularly complex and profitable
physical objects, the pressure for intensive farming methods
dictates the atrocious conditions under which many animals are
reared.

Damage to property is rather better recorded than violence
against animals, and provides additional insights into the
problems of identity within the DWL. Practically 300,000 cases
of criminal damage were recorded in England and Wales in 1977
(a many-fold increase having taken place in this category of
crime during the last decade alone). But these include such
acts of vandalism as wrecking public facilities (e.g. telephone
boxes) along with much more ambiguously 'anti-social' offences
like defacing advertising boardings; they will include malicious
damage of others' property as an act of revenge, along with,
more disturbingly, racist attacks on ethnic minorities' properties such as those which took place in the East London riot in
the summer of 1978.

It is significant that many of these activities are carried
out by young people. A study of adolescent violence in London —
which covered everything from childish pranks to vicious personal assaults — found that 11 per cent of 12 to 17 year olds
admitted to damaging cars, and 8 per cent to damaging trains,
in the preceding 6 months (Belson, cited in *New Society*, 13
December 1973, p. 664). The inscription of graffiti on public
buildings is an even more widespread facet of British youth
culture.

These data, however, are perhaps less indicative of a lack of
discipline on the part of parents and authority figures, than
of a general failure of British society to provide young people
with a meaningful way of life. Estranged from the society they
live in, often without jobs and with few prospects for the
future, they feel little identity with the sanctity of public
property or accepted codes of behaviour. Table 5.29 presents
a selection of data drawn from a survey carried out in 1976 of

the life-styles of over 14,000 British 16 year olds, which included both items relating to the opportunities to establish
an identity as well as other items relating to the problems
adolescents face in so doing.

Table 5.29
The Ways of Life of British 16 Year Olds in 1973

Proportion of teenagers reporting that they:

Have played truant from school in the past year (although 'hard-core' truancy is only around 8%)	52%
Do not have their own bedroom	39%
Have to share a bed	8%
Do not like attending school	30%
Do not take school work seriously	15%
Regularly watch TV for leisure	65%
Hardly ever, or never, read books other than for school	24%
Regularly play outdoor games and sport	38%
Regularly attend dance halls and discos	39%
Are sometimes or often involved in voluntary work	37%
Would like the opportunity to do voluntary work	16%

Source: National Children's Bureau (1976).

There is some surprising information presented here — for
example, the proportion of these teenagers lacking the privacy
of their own room, or even of their own beds. This survey also
pinpointed another source of dissatisfaction among young people:
the most popular careers were in professional and managerial
work, with variety, high pay, and opportunity to work with
others being the main criteria regarded as important in a job.
Given the actual proportion of such jobs available, this suggests that around one-third of these young people at least
were seriously disappointed by the quality of their employment.
For ethnic minorities facing discrimination, and increasing numbers
of young unemployed, even lower levels of satisfaction are likely.
    This last point suggests another way of thinking about prob-
lems of identity in British society. How many workers are able
to identify with their jobs? What sense of identity do people
derive from their work? Such questions are not commonly asked —

instead there has been a rather more narrow focus on what is
termed 'job satisfaction', perhaps because this is seen as
relevant to explaining and preventing industrial disputes. On
the basis of official data, job satisfaction may be declining
in Britain — down from an average level of 8.3 in 1971 and 1973,
to 8.0 in 1975 (as rated by a sample of workers on a 0-10 scale)
(*Social Trends*, 1976). These may seem rather high levels of
satisfaction, and, indeed, only 12 per cent of male and 8 per
cent of female workers report themselves as actively dissatisfied with their work (Table 5.30). But 'satisfaction' is always
related to aspirations; perhaps workers have tailored their
expectations to what they regard as unavoidable facts of life.
And perhaps, too, one has to be disaffected indeed to admit to
a researcher that the greater proportion of one's day is spent
unrewardingly: to do so may be regarded as personal failure.
We would suggest a rather different approach to studying problems of identity at work, based on social perceptions of the
desirability of different jobs in terms of their 'social standing'. Goldthorpe and Hope (1974) engaged in survey research to
determine the perceived desirability of different occupations
in Britain, and from their findings it is possible to calculate
that some 70 per cent of working men are in occupations which
fall into the lower half of a scale of perceived social desirability. This result lends support to the view that the sense
of identity which most workers can derive from their work in
contemporary British society is at best an impoverished one.

Table 5.30
*Perceptions of Job Satisfaction in Great
Britain, 1975*

	Very or fairly satisfied (%)	Neutral (%)	Very or rather dissatisfied (%)
Proportion of:			
Men	82	6	12
Women	88	4	8

Source: Social Trends (1977), table 5.19. Reproduced with the
permission of the Controller of Her Majesty's Stationery
Office.

It is clearly not possible to provide a neat statistical
summary of the problems of identity in the DWL. In comparison
with the relatively tangible issues of security and welfare,

the rather less tangible one of identity (and the same will be
true in respect of freedom) requires a wide-ranging choice of
indicators. However, taken together these statistics map out
the dimensions of a deep and in many respects growing malaise
in Britain's DWL. To concerns about the problems of affluence
and the persistence of inequality and deprivation, we can add
evidence relating to people's felt lack of well-being, and their
destructiveness towards themselves and others. Such social
phenomena are complex, and we would not seek to argue that they
follow in some way as a result of Britain's decline from an
imperial yet supposedly unalienated 'golden age'. Rather, they
should be related to the steady erosion and transformation of
various forms of social relationships by market and bureaucratic
forces as Britain has become a mature capitalist society. While
more and more market choice of commodities has been forthcoming
for much of the population (at least until the recent economic
crisis), traditional community structures have been eroded by
'urban development'; jobs have been deskilled and taken further
out of workers' control with working hours adapted to enable
machines to operate continuously throughout day and night; the
'bobby on the beat' has been replaced by the impersonal police
car; and segregation of social groups like 'youth' and the
'elderly' has proceeded apace. Such complex, but interconnected,
forces underlie the growing problems of identity in modern Britain —
and they in turn are rooted in the way the country is organized as a
class society. It is to the related issues of freedom that we now
turn in order to complete our statistical assessment of Britain's
DWL.

FREEDOM

If 'identity' poses problems of definition, what about 'freedom'? One person's freedom is clearly another person's license;
but restrictions on people's freedom to kill or exploit each
other are qualitatively different from the freedom to associate
with each other or to oppose the current political system. We
will thus focus on two major aspects of freedom: 'freedom to'
and 'freedom from'. Aspects of the former include the degree
of opportunity available to British people to mould or change
their occupational status or social class. Resources of
various sorts are a prerequisite for exercising such freedom,
and, in this respect, we shall consider people's access to
spare time, to economic resources, and so on. In 'freedom from'
we will consider the role of institutions that operate to limit
the activities of the large majority of the population, although
they may commonly be presented as providing a social and pol-

itical framework guaranteeing freedom. These include, for example, the use of imprisonment and institutionalization as
forms of social control (especially their application to controlling people unconvicted of any crime), and the growing
surveillance of the population by security agencies.

Access to economic resources is perhaps the central issue in
'freedom to'. Data on the ownership of wealth in Britain were
presented earlier (Table 5.9) and show that the ownership of
those forms of wealth that confer major economic control and
power in society (capital) are remarkably concentrated in the
hands of the very rich. While electoral rights and consumer
choice give British people some degree of opportunity to influence the course of future events, in each case the voter or
consumer is typically offered only a choice between alternatives
provided by others. Given the undoubted importance of private
capital as the central controlling force and motivating agent
in British industry, both political and market choices are
considerably constrained. The interests of capital therefore
have a major influence on the course of economic development —
over what sorts of products are manufactured, how, by whom, and
for whom. The concentration of such power in so few hands has
important implications for individual freedom: the financiers
and industrialists who, like puppeteers, pull the strings on
the 'invisible hand' of the market place are in many respects
more free than are consumers and workers, whose opportunities
to intervene in this process are decidedly limited. But even
the very rich do not have absolute freedom: unless they are
prepared to risk losing their wealth they have to manage their
businesses in a competitive manner. The DWL are the product
of a whole economic system rather than of the peculiar psychology of managers, financiers, and their colleagues in government
and the state.

Of course, capital is only one form of wealth. Just having
access to ready cash is itself also important — it confers a
measure of immediate power to the holder. Money, then, is a
means by which to secure 'freedom', in the sense that 'it is
he/she who pays the piper who calls the tune'. If monetary
resources were widely diffused then this aspect of economic
freedom might be fairly evenly available in Britain. But those
forms of wealth that can be easily converted into, or are
already held, in the form of cash or liquid assets are extremely
unevenly distributed in Britain. The top 1 per cent possess,
on average, forty times more cash, and one hundred times more
marketable assets *in toto*, than the poorest 80 per cent. The
inequality in the amount of freedom to make use of monetary
resources could hardly be more graphically illustrated. The
top 10 per cent of British society have access to over 60 per

cent of the marketable assets and over 50 per cent of cash
assets — not to mention their undoubtedly greater credit-worthiness when it comes to obtaining loans, running overdrafts, etc.

Table 5.31
Marketable Assets in the United Kingdom, 1975

Population group	(a) All marketable assets	(b) Liquid assets	(c) Cash assets
Percentage share of assets:			
Richest 1%	25.3	24.9	18.2
Next 2-5%	22.4	20.8	20.6
Next 6-10%	14.3	11.7	11.9
Next 11-20%	16.3	13.6	14.1
Next 21-100%	21.7	29.0	35.1
Average amount of estimated assets (£):			
Richest 1%	134,600	37,400	24,200
Next 2-5%	29,800	12,000	6900
Next 6-10%	15,200	5400	3200
Next 11-20%	8700	3100	1900
Next 21-100%	1400	840	590

Source: RCDIW (1977), table 45. Reproduced with the permission
of the Controller of Her Majesty's Stationery Office.

Notes: (c) Covers forms of cash such as bank deposits and
national savings.
(b) Covers the above, plus shares, life policies, etc.
(a) Covers the above, plus houses, land, and household
goods.

Far more than the evidence of inequalities between incumbents
of different occupational categories, such data point to the
need to see Britain's DWL as reflecting a particular form of
class society. A minority of the population belong to a class
which owns the greater proportion of Britain's wealth, in particular its industrial and financial capital. Controlling
these resources, they make their living from the profits accru-
ing to their investments. This limits the freedom of the
remainder of the population. The majority of people in contrast
depend on the sale of their ability to labour in order to make a
decent living, while their voice in the overall shaping of national
development paths is limited to irregular opportunities to vote for

candidates for parliament and local government.
But does not everyone in Britain have equal freedom to acquire
these resources? Juridicially, of course, this is (almost) true,
but in practice the unequal ownership of resources gives some
people relatively more freedom to accumulate more resources:
the system of inheritance of property ensures that the children
of the wealthy are able to reproduce this pattern of privilege.
Certainly, the self-made business tycoon can still be found,
even in an age dominated by multinational corporations. But it
is very difficult for would-be entrepreneurs to set up in producti
without access to the levels of investment that guarantee commercial success — for with the efficiency of large-scale production, and oligopolistic networks controlling markets, it is
often difficult for new manufacturers to succeed. It is not by
working for others for a wage, but by setting up in business,
that people mainly newly acquire wealth, and the main opportunities here seem to be in peripheral trades dependent on
servicing the large monopolies.
    It is not only the ranks of the wealthy that prove difficult
to join. A multitude of studies have reached striking conclusions about access to the commanding positions in such central
British institutions as the church, the military, the judiciary,
the civil service, Parliament and banking. In a comprehensive
review of these empirical studies, too numerous to detail here,
Giddens and Stanworth (1978) conclude:

> Elite positions in the major institutions in Britain are
> dominated by persons from privileged social backgrounds.
> . . . . The public schools and Oxbridge continue to play a
> pre-eminent role in elite recruitment: in most elites
> between 60 and 80 per cent have been educated at public
> schools . . . (in general) the higher the level of what is
> to count as the 'elite' is placed in any institution, the
> greater will be the proportion having public school and/or
> Oxbridge backgrounds. . . . In most elites, the proportion
> of individuals drawn from public school and/or Oxbridge
> backgrounds has remained stable or has actually increased
> over the past several decades. (Giddens and Stanworth,
> 1978, p. 222)

    These authors might also have pointed to the almost total
absence of women and minority group members from controlling
positions in British institutions. It is evident that the
ability to exercise control over important aspects of one's
own — and others' — destinies is extremely unequally distributed
within British society.[5]
    Even if access to the centres of power in business and the

state continues to be extremely closed for ordinary people —
thus in the House of Lords, the Upper House of the British
Legislature, the proportion of hereditary to appointed peers
is, in 1978, still 700 to 326 — it may nevertheless be argued
that Britain has become a more open society, that patterns of
social mobility have changed so that it is now much easier for
ordinary people to change their place in society. Proponents
of such a view will typically point to 'recruitment' to higher
status occupations, and suggest that, if the professions and
managerial posts are becoming more open to children of working-
class parents, the same will eventually become true of the
commanding heights of the economic and political system. How
well founded is this argument? What are the chances for people
to move freely from one class to another? It is again difficult
to answer this question convincingly with statistics, but
various indicators of social mobility give some idea of the
degrees of freedom available to people in Britain.

Several studies have focused on the extent to which people's
occupational status is determined by that of their parents.
Table 5.32, drawn from data presented by Goldthorpe *et al.* (1980),
indicates that in the 1970s some 70 per cent of male manual
workers (forming nearly half of the work force) were themselves
the sons of manual workers. These data do suggest relatively
high levels of mobility into the top occupational groups from
the lower status ones. Nevertheless, data produced by these
researchers indicate that 75 per cent of children whose fathers
were in status group I or II themselves had jobs of status
group I. Only 15 per cent of manual workers' sons achieved
this status, while over 50 per cent themselves became manual
workers.

There have undoubtedly been changes in patterns of mobility,
and largely through the expansion of higher status jobs over
the post-war period an increased proportion of British manual workers' children have been able to attain upward social
mobility. How much significance to attribute to this change
is another matter.[6] (Richardson, 1977, provides an analysis
which goes so far as to suggest that there has been no improvement in Britain's social mobility rate between manual and non-
manual occupations as a whole over this period.) The freedom
of children of higher status families to acquire jobs with
substantial incomes and more rewarding conditions of work within the DWL is still considerably greater than that of the
children of lower-status parents, at least when we judge it by
results in terms of jobs gained.

Of course, various theories have been advanced to account for
these differentials in performance. For many conservatives,
innate differences in intelligence are involved; for many re-

Table 5.32

Occupational Mobility in England and Wales, 1972

(Proportion of sons within each occupational group whose fathers belong to each group)

Father's occupational group (at son's age 14)	Son's occupational group						
	Higher professionals, administrators, managers, etc.	Lower professionals, etc., higher technicians, etc.	Lower non-manual and service workers	Small proprietors self-employed, etc.	Lower grade technicians and supervisors	Skilled manual	Semi and unskilled manual
	I	II	III	IV	V	VI	VII
I	25.3	12.4	9.6	6.7	3.2	2.0	2.4
II	13.1	12.2	8.0	4.8	5.2	3.1	2.5
III	10.4	10.4	10.8	7.4	8.7	5.7	6.0
IV	10.1	12.2	9.8	27.2	8.6	7.1	7.7
V	12.5	14.0	13.2	12.1	16.6	12.2	9.6
VI	16.4	21.7	26.1	24.0	31.1	41.8	35.2
VII	12.1	17.1	22.6	17.8	26.7	28.0	36.6
Proportion of fathers belonging to each group	7.9	6.4	8.0	10.3	12.5	30.0	24.8
Proportion of sons belonging to each group	14.3	12.2	9.6	8.0	12.0	22.0	21.8

Source: Based on table 2.1 in Goldthorpe (1980).

formists, the problem is one of differing social attitudes and
values. Rather than getting enmeshed in these debates here,
let us simply ask the reader to consider how powerful some of
the inequalities in security, welfare and identity discussed
earlier may prove in affecting children's school performance —
not to mention the differences in transmission of cultural and
linguistic resources across the generations, the relative
abilities of different parents to gain favour for their children,
or the attitudes of teachers to children, and employers to
school leavers, from different social backgrounds.

While education is obviously important in determining access
to social mobility, different levels of educational attainment
cannot be related unambiguously to 'freedom'. Whether education
constitutes a resource of real use depends on what kinds of
skill, knowledge and status it involves (cf. Dale et al., 1976;
Dinham and Norton, 1977). Here, recent studies have suggested
that large numbers of British school leavers lack even an
elementary knowledge of British politics. One recent survey,
for example, found that 44 per cent of school leavers believed
the Irish Republican Army to be a Protestant organization, and
49 per cent that Parliament made all the important decisions
affecting the country (Stradling, 1977). Another study concluded that the majority of school leavers were actually incapable of simple practical mathematics (Nicholson-Lord, 1978).
A recent survey of student teachers even found that most felt
that their schooling had failed to provide them with an adequate
preparation for later social and political life (Hemming, 1978).

Whatever the quality of British education, the training and
qualifications received can facilitate access to particular
sorts of jobs. There is a significant concentration of educational resources among the higher status groups in British
society (Table 5.33).

Most noticeable is the stress put by parents with high status
occupations on paying for a private education for their children.
For those who can afford it, private schools provide their
children with markedly better facilities for study than do
state schools, and with a qualitatively different kind of
education. It is here that Britain's future elites are trained:
Giddens and Stanworth (1978) cite recent studies of elite
formation which show that 85 per cent of Bishops were educated
at private schools, 86 per cent of Army officers (above the
rank of Major General), 92 per cent of Judges, and 60 per cent
of Civil Service Officers (above the rank of Under-Secretary).
Channelled into elite institutions of higher education, notably
Oxford and Cambridge, a growing web of social contact and influence provides these children with a massive head-start over
their state-educated rivals.

Table 5.33
Children's Schooling by Occupational Group, England and Wales, 1972
(percentages)

Schooling by age	Professionals	Employers and managers	Intermediate non-manual	Junior non-manual	Skilled manual etc.	Semi-skilled manual etc.	Unskilled manual
Under school age:							
at nursery, playgroup, etc.	31.7	37.6	17.6	26.3	19.2	16.1	14.8
5-10 years old:							
at state primary school	91.4	94.3	98.1	98.8	100.0	100.0	100.0
at independent or direct grant school	8.6	5.7	1.9	1.2	0.0	0.0	0.0
11-14 years old:							
secondary modern school	29.0	34.4	29.4	34.1	48.5	53.4	48.8
comprehensive school	20.4	28.6	32.1	35.8	31.9	29.3	15.1
grammar school	19.4	18.8	29.4	19.9	12.3	8.8	5.6
independent or direct grant school	30.1	15.2	7.3	2.3	1.4	0.0	0.0

Source: OPCS (1975), General Household Survey (1972), pp. 157 and 237. Reproduced with the permission of Her Majesty's Stationery Office.

Notes: Certain column totals for age groups do not add up to 100 per cent due to omission of some categories of school. Data for 11-14 year-olds of unskilled manual parents are based on a sample of less than 100 (total survey sample is over 7000). State secondary schooling in Britain was, until recently, divided largely into secondary modern schools and grammar schools, the latter selecting the higher performing children and possessing better qualified teachers and equipment. Comprehensive schools were introduced to replace this too-visible streaming, but in some places still co-exist with grammar schools. Independent schools typically possess superior resources than do state schools.

Sex is another important dividing line in the British education
system — resulting in women having far less freedom in choosing
employment in later life. While approximately equal numbers of
boys and girls take the basic '0'-level examinations, only two-
thirds as many girls as boys opt to stay on at school and take
the 'A'-level courses necessary to gain entrance to university.
Even when they achieve the requisite level of qualifications,
fewer girls than boys apply to go to university — 54 per cent of
girls, as against 65 per cent of boys, with three 'A'-levels in
1974 (Department of Education and Science, 1975). This 'opting-
out' — and 'filtering out' — increases as the academic hierarchy
is ascended: women comprise just over one-third of university
undergraduates, less than one-sixth of postgraduates, just over
one-tenth of university faculty and a mere one-fiftieth of pro-
fessors. The DWL are both context and cause of inequalities:
with media ideologies demanding 'feminine' role-playing, with
marriage typically structured around the wife's responsibility
for child-rearing and domestic work, and with few child-care
facilities available, many women see little point in pressing
forward to advance their career. When they do, the conflict
with family demands often causes them to give up in exasperation;
and prejudice still further limits their opportunities in 'un-
feminine' occupations. Girls' and women's freedom to choose
their future, then, is constrained not only by their learning
particular attitudes and roles, but also by a vast range of
social pressures and sanctions should they decide to pursue
higher education and careers. If they do opt out of work for
a time, their choices are eroded as the competitive pace of
career progression reduces the chance of re-entry into their
trained profession. When they seek work again, often the only
choice is to take the sort of insecure and low-paid jobs that
are the lot of most women. Wainwright (1978) provides an informed theoretical and empirical analysis of the sexual
division of labour in Britain, portraying a lack of freedom for
women in the educational and occupational spheres paralleled
only by that of ethnic minorities (as is demonstrated by the
Community Relations Commission, 1977). Women members of ethnic
minorities are, of course, subject to a double set of restraints
being placed on their activities and opportunities.
  Though the recent economic recession has perhaps affected
women most, in that it has reduced the number of part-time
jobs available, it has also influenced freedom, as related to
people's working lives, in more general ways. The lack of
employment opportunities clearly reduced mobility between jobs
as the crisis bit in 1974-5 — which adds further to the restrictions on freedom of choice of occupational status we documented
earlier (Table 5.34).

Table 5.34
Job Mobility in Britain, 1974-5, by Age and Sex
(Percentage of workers having changed employers in
in the past year; approx.)

Age range	Men		Women	
	1974	1975	1974	1975
16-24	34	23	30	29
25-34	23	16	18	15
35-44	13	10	11	11
45-54	8	7	10	8
55 +	5	4	7	4

Source: Social Trends (1977), chart 5.20.
Reproduced with the permission of the
Controller of Her Majesty's Stationery Office.

The rather staggering decrease in job mobility evident here
over a period of just 1 year — especially for men — suggests
that people might be much more keen on exercising the freedom
which exists in principle to change jobs, were economic conditions more favourable. Mobility is lowest among older
workers, which may indicate more about their greater incumbence
of established and relatively secure jobs (that they dare not
risk giving up), than it does about the supposed advantages of
the young in being able to pick and choose in the job market.
Whatever the case, it seems likely that older people possess
less freedom in the form of opportunity to exchange their
jobs for equivalent or better ones, while many workers of all
ages are finding it impossible even to get a job remotely to
their liking.

The discussion of 'freedom to' in Britain's DWL should also
consider the leisure opportunities available to British people.
Tables 5.35 and 5.36 document curiously contradictory effects
of the economic crisis on how people's time is spent: although
the employed are working fewer hours (note, however, the possible
reversal of this trend, and the workload of manual workers in
general), marginally fewer holidays are being taken than in the
recent past.

Since surveys (e.g. Katona *et al.*, 1971) have indicated that
many British workers, especially those with lower incomes, wish
to work longer hours — in order to obtain better incomes — the

Table 5.35
Total Weekly Hours at Work, Great Britain, 1970-6

		1970	1973	1976
Manual	Men	47.1	46.7	45.3
	Women	40.0	39.9	39.3
Non-manual	Men	39.1	38.8	38.5
	Women	37.1	36.8	36.5

Source: Social Trends (1977), table 5.21;
(1980), table 5.10. Reproduced with
the permission of the Controller of
Her Majesty's Stationery Office.

Table 5.36
Holidays Taken by Residents of Great Britain,
1966-76

Millions of holidays taken:	1966	1971	1973	1975	1976
In Great Britain	31	34	41	40	38
Abroad	6	7	8	8	7

Source: Social Trends (1980), table 11.18. Reproduced
with the permission of the Controller of Her
Majesty's Stationery Office.

freedom of increased leisure 'won', not through union militancy
but through economic recession, is a rather dubious one. Note,
too, that women's shorter average working week is more than
compensated for by the many hours of housework which women who
work almost invariably perform each week (see Oakley, 1974b).

We have already made some mention of the access to resources
which educational opportunity may make available. Other forms
of freedom may also be related to people's access to information,
and in this respect it is interesting to look at what resources
are made available through libraries. The statistics that are
available suggest that major inequalities exist here, too. In
the early 1970s there were 473 public libraries, 1001 academic
libraries and 1182 libraries in private industry and commerce

(DES, 1975). Information available through the press is also important, but again difficult to assess directly. Tracing out the links between editors, owners, advertisers, and the state, and the way these affect what news is presented, is too complex a task to be presented here. But it is easy to show that the British press is controlled by a very small number of organizations: by 1977 eight companies controlled some 85 per cent of daily and Sunday circulation (Tunstall, 1977). The national newspapers overwhelmingly tend to support the Conservative Party at elections. The number of provincial newspapers has dropped sharply in recent years, and the concentration of ownership has proceeded apace here too — the largest ten publishers control 81 per cent of evening paper circulation and 36 per cent of weeklies' circulation (Royal Commission on the Press, cited by Young, 1977). As for women's magazines, 70 per cent of the market is controlled by a single firm (White, cited by Berthoud, 1977).

It would certainly be possible to consider yet other forms of 'freedom to' — for example, the geographical mobility of different occupational groups, or the availability of contraceptive and abortion facilities to women (see *Social Trends*, 1977, for relevant data), or the limitations placed on young people's mobility by increasing road traffic (see Hillman *et al.*, 1973). A more detailed analysis of freedoms in Britain than we have space for here would need to pay particular attention to the specific circumstances of women and minority groups. But, having considered a range of general indicators relating to the ways in which opportunities to change one's circumstances are structured within the DWL, let us now consider the matter of 'freedom from'.

The first aspect of 'freedom from' which we will take up is freedom from surveillance and spying — an issue more commonly dealt with under the heading of 'privacy'. Perhaps the DWL of Britons can be ascribed little responsibility for the presence of spies from the superpowers and other authoritarian regimes who monitor (and interfere with) activities claimed to be relevant to their 'national interests'. But the limitations on individual freedom occasioned by the growth in size and activity of Britain's political police in recent decades are a different matter. In a debate in Parliament over these issues in March of 1978, the Home Secretary defined the role of one such police organization, the Special Branch, as being to collect 'information on those whom *I* think cause problems for the state'. How many people are actively monitored in this way is not public information, but the number of Special Branch officers in England, Scotland and Wales was over 1350 in 1978 (*State Research*, 1978, No. 6; this number had previously re-

mained a closely guarded secret, only released as a concession
to mounting public criticism over unnecessary state secrecy).
It is possible, however, to gain some impression of the amount
of surveillance that goes on in Britain by considering data
that exist on the incidence of letter-opening and telephone-
tapping on the part of the authorities. Bunyan (1977) reports
that over 300,000 letters in transit between Britain and other
countries were opened in 1960, with over 500,000 in 1966.
Official reporting of internal letter-openings has been discouraged since 1956, when the number of warrants granted to
open mail addressed to particular individuals or groups stood
at only 205 (although this was was a marked increase over the
ninety warrants per year of 1945; and note further that a
warrant can cover several individuals or groups). Estimates
of changing patterns in this form of surveillance clearly need
to be treated cautiously, but in 1979 some fifty-two warrants
were issued in England and Wales (Tendler, 1980). In any case,
the Post Office needs no special warrant to open mail (Ackroyd
et al., 1977), which gives even more reason to expect that a
considerable volume of mail is opened each year for security
purposes — which anecdotal evidence would tend to confirm.
Telephone tapping has trebled over the last 20 years: from
129 warrants issued in England and Wales in 1958, to 411 in
1978 (Tendler, 1980). Interestingly one group of Britons is
officially not subject to telephone tapping: Members of
Parliament. (It is claimed that they have not been 'bugged'
since 1964 by the agencies concerned, who may not be the most
reliable of sources.)
We are on rather firmer ground when we turn to the question
of surveillance via data banks. The Police National Computer
at Hendon currently carries records on around 3,800,000 people:
once recorded on it, individuals are likely to remain on file
until their death. Its capacity is some ten times larger than
appears to be necessary for present requirements. The information stored here is officially admitted to cover suspects and
associates of criminals, as well as records of convicted people,
but there is a significant discrepancy between the 3,800,000
individuals on file and the 2,200,000 sets of fingerprints
stored (although some of this is accounted for by juveniles
whose fingerprints are not recorded). Information on the
political affiliations of certain individuals is known to be
stored in this computer. The Special Branch also has its own
computer file with a capacity to store information on over
500,000 people. It is highly likely that the information
deposited here concerns people of political interest to the
state — covering everyone from militants and trade union activists to key political figures. Another data bank at Scotland

Yard is reliably reported to cover tens of thousands of suspected users of soft drugs. Immigrants are also subject to such
monitoring: some 15,000 suspected illegal immigrants feature on
one data bank. The implications of these innovations in police
practice for individual liberty will become apparent when incorrect information stored on an individual secures a wrongful
arrest. That discussions of the DWL in Britain do not seem to
be concerned with such aspects of 'freedom from' augers badly
for what might happen in the future — cases have already been
reported of overheard and untrue gossip being fed into local
police computers. (Sources for this paragraph: *State Research
Bulletin*, 1977, No. 2; 1979, No. 10; Tendler, 1977a,b.

It is likely that other computerized (let alone non-computer-
ized) data banks on Britons, relevant to monitoring political
activities rather than crimes, are in existence. 'About one-
fifth of the population has a police record, much of which consists of inaccuracies, gossip and hearsay' (*State Research
Bulletin*, 1979, No. 14). A vast amount of less sensitive data
is available — for example on local authority files — which
might potentially be made available to so-called security forces
or the police in confrontation situations. All psychiatric
hospital patients and 98 per cent of hospital in-patients are,
for example, recorded on a central computer (Ackroyd et al.,
1977). Information is already rapidly exchanged between the
government office holding records of car number plates and
police forces seeking to trace criminals and other people of
interest. Extensive information concerning individuals is also
stored in private data banks — most notably in the case of
agencies which produce data on credit-worthiness. One firm
maintains information on 14,000,000 people, and in 1970 gave
reports on more than 370,000 in response to commercial enquiries
(*Report of the Commission on Privacy*, 1972, cited in Jones,
1974). It has also been reported that British credit rating
agencies have, on occasion, traded information with the police.

Apart from the threat to liberty implied by the use of data
banks for the surveillance of people's activities, a good deal
of inaccurate information seems to be stored in them. As well
as various 'isolated' incidents and pieces of anecdotal evidence,
there are the results of a survey carried out by the British
Computer Society: over one-third of organizations using data
banks reported new problems in maintaining the accuracy of their
records. Yet only one-third of these organizations allowed
individuals to consult their own files, and most did not inform
people of the existence of such records (Report in *New Scientist*,
25 October 1973). A law was passed in 1978 giving individuals
legal access to inspect any files kept on them by a commercial
data bank (for a fee, of course, and with little redress for

discovery of incorrect information apart from its erasure) which may result in a higher standard of records being kept. But it does little to safeguard privacy, nor does it include the right to inspect police records on individuals.

It is hard to be sure just how much the practices of the security services described above represent contemporary erosions being made in people's freedom, and how much they represent contingency preparations by the state in case of future conflict. In either case, we would suspect that the state security services are hardly keeping an eye on the trade unionists and others working to change the system of privilege and power that they regard as causing the problems in Britain's DWL out of concern for these groups' political freedoms. If their task can only be carried out effectively by risking the freedom of many ordinary individuals, the political police will justify such problems as the costs of protecting the nation — as the costs of 'freedom from'. But 'whose freedom' is at stake here, and 'from whom'?

Other aspects of the operation of 'law and order' also con- stitute cause for concern over freedom in Britain's DWL. Im- prisonment, for example, is a particularly striking limitation upon one's freedom. Yet Britain stands out in Europe for its large prison population, which has grown rapidly in recent decades: from an average daily total of 33,086 in 1966 to 41,443 in 1976. This latter figure covers 143,822 'receptions' to prison being made over the course of the year. It may be argued that people whose freedom is limited in this way are only being held so as to stop their criminal activities restricting the freedom of others. But this fails to take into account the relative growth in the prison population of people as yet un- convicted of any offence: in 1966, 24 per cent of receptions consisted of untried prisoners, but in 1976 the figure was 32 per cent. More than 1 per cent of people held in prison — around 2000 people — are subsequently found not to be guilty of any offence; and about ten times this number will not be sentenced to a custodial term. (Source for these data: Church of England Board of Social Responsibility, 1978.) Other people — obviously from the poorer strata of society — are in prison not because this is thought to be an appropriate con- sequence of their guilt, but because they are unable to pay fines. The proportion of the British population affected in these ways is rather small, but in terms of absolute human misery the data suggest a rather different story. We should note here, too, that we have not attempted to raise the question of wrongful conviction, although our own experience supports social research (for example, Baldwin and McConville, 1977) in suggesting that this is by no means uncommon in the British

legal system — especially, we would argue, but by no means exclusively, where protest behaviour on picket lines or political
demonstrations is involved.

Further, we cannot take up here the question of the class
structure of British law — which extends well beyond the origins
of judges and other legal professionals in the upper classes.
Even the old adage 'one law for the rich, another for the
poor' only points to the way in which the arresting practices
of the police and the sentencing practices of the judiciary are
related to the defendant's social class, and thus their access
to legal resources, etc. There is a more general point about
what sort of social order the legal system is defending. One
does not have to see all 'criminals' romantically as Robin
Hoods struggling against the DWL to recognize that much of
Britain's law, as well as the way in which it is implemented,
is oriented to the protection of wealth and privilege; the
class composition of the prison population surely reflects this
situation. (On the points raised in this paragraph, see Pearce,
1976; Taylor et al., 1976.)

Prisons are not the only institution in which people's freedoms are restricted, of course. Three per cent of Britons
lived in institutions in 1976 (Social Trends, 1977; chart 1.3),
although many of these institutions were hotels and hospitals.
The most significant point here for our discussion of 'freedom
from' is the very large number of old people living in local
authority homes — largely because of the absence of suitable
alternative accommodation. Some 100,000 old people who live in
such institutions are estimated to be quite capable of living
privately, and of those it is likely that a majority would
prefer to live in a house of their own (Townsend, 1977). Many
old people are excluded from the benefits of the DWL once they
have finished their 'productive' life; their social support is
institutionalized as they are cut off from other people. This
'freedom' of the rest of the population — from having to cope
with the problems of the aged — is perhaps one of the most in-
human aspects of Britain's DWL. Not only the aged suffer, but
the young too, in their loss of contact with elderly people
who have a rich store of experience of other ways of life.
Certainly, provision of adequate services to old people living
alone would be both cheaper and more rewarding than institution-
alizing them (Townsend, 1977).

Other categories of people restrictively institutionalized
include homeless adults and children of all ages, some psychiatric patients — and many of the children unwillingly undergoing
compulsory education between the ages of 5 and 16. For these,
as for the aged, the limited scope of their 'freedom' within
the DWL compares strikingly with the claimed sacrifices of

freedom involved in spending national resources on providing a
'welfare state' — or indeed 'protecting' it by spending massively
more on the military.

BEYOND THE EMPIRICAL ANALYSIS

By emphasizing data that are often obscure or overlooked, our
statistical picture of the DWL is very different from that
usually portrayed in such official statistical abstracts as
Social Trends. To be sure, many of these conventional portraits
of Britain — in terms of improving overall levels of health,
material living standards and so on — are accurate enough, as
far as they go. We certainly would not want to see many of
these trends reversed — although the eventual impact of the
current world recession in Britain may in the end lead to this
being the case (for example, as social welfare provision on its
current scale is seen as a threat to profitable private
enterprise). But we would regard the official picture of the
DWL as being too one-dimensional in any case. By presenting
and assessing our data in terms of the four categories of
security, welfare, identity, and freedom, we have been able
to identify many facets of contemporary life in Britain where
stagnant or deteriorating conditions, rather than improvements,
are the rule. Furthermore, major inequalities in the distribution of the 'cake' pervade Britain's social structure. Broad
inequalities in circumstances continue to divide the social
classes, in distribution as well as in production, with those
of lower socioeconomic status (i.e. the working classes)
almost invariably having less access to the goods and services
produced in the economy, yet paying more of the social costs of
their production. We have shown, too, that women occupy a subordinate position within the DWL — although they live longer on
average than men, and less often find themselves in prison, in
most respects they clearly lose out in social, economic and
political life. And while we have attempted, as best we could
with the statistical data to hand, to assess the participation
of minority groups — ethnic minorities, the elderly and youth,
the disabled, single parents and their children, and so on — in
the DWL, it would certainly have been useful to document in more
ways than these their inferior position.[8]
Given these data, it may seem to be one of the outstanding
peculiarities of the British that according to Gallup polls
carried out in nearly seventy countries in the 1970s, Britons
were, on average, reported as being among the world's most
happy people. That 92 per cent of Britons claimed to be 'very'
or 'fairly' happy placed Britain third in the league of happiest

nations; and with 38 per cent claiming to be highly satisfied
with their standard of living, they were also seen as the fifth
most satisfied. The same survey (which involved a relatively
small sample) also indicated, however, that 21 per cent of
Britons would like to emigrate and 79 per cent to live in rural
surroundings, which suggests at the very least that people's
sources of satisfaction have little basis in their surroundings
and that the answers to survey questions need to be treated
with some caution (Gallup, 1976). Other surveys of people's
attitudes to life in Britain confirm that most people claim to
be happy with their lives — but also that majorities believe
their own circumstances to be less than they are entitled
to, that Britain is too unequal, and that people have insufficient influence on government (e.g. Abrams, 1974). Only
minorities of the British population — usually less than a
third of people surveyed — believe that important institutions,
such as trade unions, newspapers and the civil service, do a
good job, according to one recent survey (Kellner, 1977).

The points we made previously about assessing the value of
survey results in our discussion of job satisfaction are also
relevant here. It is as if people are unwilling to admit to
being dissatisfied with those aspects of the DWL in which they
are most closely involved, and have aspirations tied to beliefs
of what they might immediately expect out of the DWL in present
circumstances (which may diverge from what they actually feel
entitled to). Again, a peculiarity of the British seems to be
their penchant to tailor any expression of their feelings to a
restricted set of social responses. Those unhappy with the
type or quantity of 'cake' provided for them are told to learn
to 'like it or lump it', or to wait for more to arrive. Few
people are actively encouraged to consider the feasibility of
producing a different kind of 'cake', or how different forms of
societal organization might result in slices corresponding more
to the amount of work put into their production. This reticence
may underlie the tendency towards destructive violence in relation to both self and others, and much ill health and stunting
of creative and productive potentials. One of its most destructive results is the narrowing of people's vision to such an extent
that the very possibility of AWL is denied, with groups active
around strategies for bringing about change in the DWL regarded
as dangerous deviants — attitudes which the mass media are
usually only too happy to reflect and reinforce.

But not everyone in Britain claims to be passively content
with the DWL. Indeed, it is likely that some of those who represent themselves as happy and satisfied in polls, such as those
discussed above, are able to say this because, having rejected

the limitations of the DWL, they are striving to develop and
pursue AWL. As well as those seeking to live AWL, others are
also involved in working for the social changes that would make
it possible for other people to effect more direct influence
over their own lives. More groups seem to be developing that
take on both the role of publicizing problems in the DWL, and
that of providing support to disadvantaged groups; and many of
these may engage in such actions as occupations, boycotts and
strikes in order to press their claim for changing aspects of
the DWL which they have identified as contrary to their needs.
This diversity of strategy is also evident in the range of
policies adopted by alternative political groups: some see the
main prospects for transforming the DWL as lying in parliamentary
influence and thus seek electoral success, while others argue
that such elections are at best only a means to gain a wider
forum for their campaigns to build mass action around the workplace or in the community.

The particular strategy or range of strategies adopted by an
organization clearly reflects *political* choices made by its
members over what change is desirable: deciding upon strategy
is rarely a matter of debating rationally the merits of a set
number of policy options. Some organizations are setting out
to remove particular problems in the DWL by a 'social engineering' approach of introducing new institutions and support systems
(or restoring traditional ones that have been eroded) to help
people who suffer most from these problems. Other groups are
trying to introduce changes into the DWL that will prevent the
generation of one or other problem in the first place, thus by-
passing the need for the sorts of change advocated by those
adopting the social engineering approach. And yet others are
seeking to restructure the DWL in more fundamental ways so as
to overcome a wide range of interconnected problems simultaneously. The development of AWL has certainly, then, by no means
been the sole prerogative of radicals dissatisfied with the
DWL — many people whose ideologies are relatively conservative
or liberal have been among those pressing for change.

Confrontation with the existing system of power in Britain is
almost inevitable in any attempt at large-scale change in the
DWL. A rapid (and deliberate) transformation to a situation
where AWL can flourish is not on the immediate agenda. Consciousness concerning the possibility of AWL must first be
built so that 'realistic' deference to the existing social
order can be replaced by a realistic grasp of the possibilities
for a new society.

Innovations already made by those experimenting with AWL can
serve as an image for a future that can realistically be created
given people's commitment to participate. But it is also im-

portant to take into account *both* the possible gains and limitations of strategies to reform the existing social order: such
gains can themselves serve to broaden people's horizons, or
they may further bind them to the status quo. Certainly, important steps towards AWL can be made within the present social
framework, and such 'transitional' movements towards AWL may be
appropriate in some circumstances and situations. Nevertheless,
the overwhelming necessity at the present time is to integrate
the diverse strategies for change in all the problematic areas
of the DWL: it is of little use to gain an improved icing when
the 'cake' has crumbled away beneath. Only by uniting attempts
to change the DWL can this integration be achieved — a difficult
task, but an essential one if satisfactory AWL are to be secured.
   Bigger pieces of 'cake', and sometimes even more icing, can,
in theory, be won by individuals and groups within the existing
social order. But a share in a new sort of cake requires a
different social order: one that is not founded on the imperatives of private profit or on the oppression of women by men.
Even the size of the pieces of 'cake' available to people at the
present time is in jeopardy, and this has provided the British
with the greatest stimulus for considering change. However
peculiar the British, there is reason to believe that the growth
of the political movements necessary to organize and lead such
change is possible in Britain in the 1980s.

NOTES

1. Our section heading is derivative of E. P. Thompson's 'The
Peculiarities of the English' (1965), which is part of a debate
over the relevance for the present of the peculiar trajectory
of English history, among the contributions to which are Anderson (1965), (1969), (1980), and which is currently taken up in
Tom Nairn's essay on nationalism in the United Kingdom, *The
Break-up of Britain* (1982), and Thompson's own collection (1979).
But what do we mean by Britain? The official statistics presented here take various forms. Some concern England alone;
others England and Wales; some refer to Britain (taken as England, Wales and Scotland) and yet others to the United Kingdom,
which includes Northern Ireland. We have attempted, as far as
possible, to exclude Northern Ireland from our discussion.
Northern Ireland is better seen as a colony, than as an integral
part of the British nation. Defenders of the unity of the
nation as currently conceived by the British state will find
that inclusion of Northern Ireland among the statistics discussed below would hardly improve an assessment of the DWL in
Britain — the infant mortality and road accident rates, the

levels of social deprivation, violence, and political repression
are all considerably higher than on the metropolitan mainland.
This point also reminds us that we have not attempted to address
questions concerning the extent to which Britain's DWL dependent
upon the maintenance of repressive or impoverished conditions
in other countries — as with the case of Ireland — or the
international arms trade.

Any compilation of data involves an act of selection. With
the vast mass of official and unofficial statistics that is
available on Britain, considerable selection is called for; we
have tried to be principled in our selection, using the data
that would be appropriate to support our case but not ignoring
or suppressing them when our expectations have not been borne
out.

2. Perhaps a better analogy would be that there is a series of
cakes, the size of which has grown over time. Some people have
argued that the cake is too big, or almost too big — that it is
a strain on the Earth's physical resources. For a review of
this Malthusian debate, and evidence that the cake could actually
be much larger than at present, see Freeman and Jahoda (1978);
Gribbin (1979).

3. We shall frequently present analyses of statistics in terms
of 'social class', and we should be clear that these statistical
breakdowns correspond to the official statistician's notion of
class as a matter of occupational status. While occupational
categories have some rough correspondence to an adequate concept of 'class', they are by no means as revealing as they
might be. On the concept of class in official data, and alternatives to it, see Nichols (1979); on class in Britain see
Westergaard and Resler (1976). On general issues of problems
in interpreting official statistics, and a critique of British
data, see Irvine et al. (1979), which also includes a discussion
by Oakley and Oakley on sexism in official data.

4. Alienation deserves much more discussion than possible here.
More extended treatment can be found in Meszaros (1975) and
Ollman (1976) who present radical approaches, and Schact (1971)
who surveys the sociological literature.

5. Whether it is more appropriate to talk of elites in charge
of major institutions, or dominant classes exercising hegemony
over society, has long been an issue of controversy: see, for
example, Bottomore (1964). For a detailed study of the interests controlling the British state, see Miliband (1969).
Miliband's work has been criticized by other radical analysts for

focusing too much on who controls the state in Britain (elite theory) and not enough on how the state itself is the product of social classes in conflict (class theory). Some of the contributions to this debate are reprinted in Urry and Wakeford's (1973) collection of readings on *Power in Britain*, and in Blackburn's (1972) reader on social theory.

6. One point to bear in mind is that the nature of jobs themselves has changed — occupational categories are not timeless. On the one hand this has involved the reduction of some of the toil and hard labour of many manual jobs with increased mechanization. But it has also meant the 'de-skilling' of technical and even professional work, so that such jobs themselves become more like manual labour and further tied to the controlling power of higher management and ownership. On this point, see Braverman (1974), who re-analyses occupational statistics in the light of trends in 'de-skilling', or various other works cited in Griffiths *et al.* (1979).

7. See Bynner (1974) for an empirical account of the way parents' attitudes to, and involvement with, their children's education change over the school cycle. Working-class families appear to become aware that they lose out through the educational system, and their aspirations diverge in a downwards direction from those of higher occupational status families.

8. The four categories of needs do not yet fully assess the DWL. Take the question of waste in the DWL — were it possible to redistribute resources currently wasted, major improvements could be made in some people's lives. Thus, Roy (1976) has argued that some 35 per cent of food may be wasted with Britain's production, distribution and consumption patterns (with kitchen and plate waste the largest single factor, and manufacturing of foodstuff the next main source of waste). The Cambridge Political Economy Group (1974), who argue that some 17 per cent of Britain's GNP — involving unemployment, grandiose public projects, advertising and financial services, excess military expenditure, and luxury consumption by the rich — could be put to improving the quality of life. The role of military policies in our way of life looks like being a major political issue in the 1980s, involving not only waste but threats to life itself.

BIBLIOGRAPHY

Abrams, M. (1974) This Britain. I: A contented nation?, *New Society*, 21-2, 439-440.

Ackroyd, C., Margolis, K., Rosenhead, J. and Shallice, T.
(1977) *The Technology of Political Control*. Harmondsworth,
Penguin.
Anderson, P. (1965) Origins of the present crisis, in *Towards
Socialism* (Edited by Anderson, P. and Blackburn, R.). London,
Fontana. (Originally published in *New Left Review*, No. 23,
1964).
Anderson, P. (1969) Components of the national culture, in
Student Power (Edited by Cockburn, A. and Blackburn, R.).
Harmondsworth, Penguin.
Anderson, P. (1980) *Arguments Within English Marxism*. London,
New Left Books.
Bailey, R. (1977) *The Homeless and the Empty Houses*. Harmonds-
worth, Penguin.
Baldwin, J. and McConville, M. (1977) *Negotiated Justice*.
London, Martin Robertson.
Berthoud, R. (1977) Pressure from some advertising departments
on editors of women's magazines is criticized, *The Times*,
2 September.
Blackburn, R. (Editor) (1972) *Ideology in Social Science*.
London, Fontana.
Bottomore, T. (1964) *Elites and Society*. Harmondsworth, Pen-
guin.
Bowden, T. (1978) *Beyond the Limits of the Law*. Harmondsworth,
Penguin.
Braverman, H. (1974) *Labour and Monopoly Capital*. New York,
Monthly Review Press.
Brenner, H. (1973) *Mental Illness and the Economy*. Cambridge,
Mass, Harvard University Press.
Brenner, H. (1976) *Estimating the Social Costs of National
Economic Policy*, (Paper No. 5 for a study prepared for the
Joint Economic Committee, U.S. Congress, Achieving the
Goals of the Employment Act of 1946 — Thirtieth Anniversary
Review: Volume 1 - Employment). Washington D.C., U.S.
Government Printing Office.
Buck, D. (1977) DHSS deficiency causes rickets, *Science for
People,* no. 36, 3-4.
Bunyan, T. (1977) *The Political Police in Britain*. London,
Quartet.
Bynner, J. (1974) Deprived parents, *New Society*, 21-2, 448-477.
Caesar, H. J. (1978) We live in England, *ICI Magazine*, 56 (460),
151-155.
Cambridge Political Economy Group (1974) *Britain's Economic
Crisis*. Nottingham, Spokesman Publications.
Church of England Board for Social Responsibility (1978) *Prisons
and Prisoners in England Today*. London, Church of England.
CIS (Counter Information Services) (1977) *Crisis Special Report*

2: Who's Next for the Chop. London, CIS.
Community Relations Commission (1977) Urban Deprivation, Racial
    Inequality and Social Policy: A Report. London, HMSO.
Dale, R., Esland, G. and MacDonald, M. (Editors) (1976) School-
    ing and Capitalism. London, Routledge & Kegan Paul.
Department of Education and Science (1975) Education Statistics
    for the United Kingdom, 1974. London, HMSO.
Department of Health and Social Security (1976) Prevention and
    Health: Everybody's Business. London, HMSO.
Department of Health and Social Security (1977) Inpatient Stat-
    istics from the Mental Health Inquiry for England, 1974.
    London, HMSO.
Department of Health and Social Security (1977) On the State of
    the Public Health for the Year 1976. London, HMSO.
Department of Health and Social Security Welsh Office (1978)
    A Happier Old Age. London, HMSO.
Dinham, B. and Norton, M. (1977) Directory of Change: Education.
    London, Wildwood House.
Duncan, I. (1977) Allotments, in Big Red Diary, 1978: The Poli-
    tics of Food, or, the Digester's Read. London, Pluto Press.
Freeman, C. and Jahoda, M. (Editors) (1978) World Futures: The
    Great Debate. London, Martin Robertson.
Gallup, G. (1976) Readers Digest, October.
Gibson, E. (1975) Homicide in England and Wales 1967-71.
    London, HMSO.
Giddens, A. and Stanworth, P. (1978) Elites and privilege, in
    Work, Urbanism and Inequality (Edited by Abrams, P.).
    London, Weidenfeld & Nicolson.
Goldthorpe, J. and Hope, K. (1974) The Social Grading of Occu-
    pations. Oxford, Clarendon Press.
Goldthorpe, J. (with C. Llewellyn and C. Payne) (1980) Social
    Mobility and Class Structure in Modern Britain. Oxford,
    The Clarendon Press.
Gribbin, J. (1979) Future Worlds. London, Abacus.
Griffiths, D., Irvine, J. and Miles, I. (1979) Social statistics:
    political perspectives, in Demystifying Social Statistics
    (Edited by Irvine, J., Miles, I. and Evans, J.). London,
    Pluto Press.
Hall, S., Critcher, C., Jefferson, T., Clarke, J. and Roberts,
    B. (1978) Policing the Crisis. London, MacMillan.
Healy, P. (1977) Two babies a week die from battering NSPCC
    estimates, The Times, 6 October, p. 5.
Healy, P. (1978) Deaths are increasing among people born in
    New Commonwealth, The Times, 23 February, p. 6.
Help the Aged (1977) Death in Winter. London, Help the Aged.
Help the Aged (1978) Cry and You Cry Alone. London, Help the
    Aged.

Hemming, J. (1978) Being unprepared, *Times Educational Supplement*, 19 May, p. 25.
Henderson, H. (1976) Citizen movements for greater global equity, *International Social Science Journal*, 28 (4).
Hillman, M., Henderson, I., and Whatley, A. (1976) *Transport Realities and Economic Planning*. London, Political and Economic Planning.
Hird, C. and Irvine, J. (1979) The poverty of wealth statistics, in *Demystifying Social Statistics* (Edited by Irvine, J., Miles, I. and Evans, J.). London, Pluto Press.
Home Office (1976) *Offences of Drunkenness, 1975, England and Wales*. London, HMSO.
Home Office (1978) *Criminal Statistics*. London, HMSO.
Home Office (1980) *Statistical Bulletin*, November.
Hyman, R. and Price, B. (1979) Labour statistics, in *Demystifying Social Statistics* (Edited by Irvine, J., Miles, I. and Evans, J.). London, Pluto Press.
The Independent Commission on Transport (1974) *Changing Directions: A Report from the Independent Commission on Transport*. London, Coronet.
Irvine, J., Miles, I. and Evans, J. (Editors) (1979) *Demystifying Social Statistics*. London, Pluto Press.
Jones, M. (1974) *Privacy*. London, David and Charles.
Katona, G., Strumpel, B. and Zahn, E. (1971) *Aspirations and Affluence*. New York, McGraw-Hill.
Kellner, P. (1977) Who runs Britain?, *Sunday Times*, 18 September.
Kinnersley, P. (1973) *The Hazards of Work*. London, Pluto Press.
Layard, R., Piachaud, D. and Stewart, M. (1978) *The Causes of Poverty*, Background Paper No. 5 to the Royal Commission on the Distribution of Wealth. London, HMSO.
McKeith, N. (1978) *The Women's Health Handbook*. London, Virago.
Meszaros, I. (1975) *Marx's Theory of Alienation* (4th edition). London, Merlin.
Miles, I. and Irvine, J. (1979) The critique of official statistics, in *Demystifying Social Statistics* (Edited by Irvine, J., Miles, I. and Evans, J.). London, Pluto Press.
Miliband, R. (1969) *The State in Capitalist Society*. London, Weidenfeld & Nicolson.
Mills, I. H. (1973) Endocrine and social factors in self-starvation amenorrhea, in *Symposium-Anorexia Nervosa and Obesity*, Royal College of Physicians of Edinburgh Publication No. 42, Edinburgh.
Mills, I. H. (1974) Social pressures and attempted suicide, *The Police Surgeon*, April 26-35.
MIND (1977) *Mental Health Statistics*. London, MIND.
Nairn, T. (1982) *The Break-Up of Britain*. London, New Left Books(second edition).

National Children's Bureau (1976) *Britain's Sixteen-Year-Olds*.
London, National Children's Bureau.
Nicholson-Lord, D. (1978) Simple sums floor vast majority of
pupils, *The Times*, 9 March.
Nichols, T. (1979) Social class: official, sociological and
marxist, in *Demystifying Social Statistics*. (Edited by
Irvine, J., Miles, I. and Evans, J.). London, Pluto Press.
Nossiter, B. (1978) *Britain: A Future That Works*. London,
André Deutsch.
NSPCC (1977) *Annual Report*. London, National Society for
Prevention of Cruelty to Children.
Oakley, A. (1974a) *The Sociology of Housework*. London, Martin
Robertson.
Oakley, A. (1974b) *Housewife*. Harmondsworth, Penguin.
Oakley, A. and Oakley, R. (1979) Sexism in official statistics,
in *Demystifying Social Statistics* (Edited by Irvine, J.,
Miles, I. and Evans, J.). London, Pluto Press.
Ollman, B. (1976) *Alienation* (2nd edition). London, Cambridge
University Press.
OPCS (1975) *The General Household Survey, 1972*. London, HMSO.
OPCS. (1978) *OPCS Monitor* (DH2 78/5), 11 July.
Orbach, S. (1978) *Fat is a Feminist Issue*. London, Paddington
Press.
Pearce, F. (1976) *Crimes of the Powerful*. London, Pluto Press.
Radical Statistics Health Group (1976) *Whose Priorities*?
London, Radical Statistics Group.
Radical Statistics Health Group (1977) *In Defence of the NHS*.
London, Radical Statistics Group.
Richardson, L. J. (1977) *Contemporary Social Mobility*. London,
Frances Pinter.
Lord Robens (Chairman) (1972) *Report of the Committee on Safety
and Health at Work*. London, HMSO.
Roy, R. (1976) *Wastage in the UK Food System*. London, Earth
Resources Research Ltd.
Royal Commission on the Distribution of Income and Wealth (1977)
Report No. 5 (Third Report on the Standing Reference),
Cmnd. 6999. London, HMSO.
Royal Commission on the Distribution of Income and Wealth (1978)
Report No. 6: Lower Incomes. London, HMSO.
RSPCA (1978) *One Hundred and Fifty-Fourth Annual Report 1977*.
Hopham, Royal Society for the Prevention of Cruelty to
Animals.
The Samaritans Central London Branch (1977) *Annual Report*.
Slough, The Samaritans Incorporated.
The Samaritans (1978) *The Samaritans: 25 Anniversary*. Slough,
The Samaritans Incorporated.

Schact, R. (1971) *Alienation*. London, George Allen & Unwin.
Select Commission on Violence in the Family (1977) *Violence to Children*. London, HMSO.
Stengel, E. (1973) To die or not to die, *New Society*, 15 March, 579-581.
Stradling, R. (1977) *The Political Awareness of the School Leaver*. London, Hansard Society.
Taylor, I., Walton, P. and Young, J. (1976) *Critical Criminology*. London, Routledge & Kegan Paul.
Taylor, R. (1974) Stress at work, *New Society*, 17 October, 140-143.
Tendler, S. (1977a) Police computer files cover poaching and being suspected, *The Times*, 10 December.
Tendler, S. (1977b) Special branch to put suspects names on computer file, *The Times*, 9 September
Tendler, S. (1977c) Steady rise in number of new drug addicts, *The Times*, 10 September.
Tendler, S. (1980) Number of new heroin addicts increasing by 20%, *The Times*, April.
Townsend, P. (1977) *The Failure to House Britain's Aged*. London, Help the Aged.
Thompson, E.P. (1965) The peculiarities of the English, in *Socialist Register* (Edited by Saville, J. and Miliband, R.). London, Merlin.
Thompson, E. P. (1979) *The Poverty of Theory*. London, Merlin.
Tunstall, J. (1977) The constrained freedoms of the British press, *Times Higher Education Supplement*, 24 June.
Urry, J. and Wakeford, J. (1973) *Power in Britain*. London, Heinemann.
Vaughan, M. (1977) Schoolchildren put on drugs because class behaviour does not fit, *The Times*, 1 February.
Wainwright, H. (1978) Woman and the division of labour, in *Work, Urbanism and Inequality* (Edited by P. Abrams). London, Weidenfeld & Nicolson.
Wardle, C. (1977) *Changing Food Habits in the UK*. London, Earth Resources Research Publications.
Waugh, S. (1977) *Needs and Provision for Young Single Homeless People*. London, Campaign for Single Homeless People.
Westergaard, J. and Resler, H. (1976) *Class in a Capitalist Society*. Harmondsworth, Penguin.
Wynn, M. and Wynn, A. (1977) *The Prevention of Premature Births*. London, Foundation for Education and Research in Child-rearing.
Young, R. (1977) More power for provincial groups, *The Times*, 2 September.

6
On Ways of Life in Poland

ANDRZEJ SICIŃSKI

This chapter focuses on the ways of life (WOL) and main styles
of life in contemporary Polish society.[1]* These, of course,
result from many events and processes that took place in post-
war Poland. Let us mention here the most important of them.
First, the immediate post-war period involved the reconstruction
both of the material basis of the everyday life of the population, and of the social structure. A confrontation between
the new economic and political system and certain national
traditions has been an important factor influencing WOL and
lifestyles. Secondly, there has been a substantial shift of
the population, during the last three decades, from rural to
urban living. During this period, technological and economic
'modernization' of the country has taken place, and one could
say at the moment that a mixture of underdeveloped, developed
and overdeveloped segments is present in our economy and society.

CHANGES IN LIFE CONDITIONS

Let us first consider those changes in the conditions of life
which have been crucial for the Polish WOL, and for which we
have reliable data.[2]
The Polish population has increased rapidly over the last 30
years: from 23,900,000 in 1946 (after a high mortality rate
during the war) to 34,000,000 in 1977.[3] Accompanied by a high
spatial and social mobility, this population increase has contributed to Poland becoming a kind of 'melting pot' of WOL and
lifestyles. Another important factor is the age structure of
the population. While in 1960 33.5 per cent of Poles were
younger than 15, and 5.0 per cent aged 65 or more, the respec-
tive figures for 1974 were 24.2 per cent and 9.4 per cent. Our
society is becoming older.

*Superscript numbers refer to notes at end of chapter.

As with the most developed countries, Poland has been faced
in recent decades with a shift towards the nuclear family. An
increasing tendency to marry at earlier ages has been apparent,
despite legal restrictions (men are not allowed to marry before
21, and women before 18, without court permission.
Another important tendency is shown in the decreasing number of
children in the family. But, by and large, one can say that
the Polish population is still more 'familistic' than that of
many other European societies. Thus, the marital status of the
adult population in 1975 was that some 28 per cent were un-
married, 62 per cent married, 8 per cent widowed, and 2 per
cent divorced.

One of the consequences of the Second World War for Poland
was a drastic change in the ethnic and regional structure of
our society. Before the war, ethnic minorities (Jews, Ukrain-
ians, and others) constituted about one-third of the population.
But nowadays Polish society is almost completely ethnically
homogeneous (reflecting in part the redrawing of state borders,
involving a decrease in area from 389,700 to 312,700 square
kilometres). This homogenization of the society has been accompanied by decreased differences between social strata and
regions.

The rural-urban shift is most important from the point of
view of changes in the Polish WOL. Fifty-four per cent of Poles
lived in towns in 1974, compared with 20 per cent in 1927, 37
per cent in 1946, and 48 per cent in 1960. In consequence, an
urban WOL now embraces a majority of the population; however,
this WOL, and the lifestyles of many town dwellers, are strongly
influenced by rural patterns. Differences between rural and
urban WOL, although clearly declining, are still particularly
significant.

There is not much data suitable for the analysis of changes
in the process of work, such as the effects of automation
(which has not yet advanced far in Poland), the increasing role
of non-manual labour, etc. Three aspects of employment can be
discussed usefully here, however. The first concerns the sec-
toral composition of employment, which is not as yet very
'modernized' compared to other industrial societies. Thirty-
nine per cent of employed people in 1975 worked in Sector 1
(primary production such as agriculture), 33 per cent in Sector
2 (manufacturing industry) and 28 per cent in Sector 3 (services). While these represent a considerable shift from the
corresponding data for 1950 — the percentages were respectively
57 per cent, 23 per cent and 20 per cent — other countries have
exhibited considerably greater decline in the primary sector
with associated increases in the secondary and tertiary sectors.
Women's employment is a second factor important for the WOL. A

rather high proportion of married women are in fact employed:
76.4 per cent in 1975. Thirdly, work still occupies 6 days of
the week: most employed people work a 46-hour week, with one
free Saturday a month.
     While it is impossible to go into detail about incomes here,
two points stand out. The first is the rather small differentiation of incomes: thus the ratio of incomes of blue-collar to
white-collar workers was 1:1.12 in 1956-9, as compared to 1:2.2
in 1937. (There is a lack of reliable data for more recent
years, but it is quite evident that incomes dramatically di-
verged after the middle 1970s.) Secondly, a rapid increase in
wages over the period 1971-4, of 6.8 per cent per annum,
together with a 5.9 per cent increase in peasants' disposable
incomes, has meant that the majority of the Polish population
can be said to be on the threshold of a new economic phase, one
of 'free consumption choices'. This is reflected in changing
standards of living, particularly in 1971-4. Some data on
general consumption trends are presented in Table 6.1.

Table 6.1
General Trends in Household Consumption Patterns (Poland)

	Household expenditure of:					
	Blue-collar workers			White-collar workers		
	1959	1963	1974	1959	1963	1974
Percentage spent on:						
Food	56.4	53.6	44.3	53.2	48.0	38.2
Culture and education	4.4	6.7	7.8	6.5	9.4	11.5

     One indicator of the standard of living is consumption of
meat: this was 54 kg per person per year in 1975, compared to
22.4 kg before the last war. This improvement is, among other
factors, connected with a modernization of the WOL of the urban
population, and a reduction of the dramatic gap between rural
and urban areas. On the other hand, a serious problem for our
society is alcoholism, which is reflected in an increase in the
consumption of alcohol (100 per cent): from 1.3 litres per person
pre-war to 7.8 litres in 1975.
     Another facet of the living standard is housing, and a good
indicator of the housing situation is the average number of
people living in each room. This was 1.21 persons in 1975
(1.14 in urban and 1.25 in rural areas), compared to 2.55 per-

sons in 1938, 1.75 in 1950 and 1.53 persons in 1960.
As for health services, various indicators demonstrate improvements here. In 1975, there were 55.1 hospital beds and 17
physicians per 10,000 inhabitants. For 1938, the relevant data
were 21.7 and 3.7 respectively, while there were 34.8 beds per
10,000 in 1950, with 5.4 physicians per 10,000 in 1953. However,
health services are clearly one of the most underdeveloped sectors of Poland's economy.
      The third most important determinant of changing WOL in Poland,
after urbanization and demographic shifts, is, in our opinion,
increasing education. While about 23 per cent of the population
(a much higher proportion in rural areas) was illiterate in
1931, this problem had been practically eliminated by the 1950s.
By 1973, about 20 per cent of the population (over 14 years of
age) had received at least a full secondary education. The
relative proportions of educated men and women are interesting:
among those aged 20-24, in 1976, 15.2 per cent of men, as compared to 18.7 per cent of women, had received higher education.
The main problems at present are the quality of primary and
secondary schooling, and the accessibility of university education.
      The mass media are well-known to influence lifestyles, and
here too there has been a rapid expansion in Poland over the
last two decades, although the figures are still lower than for
many other European countries. For every 1000 inhabitants in
1972, 228 copies of the 44 Polish newspapers were sold, and
there were 223 radios and 170 television sets.

SOME ASPECTS OF WAYS OF LIFE[4]

      Here we want to give a short characterization of particularly
important or specific trends in the Polish WOL. Unfortunately,
this will be unavoidably rather superficial, and to some extent
subjective. Invariably we have to deal with some 'averages'
here, and the use of an 'average' may be more or less meaningful, depending on the level of differentiation within a group
or society, and on the particular domain of social or psychological life. In particular, in spite of the decreasing differences in Poland between rural and urban areas, it is still
necessary to discuss the WOL of people living in rural and
urban areas separately.

The Rural Population

      A major trend, started before the Second World War and now

practically accomplished, involves the shift from a traditional
peasant culture to contemporary rural culture. In peasant culture the basic values surrounded the land and work on the land.
Conformity in attitudes, thought and behaviour characterized the
traditional WOL of peasants. The local community, isolated
from other segments of the population, strictly controlled
people's lives. The present rural style of life is incomparably
more open; nevertheless some vestiges of the old tradition still
remain.

As far as basic values are concerned, the main change has involved a shift from an agro-centric to a professional system of
values. This is particularly true of the younger generation.
Work on the land has become a form of work comparable with
others, and owning land is comparable to other sources of income. (Most land in Poland remains the private property of the
peasants, who sometimes own very small plots, perhaps of only 2
hectares.) Of course, people employed by state-owned farms
fully understand work on the land to be a kind of occupation,
similar in many respects to any other occupation.

Mechanization of work has helped decrease the dependence of
farmers on the natural rhythm of life and work, and also means
that the work is now incomparably less hard than it was before.
On the other hand, the division of labour among family members,
particularly between men's and women's activities, has not yet
changed considerably. A partnership model of the couple and
family is still not popular among peasants.[5]

Despite the fact that the post-war change in politico-economic
system led to the disappearance of two segments of the rural
population — very rich farmers, and very poor agricultural
workers — the rural WOL is now much more differentiated than
previously. This is a result of more general factors and influences; today the WOL differs according to the specialization
and size of the farm, the type of family, the age of people,
and so on.

Large changes in the standard of living and consumption have
taken place. The prestige role of material commodities (status
symbols) has increased throughout the rural population, and
particularly in its younger generations. In some regions and
in some groups (typically those attached to the land) patterns
of ostentatious consumption may even be observed. Consumption
patterns are developing under the impact of urban patterns,
though these influence different aspects of everyday life to
different degrees; their influence on hygiene, health care, and
nutrition is rather limited, for example. On the other hand,
some urban family and social customs, such as the celebration
of 'name-day', which was traditionally more popular in towns,
have been extended to rural areas.

The increase of individual autonomy, relative to dependence
upon work and family, has also influenced attitudes towards
leisure. In traditional peasant culture there was no distinction between working time and leisure time. Intensive work and
production gave life meaning, and participation in traditional
culture was not strictly separated from the work process.
Today, however, leisure becomes the main object of aspirations
and desires. Difficulties connected with satisfying these
aspirations in rural areas are one of the main reasons for a
flight of youngsters from the farms to cities. On the other
hand, the spread of television, importing an urban culture, and
the development of local clubs and 'houses of culture' help to
make leisure more attractive, even in rural areas.

The Urban Population

There is obviously no clear-cut division between rural and
urban WOL. A large number of small towns exist in contemporary
Poland, displaying rather 'intermediate' WOL. The following
discussion mainly deals with quite big towns, those with over
100,000 inhabitants. The great majority of their inhabitants
are employed by state-owned (or co-operative) enterprises.
(The private sector is quite small.) The kind of work, and its
location in one or other branch of the national economy, are
among the main factors determining income and social prestige.
The character of work influences the whole life of a person:
the organization of a day, the access to different kinds of
privileges, etc. Most town dwellers working in production and
services are of peasant origin (first, or sometimes second
generation). This colours human relations in the work-place
and also, for example, relations between officials and clients,
or between shop assistants and customers.
For the first two post-war decades people desired money for
its practical importance rather than as a source of social
prestige. The standard of living of the Polish population was
rather low, in comparison with most Western European countries
(and some Eastern European countries too), but to possess more
goods did not imply greater respectability. The standard of
living of the population began to rise markedly in the early
seventies. For some people and families this has meant being
able to quit living below a 'social minimum'; but in some segments of the population it has supported a rise of consumption-
oriented values. This was rather a new phenomenon in our society,
whose values had been connected, in the first place, more with
the ideals of the 'intelligentsia' than with a 'bourgeoisie'.
The housing situation remains very difficult. This is pos-

sibly the main factor restricting options, as far as life-styles
are concerned. The kind of flat occupied, and whether or not
one owns a car and (more recently) a summer house, significantly
differentiate the urban population.

For the majority of adults, leisure time is somewhat limited
because of such factors as engagement in extra work (for an
additional income), extra-mural education, the necessity of
commuting (and inadequate transport), poor services, and the
lack of labour-saving devices in homes.

The main differences in the use of leisure time relate to
education levels and age. While television is popular with all
segments of the population, theatre and concert halls mainly
play an important role for better-educated people. Cafés,
traditionally popular as gathering places and venues for political discussion, as well as a place for rendezvous, have lost
their importance, although they are still visited by youngsters,
retired people, and black-market men (to exaggerate the situation
a bit). The cinema is also particularly popular with youngsters.
Mass media are influential agents for importing foreign patterns
of WOL, particularly those from more economically advanced
countries.

There is rather limited frequency of such forms of social
contact as visits to homes. The exceptions are some traditional
occasions such as a 'name-day', a wedding party (when there are
visits of relatives, friends and acquaintances, sometimes in a
rather great number), or Christmas Eve supper and Christmas
Day (when there are visits by family members).

EVALUATIONS OF THE WAY OF LIFE

Evaluating WOL in terms of 'costs and benfits' is not a simple
task for at least two reasons. First, the results of such an
evaluation may vary, depending upon whether we take into account
the needs and interests of a given individual, or group interests
(e.g. those of a family or local community), or the interests
of the whole society. It is not true that all that is good for
Mr. or Mrs. X is necessarily good for the groups he or she
belongs to.

Secondly, we must distinguish between 'subjective' and 'objective' evaluations. Public opinion surveys provide an insight
into 'subjective' evaluations of the existing WOL.[6] These indicate that around one-half to two-thirds of adults, when asked
to evaluate the previous year, from a personal point of view,
do so positively; about one-third are ambivalent and one-eighth
negative. While, as usual with survey results, interpreting
these data is not easy, it does seem clear that dissatisfaction

214   The Poverty of Progress

with the existing WOL is the exception rather than the rule.
As 'objective' indicators, we will consider selected physical
anthropological data, as well as some data concerning the state
of health of the population.[7] First, it is interesting to note
a significant increase in the size of an 'average' Pole. While
in 1939 the size of a male draftee was 168-169 cm, by 1976 it
was 174-175 cm, which represents an increase of about 1.5 cm
per decade. In 1976, sons (aged above 18) were found to be
about 4 cm taller than their fathers, with daughters about 2 cm
taller than their mothers. These differences were greater in
families that had ascended up the social ladder. Generally
speaking, one can say that changes in life conditions and WOL
have supported a biological development of the Polish population,
particularly its formerly underprivileged segments.

There is also evidence for an earlier onset of puberty: thus
the menarche age was about one-quarter of a year lower in 1976
than in 1966. Significant differences exist here between rural
and urban populations (where the average age of menarche is
around 14 and 13 years respectively), and between girls growing
up in families with only one child compared to those with more
children (earlier menarche occurring in the first case). Significant differences still existed between the best and the
poorest educated people in 1966, but had almost disappeared by
1976. The earlier onset of puberty probably results from
changes in WOL; its evaluation from the point of view of interests of the society, or the individual, is a difficult task.

As far as health problems are concerned, Table 6.2 presents
ten indicators which other chapters in this book argue are
relevant for studying 'maldevelopment'. What do these data
reveal?

Table 6.2
Trends in Health and Disease in Poland

Year	Deaths per million population
(a) *Deaths caused by accidents, poisoning, injuries*	
1960	430
1970	600
1975	700
(b) *Homicide and wilful injuries*	
1960	15
1972	9

(cont.)

*(c) Deaths under 1 year of age per 1000 live
births*

Year	Total	0-29 days	1-11 months
1950	109.3	43.6	65.7
1960	54.8	25.1	29.7
1970	33.4	20.0	13.4
1974	23.7	15.8	7.9

(d) Life expectancy, by sex and age

	1931-2	1952-3	1960-1	1975
Males aged:				
0	48.2	58.6	64.8	67.0
10	52.2	56.8	59.7	
15				54.5
30	36.0	38.9	41.1	40.6
45				27.7
50	20.3	21.8	23.4	
60				15.7
70	8.3	9.1	9.8	
Females aged:				
0	51.4	64.2	70.5	74.3
10	54.0	61.4	64.7	
15				61.3
30	38.0	43.0	45.5	46.7
45				32.5
50	22.4	25.3	27.1	
60				19.4
70	9.2	10.6	11.4	

*(e) Mortality from cardiovascular diseases (items 390-458 in the
WHO classification). Deaths per 100,000 population*

Year	Males in towns	Males in rural areas	Females in towns	Females in rural areas
1966	249	249	257	256
1970	308	333	308	333
1975	359	416	351	404

(cont.)

(f) *Mortality from malignant tumours (including tumour of lym-phatic tissues: items 140-209 in the WHO classification). Deaths per 100,000 population*

Year	Males in towns	Males in rural areas	Females in towns	Females in rural areas
1965	130	126	131	108
1970	150	149	137	114
1975	167	170	144	123

(g) *Diseases of urban and rural population per 1000 persons, by sex, 1967-8*

Diseases (WHO classification)	Males in towns	Males in rural areas	Females in towns	Females in rural areas
Disease of nervous system and sense organs (340-98)	271	262	125	101
Diseases of eye (370-9, 765)	66	67	31	25
Diseases of ear (391-3)	45	36	22	18
Cardiovascular diseases (330-4, 400-68)	104	150	41	56
Diseases of respiratory system (470-527, 240-1)	611	571	264	210
Diseases of digestive system (530-87)	143	157	75	69
Diseases of genito-urinary system (590-637)	50	257	20	95
Diseases of skin (690-716, 242-4, 766)	161	144	97	74
Diseases of musculo-skeletal system (720-49)	82	102	45	43

(cont.)

(h) *Deaths by suicide and self-injuries, per 100,000 population*

1960	80
1970	110
1973	117
1975	110

(i) *Mentally-ill registered for the first time in infirmaries and clinics, per 100,000 population*

1962	351
1970	498
1972	518
1975	436

(j) *Admissions to mental hospitals, per 100,000 population*

Year	First admission	Readmissions	Total
1960	99	98	197
1965	126	130	256
1972	156	155	311
1975	172	195	367

First, certain of these indicators show that a whole range of diseases have become worse during recent decades, which does not speak well about the results of changing WOL. However, some indicators which can be treated as signifying positive social development (infant mortality, life expectancy, and also number of homicides) are, fortunately, improving.

Secondly, significant differences still remain between rural and urban areas. The rural WOL is more healthy. On the other hand, the urban WOL is more favourable in terms of the rate of biological development; this may relate to nutrition, or to social factors.

A third point arising from these data concerns sex differences. A majority of indicators are better for women than for men. Some diseases — surprisingly enough, cardiovascular diseases among them — do affect women more than men.

STYLES OF LIFE IN POLAND

It is possible to look at the style of life from several

different points of view. We have, as part of our research,
worked out various typologies of Polish life-styles. For example, one is based on different socio-economic conditions (e.g.,
the life-styles of blue- and white-collar workers from large-
and small-scale industry, etc.). It is worth saying a few
words on two dynamic typologies: the first one could be called
socio-historical, the second socio-psychological.[8]

Studies of social stratification in Poland show that, despite
considerable change in the social structure, we can still observe certain types of life-style which continue those existing before the Second World War. In particular, we may find a
current version of the intelligentsia's life-style (an 'elitist'
or, rather, 'pseudo-elitist' style of life); a new version of
that of the former petit bourgeoisie ('neo-bourgeois' style of
life), and, as already outlined, a current version of that of
the peasantry ('rural' style of life).[9]

The life-style of the intelligentsia has survived to this day,
even though it has ceased to belong exclusively to that stratum
(which has increased in number and disintegrated to some extent,
so that it now differs much less from others than it did before
1939). While no longer the life-style of an elitist social
group (as the intelligentsia had been), it nevertheless functions in social consciousness as the life-style of an elite.
Thus the term *pseudo-elitist* seems an appropriate description.
The archetypal feature of the traditional life-style of the
Polish intelligentsia was the prestige of education, which
determined membership of the elite. However, this education
was not viewed as the basis of professional skills: stress was
laid on general education, and on the associated ideal of an
educated person. This model was valid both within and beyond
the sphere of professional activity; indeed the life-style was
marked by a lack of any clear distinction between the professional and the non-professional sphere of life. One's professional work and leisure, consumption of material goods, participation in culture, the upbringing of children, and housing
standards, were all supposed to prove that one is an educated
person, a man or woman of 'culture', in the sense then current.

The present day version of this life-style differs from the
old pattern, above all in the attitude toward material goods.
This is associated with the increased spread of education,
which is accordingly losing its discriminant function. Increasing importance is now attached to material objects,
especially certain consumer goods, which supposedly testify to
one's membership of the elite.

The bourgeois life-style in Poland differed from that typical
of most Western European countries; given the lack of a numerous
and economically strong bourgeoisie, the petit bourgeois style of

life, which existed in Poland between the two World Wars, was
rather more important. Its most significant feature was the
priority given to material objects and money (wealth) as opposed
to aesthetic or ideological values. (In another terminology,
there was a preference 'to have' rather than 'to be'.) This
reflected the traditional bourgeois virtues: independence of
means, and the accumulation and possession of wealth. All other
values were subordinated to these, which resulted in little
importance being attached to participation in culture or in
entertainment, for example, and in one's family being treated
mainly as a community of interests.

Even though the bourgeoisie has vanished as a socially significant class in Poland, and despite the educational and cultural policy pursued since the Second World War, the old petit
bourgeois life-style has its continuation in what we have
termed the *neo-bourgeois* style of life. To understand its
continuing viability would require a deeper analysis: it certainly does not reduce to the survival of small petit bourgeois
groups, nor is it solely due to the social influence of that
class. It manifests itself not only in treating the possession
of material objects as the source and the indicator of all
values, but also in the emphasis laid on consumption (which
makes it differ from traditional bourgeois frugality and moderation). Further, this consumption-orientation involves a fas-
cination with the modern, and with the prestige of foreign-made
goods. Other features characteristic of the neo-bourgeois life-
style are a duality of the systems of values, between the
standards officially accepted and those which are observed in
actual conduct, and also a striving for security and 'stabiliza-
tion'.

The modern *rural* life-style continues traditions of the former
peasant style only in part and to a limited extent. While the
latter is tending to vanish, some of its elements are carried
to the towns as a result of migration from the countryside. We
have noted that there have been changes in the set of fundamental
values in the rural population, so that while the possession of
farming land, and labour, are still essential, they have become
instrumental values, seen in terms of increased income, better
living standards, and materializing one's aspirations.

Modernized farming techniques have greatly reduced dependence
on the rhythm of nature. At the same time dependence on fertilizers (244.1 kg per hectare in 1976, as against 49.1 in 1961)
and machines (36.7 hectares per tractor in 1975 as against
258.2 in 1960) has increased markedly.

The rural life-style also has a clearer demarcation than
previously between the farm as the place of gainful employment
and the household. However, personal contacts remain character-

istic and traditional customs and ceremonies are still stressed,
along with ostentatious celebration of holidays and party-
making. This last feature is one of the elements to have entered the urban life-style.

The pseudo-elitist, neo-bourgeois and rural styles of life —
which we have sought to demonstrate to be continuations of
earlier life-styles — and the working class style do not, of
course, exhaust all of the macro-social differentiations of
life-style in contemporary Poland. Furthermore, each of these
has variants according to age, living conditions, etc. But to
this typology based on the origins of major styles of life, we
need to add reference to the results of other changes in Polish
society.

In the Second World War Poland's economy was almost completely
destroyed. Since the war there have been revolutionary changes
in the class and strata structure of the population, in its
ethnic composition, and in the country's frontiers. These factors have led to the elimination of some life-styles and the
intermingling of others. But they have also tended to produce
a gradual unification of styles of life, although the product
that is emerging is not yet easy to define. Perhaps several
variations of this unified style are emerging, but at present
the only one clearly visible is that shaped by the impact of
patterns spread by the mass media: in other words, a *mass media*
style of life.

The main feature of this life-style is the lack of any distinct and coherent hierarchy of values, together with the lack
of any fixed models for everyday manners, spending leisure time,
dressing, fitting out one's home, etc. Incidental elements,
drawn from various styles of life, and even from various countries, are combined syncretically, so that it would even be
legitimate to speak about a *sui generis* 'styleless ' life-style.
Hence this style of life, with all its variations, is not a
trustworthy testimony of a person's group membership or his or
her aspirations. For while it largely depends on what at a
given moment comes from the mass media, it must also depend on
the supply of the various consumer goods on the home market.
It thus also varies widely according to a person's financial
position, age group, profession, etc.

We may hypothesize that the style of life has been, over the
last decades, and will be, in the foreseeable future, less and
less connected with a person's membership of a social stratum.
Instead, it increasingly depends on other criteria of differentiation, and on people's own choices. The question arises
of what factors may come to affect such options, and what — in
place of, or alongside the social structure — will determine
differences in the style of life. It is legitimate to suppose

that an individual's personality will become such a decisive
factor.
   Thus, regardless of the typology of life-styles based on
criteria drawn from social history, future work might fruitfully
consider a typology referring to those differences between human
beings which are in the sphere of social psychology.[10]

CONCLUSIONS

   By and large, it is clear that WOL in Poland are still changing rather rapidly, and that new styles of life are emerging.
These processes are mainly a result of certain 'objective'
changes in conditions of life, demographic factors, international
relations, and so on, rather than a manifestation of people's
innovations.
   It is true that we have groups advocating a range of 'alternative' WOL and life-styles — and we intend to present their
contribution in later studies. However, such groups are as yet
not very numerous in Poland, are even less influential and, in
general, are not very original in their ideas. An explanation
of this situation could be the fact that the Polish population
is still, to a large extent, engaged in satisfying its basic
needs, in solving its 'basic' problems. Such a situation favours
an interest in improving dominant ways and styles of life, than
any search for more imaginative alternatives.

POSTSCRIPT

   This article was written before the economic problems of 1980,
and the subsequent dramatic flux in Polish political institutions
and in public life more generally. These developments will undoubtedly influence the WOL and life-styles of Poles. At the
time of writing (the end of 1980) it is impossible to forecast
the immediate consequences of this ongoing process with any
reliability.[11]

NOTES

1. This chapter represents a general reflection on WOL and
life-styles in Poland based mainly on the analysis of existing
data. Systematic empirical research on these issues was com-
menced in 1977 as a cross-national comparative project initiated
jointly by the Division for Life-Style Studies, Institute of
Philosophy and Sociology, Polish Academy of Sciences, and by
the Finnish Academy; the studies are directed in Poland by the

present author, and in Finland by Professor J. P. Roos. In these studies we have distinguished between 'way of life' and 'style of life'. 'Way of life' is understood here in the sense used by Marx (Marx and Engels, 1845-6), as an objective category characterizing human existence. 'Style of life' is a sociological category, reflecting the life of particular subjects as revealed by empirical analysis of human behaviour and its motives. 'Way of life' can embrace behaviour fully determined, or even imposed upon a subject; 'style of life', in contrast, implies the existence of alternatives, and the making of choices.

2. The main source of the statistical data presented here is *Maly Rocznik Statystyczny (Concise Statistical Yearbook)*, Warsaw, 1978. The scheme used for organizing the data was proposed by Haranne and Siciński (1978).

3. The population in 1937 had been 34,500,000, although the borders have since been redrawn. The present population density, incidentally, is 110 per square kilometre.

4. This section is based on material presented by E.Jagiello-Lysiowa (rural population) and M. Czerwinski (urban population) in Siciński (1978a).

5. A particular WOL may be observed among those peasants who, in addition to working on their farms, are employed in towns. This complex phenomenon cannot be taken up here.

6. The results here are based on surveys carried out by the Public Opinion and Programme Evaluation Studies Centre of Polish Radio and Television in the mid-1970s.

7. I gratefully acknowledge the help of the Anthropological Division of the Polish Academy of Sciences, Wroclaw, led by Professor Tadeusz Bielicki, which provided me with anthropological data. Also, I express my thanks to the statistical groups at the State Institute for Hygiene, Warsaw, led at the time by the late Professor Feliks Sawicki, for help in locating and elaborating indicators of health and disease. The main sources drawn upon are *Rocznik Demograficzny (Demographic Yearbook) (1973)*, and *Rocznik: Statystyczne Uchrony Zdrovia (Statistical Yearbooks of the Health Services)(1974; 1976)*.

8. The socio-historical typology was proposed by Aldona Jawlowska and Edmund Mokrzycki, in Siciński (1978a).

9. The workers' style of life differs again from those outlined
above, and a distinction must be made between the traditional
and modern versions of this life-style. The former was shaped
between the wars in the workers' milieux of large industrial
centres, of which only a few then existed; its values and patterns have probably penetrated the majority of life-styles in
Poland today (except for the neo-bourgeois style). But these
have been in turn overtaken by a modern working-class life-
style, which has taken shape over recent decades and is not a
direct continuation of that traditional life-style.

10. Proposals for such a typology may be found in a contribution by the present author in Siciński (1978).

11. Some prognoses concerning general trends in Polish styles
of life are presented in Siciński (1980).

BIBLIOGRAPHY

Haranne, M. and Siciński, A. (1978) *Changes of Life-Styles in
    Finland and Poland.* Research Report No. 3, University of
    Joensuu, Academy of Finland.
Marx, K. and Engels, F. (1845-6) *The German Ideology* (English
    edition, 1964). London, Lawrence and Wishart.
Siciński, A. (Editor) (1976) *Styl zycia. Koncepcje i propo-
    zycje* (in Polish)*(Styles of Life: Conceptions and Proposals).*
    Warsaw, PWN.
Siciński, A. (Editor) (1978a) *Styl zycia. Przemiany we wspolc-
    zesnej Polsce* (in Polish) *(Styles of Life: Changes in Con-
    temporary Poland).* Warsaw, PWN.
Siciński, A. (1978b) The concepts of 'need' and 'value' in the
    light of the systems approach, *Social Science Information*
    17 (1), 71-91.
Siciński, A. (1979a) Theoretical assumptions of empirical re-
    search of specific ways of everyday life-styles, *The Greek
    Review of Social Research,* no. 35, 67-74.
Siciński, A. (1979b) Ways of life, style of life, and quality
    of life in Eastern European social studies. Paper presented
    at WFSF/Poland 2000 Conference on 'Styles of Life, World
    and National Problems', Grzegorzewice, Poland, June 1980.
    (Abbreviated version of a study prepared for UNESCO, 'Prob-
    lems of Quality of Life in Eastern European Social Studies',
    mimeo, Warsaw).
Siciński, A. (1980) Tendencies of changes in the style of life:
    Introductory remarks, in *Towards Poland 2000: Problems of
    Social Development* (Edited by Danecki, J.). Wroclaw, Ossol-
    ineum.

7

Alternative Ways of Life in The Netherlands

ANNEKE SCHIPPER-VAN OTTERLOO AND PETER ESTER

ALTERNATIVE WAYS OF LIFE: AN EXAMPLE AND SOME QUESTIONS

People dissatisfied with the Dominant Way of Life (DWL) in the Netherlands can nowadays choose from a variety of alternative ways of life (AWL). Guidelines and models as to how they should, or at least could, live part or all of their lives in alternative ways are available in numerous forms. There are alternative journals, books, shops, living and/or working communities, farmers and other producers, health centres and practitioners, study and meditation centres, restaurants, schools, etc. Certain of these alternatives seem to have been increasing in number and receiving more public attention in recent years.

One notable example of this is the journal *Onkruid* (Weed). Founded in 1978, this bi-monthly publication advocates a 'natural way of life' and offers, besides the more familiar articles on organically grown food, organic cultivation, meditation and the 'Bhagwan' cult, an 'alternative encyclopedia'. This is presented as an 'alphabetic guide to the alternative life' for the perplexed. Various 'authorities' from the alternative world contribute to its columns, which cover the fields of alternative communities, agriculture, yoga and Eastern religion, food, health care, environmental issues, parapsychology, esoteric movements, astrology, and small-scale and soft technology. To those unfamiliar with the alternative literature, this presents a quite remarkable collection of subjects indeed! Such subjects, however, are quite characteristic for this journal, which is produced by a large mainstream publisher but aims at bridging the gulf between the 'alternative world' and the general public. This aim has apparently not been without success, for, according to one of the editors (personal communication), sales have risen sharply (to 30,000 copies by late 1979, half of these represented by regular subscriptions).

This is, of course, only one example of publications advocating AWL practices. In any evaluation of the overall impact of AWL in the Netherlands, one might ask, first, to what extent the subject area covered by *Onkruid* is representative of the activities of most people in the 'alternative world' which evidently exists in the Netherlands? And what subcultures are there within this world? Secondly, how did this alternative world or alternative movement originate, and which groups use the term 'alternative' in order to indicate a special way of life? Have earlier groups similarly proclaimed themselves 'alternative'?

This chapter will attempt to provide some answers to these questions. First, however, we will focus on the way in which industrialization and overdevelopment present a frame of reference for understanding AWL. This will involve considering the central value orientations that act as distinguishing characteristics of AWL. A more extensive description and analysis of several forms of AWL — those centred around problems of ecology and identity — constitutes our main empirical material. Next, we consider the New Life Style Movement, which explicitly seeks to combine all these concerns; and, finally, we end with some conclusions and critical remarks.

INDUSTRIALIZATION, FUNDAMENTAL PROBLEMS OF LIFE, AND CENTRAL VALUES

We begin our analysis by relating together three fundamental human problems in terms of the broad definition of way of life (WOL) which Galtung (1978) has posed as a question of 'what to do, when and where, how, with whom and why?' This definition implies that people are always confronted with questions or problems: their WOL is an answer or solution to them. The more fundamental problems can be considered as resulting from people's existential condition of being dependent on:

(a) *Nature*, or on one's physical surroundings - e.g. how to find food and shelter;
(b) *Other people*, or on each other - e.g. communication, power relations, authority, participation, emancipation;
(c) *The inner self*, or on oneself - e.g. psychic and religious problems; problems of self-control and identity.[1]*

Let us try to clarify the complex relationship between these three levels of human problems using the example of natural resource depletion. This can be considered as a problem of inter-

---

* Superscript numbers refer to notes at end of chapter.

action with our physical environment. We cannot succeed in exercising some control over this problem, however, without some form of co-operation with other people. Therefore, governments may need to enlist the co-operation of their citizens, and of other governments to conserve resources. This interdependence in itself creates a host of problems, of which those concerning power differences and their consequences are most crucial. On this inter- and intra-societal level we only have to look at oil politics, for instance, to get some idea of the complicated character of these interdependencies. But in trying to solve the problem of distributing scarce natural resources we also meet with the problems posed by our own inner selves. Limits to energy consumption, for example , may evoke fears, wants and other emotional feelings within individuals. At any rate, considerable self-control or self-discipline seems necessary to overcome these problems of scarcity: we have to learn temperance in driving, in heating, in eating, indeed in our whole WOL.

In the historical course of Western societies, very specific solutions have been worked out for each of the above-mentioned problems, resulting in rather distinct WOL. The most characteristic solution to our first level problems — those concerning nature — over recent centuries seems to have involved industrialization and technological development. Industrial and technological development, although originally initiated by groups of individuals, have nowadays become relatively autonomous processes. They were, and still are, accompanied by several other developments, indicated by such terms as 'modernization', 'democratization', 'urbanization', 'rationalization' and 'secularization'. It is now merely a platitude to say that since the onset of industrialization, people's relationships to nature, to each other, and to their own selves have completely changed. It is not our intention to expand upon these changes here, although we will demonstrate that the various forms of AWL described in this paper are intimately linked to the very beginnings of industrial development. This is not to say that AWL began with industrialization. Alternative ways of life and countercultural movements have been built on traditions preceding industrial developments, such as medieval ascetic cloisters.

Dominant (i.e. industrial) solutions, and thus the DWL in Western industrial countries, are described by Galtung, Poleszynski and Wemegah (Chapter 1) as reflecting 'overdevelopment'. Roughly speaking, they use this term to refer to an imbalance between the increasing production of material goods and a decreasing degree of satisfaction of personal needs. Overemphasis on material consumption, at the expense of non-material needs,

leads to a very lop-sided quality of life in these countries.
The concept of 'overdevelopment' can be regarded as presenting
an alternative socio-economic theory, countering dominant growth
theories and the use of GNP per capita as a measure of development and welfare. Personal growth, which can be achieved by
fulfilling all fundamental material and non-material needs, is
the alternative criterion of development (Galtung *et al.*, 1974;
Galtung, 1978).

But AWL phenomena, while seeming to present useful possibilities for coping with many of today's pressing social problems,
are not only recognizable in the contemporary stage of overdevelopment. AWL have been attempted before the development of
our present highly industrialized and technologized societies.
In general, those groups and individuals feeling ambivalent to,
or actually disadvantaged by, socio-economic changes have always
sought to oppose them in many different ways. Previous counter-
cultural and counterstructural activities are comparable in
approach and concern to the more recent AWL movements of the
1960s and 1970s. It is clear that a historical perspective is
necessary in any attempt to study AWL. This has, unfortunately,
been lacking in many previous studies of the subject.

While the three fundamental human problems mentioned above
form one criterion for the selection and description of AWL
in the Netherlands, we also need to take into account a second:
the *central value orientations* of this movement. Invariably the
particular solutions people choose in dealing with urgent problems need to be legitimized in the face of competing solutions
and criticism. Thus, in searching for solutions, people develop coherent sets of knowledge and belief systems (which
since industrial times have become more scientific in nature);
these present clear value orientations. Often such systems of
thought are expanded to form ideologies, religions or world
views, which, we would argue, are crucial elements in distinguishing between DWL and AWL. We will therefore concentrate
upon such value differences here.

Although some differences in conception as to what AWL are,
or should be, appear in the literature, the following clusters
of value-orientation principles seem to be regarded as essential
elements.[2] These are: (i) *restraint, moderation* and *smallness*
(as opposed to *insatiability* and *gigantism* — which both charac-
terize 'overdeveloped' societies); (ii) *participation, justice*
and *sustainability;* and (iii) *security, welfare, identity* and
freedom.

These rather abstract terms become meaningful when seen in
the context of the wider theoretical frameworks into which they
fit. They are not mutually exclusive: on the contrary, they
overlap and may be partially reduced to each other. Moreover,

they are not all at the same level of abstraction, referring respectively to (i) *structural* and *cultural conditions* of development; (ii) *means* and *ends* to realize a just, participatory and sustainable society; and (iii) material and non-material *needs* which call for an alternative society. Whether expressed as needs, means or otherwise, value criteria are at the base of all these terms and principles. In Fig. 7.1 we attempt to schematize the relationships between the three problem levels distinguished previously and the central value orientations around which AWL are structured.

Fundamental human problems	Clusters of central value orientations	Forms of AWL
People's (dependent) relationship with nature	Smallness sustainability restraint/moderation	AWL/movements concerned with mainly ecological problems
People's (dependent) relationship with other people	Participation social justice	Democratization and Emancipation movements
People's (dependent) relationship with themselves	Security welfare identity freedom	AWL/movements mainly centred around identity

Fig. 7.1   A preliminary classification of AWL.

Alternative groups and movements develop around these different concerns: the different sets of value orientations legitimate the various alternative solutions. AWL primarily centre around particular sets of values, underlined in Fig. 7.1, but these are not necessarily exclusive: other values may also be involved to a lesser degree. It is our impression that groups and individuals in the Netherlands considering themselves 'alternative' are not equally strongly concerned with all the value orientation principles mentioned above. Research findings presented in the following sections confirm this impression.

Although the three forms of AWL are interdependent, manifestations of AWL centred around concerns about ecology and identity have, in our opinion, more to do with 'overdevelopment' than has the tendency towards democratization. Moreover, analysis of material on AWL reveals, as we shall see, a conspicuous coherence of ecological and identity concerns. For this reason, we will discuss AWL concerned with ecology and identity together, after first briefly considering democratization issues.

*AWL CENTRED AROUND PROBLEMS OF DEMOCRATIZATION AND
EMANCIPATION*

The most appropriate sociological concepts to describe and
analyse changed social relations in Western industrialized
countries since the last century are: *democratization* and *emancipation*. The balance of power has shifted in numerous areas
of social life but especially in working relations.[3] In all of
these areas, dominant conceptions of social injustice and acceptable life-styles have been criticized, in various ways, by
different social movements. Alternatives were conceptualized,
fought for, and sometimes realized. Balances of power shifted
gradually in favour of those holding more inferior positions:
power differences diminished between social classes, governments
and citizens, men and women, older and younger people, etc.
These developments frequently involved violent struggles where
terms like democratization and emancipation were guiding principles. Industrialization provided a new impulse for these
movements, which repeatedly came into existence. Most recently,
in the 1960s, concern about participation and decentralization,
as opposed to bureaucracy and technocracy, has also been clearly
expressed. At about the same time the idea of social justice
was extended to a global scale, as shown by opposition to the
wide gap between rich and poor countries.

Unlike such contemporary criticism of the DWL, the democratization and emancipation movements did not point to overdevelopment tendencies. On the contrary, they criticized the lack of
access of particular social strata in society (labourers, women,
students) to political and economic power. Some examples of
the movements involved in this type of criticism of the DWL
over the past century can illustrate this point quite clearly.

Since the late nineteenth century, radical changes have taken
place in *working relations*. Of course, the labour movement
with its main social institution, the trade union, has played a
crucial part here. Unions were founded from 1871 onwards (the
ANVW was the first general union). Like industrialization, the
development of trade unionism started relatively late in the
Netherlands. In fighting often rather ignominious working conditions, the labour movement succeeded in improving working
life, quite markedly in many areas — for example, with shorter
working hours, abolition of child labour, higher wages, better
working conditions and the establishment of works councils.
These successes — confirmed by law — were mainly obtained in
the period between 1906 and 1940.[4] Renewed economic growth
since the Second World War made substantial rises in workers'
incomes possible, and this facilitated a process of embourgeoise-
ment and the integration of workers into welfare society. But

in the 1960s, trade unions began to adopt a more critical
stance towards the distribution of power and participation in
society.
Broadly similar developments can also be seen in regard to
authority relations. Already at the beginning of this century
a number of social groups were expressing resistance to existing
authority relations, arguing that radically new social conceptions were needed. For example, the movement for universal
franchise achieved marked successes when, in 1917, a change in
the law enabled men to vote independently of their social
position, with the general franchise for women established a
few years later. Drastic changes in authority relationships
have again been taking place in Dutch society since 1960 within
a wide range of social settings. The 'Provo-movement', which,
often by bizarre methods, ridiculed the establishment (mainly
in Amsterdam) should be mentioned in this respect.[5] Some of
the former leaders of this movement later founded a very non-
traditional political party, the 'Kabouters' (Gnomes), which
succeeded in gaining a number of seats on the Amsterdam municipal
council. Important themes in the programme of this party were
direct democracy, environmental protection, soft technology,
small-scale organization, liveable cities, free public transport, and the like. Many of their political issues and conceptions have since been taken over by the other political parties,
and as such can be said to have had an effect on the DWL.
The student movement, too, strongly criticized traditional
patterns of power and authority relations; in particular, it
fought for more democratized universities, much of the impetus
here being derived from earlier involvement in anti-Vietnam
war activities. The movement for the democratization of universities has functioned as a crucial medium for the political
socialization of many students, and, while its ideals were only
partly realized, the administrative organization of the universities has been drastically changed. Again, this change was
confirmed by law, and shows the way that the DWL can accommodate
to change.
Another social movement that has undoubtedly had important
consequences for the relationship between generations was
shaped by several youth subcultures which were very active in
the 1950-70 period: especially the rock and roll, and 'flower
power' movements. By the end of this period Amsterdam was
well-known as an international centre for all kinds of youth
subcultures, whose adherents would gather in certain spots in
the city and sleep in the parks. They had their own life-
styles, philosophies, forms of dress and communication, and,
later, their use of drugs. Although it is difficult to describe exactly the influence these subcultures had on the DWL,

one could say that the relationships between older and younger
generations have perhaps become more open, tolerant, and flexible. The tuition of parents by their children, for example,
and a more informal way of dressing, are much more common now.
Finally, democratization and emancipation processes during
this century could also be said to have had an impact on *relations between the sexes*. The feminist movement, already active
early in this century, has served as an important 'consciousness
raising' movement to many men and women alike. Though feminism
covers the activities of many divergent groups, it has certainly
contributed to changes in traditional sex roles. At first,
changes were restricted to achieving a more equitable position
for women within the family. (Not until 1968 did a ruling remove from law the exclusive masculine headship of marriages,
for instance). However, more recent waves of feminism — starting at the end of the 1960s — have demanded and achieved
changes in the overall societal positions of women. Women are
now catching up with men as far as their participation in
formal education, and to a lesser degree in employment, is con-
concerned.[6] Thus, social relations have changed quite drastically across a whole range of different areas in society. These
changes have clearly been influenced by alternative ways of
thinking, acting and feeling.

AWL CENTRED AROUND PROBLEMS OF ECOLOGY AND IDENTITY

By about 1870, the Netherlands had successfully mastered the
process of industrial and technological innovation, so that the
natural environment no longer seemed to pose important problems.
Except for farmers and a few other groups remaining directly
dependent for their livelihood on it, nature disappeared, as
it were, from most people's visual field. Yet certain groups
of people began to oppose industrial and technological development as the effects of such change became clear. A romantic
back-to-nature movement originating in circles of artists,
authors and painters developed. Earlier centuries, of course,
also had their revaluations of nature; but at the end of the
nineteenth century such ideas again gained in strength. More
recently, in our period of overdevelopment, consciousness of
the fundamental survival value for human existence of a balanced
natural environment has broken through: nature has become a
problem again. Various forms of AWL develop around principles
of smallness, restraint, moderation and sustainability.
Forms of AWL concerned with identity issues are harder to
distinguish. Questions about the purpose of life and the
meaning of relationships with others and the world, and a search

for identity, seem to become especially prominent when self-
evident answers have disappeared or have lost their plausibility,
as happens in periods of accelerating social change. Further,
overdevelopment of material, and an underdevelopment of non-
material or emotional, aspects of life was among the outcomes
of industrialization. In the Netherlands, as in other countries,
a number of revivalistic and esoteric movements attempted to
counter this imbalance in the late nineteenth century. Similar
movements are currently regaining importance and can be considered as manifestations of AWL centred around identity. In
looking at these developments in greater detail, we shall see
that identity concerns have been strongly linked to concern
about ecology.

Even at the turn of this century, when the Netherlands was
experiencing an increase in affluence, improving dietary and
housing conditions, decreasing illiteracy, alcoholism and birth
rates, and expanding its cities, phenomena that can be viewed
as relating to 'overdevelopment' had already begun to manifest
themselves. Wealthy people were fleeing from the cities into
the countryside, while a renewed romantic appraisal of nature
was budding in certain circles of painters and writers. In the
movement of 'De Tachtigers', the effort to reform literature
had a much wider impact than on poetry alone, for it also put
stress on social reform. The founding, in 1906, of the first
important society for environmental protection — 'Natuurmonumen-
ten' — is another case in point. This 'back-to-nature' trend
of several elite groups can be considered as a reaction to
processes of differentiation and specialization which were
spreading rapidly with the industrial WOL.

At the same time, another trend became discernible: the incidence of nervous and psychic complaints began to increase.
Also, increasing numbers of people were leaving the traditional
Christian churches — whereas only 2.2 per cent of the population
did not belong to any church in 1899, this figure has risen to
around 30 per cent by 1980. People were already beginning the
search for alternative solutions to problems of identity at the
turn of the century. Thus, Jelgersma, a well-known Dutch
psychiatrist working around 1900, opined that:

> We experience today the remarkable phenomenon that
> people who lost their old beliefs, accepted new ones:
> the spiritists and theosophists and many others prove
> this. . . . Most people have an intense need . . .
> for certainty and to this goal only a belief or some-
> thing that resembles it, can serve . . . this other
> 'something' can take very different forms . . .

vegetarianism, Christian Science, anarchism, theosophy,
faith healing, pure life, antivivisectionism . . .
this is no complete list at all. (cited in de Boer,
1972, p. 29)

Among these new beliefs we can note the striking influence of
Eastern-inspired religions and philosophies: an 'Eastern Renais-
sance', which originated in the late eighteenth century, gained
a new impulse in Western countries at the end of the nineteenth
century. Thus societies for theosophy and anthrosophy, where
restrictive food rules play a major role, were formed. A sociological inquiry into these new religious groups in the Netherlands, reporting in 1927, mentioned about thirty different
groups. These were divided into spiritualistic-occultistic
groups (Rosicrucians, Sufis, Mazdaznans, Psycho-Synthesists, etc.
and groups based more on 'intuition and spontaneous religious
and social feelings' (such as Woodbrookers, religious-socialist
groups, and the 'New Thought' Association which was characterized by an optimistic mood and enjoyment of art and nature)
(Hofstra, 1927). These new groups often received more attention
than their numbers might warrant, and were restricted mainly to
elite or at least middle class circles.

A distinctive aspect of this period, aptly labelled by the
historian Romein (1976) as 'the era of a hundred-and-one prophets'
was the blending of both developments touched on above: concerns
about nature and ecology interpenetrate with those of religion
and identity. Thus, the wealthy people, mentioned earlier as
settling in the countryside, are described as:

> the drop-outs of nobility and the bourgeoisie who
> couldn't adapt themselves and left their own community
> . . . to fight for a better world. Their lifestyle
> was extraordinary, they were strangely clothed in the
> so-called Reform dress, slept with open windows, fre-
> quently prepared their meals according to vegetarian
> principles and abstained from smoking and alcohol.
> Handicrafts like pottery, weaving and forging of iron
> ornaments were popular among them, as were spiritual-
> istic seances. They were fighting for a better world
> against all kinds of evils — animal torture, child
> and female labour, harsh prison conditions, inequality
> between the sexes. They were filled with a hatred
> against the commercializing and industrializing so-
> ciety that was destroying the landscape, polluting
> the air and poisoning the food for the sake of profit
> and gain. (De Rek, 1978, p. 20)

Other settlers in the countryside were still more radical,
adding to these concerns AWL centred around problems of democ-

racy, equality and emancipation. Intellectuals and artists sought to practice agricultural living in communes, frequently based on anarcho-socialist ideals. Private ownership was repudiated and communards shared vegetarian principles and a repugnance of modern industrial life. Walden, the most famous of these communes, involving about 10-15 people around 1900, was intended to form a 'counterweight to the prevailing disorder based on the blind quest for personal profit that was causing millions to starve amidst affluence.[7] It lasted for 9 years, in the end failing due to an insufficient sense of responsibility on the part of the communards, an inadequate knowledge of agriculture, financial problems, and finally a flow of social 'misfits' to the commune.

A similar blend of concerns can be recognized in the 'red and blue' — socialist and temperance — youth movements that flourished in the Netherlands in the 1920s and a few decades hence. Romantic longing for natural and simple WOL went together with an optimistic and idealistic view of the possibilities for reform. Instead of smoking, drinking and/or eating meat, the 'blue' young people undertook a crusade 'against the lazy and banal hedonists of our civilization in decay' (Harmsen, 1975, p. 96). A comparable spiritual emphasis was characteristic in general of the 'red' movements too. In the 1930s the lofty ideals of purity and inner reform, advocated by the 'blue' movement, evolved into radical pacifism and socialism; 'blues' and 'reds' met each other here, and their practices such as camping clearly did affect the DWL.

It can thus be seen that many of the elements characteristic of these movements during the first three decades of this century present a clear indication of the existence, and the interrelation, of concerns over problems of ecology and identity. (Frequently, too, these movements took up issues related to democratization and equality.) Conceptions and orientations central in modern attempts to develop AWL — such as 'smallness', 'restraint', 'identity', sometimes combined with 'participation' and 'social justice' — were already recognizable in these early AWL movements. Then and now, one can identify a striking preoccupation with a simple and natural way of life, promising better mental and bodily health or stability, often setting this in the context of a turn to the esoteric and occult. The question that arises in both cases is whether we are dealing with retreat from and compensation for, or with active resistance against, the DWL. Definite answers are difficult to come by, although it does seem that esoteric culture invariably comes to play a creative role during periods of major sociocultural transition.

During the next few decades other, more material, problems came to occupy the Dutch nation. Depression, war, and the period of ensuing economic reconstruction forced people to moderation and restraint through necessity rather than choice: the struggle for naked existence claimed most efforts. By the second half of the 1950s, new signs of AWL began to appear. In this more recent period, a real outburst of AWL activity has addressed all three problem areas, though not always at the same time. Roughly speaking, there seems to have been a shift in emphasis from the problems of democracy and emancipation (which were preoccupations of the 1960s and first half of the 1970s) to those of ecology and identity during the last decade. In the first period there was a great deal of very open public activity, frequently taking place in the streets and receiving much attention from the mass media. Often through demonstrations, students and other sections of youth voiced their criticism of all aspects of the 'technocratic society'. 'Participation', 'decentralization' and 'social justice' seemed to be the main issues at stake. These developments, which took place in practically all Western countries, and which have been extensively described by a variety of journalists and scholars, need no further elaboration here.[8]

There is some debate, however, as to the origins of present concern with AWL: is this to be considered as a more moderate, and sometimes introverted, continuation of the movements of the 1960s? Or are we witnessing a withdrawal from political action, directed to 'structural' change, into activity mainly focussing around individual concerns? Certainly, ecology-oriented AWL seem to express more 'structural' aims and can thus be considered in some way as successors of the 1960s democratization movements. But this concern is rather less evident in identity-oriented AWL.

Ecological problems really began to attract attention in the Netherlands after publication of the *Limits to Growth* study (Meadows *et al.*, 1972). At this time, a host of new organizations and initiatives concerning the environment sprang up, while political parties and government agencies also became preoccupied with the new topic: a true ecological movement had been born. The Provos, although mainly concerned with authority problems, had already addressed these concerns in their 'white plans': thus white bicycles and small electric cars, to be used freely by everyone, were their solutions to city traffic and pollution problems. A few years later an extra-parliamentary opposition was to develop and begin a long fight against the asphaltization of what green countryside was left in this extremely urbanized and densely populated country. They were at least partially successful: road constructions were postponed; the extension of polluting industries was prevented. Another consequence was the establishment of new 'inspraak' (participation) procedures by local government. At the same time, countercultural groups also became more preoccupied with 'nature'. Simple and natural living of several varieties — sleeping in the open air in Amsterdam (Dam Square, Vondelpark), eating organic food, founding agrarian communes and co-operatives in the country, and so on — gained in popularity, mostly among young people.

Identity problems seem to have been taken up in a broad sense in other aspects of the counterculture. In particular, interest grew in magic, in Eastern knowledge and religion, and in folklore and astrology, accompanied by widespread usage of drugs. An esoteric and occult cultural climate prevailed, with Amsterdam as its 'magical centre'. Again, a common set of alternative solutions to ecological and identity problems, comparable in many respects to those developed earlier in the century, is clearly evident.

Developments over the last few years show that the concern with both these problems has continued, although activities in these fields are less frequently 'hot news'. The ecological movements became channelled for the great part into more organized, overarching structures, functioning as pressure groups trying to influence government decisions. The actual practice of ecologically conscious AWL seems to be carried out on only a very limited scale. Perhaps this is related to the fact that the general and widespread feelings of crisis and anticipation of imminent ecological or energy disaster, so evident around the time of the 1973/4 oil crisis, seem to have become somewhat less intense since then. The worsening economic situation has also directed people's attention to other, more short-term, problems like wages and unemployment. Notwithstanding these material concerns, the number of new cars sold reached a peak at the end of the 1970s, while few people worry about speed limits any more. As to identity issues, there is an extensive psycho-therapeutic industry, while yoga, meditation, and similar techniques, as well as more 'natural' food habits, seem to have also spread to older and more 'established' people — middle-class housewives, for example. The readers of *Onkruid* can presumably be found in these groups too. This trend reflects changes in fashion and commerce, and, perhaps, a shift in priorities from more structural types of changes to more individual ones.

Evidence for change during this period also comes from the activities of the elites within the AWL groups originally

raising matters of democracy, ecology and identity. An example
is found in the career of Roel van Duyn. Starting as a Provo
in the 1960s, actively opposing authority relationships, he
founded an imaginary state within Amsterdam — the Orange Free
State, populated by so-called Gnomes — in which freedom and
alternative goals were to be realized. He was subsequently
confronted with political responsibility when his Kabouter
party won five out of forty-five seats in the city council
elections of 1970. The 'Gnomes' disappeared and Van Duyn joined
the PPR, a new radical left-wing party oriented to many AWL
concerns, especially ecology. Though he was to hold the office
of Alderman of the city of Amsterdam for several years, the
realities of administration and the deteriorating economic
climate during the 1970s made realization of his ideas rather
difficult.

More recently he retreated from political and city life to
start a new existence in the countryside. With his wife, he
has tried to make a living out of their small alternative mixed
farm. He confessed to other founders of alternative agrarian
enterprises:

> At this moment I don't think an alternative world ex-
> ists which has any political power. We are thrown back
> upon ourselves and what importance we can possibly have
> in the future. Afterwards a movement might originate
> from this, which could be offered as an alternative for
> the whole world. But now one has to resist the tempta-
> tion of joining an authoritarian clan (like the Jesus
> Movement and Bhagwan Shree Rajneesh) again.[9]

Let us now consider some examples of ecology and identity-
oriented AWL existing in the Netherlands today. People engaged
in these experiments are struggling with both orientations,
but they emphasize different aspects of them.

A CASE STUDY OF ECOLOGY-ORIENTED AWL: DE KLEINE AARDE

De Kleine Aarde (DKA — 'Small Earth') is an agrarian work
collective founded by Sietze Leeflang, formerly a well-known
journalist, who gave up his career to pursue practical, rather
than paper, solutions to ecological problems. DKA is essentially
an educational project seeking to direct attention to AWL
based on alternative agricultural and gardening methods, new
dietary habits and selective consumption, the application of
soft technology, and respect for the environment with non-
polluting energy use and conservation. Its activities include:

research (on organic gardening and solar energy); running an
ecological shop; editing a journal and producing pamphlets; offering courses and educational visits to school pupils, housewives, and officials; and keeping in contact with friendly
communities, extra-parliamentary groups, political parties,
government agencies, the mass media, educational institutions
and the general public.
    DKA is a working, rather than a living, community. Most
participants/co-workers do not feel like investing their energy
in the development of social relationships — their work is intensive enough in itself — though some live together. There
has been an evolution towards decentralization and a relatively
high turnover of co-workers (none of the original founders of
the project still participate in the work) largely because of
problems of organization and social interrelationships. Most
co-workers now are young people who, earning minimal wages,
stay for about 3 years on the project. Work is organized in
groups — on food, the garden, and energy, for instance — which
employ decentralized decision-making structures, since the
growth of the project caused certain co-ordination problems.
Household activities and meals are shared. The financial
position of DKA is never sound. Resources come from the sale
of organic foods, as well as from a small government subsidy
given in recognition of the project's educational importance.
    Despite these minor problems, DKA's activities have expanded
enormously since it was first set up in 1971. During this
period the working-group has grown from five to thirty-five
co-workers, while its journal has grown in circulation from
500 copies in 1972 to 25,000 in 1979. Leeflang attributes this
rapid growth to 'an intense need of people for information on
ways of life that enables them to make themselves independent
of the consumption society' (Meijer, 1978, p. 270). Experiments
with alternative energy supply have, however, been less successful than expected (according to reports in De Kleine Aarde, no..
27, pp. 34-35, 1978), though this does not diminish its overall
impact. Readers of DKA publications, such as students, mostly
belong to elite groups, but some have reported changes in WOL
such as reduced meat consumption, eating organically grown food,
more selective use of cars, energy saving, recycling, making
compost heaps, and being generally critical in matters of consumption. The number of visitors and course members rose from
10,000 in 1976 to 18,000 in 1978. The success of DKA is —
according to its founder — due to the following principles:
offering simple practical alternatives, absence of a sectarian
world view, recognizing our common responsibility for the
present situation, no 'professionalism', no sudden and forced

change, and co-operation of the younger and older generations.
However, he admits that 'a large part of the Dutch population
doesn't seem to be aware of necessary changes. . . . (Meijer,
1978, p. 272).

A CASE STUDY OF ECOLOGY- AND IDENTITY-ORIENTED AWL:
THE HOBBITSTEE

The Hobbitstee, a community of around twelve people, founded
in 1969 at about the same time as DKA, lives and works together
in the northern, more agrarian, part of the Netherlands. They
cultivate a biological garden, run an ecological shop and
practise handicrafts. The Hobbitstee was the intended nucleus
of an alternative village where new social forms could develop,
fostering human values in contrast to technocratic ones. In
1973, they distributed unfluoridized water in Amsterdam, with
a pamphlet explaining their intention 'to provide ever more
people with clean water, clean air, organically grown food and
a new way of life'. Thus originated their journal, *Waterman*.
  Though originally set up to communicate between the Hobbitstee alternative village and other similar communities and interested people in the 'old world', the current philosophy implicit in *Waterman* has a more identity-oriented, vaguely religious flavour. Its goals are: to give inspiration to the
renewal of man and society; to forge bonds between experiences
in the spiritual domain and the practical shaping of a New
Culture; to communicate with 'thousands of people'; to spread
Good News from the ecologically conscious society that is
developing in the Netherlands and to follow critically the
endeavours and activities in that small world (*Waterman*, no.
25, 1978).
  In marked contrast to DKA, the Hobbitstee represents not only
a working, but also a living, community, and has remained small.
There is, however, a similarity in the high turnover of community members because — as one of the founders, looking back at
the past admits — 'living together appeared to be not only
beautiful, but frequently too difficult to endure very long'
(*Waterman*, no 26-27, 1978/79, p. 25). Both the original founders have now left the Hobbitstee, experiencing inner changes
which made them look for salvation in different directions: one
became a follower of Jesus, the other of Bhagwan. Although the
'alternative village of the New World' never really escaped
from the realm of Utopia, the Hobbitstee continues to exist.
In view of the problems concerning social relationships — to
which one of the initiators alludes — this seems an achievement
in itself. *Waterman* has gone on to achieve an independent

position and a more professional character, its circulation
rising from 500 in 1973 to 6000 in 1979. In a recent issue
(June/July 1979) the group at the Hobbitstee has expressed its
desire to continue everything that has been built up over the
past 10 years. New initiatives, such as that to establish an
alternative bank, have finally led to the formation of the *Memo-
Foundation* (Human- and Environmentally-Conscious Enterprise),
which intends to facilitate the financing of small-scale enterprises.

DKA and the Hobbitstee both attempt to express and advocate
environmentally conscious AWL, but differ in the emphasis placed
on living together, and on the degree of involvement in matters
of religion, and 'expansion of consciousness' (i.e. identity
concerns). *Waterman* displays an amazing variety of more or
less esoteric and occult subjects — for instance, astrology,
myths and traditional celebrations, folklore, and fortune
telling, accompanied by articles on organic gardening, natural
childbirth and babycare, small-scale enterprises, to name but
a few. There are anthroposophic, Zen, Bhagwan, and Christian
authors. DKA's articles are, in comparison, much more rationally based and restricted to ecological concerns without explicit reference being made to a definite world view.

Numerous other experiments with AWL of the so-called 'New
Culture', combining ecology and identity issues, are going on
in the Netherlands and Flanders. Out of twenty-five major
initiatives originating at the beginning of the 1970s, only
two had been dissolved by 1978 (Meijer, 1978). A few of those
twenty-five are living communities, following more or less the
pattern of the Hobbitstee. Although there seems to be a continuing eagerness — as is apparent from advertisements in alternative journals — to initiate AWL in a communal setting, problems of ongoing social relationships often hinder the growth of
alternative communities. Some idealists cannot even find people
to work or live with at all. The editor of *The Ark,* for instance, continues to produce his journal to spread his anthro-
posophical and strict vegetarian ideas, in search of followers
to share a frugal WOL and an accompanying philosophy in his
New Community. Other problems of founding an alternative
agrarian community are the scarcity and cost of suitable land.

Most groups belonging to the New Culture are working co-
operatives, small-scale enterprises, organic agricultural
enterprises, distribution centres of organically grown food,
ecological shops, tea houses and restaurants, etc. Some of
these have grown considerably in number during the past decade,
which seems to indicate a diffusion of more ecologically conscious WOL — though mainly centred around food — to a larger

public. The number of 'ecological shops', for example, increased from 4 in 1969 to 126 in 1978 (de Groot and Uyttewaal,
1979), and over the same period the number of organic farmers
increased from 30 (exclusively biodynamic) to 220 (biodynamic
and ecological farms taken together). About nine distribution
centres are now co-operating (the largest of which has an annual
turnover of 1,500,000 guilders) and a research foundation on
the quality of 'alternative goods' has been active for several
years.[10] Moreover, older organizations are prospering: the
Association for Reform Food Shops, founded in 1894, reports a
remarkable 300-400 per cent increase in sales of Reform goods;[11]
and membership of the Vegetarian Association has now risen to
3000, many of these being young people.[12] It is also interesting to note that information brochures on alternative food and
agriculture, sold by NOS television as summaries of the programmes on these subjects, sold far better than their brochures
on any other subject in 1977 (60,000-80,000 as against 1500-2000).
      These figures indicate the existence of far wider interest
in alternative eating habits than would have been found 10 years
ago. Larger numbers of people have become conscious of the
consequences of industrial agriculture on nature, and of the
effects of chemically processed food on their health. Interest
in alternative medicine is similarly spreading. These changing
attitudes towards food and health — sometimes accompanied by
the desire for more frugal WOL — are often coloured by religious
or philosophical beliefs, as in macrobiotic, theosophical and
vegetarian 'systems'. The romantic longing for simplicity and
harmony adds its own flavour to 'whole' food! Books and journals on alternative food and medicine (from herbalism to acupunc-
ture) abound, alongside those on Eastern religion and philosophy,
and occult and magical subjects. As is the case with most
alternative ideas and ideals, fashion and commerce have not
left unattended this increasing interest in food, health, nature
and occult/religious topics. Apart from the impact on mainstream commercialization, with new commodities appearing in
high-street shops, this climate accounts for the success of
Onkruid, which displays precisely the mix of subject issues
presented in this section as being characteristic of AWL concerned with problems of identity and ecology.

*A CASE-STUDY OF IDENTITY-ORIENTED AWL: THE KOSMOS
MEDITATION CENTRE*

      The Kosmos centre is a state-subsidized institution for youth
welfare and education, situated in Amsterdam. In the 1960s
Provos and Hippies were frequent visitors, enjoying the psyche-

delic music and subcultural atmosphere; use and trading of drugs
was both commonplace and encouraged. Fantasio, as it was then
known, rapidly became an overcrowded counter-cultural meeting
place with an international reputation. In the 1970s, however,
changing youth movements, and a new management, both contributed
to reorient the centre's activities towards more esoteric and
occult issues, as well as towards Eastern religion. Its goals
are now primarily educational, seeking to help visitors gain:

> (a) insight into their own being as intimately connected
> with all life on earth; (b) knowledge of oneself as a
> thinking and feeling human being who can consciously search
> for the origins, causes and consequences of one's own ac-
> tions; (c) recognition of the apparent contradiction between
> life and death — reconciling this contradiction by thinking
> and acting; and (d) developing the ability to act in
> reality according to these insights.[13]

The methods used to foster such understanding are 'daily courses
on meditation, yoga, philosophy, massage and other forms of
healing, Tai-Chi, lectures and other forms of study on Western
and Eastern philosophical and religious systems'.

The Centre's activities are threefold: general cultural activities (music performances, films, workshops); consciousness-
raising activities (courses in alternative health care and
alternative cooking, sensitivity training); and religious activities (astrology, Kabbalah, the Lord's supper, and a variety
of Eastern religions and meditations). These latter religious
activities (religions should not be interpreted here in the
narrow Christian sense) have now grown in importance so much
that they constitute the largest element in the Kosmos programme
of courses. Other facilities provided by the Centre include a
library (containing mainly religious literature), a macrobiotic
restaurant and ecological shop, and offices with equipment enabling them to produce pamphlets and their own newspaper (*Cosmic
Papers*). The Centre has also been able to organize events like
'The World Symposium on Humanity' in April 1979.

The philosophy of Kosmos is mainly determined by the small
(four to six persons) permanent staff. A large, though fluctu-
ating, number of teachers and lecturers is connected with the
Centre, many of these being quite well-known activists or
specialists in their field of AWL. Kosmos issues annual membership cards entitling holders to reduced entrance fees and to
the right to attend any of the programmes of courses. In 1977,
there were approximately 2000 members, mainly younger people;
the total number of visitors in that year was about 45,000.

It is, however, difficult to establish the extent to which
acquaintance with Kosmos contributes to a higher degree of

'self-realization' among the numerous course members and visitors — it is hardly an observable state! One might, of course,
point to changed patterns of consumption of counter-cultural
products as a measure of Kosmos' impact in this area, but staff
members are quick to emphasize that a higher level of consumption
(albeit of different products) paralleling the DWL is no good
thing in itself. One problem here is that the enormous variety
of ways offered to reach self-realization probably produces a
fashionable superficiality on the part of some of the visitors.
One could argue that meditation and yoga techniques act to
stimulate a more moderate and frugal WOL (as is suggested by
associating meditation with personal detachment) and therefore
the numbers of people practising such activities is a measure
of success in itself. However, practitioners again admit that
achieving real change is a long process and that a frugal WOL
need not necessarily be an end stage. Thus the effectiveness
of solutions to identity-related problems, as offered by Kosmos,
is hard to establish with any certainty.

  Whether Kosmos is the cause, or the result, recent years have
seen the development of a huge consciousness-raising 'industry'.
There is now on offer a confusing variety of growth, meditation,
yoga, therapy, and human potential groups, all claiming to
offer their particular solutions to identity-related problems.
Intimately connected with this consciousness-industry is the
renewed abundance of Eastern religions. Some of these, like
Transcendental Meditation, Zen Buddhism and Hare Krishnaism are
new to the West; others, like Theosophy and Sufism, testify to
a revival of earlier esoteric and occult trends in a wider,
though mostly young, public. An important characteristic of
many such religions is a much stricter concern for food rules
and food restrictions than most of their Western counterparts.
Perhaps this is one of the reasons why this Eastern trend fits
so well into the ecological movement; the popularity of macrobiotic restaurants is a case in point.

  The sometime fashionable aspects of this 'consciousness'
trend must not obscure the sincere efforts of an increasing
number of people to solve their identity problems in alternative
ways. Here, too, we can observe during the last decade, as was
the case with ecological forms of AWL, a shift from small elite
groups to a larger public. The Kosmos undoubtedly pioneered
this development, at least as far as religiously-oriented
solutions are concerned.

THE NEW LIFE STYLE MOVEMENT

  The search for, and advocacy of, AWL in the Netherlands is

the explicit goal of the 'New Life Style Movement'. This was
set up after a conference held by the Dutch Council of Churches
in 1974 adopted a resolution calling for a new, more responsible,
ecologically conscious WOL. The result was the foundation of
the New Life-Style Working Group (WNL) — a committee of about
fifteen people, mainly active church members, whose role was to
structure and co-ordinate the search for AWL, both inside and
outside of the church, and express solidarity with others
attempting to do the same.[14]

The WNL sees contemporary social problems (alienation, environmental pollution, resource depletion, stress, overconsumption, energy problems, unemployment, and hunger in Third World
countries) as requiring radical changes in the DWL. Effective
long-term solutions, argues the WNL, must be based on new and
more enlightened attitudes towards money and consumption, towards people, towards time, and towards nature. Such issues
are treated at length in a number of the group's publications
which relate both domestic malaise and world inequality to
Western overconsumption, take up the problems of minorities
and of people's unfulfilling leisure activities, set out the
possibilities for changes in the dominant economic system and
the development of small-scale alternatives, and argue for a
New International Economic Order. The WNL has also published
a practical manual on *Models of New Life-Styles* to be used by
groups seeking to practice AWL. We should note here that a
crucial activity of the WNL has been, and to some extent still
is, to stimulate the formation of small local groups (mainly,
but not only, within the church) to discuss problems with the
DWL and how to establish AWL.

Another important activity of the WNL has been to confront
existing political, economic and social institutions with the
ideas of the New Life-Style Movement. Thus, political parties,
labour unions, youth and women's organizations, the mass media
and action groups, as well as churches, have been contacted to
discuss dominant life styles and the need for AWL. The WNL
has also participated in public debates on issues relevant to
its ideas, such as the debate on selective economic growth and
nuclear energy.

By all accounts, the WNL seems to have had a marked impact,
within the church at least. The number of formally affiliated
groups had reached 350 by 1976, though the total number of
active groups within the overall WNL network was then estimated
as around 800. Growth had been rapid, and in order to get an
impression of the activities, impact, difficulties, and possible
frustrations of these groups, the WNL sent questionnaires to
each group. Some of the findings are interesting enough to be
mentioned here. It turned out, for instance, that the motiva-

tions of the groups were rather divergent. One-third started
as discussion groups, while the others aimed right from the
beginning at some form of practice. Regarding effects of participation in the New Life-Style Movement, 29 per cent reported
feelings of powerlessness to bring about change, 31 per cent
said they were motivated to continue the search for alternatives,
48 per cent mentioned an increased awareness of certain habits
and 20 per cent reported actual change of habits. Feelings of
powerlessness were also cited among the main problems of the
groups, while some 14 per cent reported that they found it very
hard to convince people outside the group to change their life
style, and 10 per cent mentioned problems such as shallowness
of discussion and commitment, and different motivations, within
their group. Interestingly, given that the WNL argues that
structural change should go along with individual change and
vice versa, 23 per cent of the groups identified the New Life
Style Movement primarily with individual behaviour modifications
whereas 66 per cent also thought it should be centrally involved
in fighting for structural change.

The sorts of attitude change reported by groups included, for
instance, those relating to desirable consumption patterns,
employment problems, developments in Southern Africa, and the
causes of food problems in Third World countries. Behavioural
changes cited included the use of public transport, reduced and
changed consumption, recycling, energy saving and communication
about such issues with others. And among the range of collective actions organized by local groups were the following:
organizing Third World shops, solidarity action with migrant
workers, support for political refugees, the adoption of Third
World projects, and participation in anti-nuclear power activities.

It is difficult to be precise about the particular impact of
what is part of a broad social, political and cultural current,
not just a unique and isolated movement. In addition, the
search for AWL is essentially a process with no definite beginning and certainly no definite end. However, some tentative
conclusions about the relative success of the New Life Style
Movement can still be drawn. First, it is clear that the movement succeeded in initiating and structuring the debate within
the churches on the need for AWL, and in mobilizing and activ-
ating many church members to discuss the DWL and alternatives
to it. One consequence is that several official church documents now call for a new, less materialistic, more responsible
and stable WOL. Secondly, one could also argue that the New
Life Style Movement has contributed to what one might call a
'radiation' effect. An indication of the overall political
impact can be seen from the fact that in almost any contemporary

debate on economic and energy issues a plea will be heard for
AWL.

SOME CONCLUDING AND CRITICAL REMARKS

We began this chapter by asking whether the journal *Onkruid*
was representative of AWL concerns in the Netherlands. The
answer here must be a qualified 'yes'. This journal provides
a good guide to the ecology and identity types of AWL. It is
also an interesting example of two developments which character-
ize a whole range of contemporary attempts to develop AWL: the
focus on private, non-political spheres of life; and the intention to reach a larger, non-elite public. Such practices, of
which alternative diets, healing and therapies are other examples, are apparently able to penetrate dominant society without fundamentally changing its course. Advertising and TV
commercials, accordingly, are very receptive to concepts and
slogans like 'handmade', 'ecologically conscious', 'energy
saving', 'healthy' and 'natural'. However, *Onkruid* generally
lacks reference to questions of democratization and emancipation — in short, to 'inequality' problems (excepting those of
women). These concerns, forming a second broad strand of AWL,
were more characteristic of the turbulent 1960s and have been
less prominent subsequently.

This shift of emphasis over just one decade relates to our
questions about the origin of the alternative world and of the
societal groups practising and/or promoting AWL. Our historical
perspective offers a view of continuities and changes in the
phenomena of AWL. Although the use of the term 'alternative'
to indicate a special WOL does not seem older than a quarter of
a century, life-styles in opposition to the DWL have a rather
longer history. Our limited study of concrete examples does
suggest, however, that new forms of WOL based around identity
and ecology do tend to arise together in periods of successful
industrialization, and seek to oppose overdevelopment tendencies.
These are different from WOL concerned with equality. It is
perhaps best to consider as AWL those practices countering an
overemphasis on material production and consumption, and aiming
at 'moderation' and redressing the neglect of non-material and
'identity' needs. Practices centred around issues of equality
are less clearly subsumed under the heading of AWL, at least as
this term is used by groups identifying with it.

Further historical research might yield more insights concerning the origins and diffusion of different forms and combinations of AWL in different periods. The questions to ask
in such research are clear: what leads to the formation and

abandonment of AWL, and to their acceptance by different social
groups (typically diffusing from elite groups to the broad
population)? Why do people focus on personal behaviour modi-
fication, on structural change at the societal level, or on
both? The social, economic and political conditions for (and
the consequences of) AWL movements await more detailed study.
Nevertheless our research seems to provide reasonable support
to the proposition that AWL develop primarily in times of affluence and less in periods of economic crisis.

   If this is correct, and if during periods of economic stagnation or depression people do look for certainty and safety,
and are keen to keep what they have, what does this suggest for
the future of AWL in the Netherlands? The media are now, at
the beginning of the 1980s, discussing what has been termed
'the great dullness of the 70s'. This debate has drawn attention to the waning of public interest in the wider political
sphere and the demise of political action aiming at fundamental
social change. A fragmentation of the far-reaching goals of
former movements has taken place: people prefer to limit concern to their immediate personal interests, as in the present
movement around 'alternative' family relationships. This could
possibly be interpreted as a manifestation of the more generally
observed pattern of 'privatization' of social affairs. Whether
privatization is really taking place, and how it relates to the
present economic situation, requires further study, which might
provide us with some ideas on the conditions that favour either
acceptance or rejection of alternative ways of feeling, thinking
and acting.

NOTES

1. For this list we follow Elias (1971) and Goudsblom (1977).
We might also identify a fourth fundamental human problem, resulting from people's feeling of dependency on extra-empirical
realities. As becomes evident from *Onkruid's Alternative Encyclopedia*, these realities are not unknown in the alternative
world. We subsume this fourth problem, however, in the third
type of dependency, because it is so intimately linked to feelings and inner experiences.

2. We here draw upon contributions Galtung and Wemegah have
made to the UNU/GPID project on AWL.

3. A very important change concerning all the areas mentioned
is that of family and marital relationships. So many forms of
alternative living patterns have developed that we can pay only
minimal attention to them here.

4. The Socialist Federation of Unions (NVV) was founded in 1906, followed in 1909 by the Protestant and Roman Catholic Federations.

5. Cf. Boehmer and Regtien (1970), Frenkel (1966) and Von Weerlee (1966).

6. Between 1960 and 1971, the proportion of women in employment increased from 20 to 27 per cent, mainly as a result of married women entering the labour market. See: Atlas Sociale Van de Vrouw, Ryswyk, (1977).

7. Quotation from De Haagse Poste Extra, 'De Nieuwe Vrijgezellen en Andere Berichten uit de Moderne Samenleving', p. 29, (1979).

8. See, for example, Roszak (1970), Skolnick (1969) and Stansill and Mairowitz (1971).

9. In Waterman, no. 25 (1978), p. 14.

10. Oral information from A.v. Genderen of SAW.; see also Organic Agriculture, SAW, Amsterdam (1979).

11. Oral information obtained from the Secretary of the Association.

12. F. G. de Ruiter in NRC Handelsblad, 13 October 1979, p. 20.

13. Quotations from Overzicht van Vaste Cursussen in de Kosmos. Other data are taken from conversations, Kosmos brochures and news bulletins, the work of two students (W. Jansen Heytmeijer and E. Tuboly) involved in a research project on subcultures at the University of Amsterdam, and from Kranenborg (1974).

14. See Ester (1980), where this movement is discussed in more detail.

BIBLIOGRAPHY

Boehmer, K. and Regtien, T. (1970) Vøn Provo naar Orange Vrijstaat. Amsterdam/Nijmegen, Sunschrift.
de Boer, D. (1972) Nederland Rond 1900. Bussum.
Elias, N. (1971) What is Sociology? (Dutch version), Utrecht.
Ester, P. (1980) Attitudes of the Dutch population on alternative life-styles and environmental deterioration. Tokyo,

United Nations University Working Papers from the GPID project.

Frenkel, F. E. (Editor) (1966) *Provo, Kanttekeningen bij een Deelversncijnsel.* Amsterdam, Van Gennep.

Galtung, J. (1978) Life-styles: irrelevance or necessity? (Paper presented at World University Service Workshop on 'Rethinking Development'. Colombo.)

Galtung, J., Guha, A., Wirak, A. H., Sjølie, S., Cifuentes, M. and Løvbraek, A. (1974) Measuring world development. Mimeo, University of Oslo.

Goudsblom, J. (1977) *Sociology in the Balance.* London, Blackwell.

de Groot, J. and Uyttewaal, M. (1979) De ruimtelijke diffusie van ekologische winkels in Nederland. Mimeo, VLVU, Amsterdam.

Harmsen, G. (1975) *Blauwe en rode jeugd.* Nijmegen, Sun reprint.

Hofstra, S. (1927) De nieuwe religieuze bewegingen in ons land, *Mens en Maatschappij,* 519-43.

Kranenborg, R. (1974) *Zelfverwerkelijking, Oosterse Religies Binnen een Westerse Subcultuur.* Kampen.

Meadows, D. L., Meadows, D. and Randers, J. (1972) *The Limits to Growth.* New York, Universe Books.

Meijer, K. (1978) *De Aarde, Je Leven.* Boxtel.

de Rek, J. (1978) *Koningen, Kabinetten en Klompenvolk.* Baarn.

Romein, J. (1976) *Op Het Breukvlak van Twee Eeuwen,* (2nd edn.). Amsterdam.

Roszak, T. (1970) *The Making of a Counter-Culture.* London, Faber & Faber.

Skolnick, J. H. (1969) *The Politics of Protest.* New York, Ballantyne Books.

Stansill, P. and Mairowitz, D. Z. (Editors) (1971) *Bamn! Outlaw Manifests and Ephemera.* Harmondsworth, Penguin.

van Weerlee, D. (1966) *Wat de Provo's Willen.* Amsterdam, Bezige Bij.

8

Alternative Ways of Life in Denmark

JENS FALKENTORP, DINO HANSEN, STEEN JUHLER, MOGENS KLØVEDAL AND
PER LØVETAND

INTRODUCTION

Alongside the dominant way of life (DWL) in Denmark, new trends
indicate the emergence of alternative ways of life (AWL). This
chapter discusses some manifestations of AWL, but first it is
worth outlining some aspects of the DWL.

Since the 1960s, Denmark has moved from high economic growth
to the beginnings of economic breakdown and associated high
unemployment. The problems of the 'overdeveloped' countries
have now been acknowledged in addition to those of the 'underdeveloped' ones in contemporary thinking about the global context. The Third World is fighting for greater independence;
meanwhile the West engages in fierce competition and continues
to strive to increase its production at any price. (Note, for
instance, the booming armaments industry, which consumes nearly
half of the USA's federal budget, or the production of tran-
quilizers by the medical industry).

The crisis is upon us, and the result, even in nice little
Denmark, is human demolition and environmental despoilation.
Every fourth admission to psychiatric hospitals is now due to
problems rooted in unemployment (Fruensgaard and Juel-Nielsen,
1977). A growing proportion of the population are social workers, taking care of the remainder.[1*] Industry produces more and
more unnecessary products and creates more and more pollution;
people suffer from over-eating while elsewhere others are
starving. Our national debt is reaching astronomical heights
and we are increasingly dependent on the EEC, NATO and transnational corporations.[2] Given all these trends, it would not
be strange if confidence in established values is dwindling,
and indeed this has been apparent since the 1960s. The 'youth
revolt' expresses this dissatisfaction in spontaneous and
emotional forms; and an increasing political, environmental and
human consciousness has been shown by demonstrations against

---

* Superscript numbers refer to notes at end of chapter.

the U.S. in Vietnam and more recently big campaigns against the
EEC and nuclear power, as well as in environmentalism and the
women's liberation movement. The DWL encourages a centralization of state and economic power and a drive for robot-like
discipline: in reply people demand decentralization, joint
decisions, and autonomy. Activists and squatters put action
behind such words, and everywhere the result is a stirring of
conscience saying that we only have ourselves and a common
solidarity to trust, if the 'Huge Machinery' is not to grind us
down. All sorts of participatory movements are emerging, such
as tenants' unions, communes, collectives, and free schools.
Strikes, boycotts and workers' struggles are supported by
students and through research and solidarity action in colleges.
These are all aspects of a protest against absurdity, a claim
for human dignity and self-respect — a protest and a claim that
increasingly gain the character of a popular movement for new
values and quality of life.

One more indication can be seen in the conference held in the
Danish National Museum in 1978 under the theme 'Possibilities
for Alternative Society Experiments in a Pluralistic Democracy',
which involved researchers from a wide spectrum of disciplines.
In their report (Blum and Sjørslev, 1978), the organizers state
that the conference delineated three complexes of problems: the
alternative societies as such, established society, and the relations between them. They concluded that, while alternative
societies are nothing new and not a specifically Danish phenomenon, in our part of the world they must be seen in the light
of development of the industrialized technological society, of
whose crisis they form a part rather than a solution. They also
argued that research would produce much knowledge about these
experiments that would be valuable both to established and
alternative societies; that no Danish alternatives are completely
independent of established society; and while participants did
not agree whether Denmark was actually an active pluralistic
democracy, they did feel that the coexistence of alternative
societies would be both reasonable and necessary in a pluralistic democracy.

The rest of this chapter considers some alternative society
experiments in AWL. We do not examine here the 'movements'
like environmentalism and feminism, even though these are important influences upon such alternative activities. Likewise,
we focus on attempts to build physical alternatives, rather
than on attempts to change consciousness, or on the part-time
action around AWL in which many people are deeply involved.
We focus here on five significant cases of AWL in Denmark: the
Tvind Schools, communes, the Free Town of Christiania, the Thy
Camp, and Island Camps.

TVIND: A NECESSARY SCHOOL

Tvind Schools have set themselves the task of making themselves better than any other schools in Denmark. They work
within the framework of the Danish Education Act, but build on
it to such a degree that some Danes feel this commitment is
strained practically to the breaking point.

Tvind started in the late 1960s as Den Rejsende Højskole (the
Travelling High School), an initiative taken by a group of
young people, some of them teachers, who had found world travel
to be the best education they had ever received. Seeking to
use these experiences in their own teaching they set up the
Travelling High School. (A high school in Denmark is an exam-
ination-free school open to anyone over 18 years old, with
courses usually running for 6 months of the year. Provided a
number of conditions are fulfilled, public funding is provided
on a par with other schools; thus groups with diverse aims have
established their own high schools.)

The Travelling High School sends groups of young people on
bus tours to the Third World, with the goal of relating their
experiences, and communicating them, to Danish society. Young
people themselves plan their own courses within a structure
prepared by the Teaching Group of the School; they decide their
route and the particular problems they are to study, and repair
and maintain their own bus.

The Teaching Group behind this venture has since set up a
teacher's training college (Der Nødvendige Seminarium) for the Tvind
Schools. Tvind Continuation Schools (Tvind Efterskole) for 14-
18 year olds have now been established in all parts of Denmark,
and the number continues to increase. The first three schools
were built by the Teaching Group themselves — and despite inflation, learning from experience, they made the third school
cheaper than the first. More recently, existing buildings have
been purchased and reconstructed — and ships, too, are being
converted into sailing schools. Travelling is part of the
education in all schools.

The Teaching Group consists of more than 100 people who have
committed themselves to it for life. In line with legislative
requirements, titles like principal, headmaster, teacher, por-
ter and secretary are taken. But, in practice, all members of
the Group not absent on travel are obliged to participate in
major decisions; generally there is one meeting a week. All the
schools are considered as a whole, with Group members expected
to be able to take part in any work anywhere. (This means that
conventional nuclear family couples cannot exist, and the members' children form a special group which is not necessarily
where the parents are.) However, at the new schools it has

been necessary to take on teachers on 2 year contracts. Such
teachers neither have the same rights with respect to general
decisions as the Teaching Group, nor do they enter into the
Group's common economy.
    In the early years the schools kept a low profile, with pupils
recruited through personal contact. But since the Teaching
Group decided to build the world's largest windmill, Tvind has
become the subject of public debate in Denmark. As everything
else, the decision to build the mill was taken because it was
necessary: it could provide power and heating for the three
schools at Tvind more cheaply than could be provided by electricity or oil. (Tvind does not claim to be against nuclear
power as such but just prefers an energy which no-one can
monopolize.) The mill was built by the Teaching Group, with
considerable outside help. All available know-how was utilized:
the Danish atomic research plant at Risø, technical universities,
and foreign experts all contributed necessary expertise. The
experience gathered during the building of the windmill has
been written up and deposited at the Energy Office of West Jutland (Vestjysk Energikontor) and is passed on without charge
to anybody interested.
    A certain amount of land is cultivated around some of the
schools, in an attempt to be self-sufficient in worthwhile
crops, just as each school has its own workshop, printing
machine, computer, etc. So far no special stress has been put
on ecological cultivation: the goal is to produce as good and
as cheap foodstuffs as possible.
    The core of the Tvind attitude is to go against the stream.
When sexuality occupies an important place in people's consciousness, Tvind goes ascetic. When society practices throw-
away culture on a massive scale, Tvind starts to buy up secondhand equipment. When the state is about to opt for nuclear
power, Tvind builds the world's largest windmill. And when the
Danish school system begins to isolate itself from economic
development, Tvind introduces economy and production into its
curricula.
    With the onset of youth unemployment, the Teaching Group
sought cooperation with SID, the biggest trade union in Denmark.
The very practical approach — combined with necessary theory —
of its training has, over the past few years, put Tvind in a
very strong position within the Danish educational system.
Teachers trained at the teachers' college have the reputation
of being able to cope better than most with the disciplinary
problems which haunt large sections of the school system. They
themselves think that the main reason for this is that an essential part of their training is paid work at ordinary work-

places like those of most children's parents. Undertaking
frequent periods of paid work is a duty for all members of the
Teaching Group too. (Tvind was also asked to provide a Danish
proposal to the EEC for a special training programme for unemployed youth, and this is now underway.)

From the outset, the Tvind schools wanted to influence or
take over the Danish educational system as much as possible.
They have succeeded beyond all expectations so far. Thousands
of pupils have been trained at the schools, not one without
being strongly influenced by the experience. They are already
making their mark on the whole of Danish society.

In another society or time it is uncertain whether the drive
behind the work of the Teaching Group would have resulted in a
steadily expanding school system. The working methods and the
goals of the teaching group embody a strong will to change
society which, under other social conditions, might have taken
a quite different course. But, because there is a Danish tradition of using high schools for starting popular social movements, the Tvind people concentrate all their energy and inven-
tiveness on this — not because they see the making of schools
as a goal in itself, but because education is still an accepted
way to change society.

In a basically liberal society like Denmark, one cannot build
up a school system as disciplined and — compared with the
standards of the rest of society — ascetic as Tvind without
running into problems. Media curiosity did not stop with the
great windmill. During the last few years a 'Tvind debate' has
hit the front pages and TV screens.

It has been claimed that the discipline of Tvind actually
involves the dictatorship of a small elite within the Teaching
Group. Stories have been told about the hardships some pupils
have suffered because they could not adjust to the collective
rules forced upon them by the majority or, covertly, by the
teachers. Such stories range from pupils being forced to 'con-
fess' in front of the rest of the school, being sent home alone
from a foreign country, etc. Another sensation was caused when
an expelled Tvind member leaked to a newspaper a document
written some years ago by the man who the press subsequently
portrayed as 'the real leader of Tvind'. The document in
question was meant to stimulate discussion among the teachers
on how to bring up children capable of changing society, making
it more democratic and solidaristic towards Third World countries. In the press Tvind was portrayed as a secret revolutionary organization indoctrinating innocent children.

Certainly Tvind has felt the results of these debates. It is
no longer so easy for them to attract the necessary student

numbers as it used to be. Nevertheless, the schools are still growing. It is not difficult to understand why. Outside the schools there is a Denmark characterized by huge economic problems and social clashes. But these economic problems and social conflicts are among the things the schools teach about, relating them to their global context. Thus they are training a new generation of youth who can be found in any of the large number of people's movements in Denmark.

COMMUNES

Some 30,000 of Denmark's 5,000,000 inhabitants live in communes. In 1968 there were perhaps as few as 10 communes, but by 1971 the number had grown to around 700 and there are now several thousand (although this includes groups sharing accommodation as well as those engaged in more integrated collective living). A typical Danish commune consists of five to eight adults and three to six children living in an old house in the suburbs of Copenhagen or a smaller town. Each adult will have his own private room, and the kitchen and living room will be communal. Commune dwellers are typically middle-class people, mostly students, teachers, academics, and social workers — that is, people employed or supported by public institutions. But more working class people are now joining communes.

The relatively high number of communes in Denmark may be related to the fact that suitable housing can be readily acquired. For only a small deposit, it is possible for a group collectively to purchase a large house, provided of course that the commune can afford to pay the interest on the associated mortgage, which is nowadays at a very high level.

Very few of these communes are actually involved in production, although some are organized around intellectual activities in the media, theatre, or music. Others function as therapeutic enclaves helping addicts, alcoholics and criminals. Some communes (e.g. the Tvind schools) work in education, and some in agriculture or making clothes and handicrafts.

Communes were much discussed in the mass media during the late 1960s — mostly indignantly — being portrayed as a threat to the DWL and its nuclear family structure. As this attention faded, the general opinion was that communes were for young people, who would leave for traditional families as they finished their studies and had children. However, it gradually became clear that the movement was growing, that it included a significant number of people from 25 to 40 years of age, and that those leaving one commune would often move into another. So more recently the media and cultural debate have taken up

communes again, not because of any controversial development or
achievement but because the ideas and experiences they represent
may be of value in coping with certain fundamental problems in
modern society — problems of production, of daily life, of privacy, caused by the economic and structural crisis of capitalism.
The impact of the communes movement over the past decade has
been well summarized by some commune-dwellers as follows:

> From a general viewpoint the communes seem to offer two
> things: on the one hand a way of living together that
> meets the demands of society (i.e. capitalism) on the
> individual — mobility, flexibility and low-cost social
> care; on the other hand a tool that *might* be used for
> political mobilization, to overcome privatization,
> isolation and narrowness, and to build up a solidarity
> and responsibility going beyond the unity of father,
> mother and child.[3]

The ideology of the commune movement is overwhelmingly left-
wing; its proponents have found their political platform since
the 1960s (most of them not having working-class backgrounds).
An essential thesis in this ideology is that to change society
one must be able to change oneself, to seek to carry out the
values one believes, to test theories out in practice. But
perhaps a major reason for people being frustrated with commune
life is that it does not just work — snap! — like that. Even
in a commune one cannot change oneself completely. For example,
communes were not able fundamentally to question traditional
sex roles before the emergence of the women's movement. This
sort of limitation might be thought to support those on the
orthodox left, in particular, who portray AWL as naive idealism,
and argue that nothing can be done before the revolution, to
which goal all efforts should therefore be directed. However,
there are many indications that, on the contrary, future aims
are anticipated through our present means — that the way *is* the
destination.
   There has, unfortunately, been rather little serious analysis
of communes from a socialist perspective, because 'subjective
factors', psychological and ecological issues, are still not a
concern of the left (outside those movements focusing on such
concerns). Rudeng (1976) has argued that:

> It is important to remember that material suppression
> includes emotional suppression as well. Capitalism has
> become incredibly advanced, especially in fields of
> culture and privacy, through the development of mass
> media and the organization of our preferences. A coun-
> terweight is necessary. Thus policies for culture and

privacy require higher priority than previously. Most
of us male socialists may still be 'progressive in our
head' and 'reactionary in the rest of our body'.

Far more attention is now being paid to the ideas of community
life from the centre-right of the political spectrum, the
so-called establishment. A number of Danish politicians recently
suggested that communes should become involved in production
as a solution to youth unemployment. Another factor stimulating
sympathy for communes is the crisis of the isolated nuclear
family, which finds it hard to deal with the social and psychological problems created by society (the capitalist process of
production, mainly). Thus some American futurists advocate
communes as an appropriate way of living together in highly
industrialized society.
But one commune-dweller has commented on such reformist implications by pointing out that:

> You don't eliminate alienation by making a commune, but
> you may be able to endure it for a while. In a family
> you might have had a feeling of *existing* through identi-
> fying yourself with someone else, by owning that person.
> In the commune you can get the same feeling by utilizing —
> or consuming — other people. Community replaces love.
> Uncommitted togetherness and amusement replaces identifi-
> cation. Consuming each other replaces owning each other.
> . . . The family needs *stability*. The commune can sur-
> vive on *flexibility* and *continuity*.[4]

THE FREETOWN OF CHRISTIANIA

Christiania, an alternative society of more than 1000 people,
situated in the middle of Copenhagen, has been in existence
since 1971. Its origins were spontaneous and unplanned, and
it has provoked a wide range of reactions and counterreactions
in Denmark. Practising an alternative to our contemporary norm
of unrestrained consumption, and establishing the principles of
the right to use, rather than the right to own, Christiania has
stimulated a debate on social issues and helped to expose contradictions in the wider society. But above all, it has demonstrated the strength inherent in 'holding together' and in
mutual trust. These experiences can certainly be of use in our
cold and crisis-stricken world.

Christiania's Origins

Christiania covers an area of 22 hectares in the district of Christianshavn, near the centre of Copenhagen. Its site, with ramparts and moats, was formerly used for military purposes, but when the military moved out in the spring of 1971 the area was left derelict due to lack of money and planning. The site contained over 170 buildings, including barracks, huts and large and small workshops. It was badly guarded and there was some vandalism, but people fairly rapidly began to move into the site: the homeless, squatters, students, dissidents, members of minority groups.

By the beginning of 1972 several hundred people had arrived. Facing common problems — such as needing to reach agreement with the authorities (who could not decide among themselves whose responsibility the situation was) about electricity and water supplies — the inhabitants started to hold joint meetings and to set up work groups. Other practical problems faced the 'Christianites': who was to live where, sanitary questions, drugs, common living regulations, and so on. It was agreed that cars would not be allowed in the Freetown; the sale of hard drugs was banned (although hashish was accepted); and a 'peace-guard' was established to stop crime before it could begin. An assembly house with an information office and a weekly newspaper was set up, and in a short time a number of small workshops and a 'flea-market' had opened.

In May 1972 a ten-point 'Temporary Agreement' covering payment for electricity and water, etc, was signed with the authorities, representing their acceptance of the situation. The Defence Ministry (the owner of the site), the Ministries of Culture and Social Affairs, and the Municipality of Copenhagen set up a 'contact group' to negotiate with the Christianites. At this time Christiania was divided into a number of independent areas. Decision making was decentralized, and each area had its own treasurer, although joint meetings were retained to deal with emerging common problems such as medical care, social assistance, and the unreasonable behaviour of the police. The continued existence of Christiania was, however, opposed by right-wing parties, who warned of threats of crime and disease, and by city politicians, who found their own plans for the area forestalled. In the political development of the mid-70s, plans were drawn up to demolish half the buildings of Christiania, but a 'Support Christiania' movement, formed in 1974, helped to get the plans rejected through a non-violent strategy of raising a 'Women's Army' and a 'Peasants' Army', to help from outside. The Christianites sued the government for unjustly demanding the closure of the Freetown, in a High Court case begun in December 1975.

Life in Christiania

While the political struggle unfolded, the Freetown was being consolidated. The attacks from outside helped create solidarity and a common identity within Christiania. Meanwhile outside groups were active in rejecting the allegations levelled against Christianites: the Criminological Institute of Copenhagen University showed that the Freetown had a decriminalizing function; the Department of Social Welfare in Copenhagen discussed the resocializing function of Christiania in their magazine *Kontakt;* the Department of Child Welfare supported the runaways who went to join 'Child Power' in Christiania; and the City doctor and public health nurse pointed to its good levels of health. Cultural life in the Freetown was shared with the outside world through festivals, celebrations, theatre and music groups. The Freetown became something of a recreation area, enjoyed by thousands in Copenhagen. During the summer the population doubled to nearly 2000 with visitors from near and far.

In the year up to April 1976 the threat of eviction still hung over the Christianites. They responded to a demand from the Ministry of Defence for building improvements by doing the work themselves. With 'Support Christiania', a popular campaign was initiated throughout the mass media, culminating in a public enquiry chaired by the Ombudsman. This all increased public understanding so much that opinion polls revealed that more than half the population, as April approached, supported the continuation of the Freetown. Sympathizers joined the nonviolent 'Rainbow Army' — they wore armbands whose colours symbolized a number of related functions they could perform, thus helping them locate other helpers, too. A huge Spring Festival was attended by thousands who, on the day of decision, formed a demonstration joined by 30,000 to the Folketing (Parliament) and the City Hall. In the event, the eviction of Christiania did not take place, though the legal and political tug-of-war has since continued, with varying fortunes.

Despite the continuing uncertainty, construction of the Freetown proceeded through the 1970s. In summer 1977, for example, workshops were busier than ever before; a windmill was erected; the health centre and children's house (over a hundred children now lived in Christiania) were extended; dome- and pyramid-houses were built; and caravans moved in. Stalls of different colours applied the rainbow strategy. Recycling was performed in the Green Hall as a modest contribution to combatting the meaninglessness induced by youth unemployment. Political

groups met in the Blue House, and the Grey Hall was used by
community activists, minority groups, and striking workers.
A Work Festival in the late summer engaged visitors in cleaning
up the town, renovating buildings, and constructing an amphi-
theatre.
   Problems continued with the police, nonetheless. It seems
that they stay away in the summer and carry out raids in the
autumn so as to be able to report 'increasing crime' in Christiania. Many tourists are interested in hash, which is openly
sold, but so many pushers came from outside that it was impossible for Christianites to control them. More beer is sold,
which may benefit the restaurants, but this only increases aggression, the hopelessness of unemployment, and the uncertainty
in the situation. Increased contact with Copenhagen psychiat-
rists, along the lines already established with the organization
for the care of runaway children, has been achieved by social
and health groups from Christiania. With the help of 'Support
Christiania' in Århus, a convalescent project for former drug
addicts and alcoholics has been set up at Thy in Northern Jutland; ten to fifteen Christianites now live and farm the land
there, continuing work begun during 1972-3 when a 'withdrawal
trip' was organized for a group of drug addicts — over half of
whom were still off drugs more than a year later.

The Future of Christiania

   Even during the periods of greatest uncertainty and threat,
cultural activities have flourished within Christiania. For
instance, on the Freetown's sixth birthday in September 1977
(in the shadow of the general rightward political swing in Denmark) a festival was staged to stimulate discussion about its
social and cultural functions, and its ties to parallel alternative movements. As well as performances and exhibitions, a
wide-ranging debate was initiated. The festival became a broad
display of solidarity with thousands of visitors and representatives from all popular movements: tenants, trade unions,
strikers, the unemployed, ecological groups, and so on. A
large amount of money was raised for Christiania's working fund,
together with declarations of solidarity from abroad — and a
deafening silence from the press, despite all the newspapers
having been invited. But the festival did demonstrate to the
participants that a growing number of Danish youths are working,
individually and collectively, for a better world, and for the
ways of life appropriate to this.
   In February 1978 the Supreme Court confirmed an earlier verdict of the High Court that after April 1976 the Christianites

had no legal right to stay in the area. At the same time, however, the Court pointed out that this judgement was made on a legal basis only, and any final decision would have to take into account all the social and human aspects, responsibilities that were the concern of the Folketing and the government. These problems were more than the social democratic government wanted to take on. Its doubts about being seen as responsible for terminating Christiania were reinforced by the publication by Christianites and 'Support Christiania' of a remarkable plan for non-violent resistance which looked as if it might be rather effective. So, with the votes of the left parties, the government overturned the legal decision in the Folketing. Christiania was given a respite of several years, until plans for the area could be settled. This agreement has, however, proved rather unstable, due to differences between the state and the City of Copenhagen. After only 2 years all plans were cancelled, and instead the new Minister of the Environment and the Lord Mayor of Copenhagen asked a 'cultural personality', the director of the Tivoli amusement park, to cut this 'Gordian Knot' and singlehandedly construct a plan for the future of the city areas now occupied by Christiania.

    In the meantime, partly as a result of the general social crisis in Denmark, social and criminal problems have arisen in the Freetown in increasing numbers, and are now nearly out of control. Shortly after the government's decision to let Christiania continue, the open sale of hard drugs in the Freetown became endemic, without serious interference from the police. When an attempt was made by certain Christianites to expose the dealers in co-operation with the narcotics police, they were betrayed by a premature police raid, which resulted in heavy internal differences within Christiania and precluded further investigation taking place. In November 1979 a big, public 'narco-hearing' resulted in hundreds of Christianites setting up a blockade against dealers within Christiania. At the same time, all junkies in the Freetown were offered help with 'withdrawal', and all of them had to leave for 6 months before returning.

    This strategy has proved relatively successful until recently, but the continual importation of social problems into the Freetown is still considered to set the biggest challenge to the future of Christiania — beside the so far thwarted plans of the state and of the City for alternative use of this attractive part of Copenhagen. To help solve these social problems in a constructive way, more workshops are being established alongside the existing shops, restaurants and workplaces (which already provide a living for 260-300, not to mention the hash pushers). It is against this background that Christianites

have continued to debate options for the future, trying to
reach agreement on a common structure and plan for the Freetown.
This may very well be a process of increasing integration with
the wider society, probably involving an elaboration of Christiania's existing social and cultural functions — in an alternative way, of course.

THE THY CAMP

Unlike Christiania, the Thy Camp began in 1970 in a completely
legal and ordinary way. The association, Det Ny Samfund (DNS,
The New Society), representing the most un-authoritarian wing
of the late 1960s New Left, bought 17 hectares of land in Thy,
a beautiful but stern northwestern corner of Jutland, and set
up a summer camp. 'This is the first time the people have
owned land', they proclaimed. The 1970 Thy Camp developed into
the Danish equivalent of Woodstock, with many thousands of
people attending over a period of a couple of months. It was
a powerful protest against the 'plastic culture', arousing a
good deal of public interest in the process. A new subculture
manifested itself with its Asian bric-a-brac, its new music,
its psychedelic drugs, and its will to develop new forms of
consciousness and direct democracy. The media followed developments in the camp on almost a daily basis, with tens of thousands of Sunday drivers passing by to have a look at the hippies.
In general, the local population took a composed attitude of
'let's wait and see', though local indignation was aroused towards the end of the summer when a small group of young people
occupied a nearby church at Hjardemaal. The police were called
in to evict the occupants. While DNS and a mass meeting of the
camp condemned the occupation as meaningless, the incident has
nevertheless been a stain on the image of the camp ever since.
    Since 1970, a camp has been held at the site every summer,
attracting between one and two thousand participants — mainly
young people from cities in Denmark and abroad. These camps
are now rather more quiet and better organized than the first
one was, with decisions taken at mass meetings. Special meetings are often held within the camp period: for example, women's,
gay people's and China weeks; congresses for communes; anarchist
rallies; lectures on magic, ecology and socialism; music festivals, etc.
    Since 1972, a smaller group has settled permanently on the
site. Calling itself the Northern Lights Survival Commune
(Nordlyset), this group lives a frugal life in self-constructed
huts, gypsy wagons and teepees, cultivating the land and keeping
horses, cows, sheep and chickens. During 1973-75, however, a

split developed between Northern Lights and the administrative
group of DNS in Copenhagen. As the economic, social and political crisis set in, the latter tended to adopt a classical left-
wing attitude to dealing with problems, trying to keep the Thy
Camp uninhabited over the winter because the people gathering
there were seen as too undisciplined and this would only result
in greater political opposition to the project. The Survival
Commune, on their part, accused the Copenhagen comrades of for-
getting the vision and only practising 'the new society' in
their summer holidays.

An attempt to bridge this divide was made in 1976, using the
'rainbow' approach developed at Christiania. During the great
pro-Christiania campaign in the winter of 1975/6, the 'Rainbow
Army' was born (as described above). Each of the six colours
of the rainbow was defined as representing a type of temperament
and a type of work. In this scheme, all colours are of equal
importance: red, which means 'taking initiatives, developing
ideas, organising, leading without manipulating', is seen as no
more or less essential to the whole than, for instance, blue,
which means, 'untying the knots of consciousness, loosening the
mind from the ties of the body, spreading the highest knowledge,
increasing the highest love, researching into the unspeakable'.
During the 1976 Summer Camp both the 'red' Copenhagen group and
the 'blue' Northern Lights were reconciled as being part of the
same rainbow and equally indispensable — and maybe even able to
learn something from each other. At the time, this new integration was urgently needed, because the local authorities had
escalated their attempts to get rid of the Thy Camp and internal
agreement was crucial to cope with this threat. Right from
1972, DNS has been fined increasing amounts for arranging
summer camps without permission (which would not have been
granted, even if it had been requested). On top of this, the
local authorities sued DNS for having erected huts without obtaining the authorization required under the Zoning Law and
Building Code. DNS responded by defending their right to experiment on their own land. In a letter to the authorities
written in 1977, DNS argued that the people living in the condemned huts had nowhere else to go, and that the authorities
must take part of the social responsibility for this situation:

> We want to use our piece of land for experiments in
> new social and cultural ideas. Our basic attitude is
> awareness of the necessity of renewal in society, in-
> cluding renewal of fundamental principles, habits and
> ways of thinking. But renewal must take place through
> practical experiments, not through enforcement of un-
> tried theoretical principles, as has been and is the

case in many places in the world. That sort of renewal we consider one of the major sources of human
unhappiness.

In 1977 the court found DNS guilty and decided that nine huts
and other buildings must be cleared by 1 January 1978, after
which daily fines of 150 kr. were to be paid until the directive was complied with. DNS pressed the local authorities for
negotiations on the longer-term future of the camp and, when
such negotiations were promised, agreed to take down the nine
huts. The negotiations had reached a point at which the authorities seemed to have accepted some kind of continuation of the
camp when, unfortunately, a few people in the camp caught hep-
atitis. This changed the situation completely: the local press
played up the outbreak, while opponents of the camp organized
themselves into a committee and collected 600 signatures to a
petition that the camp be closed. The camp was quarantined and
negotiations dropped, the authorities instead beginning preparations for a new lawsuit. As a result, that year's summer camp
was held at another site.

In 1979 a new court order directed DNS to clear all huts and
constructions by 1 April 1980. At the time of writing (July
1980) DNS has not yet complied with the directive, but is facing
an ever-growing debt of 200 kr. per day in fines. This debt
may eventually lead to compulsory sale of the property. In this
rather difficult situation, the 'red' faction has advocated the
strategy of asking the authorities to evict the fifty inhabitants
of the camp, since DNS has no power to do so. This way, they
argued, the spectre of compulsory sale would be dealt with,
while the eviction would probably be too drastic an action for
the authorities to actually carry out. However, an overwhelming majority of the DNS general assembly turned down this line
of action as 'schizophrenic', doubting, in any case, that it
would save the place from demolition. Instead DNS chose openly
to defend the camp and to try to gather broad public support
for their action. As part of this strategy, the administrative
organization of DNS was moved to the camp, thus finally ending
the 'remote control' of the site by the Copenhagen group.

In the campaign to win support for the continuation of the
project, DNS is arguing that the camp represents a necessary
experiment in collective living in harmony with nature, and
that the Zoning Law used against them could just as well be
used to grant the necessary authorization. DNS points out that,
perhaps even more than Christiania, the camp is the only alternative many people have to psychiatric hospitals or complete
social breakdown. An appeal is being made to the Danish public
and to politicians to keep Denmark an 'open society' where
social experiments are welcomed and respected.

There exist close links between Christiania and the Thy Camp,
with many people moving between the two. Unlike the Christianites, the members of DNS have legal rights to the land they
occupy and this has been used by the authorities in an attempt
to isolate 'responsible leaders' and enforce their will through
them. But DNS refuses to exercise its property rights internally
— for instance, to evict people who live on the property.
The fact that the fortunes of Christiania and Thy have mirrored
each other so closely, in spite of this legal difference, shows
that both represent expressions of a deeper political conflict
within Danish society. The decision (in 1978) of the Government
not to use its legal right to evict Christiania seems indirectly
to suggest a possibility of a 'peaceful settlement' also being
reached for the Thy Camp through negotiations with the authorities.

ISLAND CAMPS

Geographically, Denmark consists of the peninsula of Jutland,
together with a number of islands of different sizes, including
about a hundred small islands (each supporting up to fifty
farms). These small islands have been depopulated in the course
of the emigration from country to city associated with industrialization. As a result, many no longer have their own school.
The inhabitants are very dependent on transport facilities, and
although the state has subsidized many ferry routes, depopula-
tion goes on. Many of the old houses now serve as holiday
homes for town dwellers, while numerous summerhouses and camp
sites have been established to take advantage of the great
scenic beauty.
In 1970, the International Year of Nature Conservation, the
Danish committee entrusted with spreading ideas relevant to
this goal proposed that summer camps be established on some of
the smaller islands to give people a chance to have closer contact with nature during their holidays. Conservation was seen
as more than just keeping nature untouched but also including
making nature more accessible to the public. But highway construction and new camp sites — not to mention 'deserts' of
summerhouses and resort centres — can undermine conservation.
Thus it was planned to situate summer camps, which would be
neutral in the landscape, in rather unspoilt sites — and in
some cases to prevent access by cars. In the summer of 1970,
then, island camps were set up on six small islands, funded by
the Ministry of Culture. Participants were able to have a
cheap holiday, paying only for the running and maintenance costs
of the camps. This fitted in with the aim of reaching as many

people as possible who lacked other opportunities to be in contact with nature.
Each camp offers a main activity around a specific theme to participants. This could be, for example, restoring an old windmill, arts and crafts, or making an ecological mini-society. In addition, there are such options as ball games, learning to dye with herbs, to bake bread, maintenance and improvement of the camp, and, of course, such daily jobs as fire making, cooking, and cleaning up. Finally, there are traditional relaxations like swimming, cycling, making love, talking and reading.

Summer camps are open for the seven weeks during the school holidays from the end of June to mid-August. Fifty to eighty participants will each stay for a week or more. The life is rather primitive, twenty people sharing a large tent (a secondhand military tent). Since the idea is for people to live together, bringing one's own tent is discouraged. We are used to isolating ourselves from one another, and traditional holidays reflect this with their private rooms, cars, trailers and tents. The island camps experiment with living closely together, without the possibility of hiding oneself, except for special occasions.

Decisions are made by common meetings in which all can take part. While the first camps had previously-appointed teams of volunteers to deal with finances, food and the main activities, this structure is now less formal, and participants from one year's camp form groups to plan and initiate that of the subsequent year. Thus many participants accept responsibility for camp life, though problems of adaptation sometimes occur. Since 1970 island camps have been arranged every summer, and some 10,000 participants have undergone the experience (though some of those will be people coming a second time). The camps are now organized as an independent institution without public grants. Some are arranged by groups belonging to the 'movements', reflecting a tendency to give the camps a more political (predominantly socialist) basis.

The participants do not represent a broad sample of the Danish population: the majority are young people still receiving education, and people from the larger cities. But more than 25 per cent are over 30 years old, and almost this proportion is composed of skilled workers, clerks and people with less education (1973 data). Thus they are more typical of the population than, say, commune dwellers. The camps bridge the gap between people living in conventional family structures and those living more collectively. Prejudices about camp life (drugs, dirtiness, promiscuity etc.) have been eroded by personal experience, while the 'primitive' way of life is making people conscious of the merits of human, as opposed to material, values.

NOTES

1. According to official statistics, the expenditure on social and health services doubled as a proportion of GNP (to 13 per cent) between 1965-75, most of this expenditure being accounted for by wages.

2. Thus the 'Danish' company A. P. Møller is guaranteed huge reserves from North Sea oil and gas while the Danish state will receive only a fraction of this amount.

3. This is taken from 'Ventrebevaegelsen: Skandinavien' (The Left Movement in Scandinavia) in *Hug*, 15/16, 1977, which has been a major source for this section.

4. Source as Note 3 above.

BIBLIOGRAPHY

Blum, J. and Sjørslev, I. (1978) *Spirer til en ny Livsform (Sprouts for a New Way of Life)*. København, Nationalmuseet.
Fruensgaard, K. and Juel-Nielsen, N. (1976) *Ugeskrift for Laeger*, 129/30.
Rudeng, E. (1976) article in *Paxrevy*, No. 1.

9

From Things to Experiences - Changing Values in Contemporary Japan

HIDETOSHI KATO

DETACHMENT FROM MATERIAL THINGS

In 1977, *The White Paper on National Life*, published by Japan's Economic Planning Board, drew attention to a significant change in the life style of the Japanese people since 1975. What has happened seems to be that people in general have become less interested in the consumption of material objects, especially consumer durables. Manufacturers of automobiles, electric appliances, and even textile products have discovered that their markets have become less flexible and that they can no longer sell their products so easily. The authors of the *White Paper* termed this change 'a detachment from things'.

There are several ways to explain this development. In the first place, it should be noted that the consumer market in Japan has already reached its saturation point. For example, electric and electronic appliances, such as refrigerators or TV sets, are now owned by almost all households, and there is practically nothing here than people are eager to buy. Moreover, because of technological innovation and better production control, the quality of products has attained such a high standard that durable goods have become more durable. For example, automobile manufacturers found that, on average, a consumer now carries on driving the same car for 7 years after its purchase; until recently, the average had been less than 5 years.

Second, the economic recession which began in late 1973 affected both people's purchasing power and their purchasing patterns. There has been a strong tendency to reduce consumption, in order to save more, on the part of individual consumers who have felt uneasy about future economic conditions. Indeed, since 1975 unemployment has become one of the most crucial political issues in Japan, the high economic growth which characterized the Japanese economy from 1950 onwards clearly having come to an end. Though exports still prosper, no one can be

269

too optimistic about the future of the Japanese economy. Less
material consumption, therefore, may be seen as an instinctive
defence mechanism in the minds of the public.
 Third, and probably most significantly, the Japanese people,
after 20 years of material affluence, may have finally found
consumption boring. Until the early 1970s consumption was more
or less 'conspicuous', with the ownership of consumer durables
thought to be a symbol of prestige. Indeed, it was said in the
1960s that, in order to show off to the neighbours, some people
even installed television aerials on top of their homes although
they did not actually own television sets! According to the
statistics, it was in 1971 that the peak in consumption of consumer durables was reached. Automobiles, electrical appliances,
and so on, could not continue to serve as status symbols once
everybody had them. In short, consumption ceased to be a goal
in the minds of the people. It is even pointed out that 'non-
ownership', rather than ownership, can be more conspicuous and
prestigious today. For example, not owning a TV set may be
regarded as a sign of culture rather than indicating poverty
or meanness. Someone driving a big American automobile, previously seen as rich, is now thought to show bad taste, if not
ignorance. In this sense, ethics and value orientations vis-a-
vis material consumption are undergoing drastic change. To
make the point clear, material consumption, which was once a
virtue, has turned out to be a vice today; in other words,
Japanese people are 'graduating' from material affluence.
 However, it is dangerous to regard this 'detachment from
things' as a general trend, because, as in any society, there
are several strata in contemporary Japan. While people in the
upper-middle and middle-middle classes, who have already experienced material affluences, are more or less detached from
'things', others at the same time are still eager to acquire
tangible possessions. Two groups can thus be seen as co-exist-
ing in Japan today: 'materialists' and 'post-materialists'.
But the important point is that the number and proportion of
the latter is increasing significantly.

CHANGES IN THE SERVICE SECTOR

 Around 35 per cent of Japan's population is today employed in
the service sector. Of course, the major activity of many of
these workers (as in retail services) is the handling of things.
But an extraordinary growth has taken place in non-material
transactions.
 Leisure is a good example. On average, each Japanese person
travels twice a year for pleasure. The distance travelled may

be very short, but people typically spend 2-3 days and the
equivalent of $150 on such holiday trips. The sum of money
involved here, needless to say, is more than enough to purchase
a small electrical appliance, such as a washing machine or a
black-and-white TV. Until 10 years ago, most people would have
preferred to purchase such tangible goods, but the general
trend now indicates that people are willing to spend their money
on intangible 'experiences' of the sort that may be gained from
travel. In particular, Japanese today venture overseas a great
deal more than before. Over 3,000,000 Japanese went abroad in
1977, and it was estimated that some 80 per cent of travellers
were tourists who had decided to spend their holidays in foreign
countries. In short, there has been a shift in the objects of
consumption, a change that may be termed 'from things to experiences'.

A similar trend can be found in education. As many observers
have noted, the Japanese have been extraordinarily interested
in education, and affluence has brought another explosion in
this area. After 9 years compulsory public education (6 of
primary school and 3 of junior high school), 95 per cent of all
young Japanese today decide to go through another 3 years of
senior high school rather than to take a job at the age of 15
or 16. Because of this, factories and firms who want to hire
young junior high-school graduates face a severe labour short-
age. Even senior high-school graduates are difficult to find,
because approximately 40 per cent of them choose to go on to
higher education. From an economic viewpoint, however, the
average total lifetime income of an individual is much higher
among senior high-school graduates than university graduates;
this is because the level of education does not affect the
salary scale much, and high-school graduates are earning for at
least 4 years longer than university graduates. As far as
financial benefits and rewards are concerned, university education does not necessarily mean more gain. Yet, even at the
sacrifice of total economic gain, more and more people have
become interested in going through university education. University graduates today also know that their future is not
bright. Some are only able to find such jobs as driving taxis,
selling goods door-to-door, or manual work which, only yester-
day, would have been thought unbecoming for graduates. Nevertheless, many young people remain eager to undertake university
education: higher education and intellectual achievement are
the dominant values for them.

The same trend can be seen in adult education. Several thous-
and non-official schools specialize in vocational, artistic,
and liberal education; in Tokyo alone, 750,000 people (7.5 per
cent of the total population of the city) are engaged in such

activities. The curriculum of such informal schools is diverse:
some specialize in foreign language instruction, others offer
piano lessons or flower arrangement. Many people, including
housewives, take these courses; for example, the Asahi Culture
Centre, sponsored by a leading newspaper, has 10,000 enrolled
students, and expects more each semester. Most students in
these institutions are taking courses without any anticipation
of economic return. They are simply looking for intellectual
and/or emotional satisfaction from their studies. For instance,
at the Asahi Culture Centre, hundreds of students (mostly housewives) practice oil painting; all they seek in the classroom is
a sense of artistic achievement. Tuition fees for these classes
are rather expensive, but the students feel that their satisfaction is more than worth the money involved. Such experiences,
which bring inner satisfaction to individuals, have become a new
kind of commodity which has somewhat displaced material goods.
This new market is still rapidly growing; the consumption of
information, in terms of books, magazines, newspapers, records,
etc., is also increasing, for example.

Another aspect of this trend towards 'post-materialism' may
be seen in the cult of pre-industrial values. In the early
1970s, for example, the National Railways started a campaign
with the slogan 'discover Japan'. This has been very successful, with more Japanese becoming interested in visiting the
small local towns and villages where they can experience the
ambiance of an old, traditional Japan which city dwellers have
forgotton. Accompanying this nostalgic movement, handicrafts
and other folk arts have become another fad. People often say
that they are bored by mass-produced products, that they prefer
the more humane feel of handicrafts. The overall effect, then,
is that those who 'graduated' from material affluence are now
on a new journey to more personal and inner values (as opposed
to those of impersonal mass-society), and both tourism and education are among the social expressions of this new mood.

CHANGES IN VALUES

It is interesting to compare these changes in people's activities with data on changing values. In 1977 I conducted a
survey among young people in Japan to parallel a study by Morris (1956) which contrasted the value choices of students in
different countries. Morris had asked respondents to choose
between thirteen different ways to live: Indian students, for
example, tended to cite most often Way 1 (to preserve the best
that man has attained), Americans, Way 7 (to integrate action,
enjoyment and contemplation), and Japanese, Way 3 (to show

sympathetic concern for others).

Comparing the original study with more recent data, an obvious and drastic change has taken place in the values of young Japanese. In 1953-55, the four values most frequently chosen were Ways 3, 10 (to control the self stoically), 6 (to constantly master changing circumstances) and 1, receiving respectively around 18, 15, 13 and 12 per cent of first choices. The Japanese pattern of choices, then, was much like the Indian, although the most widely preferred 'Way' tended to receive a much higher proportion of first choices in both the American and Indian groups than among Japanese. In 1977, however, the ideal of the good life had changed considerably in Japan. The most frequent first choices were now Ways 4 (to experience festivity and solitude in alternation), 3, 7, and 8 (to live with wholesome, carefree enjoyment), receiving respectively about 22, 15, 9 and 9 per cent of first choices.

This seems to indicate a shift away from values of altruistic empathy, self-sacrifice and asceticism, and toward individual-centred, liberated, joyful altruism. The decline of Way 6 (to just over 1 per cent of first choices) may suggest a shift from concern with change, toward interest in comfort; or it may mean that young people are less aggressive than their counterparts of 20 years ago. There seems to be a tendency towards 'privatization', towards more concern for one's private self than with social commitments and reforms.

Turning away from survey studies, one striking symptom of a rather pathological aspect of 'privatization' is the phenomenon which has won the name of 'evaporation'. Very often, especially in urban areas, certain individuals simply disappear. These 'evaporated' individuals are neither young runaways nor cases of kidnapping: most are mature adults with middle-class backgrounds, who disappear overnight from their families and work. Their motives are not well understood, but it is possible that these people are bored with their daily routines and complicated social relationships, and have decided to escape in search of unknown values and freedom. Sometimes they change their names and find new homes and jobs. It is quite possible that these 'evaporated' people are interested in living another totally different life, having discovered their 'first life' of many years to be unsatisfactory or actively frustrating. Perhaps the temptation to 'live twice' arises in part from prolonged life expectancy (male 77, female 82). Whatever the case, such 'evaporated' people are usually very difficult to locate, despite the efforts of the police and other agencies asked by their families to find them.

More generally, it is doubtful if the tendency towards 'privatization' is well integrated with the 'graduation from material

affluence' and the accompanying search for inner satisfaction
discussed above. Furthermore, one may be sceptical of these
characteristics as necessarily indicating a better future. But
it is hardly surprising that some disintegration and confusion
is apparent while Japanese values are undergoing such tremendous change. The people of Japan are today experimenting with
adjusting to an era of 'post-materialism' — and this may eventually lead them to a new philosophy of life altogether.

BIBLIOGRAPHY

Economic Planning Bureau (1978–80) *Kokumin Seikatsu Hakusho*
    (White Paper on the Lives of People). Tokyo, EPB
Fujitake, A. *et al.* (1979) *Sengo Nihon no Yoron Chosa (Postwar
    Japan as seen from Public Opinion Surveys)*. Tokyo, NHK
    Publications.
Morris, C. (1956) *Varieties of Human Values*. Chicago, Univer-
    sity of Chicago Press.
Office of the Prime Minister (various years from 1960) *Kokumin
    Seikatsu ni Kansuru Yoron Chosa (Series of Public Opinion
    Survey Statistics)*. Tokyo, OPM

10
Another Development for Europe in the 1980s

RICHARD JOLLY

INTRODUCTION

Europe, like most of the industrialized world, is in the midst of crisis and faces profound choices over its future. At the onset of the 1980s, unemployment in Western Europe averaged 6 per cent of the labour force, about double the average of the 1950s and 1960s, and higher than at any time since the 1930s. Yet, counting involuntary part-time employment and under-utilized labour, the true rate of unemployment is much higher than the open rate — and most forecasts suggest unemployment will increase further over the 1980s, if there are not major changes in current policy. Inflation levels in most countries, East and West, have been at the highest levels ever recorded (apart from brief periods of monetary collapse, usually in war or post-war situations). Energy costs and problems have become a matter of public preoccupation, in almost total contrast to the previous era of cheap oil and blissful neglect of the risks of nuclear power. In short, the steady growth of the 1950s and 1960s changed in the 1970s to a period of overcapacity in a number of basic industries (especially steel, shipbuilding, textiles and clothing), with underproduction and serious short-ages in others (notably in oil supplies). This has led to fit-ful and uneven growth, instability in the short run, and enor-mous uncertainty over the future.

These major economic concerns show up almost dàily in the newspaper headlines in every country in Europe. Yet too often the solutions proposed — by political parties, politicians and civil servants — seem little more than a superficial attempt to return to the more rapid growth of the first two post-war decades, without asking whether this is either feasible or desirable — or what its effects would be on the Third World.

For several years, official thinking maintained that a return to rapid growth was perfectly feasible, but with every year of

---

* Superscript numbers refer to notes at end of chapter.

continuing difficulty, doubts have crept in. The world politics
of oil, and the domestic politics of inflation, have combined
to constrain severely the capacity of the main industrial powers
to agree on an effective and coordinated strategy of economic
recovery. Recession is now with us — and, at best, slow growth
is forecast over the foreseeable future. But if rapid growth
is no longer feasible, what sort of society does this imply?

Less publicized, but perhaps in the long run no less important,
has been a growing public disillusionment with many of the
goals of this struggle for growth. A significant fraction of
youth in Europe openly despises the 'rat race of consumerism',
and drops out into the alternative society, at least for a
period. Other groups focus on other weaknesses such as enforced
choices between work and family; the tendency to ever larger-
scale activities where human values are lost and people reduced
to statistics; the increasing dominance of multinational companies and technologies which use up vast amounts of resources
but provide few jobs; patterns of life which offer only marginal
roles for women and older persons. It is far from clear how
widespread is such dissatisfaction, but in a recent poll in
Sweden and Britain, nearly half the adult population said they
thought that living standards and life-styles in their country
were going in the wrong direction: barely a third thought they
were going in the right direction (Gallup and Sifo polls, May
1979).

But if things are going in the wrong direction, what development patterns would be better? And to what extent might a
change in Europe's patterns of development make possible more
rapid and balanced development in the poorer parts of the world,
in which some 800 million persons — far more than the population
of Europe — are living in poverty and destitution and, given
present trends, are likely to continue to do so until the end
of the century? These important questions urgently call for
thought and action.

NEGLECTED ASPECTS OF DEVELOPMENT IN EUROPE

From the start, we will accept as given the obvious evidence
of economic difficulty and crisis in most of the European
countries. We will concentrate here on some *neglected* aspects
of the problems facing Europe at the present time.

Societal Overdevelopment

Johan Galtung[2] has epitomized the idea of 'overdevelopment'

as the development process gone wrong. He has suggested that
the idea of overdevelopment can best be approached through a
simpler concept, that of 'overconsumption'. Just as a person
can be underfed, in relation to nutritional needs, so also one
can be overfed, moving beyond an adequate diet to a condition
of obesity, with its concomitant physical and psychological
problems. Overdevelopment extends this concept to a general
state of maldevelopment in which overconsumption of material
goods in relation to one's needs is combined with underfulfill-
ment and underconsumption with respect to non-material needs.
Applied to the Western economics of Europe today, overdevelopment is not yet the typical condition of the majority of the
population, but, argues Galtung, it is a tendency of the pattern
of maldevelopment which has been let loose. Without fundamental
change it will increasingly spread its material obesities and
non-material, anti-human, anti-social, and anti-spiritual deficiencies throughout these societies.

    At the same time, it is not evident that the excesses of this
pattern of development can continue much longer. The present
high levels of material consumption in Europe and other industrialized countries have been built up, over the decades of
industrialization, through four processes: (i) a tremendous
increase of labour productivity through sustained technological
advance; (ii) exploitation of the 'internal' proletariat, paying
wages which were low in relation to worker productivity; (iii)
exploitation of the 'external' proletariat, obtaining cheap
goods and resources from abroad on favourable terms of trade
which in part reflected very low wages and incomes for workers
and peasants in developing countries; and (iv) exploitation of
nature.

    It was always a precarious balance, and one by one each of
these four props has been put under increasing strain and
challenge: from organized labour in the North, from increasing
demands for higher prices and fairer relations from the South,
and from the very exhaustion of nature's unreplenished abundance.
It is not clear whether any of the props will continue to sustain the pattern of past development in the future. However,
the attempt to maintain momentum by further technological advances is likely to throw society more into the hands of experts, researchers and technicians, with labour becoming ever
more redundant and people reduced to the role of passive consumers. 'The old homo faber will be split into two: a homo
sapiens designing the non-human forms of material production;
and a homo ludens engaged in, hopefully, playful enjoyment of
the role of consumer.'

    Suffice it to say that Galtung finds this portrait of the
future neither desirable nor sustainable. To split humankind

in this way leads to serious alienation, in which the very basis
of society will soon show serious cracks.
This challenging critique of so much of existing society can,
of course, be questioned. Following the unclouded optimism of
the 1950s and 1960s, might we now not be in a phase of over-
reaction, a dark and unjustified pessimism in which almost
every aspect of industrial society is condemned? Ironically,
the desire for alternatives today might be more a reflection
of current economic problems and recession — more a result of
the *failure* of the existing patterns of development to continue,
than a genuine reaction to overdevelopment and excess consumption. Indeed, as Gösta Dahlström of the Swedish trade union
movement put it: 'Certainly economic growth brings with it
negative effects.' But one cannot 'just presuppose that (all)
increasing problems are due to our materialistic strivings'.
Moreover, it is still strongly argued that, in many respects,
some increase in economic growth may actually be needed in the
industrialized countries (like Britain) to generate the resources required to deal with their current problems, and to
achieve the economic and political conditions which would make
possible the alternative development patterns they seek in the
long term.[3] Others suggest that the overdevelopment debate
may represent little more than the reaction of the bored and
rich to excessive affluence — far removed from the practical
worries of the mass of ordinary people in Western Europe, for
whom inflation and the risk of unemployment bring continued
concern over their ability to purchase what are genuinely felt
to be basic needs. In this respect, a recent survey in Finland
showed that many of those who have enjoyed an increase in
material consumption in no way regard their material wealth as
overconsumption.
    In spite of these important qualifications, it is increasingly
being accepted that some form of maldevelopment now prevails
in the rich countries, and that, in important ways, new development patterns are needed. The waste and misuse of human resources is a major symptom of this maldevelopment.

Underdevelopment of Personal Roles and Relationships

    Industrial society is too often a world divided — with women
limited to housework and family, even to the home. By participating so little in decision-making, women cannot voice the
needs of children and end up lacking opportunities and respect
both in their workplace and in public affairs.
    Is this an unavoidable result of our present economic system?
It has been calculated in Scandinavia that the time required

for a family to attain the average income amounts to 16-18 hours of work a day, inclining, if not forcing, both parents to work. In Sweden, for example, 63 per cent of mothers with small children work, leaving little time and energy for other activities, especially political participation. Also, the stress put on families to attain a desired standard of living, coupled with possibilities for women to sustain themselves economically, has resulted in ever-increasing divorce rates.

Too much of modern Western working life is arranged on male conditions and at the expense of the potential development of men, women and children. Both men and women feel torn much of the time, carrying a sense of guilt for not being able to fulfil properly their roles either at home or at work. The negative effects on children are also striking. Too often children appear to have only three functions: to keep their parents happy, to prepare themselves for production, and to consume. During the United Nations' 'Year of the Child', 1979, we talked about what adults can do for children. Instead, we should have asked what part children should have in modern society and in their families.

Most people seem to be happiest when they are doing things together with people they like. Most work and family patterns do not match up to that end. One suggestion is to give up the sharp divisions between family and work by bringing back work to the house or neighbourhood and to humanize work relations. The family farm and the family shop manage to combine work and family life, enabling children also to have a meaningful function. Integration between work and family needs to be extended into other areas of economic activity. Alternative ways of life will require a different technology, eliminating drudgery, but not skill. However, such suggestions are far from unanimously accepted as the solution to these problems. Fears have been voiced that moving the focus of economic activity back to the home would not improve the situation of women and children. Others have argued that more fundamental solutions are needed to deal with the restless individualism which characterizes Western society. The drift from rural to urban areas has often broken up families and kinship relations, while substitutes for these have failed to emerge. But we have also failed to come to grips with consumerism, to realize that material consumption often functions as a substitute for real life.

Poverty in the Midst of Plenty

Whether overdevelopment is the condition of only the top affluent elite or also affects in a lesser way a large majority in the

The Poverty of Progress

industrialized countries is debatable. What is not in dispute
is the continued existence of a significant margin of people in
Europe who are in real poverty — on average, somewhat over 10
per cent of the total population in the early 1970s. The figures for some seven countries of Western Europe — and for three
other industrial countries, for reference — are given in Table
10.1. These data relate to two different poverty lines — one a
national definition based on the poverty line as each country
itself chooses to define it, the other an international definition, standardized across various OECD industrialized countries.

Table 10.1
Percentages of Population below 'Poverty Line' in
Various OECD Countries Contrasted with Expenditure
on Income Maintenance Programmes, During the Early
1970s

	Percentage of population below 'poverty line'		Percentage of national product spent on income maintenance programmes
	Standardized definitions	National definitions	
Europe			
Belgium	—	14.4	14.1
France	16	15.2	12.4
Germany	3	—	12.4
Ireland	—	24.0	6.4
Norway	5	—	9.8
Sweden	3.5	—	9.3
UK	7.5	13.2	7.7
Reference countries			
Australia	8	8.2	4.0
Canada	11	15.1	7.3
USA	13	11.9	8.0

Source: OECD (1976).

The amount by which the incomes of those in poverty fall
short of the poverty line is in fact quite small in relation to
total resources — a little more than 1 per cent of GNP in most
OECD countries. Yet, for various reasons, the mobilization of
these additional resources for the poor has proved difficult.
An increase in low wages often touches only a small fraction of
the poor, since many of those in poverty are over working age
or unemployed, and thus not in receipt of wages. Moreover,
many poor families are poor because of special family circumstances, as is the case with single parent families and those
with above-average numbers of dependent children.

Many of the industrial countries spend significant fractions
on income maintenance programmes to deal with such problems,
as Table 10.1 shows. But widespread 'leakages' mean that, in
most countries, a large proportion of the resources provided
for income maintenance are in fact directed to persons other
than the poor or, if they do reach the poor, are offset by
other reductions in their incomes. Other things being unchanged,
it has thus been estimated that, to provide the additional 1
per cent or so of GNP required to bring those in poverty up to
the minimum defined by the poverty line, would require, after
allowing for 'leakages', some 8 per cent of GNP. This under-
lines an important conclusion: the eradication of residual
poverty in the industrial countries is less a question of growth
and additional resources than of structural and institutional
changes to enable resources that already exist, but are so often
misused, to be distributed more evenly and used more effectively.

UNDERLYING IMBALANCES AND CONSTRAINTS IN EUROPE

Unemployment, inflation and poverty are merely the obvious
and recognized tip of a much larger iceberg of contemporary
problems. Some of the deeper problems — especially major imbalances within the European economies and within the whole
pattern of global development — are officially acknowledged,
if not widely publicized. Others, like overdevelopment, are
as yet recognized by only a minority, and even then their existence, scope and seriousness are often hotly disputed.

A central issue concerns the future consequences of a changed
international division of labour in the highly-industrialized
countries of Western Europe. The 1960s were characterized by
high growth and structural adjustment, the 1970s by low growth
and many adjustment problems. The 1980s are fast becoming a
period of considerable instability in national and international
relations.

The coming decades seem likely to be characterized by heavy

global population growth and by a correspondingly steep increase in the labour force in many countries. Thus, in these
countries, there will be an incentive to develop the traditional
production basis at the same time as attempts will be made to
develop new production processes. This will lead to a continuously evolving international division of labour, in which an
increasing part of the overall industrial production of the
world will be located in countries having low real incomes.
This points towards the 1980s as being a period of major adjustment problems, which may bring about political and social un-
rest in most of the industrial countries.

The increasing structural problems of European industry have
already contributed to a marked growth of protectionism, particularly directed towards the fields in which the developing
countries have, or can be expected to have, comparative advantages: textiles and clothing, steel and ships, and to a wide
range of agricultural products. It was, however, only after
the recession in 1973-74 that these fundamental economic problems were acknowledged by most of the industrial countries,
despite much earlier indications of their existence.

Recession in the Western world has increased the problems of
adaptation in several Western industrial sectors. The original
expectations of many industrial enterprises, that the growth
trends of the 1960s would continue, have given rise to considerable overcapacity in several sectors. This is being compounded
by policies of restraint and deflation in the attempt to combat
inflationary pressures. Overcapacity is further extended by
the tendency to protect industrial sectors, which are up against
keen international competition, rather than to take active
steps to encourage structural adjustment. These current structural difficulties are likely to extend into other sectors
during the 1980s. Synthetic fibres, paper, footwear, automobile and electronic industries are only a few of the fields
in which problems can be expected.

The structural problems of the industrial countries can only
to a very small extent be ascribed to the importation of labour-
intensive products from the developing countries. Most of the
problems are clearly due to changes of technology and demand
structures, or to changes in the structure of trade among the
industrialized countries. Moreover, only a small number of
developing countries can at present challenge even the newly-
industrializing countries — Hong Kong, Taiwan, South Korea,
Singapore, Mexico, Brazil, Argentina, perhaps Colombia, and a
few countries in the Mediterranean region. These economies are
characterized by explosive increases in exports, together accounting for 75 per cent of the developing countries' exports
of finished manufactures.

Simultaneously with the shift of West European production
processes to other parts of the world, technological capacity
and industrial techniques are likely to move to even higher
levels within Western Europe. This in its turn means that
there will be a tendency towards greater concentration of activity in technologically-based industries and towards forms
of production offering ever more limited employment opportunities.

In the 1980s, the West European countries will therefore face
changes in production as well as demand structure towards:

> greater production of investment goods;
> increased social pressure to reduce and discourage labour-
> saving innovation, possibly leading to public intervention
> to this effect;
> heavy investments in energy-saving capital requirement;
> equipment using fewer raw materials;
> greater research and development efforts;
> environmental requirements which may entail needs for fresh
> production equipment.

Competition among the European countries is likely to inten-
sify over the 1980s, especially in the supply of technologically
highly-processed goods. These and other changes in the international division of labour are likely to have an extremely uneven impact on the different countries of Europe – in the future
perhaps even more than in the past. As Kimmo Kiljunen has
argued:[4]

> The core countries of Western Europe – notably West
> Germany and France, but also some of the stronger, smaller
> economies – are likely to be in a strong position to re-
> spond to their industrial challenges, and thereby themselves
> to grow stronger. In contrast, the peripheral economies –
> Portugal, Spain, Greece, Ireland and Finland, increasingly
> perhaps Britain as a semi-peripheral country – may well be
> weakened, rather than strengthened, by being squeezed by
> competition from outside as well as from within.
> Without strong offsetting measures, much stronger than
> any which exist at the moment in the European Economic
> Community, or are even contemplated by it, divergences be-
> tween the richer and the poorer countries of Europe are
> likely to grow even wider in the future than in the past.
> It is not clear where the countries of Eastern Europe
> will stand in this process. After their own period of post-
> war rapid growth, there has been in the last few years a
> slowing in the growth rate – and a greater integration

through trade, technology and financial flows with the
economies of the West. Energy pressures will also be a
constraining factor — as they are already, though not to
the extent that they have been in Western Europe. To what
extent does this suggest that the economies of Eastern
Europe will be part of the same worldwide shift in the
international division of labour, and to what extent will
the process be subject to the same tendencies as the market
economies of the West?

ALTERNATIVE APPROACHES AND STRATEGIES

Despite the enormity and complexity of the issues cited above,
we can point to a number of alternative strategies that have
been put forward as positive ways to tackle the underlying
problems now beginning to be identified.

Solutions to Employment Problems in Industrialized Economies

Unemployment is almost certain to be a long-term problem for
the industrialized countries — the inevitable result of lower
economic growth rates on the one hand, and rising numbers of
persons seeking jobs (especially women) on the other. Conventional policy instruments will have a clear part to play in
ameliorating the problem, especially international policies to
stimulate demand from developing countries. So also will
measures which create employment in the local or informal sectors of industrial countries. Nevertheless, however successful
such policies are, especially in terms of improving the quality
of life in industrial societies, it would be naive to believe
that they alone will create sufficient employment opportunities.
In the face of these problems, Louis Emmerij[5] has proposed an
alternative global approach, resisting protectionist pressures
and encouraging adjustment and restructuring in the industrial
countries along lines of international comparative advantage.
On the supply side, this approach would be bolder — breaking
down the watertight partitions between school, employment and
retirement, and thereby encouraging a more flexible and responsive attitude to employment, so as to achieve a balance between
people seeking work and the jobs on offer. His proposal is to
transform the present rigid segmentation of education and work
into a more flexible system, with recurrent education as a main
feature. The aim is to make it possible to combine, or alter-
nate, periods of education, work and retirement throughout a
person's adult life. This of course has major implications for

education, labour market policy, income distribution and social security. For education, it means carrying much further the proposals for recurrent education, keeping options open for students of all stages and ages, and integrating non-formal education with the rest of education rather than denigrating it. As regards labour market policy, flexibility is again the strategy, as well as being a positive means for responding to the mismatch which often exists between the skills required by a dynamic economy and the qualifications possessed by the labour force.

Although the approach implies a major harmonization of the social security system to cover education, retraining, unemployment and retirement, this is seen as a double virtue. First, it makes is possible to ensure that there will be a systematic and coherent impact on income distribution. Secondly, it makes it possible for the whole scheme to be introduced without additional cost by using money now invested in social security to finance the new elements of recurrent education and paid leave. Put another way, the scheme turns unemployment, which at present is involuntary, into a freely-chosen, 'voluntary' period of further education, creative paid leave outside the labour force, and more flexible retirement.

Industrial Restructuring

The widespread persistence throughout Europe of the industrial problems and imbalances already outlined raises further questions about future industrial policy. In spite of the depth of complexity of these problems, European governments too often seem to be looking no further than to a revival of economic growth as the over-simple solution.

But what are the alternatives? A case can be made, for example, for 'restructuring behind tariff barriers'. Perhaps international agreements could allow such barriers specifically for this purpose. But it is widely felt that this option is not open to the industrialized countries, either because of international opposition and threats of retaliation, or because of internal pressures which would lead temporary barriers to become permanent ones, ultimately solidifying present structures rather than helping to change them.

In fact, a growing weight of evidence suggests that jobs endangered by competition from newly-industrialized countries are far fewer than generally supposed. The real threat to employment, and the forces creating a need for restructuring, are from technological developments and competition within other industrial

countries. These threats are infinitely graver than the threat of
Third World competition. Ultimately, the main adjustment problem
may well be the *permanent* displacement of much unskilled and underemployed labour (in terms of hours and effort required) throughout
conventional industry as a result of continued automation.

To encourage rather than resist the adjustment process may
well be the most favourable alternative, but there are many
difficulties in following such a policy. Popular support might
not be easily forthcoming in the midst of high unemployment.
Government planning to anticipate and guide the adjustment process has not enjoyed a good track record. Nor are most governments the benign, all-powerful mediators they are sometimes
thought to be. They often lack effective power in critical
areas of policy, while their motivation and intervention often
reflect crude sectional interests.

There is no single solution. Rather there is a process to be
influenced and encouraged at a number of points by a variety of
agents and policy instruments. But for this to be a serious
improvement on the present, several changes are needed. Greater
involvement of unions and employers in *anticipatory action* has
a clear part to play, and for this governments have a major
role in *stimulating a flow of better information*. They must
also provide assistance to prevent the burden of adjustment
falling primarily on individual workers. A major requirement
is to *lower the resistance to adjustment and restructuring by
devising more adequate forms of compensation and incentives*, to
encourage individuals and enterprises to shift into new activities. Finally, much further thought has to be given to *alternative development patterns*, not merely focussing on employment
but on working and living more generally. An efficient modern
sector may only be possible in conjunction with an 'informal'
sector which provides an adequate life-style for those displaced
or underemployed by a largely automated 'formal' sector.

We should also note that major changes are also needed inter-
nationally. The present process of adjustment is marked by intense competition, and sometimes by violence and aggression.
A move to a more harmonious process will require more than
international goodwill. New institutional structures are needed
for integrating trade and production decisions at both national
and international levels. Concerted international planning, in
any comprehensive sense, is hardly realistic, though much might
be done in *ad hoc* ways. International initiatives to stimulate
world economic activity are the most immediate and obvious
solution to present world underemployment, and would also encourage structural adjustment. The raising of consumption
standards in the poorer parts of the world is the most obvious
focus for such a stimulus, and would also encourage long-term

adjustment in useful directions.

Agriculture and Food Security

As important as industrial adjustment, but usually less empha-
sized, is the need for measures to tackle the major imbalances
in world agriculture and food production. Both developed and
developing countries have an interest in this — and European
countries are no exception.

While adequate nourishment is one of the basic human needs,
there are gross imbalances in the current situation. At the
present time, some 500 million to 800 million people in the
world are hungry and without adequate nutrition, yet agricultural development and particularly plant breeding have achieved
such results that there is now, from the technological point of
view, no need for hunger. One problem here is that agricultural
resources and production are extremely unevenly distributed and
utilized, both between countries and between farmers and regions
within countries. There is a pressing need for economic and
social reform in many developing countries.

In many of these countries, agricultural production has remained stagnant. At the same time, production of cash crops
has increased. The emphasis within the green revolution on new
varieties of wheat and rice has reduced the cultivation of
other nutritionally valuable crops which play an important role
in the diet of the people in the Third World. Moreover, because
of expensive factor inputs, higher productivity has tended to
benefit the better-off large farmers.

Drastic changes are also needed to correct the international
imbalances between rich and poor countries in production, resources and consumption patterns. The terms of trade in agricultural products are often unfavourable to developing countries, leading to enormous balance-of-payments problems, particularly since all the continents of the Third World are now
food-grain importers, along with Eastern and Western Europe,
Japan and China. Over 95 per cent of net food-grain exports
come from four countries: the US, Canada, Australia and New
Zealand. This is highly unsatisfactory, both politically and
in view of a possible decline in production due to energy
scarcities. At the same time, the grain used as feed for live-
stock in the developed countries exceeds the total grain consumed as food by more than 100 developing market economies (see
Table 10.2). This overconsumption of animal products should be
changed — both to improve global food availability and for
health reasons.

These and other unsatisfactory features in the present situ-

The Poverty of Progress

Table 10.2
Actual and Projected Annual Grain Consumption
by Main Types of Uses, 1970-90

(million metric tons and kilograms)

	Actual consumption 1970	Projected demand[a]		
		1980	1985	1990
Developed countries	(million metric tons)			
Food	160.9	163.1	164.1	164.6
Feed	371.5	467.9	522.7	565.7
Other uses	84.9	100.6	109.5	116.4
Total	617.3	731.6	796.3	846.7
	(kilograms)			
Per capita	576	623	649	663
Developing market economies	(million metric tons)			
Food	303.7	409.3	474.5	547.2
Feed	35.6	60.9	78.6	101.9
Other uses	46.4	64.1	75.4	88.5
Total	385.7	534.3	628.5	737.6
	(kilograms)			
Per capita	220	233	240	246
Developing centrally planned economies	(million metric tons)			
Food	164.1	200.5	215.2	225.3
Feed	15.3	38.7	48.7	61.4
Other uses	24.6	32.6	36.0	39.1
Total	204.0	271.8	299.9	325.8
	(kilograms)			
Per capita	257	290	298	304

Source: Food and Agriculture Organization of the United
Nations (1975), p. 28.

Note: [a] FAO projections based on 'trend' GDP growth and UN
'medium' population projections.

ation point to a number of broad goals for change. First, a
revolution in food consumption patterns in Europe is necessary.
This is likely to take a long time to realize, but a start
should be made now, through information campaigns and government initiatives. The basis for this already exists in various
movements and organizations. Secondly, a higher degree of self-
sufficiency is desirable — both in countries and regions —
especially in the light of rising costs of resource transportation. A third point, also related to rising costs, is that
new production techniques, consuming less energy and utilizing
waste and by-products, are required; and to these may be added
a better use of sea food (e.g. mussel cultivation on a large
scale, fish farming) and of less conventional foods (such as
mushrooms).

The status of agriculture has historically diminished with
the growth of towns and modern industry. A fourth goal involves
changing these attitudes, so the political process puts more
emphasis on the agricultural sector, including the retention,
where possible, of the family-size farming unit. Finally,
whilst recognizing that some agricultural trade will be reduced
as a result of higher degrees of self-sufficiency in food, a
fifth goal can still be profitably pursued — that of promoting
trade in certain tropical products so as to yield income to
their producers. In these cases, the trade must be governed
by commodity agreements which ensure fair and stable prices to
the producers without the intervention of exploitative intermediate agencies.

These goals could be widely applicable in developing as well
as developed countries, West as well as East. Self-sufficiency
in food and agriculture as a universal goal is, however, more
controversial, especially when applied to industrial countries
like those of Western Europe, whose current agricultural policies have raised the prices of many foodstuffs far above those
of imported foods. The costs and benefits of these policies
to particular groups within Europe, and to countries which
might otherwise be exporting to Europe, have been considerable.
It is far from clear whether these should simply be continued
rather than extensively modified — the whole question of the
extent to which self-reliance should mean economic self-
sufficiency is complex and difficult.

Disarmament and Alternative Development

The high levels of spending on armaments and military activities in Europe, East and West, are rarely given sufficient
emphasis as a cause of current economic constraints and diffi-

culties — whether of inflation, taxation, excessive public expenditure, or the diversion of scientific and technological personnel. Even some part of unemployment can be attributed to military spending, because such expenditure generates rather fewer jobs than the equivalent spending on domestic private consumption — and considerably fewer than those which would be generated if military expenditure were diverted into development expenditures in the Third World.[6] It is clear that disarmament must become a priority area for restructuring in the 1980s. Apart from the fact that many of the economic issues involved in restructuring in general apply *a fortiori* to disarmament, the current arms race is putting the whole future of the world in severe jeopardy. There is sufficient reason to fear that, if no real breakthrough is achieved in the arms talks during the next decade, the result will be new and more extensive proliferation of nuclear weapons, implying a most serious risk of nuclear war before the end of the century.

In addition to its corrosive effects on security and social well-being, the arms race is the most wasteful use imaginable of mankind's limited resources. In 1980 the annual sum of money consumed by weapons manufacture was about $450 billion. This means that at least $51 million is wasted on arms every hour of every day of the year. At least 60 million people are directly employed in military activities on this globe. The creative energies of about one-half of all scientific workers are tied up in the essentially destructive pastime of arms research.

The arms race, and its enormous costs, are closely related to the East-West conflict in Europe. These costs are furthermore one of the main obstacles to giving sufficient attention to worldwide problems of development, resources and environment. Not until the East-West conflict has been de-escalated can we hope for increased attention to be paid in the North to the North-South relationship. On the other hand, the development processes in the Third World are bound to create possibly severe clashes and conflicts, both internal and external, in a world of growing interdependence. The outcome of the North-South dialogue is therefore of great, perhaps decisive, importance to the overall global security situation.

The primary task in the struggle for putting an end to the arms race is to demonstrate the immediate and long-term gains from, and the concrete steps necessary for, converting military production to economic activity for peaceful purposes. Disarmament will require profound, though essential, restructuring of the economic foundations of many powerful and populous Western societies, and reforms in the military and security policies of these nations. Both in turn are linked to alternative patterns

of development and ways of life: armaments and military activities have severe consequences for the local, national, regional
and international levels of the energy and raw materials situations and trade relations, for the demand for science and
technology and the transfer of technology, for employment, for
the social and industrial infrastructures, for the environment,
and for the formulation and implementation of development programmes for improving well-being and for the elimination of
poverty, unemployment, disease, hunger and illiteracy. Information concerning the nature of these consequences must be
spread among the general public, and made use of in weighing
and evaluating the options and constraints relating to alternative patterns of development during the next decade. Education
for peace should become an essential part of our education
programmes and be formally incorporated in school curricula.
Historical experiences indicate that real possibilities exist
for a widespread conversion of military technology and productive capacities to peaceful means, but action will depend on
both serious commitment from governments and support from an
informed public.

Changes in Ways of Life and Development Strategies[7]

Partly in reaction to 'overdevelopment', there is a growing
tendency in a number of European countries for the emergence
of new social movements whose main focus is on alternative ways
of life. In terms of political impact, however, these movements
must as yet be regarded as only marginal. Most of the bigger
existing institutions which normally provide a channel for
people's participation — political parties, trade unions and
parallel organizations — still follow a traditional way of
thinking emphasizing economic growth and improvement in the
material standard of living. In a few cases, however, workers
within hard-hit industries such as steel, shipbuilding, pulp
and paper, have been willing to reduce their standard of living
to be able to keep their jobs. A reorientation towards new
life-styles may thus also be related to the economic crisis of
recent years.
In a number of countries, it now seems that young people are
tending to reorient their values in new directions, but en-
counter difficulties in expressing and directing them in practical ways. This view can, of course, easily be overstated.
It is also possible to present evidence showing that most young
people in European countries are relatively happy with their
existing way of life and that fundamental changes are not
generally wanted, though it is perhaps the case that such views

are primarily found in those countries still characterized by
low inflation and continuing growth. There is little doubt,
however, about the rising number of new movements in specific
areas, such as energy, environment and women's emancipation.
Individuals participating in these movements come from all
walks of life, though there is usually an especially strong
representation of young people, women, intellectuals and
students.

Discussion within these movements is often linked to debate
on how future society should be organized so as to permit the
realization of more humane values in the society as a whole.
Within them, too, there is an increasing awareness of the interdependence between nations and a desire to improve information
availability about the developing countries and their interdependence with the industrialized world. The values and objectives of these new movements can readily be conveyed by
listing the social goals which many of these movements seek:

> a more humane society;
> more equality both on the national and international levels;
> a better distribution of economic and natural resources;
> less preoccupation with economic progress, and more stress
> on qualitative aspects of life;
> increased self-reliance;
> a society in better ecological balance;
> conservation of nature;
> a greater stress on culture;
> equality among men and women;
> a society in which individuals can more directly participate
> in decisions which influence their own lives and shape the
> society in general;
> less bureaucracy;
> less centralization;
> more control of the direction of technological change;
> more international solidarity.

The selection and mix of these goals naturally varies in
different countries and in different situations. Since different movements put the main stress on different goals and values,
the question of joint action and possible coalitions has to be
carefully weighed in each particular context. The main movements currently seem to be: women's movements, environmental
movements, groups searching for alternative ways of life, and
movements against high taxation and overcentralization. One
movement of particular interest is 'The Future in Our Hands',
founded in Norway in 1972. This movement is clearly committed
both to new life-styles in the industrialized countries and

more positive policies towards the developing countries — the two goals being seen as already linked. At least 20,000 people in Norway currently align themselves with the movement; its bimonthly newspaper has a circulation of 35,000, and parallel groups have been established in other Scandinavian countries. Movements of this sort can have a positive impact in the sense that they stimulate awareness among the population that something is wrong in today's society. Such movements, furthermore, have a 'nuisance capacity' in confronting political decision-makers with public support for new values and specific issues. They exert a pressure for new ideas to be incorporated into party programmes and the decision-making process. They can also provide a countervailing force against more traditional ideas, thus widening the margin of manoeuvre of decision-makers; the final outcome depends on whether or not the decision-makers want to take the new ideas into account. Certainly, politicians tend to respond to new movements if they are growing rapidly — but there will always be a time lag until new values among the population are incorporated into party programmes and the policy decision process, and because of this it is difficult to evaluate the direct influence of these new movements on national decision-making. To get a better insight, it would be necessary to undertake some historical research regarding the extent to which party political programmes have changed during the last 10 years, how values have evolved among the population, and the extent to which new programmes were actually implemented.

IMPLICATIONS FOR INTERNATIONAL POLICY AND THE THIRD WORLD

    This chapter has so far largely focussed on alternatives within Europe, and only dealt indirectly and in part with measures primarily chosen to accelerate development in poorer countries. This does not indicate any lack of concern with the impact on the Third World, let alone a complacent acceptance of the existing international economic order. Rather it reflects the conviction that any serious proposals for international reform must be built on the enlightened self-interest of all the major countries involved. In Europe's case, this means identifying Europe's own stake in changes of development patterns, both national and international. It is, however, possible to identify in broad terms a few of the international directions along which new approaches might lead.

    First, there will be a need for *international restructuring.* This is a priority, whether major or only minor changes are made in the development patterns within industrial countries. Indeed, some restructuring — in energy, in industry and in

certain commodities — will be needed to avoid bottlenecks in
supply, even if there were no change in the pattern of development and only a modest increase in the rate of economic growth.
Changed development patterns within industrial countries would
require greater international restructuring, some of which
would primarily involve other developed countries, though many
of the necessary changes imply shifts in the balance of production being made to countries in the South.

Second, it may be desirable for the industrialized nations
to consider tying their international restructuring efforts
to policies attempting to cope with their own economic problems.
At present, the advanced industrial countries are in the midst
of the worst recession since the 1930s, and this grim scene,
with the domestic preoccupations and the pressures to reduce
public expenditure which accompany it, provides an obviously
pessimistic background against which to propose major new
initiatives for restructuring towards the Third World. Certainly this is true if one is thinking primarily of conventional
measures dependent on increased flows of publicly-financed aid.
But such a reaction is both analytically misguided and strat-
egically wrong at this moment of history. Solutions to the
problems of the industrial countries and the need for a whole
new approach to Third World development are related, not separ-
ate, issues. They could and should be combined into a general
programme of mutual recovery and structural change over the
longer term: *restructuring out of recession*.

A good part of the present difficulties within the industrial
countries are due to the failure of existing international
economic mechanisms to harmonize adequately domestic and international policies, especially those relating to North and South.
Recession in the industrial economies is one measure of the
price of this failure; stagnation in the poorer countries is
another; and financial uncertainty and externally-induced inflation, even in the relatively successful oil and manufacturing
exporting economies, is a third. By the same token, joint
international action to remedy these failures could offer enormous economic and political gains to many countries in both
North and South. Indeed, without major reforms of this sort,
it may not be possible to solve many of the internal problems
of the advanced economies.

Taken together, underutilization of capacity and the need
for restructuring provide the possibility, and underline the
need, for a new international initiative under which a major
increase of transfers from developed to developing countries
would be combined with measures to stimulate investment in
developing countries in projects or sectors which would ease
structural bottlenecks in the medium and longer run. On a

reasonable scale, such transfers and investment could provide an important stimulus towards higher levels of economic activity in the industrial economies of the West — though their probable scale and timing suggest that any initiative should primarily be judged for its medium-term impact than for its short-term counter-cyclical efforts.

Thirdly, and directly related to the arguments presented in this book, the industrialized nations might consider carefully the *implications of new developed-country development patterns for the Third World*: What would be the impact on the Third World of a major swing towards the sort of alternative ways of life and new development patterns sketched in earlier parts of this chapter? This is an issue on which it is impossible to generalize. The implications for the Third World must be related to *specific* alternatives of new life-styles in the industrialized countries.

For instance, if actions are taken in the energy field in developed countries, what will be the implications for the Third World? Alternative policies within the transport sector might, for example, involve less energy use, longer availability of oil reserves and improved environment. Less private consumption within the industrialized world could imply availability of scarce natural resources for a longer period and might give rise to new technologies as well as a reallocation of resources within both developed countries and the Third World. This link, however, is not necessarily positive for development within the Third World.

Similarly, marginal reductions in consumption in developed countries would have different impacts on the Third World depending on the pattern of consumption in both groups of countries. A reduction of private consumption in the developed countries, for instance, might directly hit the exports of goods from the Third World. Alternatively, however, it might have consequences primarily on production in the developed world, if the reduced consumption were of domestically-produced luxury articles. But even when the initial direct impact is clear, there will be secondary impacts, which could make the total impact on the Third World very different. Generalizations about the possible implications for the Third World should, therefore, be avoided, though research on the likely effects of some specific changes could usefully be undertaken in the area.

More specific, but still not certain, are moves towards a greater degree of self-sufficiency and self-reliance, either on the side of developed or developing countries. To some, such moves involve reducing economic linkages between the North and South, and for this reason seem bound to have a deleterious effect. To others, the very reduction of linkages implies a

beneficial effect. The positions people take on such questions
of course largely reflect how they choose to look at the world —
through the orthodox economic eyes of the major Western countries, through the different orthodoxies of East European countries, or through some more eclectic perspectives in which
generalization is dangerous, and only analysis of the specific
issues in hand and the orders of magnitude will indicate the
likely result. However annoying such indeterminacy may seem
to be, it does correspond to a diversity of positions and policies which countries actually adopt.

To conclude, we should stress that these new perspectives
concerning the future in the industrialized world need not imply
any turning away from concern, in developed countries, for
accelerating development in poorer countries as a goal in
itself. There will remain a continuing need for *sensitive
action and political commitment by European countries clearly
directed towards the goals of Third World development and
international justice.*

The global challenge for the rich countries — in the medium
term, at least — is to produce more and consume slightly less.
But reductions in consumption in the rich countries will not
automatically lead to greater transfers of resources and increased production in the less-developed areas of the world.
Indeed, economic restraints in the North, as at present, with
rising Third World debt and few special measures to stimulate
transfers, will only reinforce recession. In contrast, a massive transfer of resources, combined with active restructuring,
could make the South the 'engine of world economic growth' —
and help restore dynamism to the world economy and promote new
patterns of development in both North and South. There is thus
an urgent need for special initiatives, national and international, to encourage adjustment and restructuring as well as
to stimulate increased transfers.

To achieve changes in development patterns and structures
will still be a vital issue. Poverty in the Third World is
acute. Agriculture is often stagnant, industrial development
often slow and frequently misdirected. The gap between population increases and food production is growing. Similarly, in
the rich countries, production is increasingly geared to types
of products and services that are less and less relevant to
human conditions: increased armaments production, excessive
technological concentration on space and nuclear energy, and
many wasteful preoccupations of overdevelopment coexist with
unmet human and commodity needs, often also with basic poverty.
Armaments are the single greatest distortion of the world's
productive system. Hundreds of billions of dollars are injected
every year into the production of goods that nobody can consume.

Until this fundamental issue is tackled, there can be no security between the North and South — and only limited development.
There will always be debate about the details of different
ways of life and development strategies. But there can be no
doubt that, in these fundamental respects, *alternative development patterns* are needed. And it is **in** these fundamental areas
that development concerns in countries of both North and South
are ultimately linked and which make the achievement of new
development patterns a common long-run endeavour.

NOTES

1. This chapter is based on discussions at the European
Regional Conference of the Society for International Development
(SID), June 17-20, 1979. The conference, entitled *'Alternative
Development Strategies in the 1980s and New Life-Styles in
Europe'*, was hosted by the Finnish Chapter of SID with the
support of the Ministry for Foreign Affairs and financial and
professional support from the other Nordic countries. Some 125
persons from 17 countries participated. This chapter summarizes
the themes considered, the main issues of debate and, where
conclusions could be reached, the nature of those conclusions
for policy and action. It draws on reports of the five working
groups of the conference prepared by six rapporteurs: Mrs
Marja-Liisa Kiljunen, Ms Kari Lotsberg, Mrs Eleonora Masini, Ms
Birgitta Nygren, Ms Gunnel Mellring and Mr Hannu Valtanen, as
well as the papers and plenary addresses delivered to the conference. The chapter has, by agreement, been prepared as a
unified argument rather than a comprehensive or detailed account
of the conference itself. For this reason especially, responsibility for the overview presented rests with the author, not
with the many whose help and comments on an earlier draft he
gratefully acknowledges.
      Summaries of some of the conference papers and further articles
on the themes of this chapter will be found in the quarterly
review of SID, *Development*. A slightly fuller report of the
conference and a full list of the conference papers is given in
Alternative Ways of Life: the SID/UNU Project Report, mimeo,
SID, Rome, 1979.

2. In a presentation at the SID conference. See also Chapter
1 in this volume by Galtung, Poleszynski and Wemegah. Other
quotations, unless specifically referenced, are also drawn from
conference presentations.

3. This case was argued at the SID conference by the British
Chapter of SID.

4. See the SID conference papers (Note 1).

5. See the SID conference papers (Note 1).

6. These paragraphs draw upon a paper by Sandor Rajki, and a commentary by Jacqueline Mondat, at the SID conference.

7. This section draws on an address to the SID conference by Mrs Inga Thorsson.

BIBLIOGRAPHY

FAO (1975) *Population, Food Supply and Agricultural Development.* Rome, Food and Agriculture Organization of the United Nations.
OECD (1976) *Public Expenditure on Income Maintenance.* Paris, Organization for Economic Co-operation and Development.
SID/UNU (1979) *Alternative Ways of Life: The SID/UNU Project Report.* Mimeo, Rome, SID.

11

On Establishing Alternative Ways of Life

IAN MILES AND JOHN IRVINE

INTRODUCTION

The first six chapters of this book document a wide range of problems deeply rooted in the dominant ways of life (DWL) of industrial societies. The point that 'something has gone wrong, somewhere', argued in Chapter 1, has been abundantly substantiated as far as people's security, welfare, identity and freedom are concerned. Later chapters of this book, in contrast, largely concentrate on attempts to live alternative ways of life (AWL) and on factors that are promoting change in ways of life (WOL). That alternatives are possible we have no doubt. The problem lies in realizing them, in going from the desire to overcome problems to concrete strategies for achieving change.

Proponents of AWL must face a number of questions, both theoretical and practical, if they are to realize their alternatives. This is the case even if we consider the prospects for actually living out AWL in the here and now, but is especially so if any longer-term arrangement is to be established, and is true *a fortiori* for those seeking to secure lasting changes in the DWL. What *strategies* are needed? What *tactics* should be used? What *resources* will be required. And *who* might be willing and able to act as agents of change? What sorts of *alliances* between which social groups will be needed, and what *opposition* may be expected? *For whom* are the alternatives proposed? These are the questions that we shall address in this final chapter, as we consider the possibilities for establishing AWL.

The answers to such questions, are, we repeat, both theoretical and practical. This means that we cannot hope to provide a step-by-step 'guide' to establishing AWL. The nature and outcome of actual attempts to promote change will largely determine our future limits and opportunities for action. But we can learn from what has already been ventured, from past failures and successes. Most importantly, we need to relate

---

*Superscript numbers refer to notes at end of chapter.

300 The Poverty of Progress

our actions to achieve AWL to our explanations of what is wrong
with the DWL, so that each can inform the other. To put this
point another way, we have to try to grasp both the processes
which reproduce basic features of the DWL, and those which con-
tinually tend to undermine them. Without such a grasp, our
initiatives are likely to achieve little more progress than
simply resigning ourselves fatalistically to the present state
of welfare, security, identity and freedom (or is it disease,
insecurity, alienation and subordination?).

EXPLANATIONS AND ACTIONS

People's explanations of the central problems of the DWL are
intimately linked to the sort of action they are likely to
engage in to achieve AWL. Establishing AWL cannot be reduced
to the selection and application of self-evident strategies
that any person concerned by the problems of the present world
would accept. Different accounts of these problems, and different explanations of their underlying causes, lead to different solutions being proposed. Particular strategies are
grounded in particular explanations.

Earlier chapters of this book demonstrate something of the
diversity of explanations and action which are manifest among
critics of the DWL. Perhaps a majority of the contributors
(especially Galtung, Poleszynski and Wemagah; Otterloo and
Ester') subscribe to some extent to the notion of 'overdevelopment', arguing that the malaise of the industrial countries
reflects their having passed some optimal level of production
of material goods, the over-provision of material satisfiers
being accompanied by an under-provision of the less material
components of well-being. From this perspective of *overdevelopmentalism*, the term 'maldevelopment' may signify the coexistence
of overdeveloped rich nations with underdeveloped poor
countries. However, a second perspective, which we label
maldevelopmentalism (perhaps most explicitly presented in
Irvine and Miles' chapter) tends to reject notions of over-
and underdevelopment. From this viewpoint, all 'development'
in the world today is predominantly constrained by the fact
that the goals of production are set by profit-maximizing
firms or large bureaucracies, for their own purposes, and
thus only indirectly bear on the satisfaction of human needs,
material or non-material.

A third perspective receives less of an airing in this volume,
for reasons that will be apparent, but is particularly prevalent
in those industrial countries currently facing the greatest
economic difficulties (thus reference to such views is implicit

both in the Polish chapter and in Jolly's discussion of British
thinking on development). This is *underproductionism*, which
holds that poor economic performance, typically attributed to
sectional interest groups imposing too much on the operation of
market forces (or, in the East, on rational central planning),
is a major source of present discontent and slowness to cope
with social problems. In some ways, then, the first and third
perspectives are the inverse of each other: one sees the problem as too much production, the other as too little. The
second perspective, in contrast, focuses attention on the
meaning of production: what and who determines what is produced,
under what conditions it is produced, and how it is distributed?
   Let us enlarge on these three perspectives. It is only possible here to give a summary outline of each, and numerous
nuances, refinements and subtleties could easily be added to
take into account the many different versions of these perspectives that have been propounded at one time or another. However, our aim is to provide the material necessary to distinguish
between significantly different, and politically distinct,
types of explanation of the problems that people face with their
welfare, security, freedom and identity.[2] In presenting this
outline, we shall begin by discussing underproductionism, for
the strategies embarked upon by the dominant groups and governments in practically all regions of the world actually correspond to this perspective. We shall concentrate on the expression of this viewpoint in the industrial West, however, for
there are necessarily significant differences in the organization
of production in different parts of the world economic system.

Underproductionism

   According to this viewpoint, many of the problems currently
confronting the world (and this includes the industrialized
parts of the world) can only be alleviated by the creation and
deployment of more wealth. But, since the early 1970s, the
world economy has been beset by severe problems which threaten
continued growth and have led to increased conflict over the
distribution of what wealth there is. It is argued that during
the prosperity of the 1950s and 1960s, people became rather too
interested in consumption at the expense of production. The
welfare state has likewise grown into an unproductive bureaucratic monster: parasitic on, but interfering short-sightedly
with, economic growth, it has sapped enterprise by overtaxation,
and spawned inflation by printing money. The work ethic,
discipline, thrift and self-reliance have all been undermined,
and the DWL suffers in consequence. Even the wealth that al-

ready exists is used most inefficiently.

The necessary change in Western societies pointed to by under-productionists centres around re-establishing efficiency and productivity as the motor forces of our economies, in place of short-sighted government protection of unprofitable firms. The ultimate aim is depicted as being the creation of societies in which the most modern technologies, such as microelectronics and biotechnology, can be rapidly developed. This, it is argued, will enable an ever-increasing variety of social needs to be freely expressed and provided for through consumer sovereignty in the market. The most immediate means seen as necessary to achieve this state of affairs include the removal of government obstacles to free enterprise and a reduction of state overexpenditure and thereby inflation — although govern-ment intervention is still seen as playing a useful role in providing an environment conducive to the development of inno-vative industries and in facilitating change in people's atti-tudes and WOL. Thus, people in the West must be encouraged to accommodate to the industrial restructuring that is much needed for economic recovery. Politicians must promote longer-term interests rather than promising vote-catching handouts; managers and state officials must be prepared to encourage excellence and prune waste; and workers must recognize that unrealistic wage demands will create unemployment, and learn to be flexible in accepting jobs in new locations and technological change. Respect for authority has also to be restored well beyond the workplace, and lawlessness, of wayward youth and political hooligans alike, combatted by measures to reinforce such central social institutions as the family. More immediately, this may also require improved policing and reorienting the mass media towards concern with moral values and away from preaching in-stant gratification.

Figure 11.1 is a schematic representation of the unproduction-ist strategy, which requires change in the DWL around work (to secure greater efficiency) and consumption (to free more re-sources for investment, and revitalize traditions of self-help).[3] Some short-term discomfort must be put up with in order to allow for the production of more wealth, and thus the satisfaction of more needs, in the future. This is probably beginning to sound like a familiar story. But who advocates such views as these? And what visions of AWL are implied?

One clue to the answers to these questions lies in the fact that underproductionists typically portray the present social system as predominantly sound, as merely suffering from hedon-ism, bureaucracy, and creeping socialism. In the West, then, the need is not for structural change, but rather for reforms

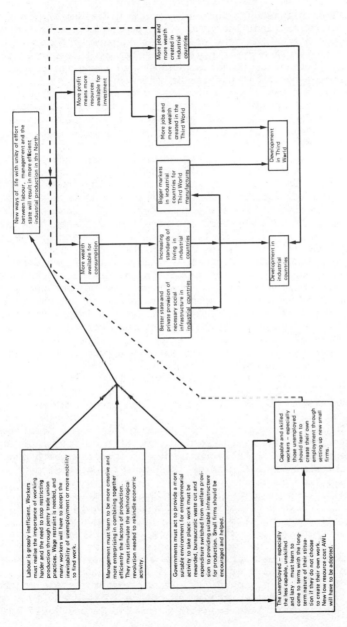

Fig. 11.1   The underproductionist view of changes required in the DWL.

that will simultaneously increase economic freedom and restrict political and cultural license. This perspective thus tends to endorse the status quo, the existing structure of power in society; it is not surprising to find that it is endorsed by representatives of big business and by the leadership of most establishment political parties in the West.

We can uncharitably interpret underproductionism, then, as the theoretical rationale for attempts to win back many of the gains in welfare and workplace rights that have been achieved by labour movements in the social democratic West. But then we face the paradox that underproductionist views are very widely spread throughout Western societies; they are far from being exclusively promoted by industrialists and conservative politicians. Union leaders often take up this viewpoint, for example, and the Italian Communist Party has declared its support for a period of austerity in order to boost national productivity. Although the mass media certainly disseminate such arguments, it is too facile to attribute their hold to the manipulations or conspiracies of opinion-forming elites. Underproductionism does resonate to many of the lived experiences of ordinary people. Strikes may inconvenience us as consumers, public services are often far from responsive to our needs, and, in a period of intensified economic competition, it may well be that — short of effecting fundamental changes in the structure of our firms — the only way to protect our jobs is to agree to higher workloads and limited wages. It is all too easy to identify our immediate interests with what amounts to a renovation of the status quo.

We have stated that underproductionism is generally associated in the West with proposals for reform rather than with structural change — and it should be noted that these problems are being widely implemented in the 1980s, with conservative parties displacing social democrats from government in many countries, with attempts to cut taxes commonplace, with policies for full employment being officially renounced as obsolete, with monetarism eclipsing Keynesianism as the conventional wisdom of economists, and so on.

In the Eastern bloc, too, underproductionism is a prevalent viewpoint, though with local variations: emphasis is placed on the need to catch up with the West, and free-market ideology is replaced by rhetoric about conforming to the directives of central planning. The economic problems of Eastern Europe are surely more than just a consequence of inefficiency yielding levels of industrial production well below those necessary to achieve Western standards of living. But the state control of economic discourse in academia and the media means that the underproductionist views emanating from the Second World are

also largely reformist and status quo oriented. The assumption
that the existing political leadership and structure of control
is itself capable of the necessary reforms is unquestioned. As
in the West, then, change in the DWL is to be brought about by
reforms undertaken gradually.

In Third World countries the situation may be somewhat different. Here, there have been cases where free market oriented
underproductionism has been embodied in non-reformist change:
most dramatically, the military coup in Chile when Allende's
government was seeking to establish a planned path of social
development. More generally, the poverty of most of the Third
World makes increasing production an obvious priority for
regimes of all shades. But the variegated ties of the dominant
groups within these countries to international capital, to
traditional oligarchies, or to worker's and peasant's movements,
means that any simple formation of underproductionism around
free market perspectives is quite uncommon. While such cases
certainly do exist, many other countries pursue a measure of
economic nationalism backed up with populist policies, and an
increasing number are headed by revolutionary governments seeking socialist development strategies.

Returning to First World countries, hopefully with a clearer
insight into the specific grounding of underproductionism in
the particular organization of political and economic power in
the West, we may ask what forms of AWL are proposed here from
this perspective? In part, what is sought is a restoration of
the DWL to its 'prime': regaining traditional values and
strengthening established institutions like the family.
Together with this, there is something of an appropriation of
certain features of some AWL (often originated by people with
quite different perspectives) which seem to provide low-cost
alternatives to the welfare state, to demonstrate the viability
of reduced consumption levels, or to relieve potentially dangerous discontent with the DWL.

In Chapter 5 we noted how notions of preventive medicine, of
changing WOL to improve health, have been employed in Britain
to justify reduced support for public health services. Many
more examples could be cited of conservative politicians
drawing upon AWL to support underproductionist strategies. For
instance, worker cooperatives, or the development of the local
informal economy, may appear to offer prospects of containing
the unemployed — and perhaps simultaneously cutting welfare
costs or providing cheap services to industry.[4] Self-reliance —
to a certain extent — is seen as a good thing, promoting thrift,
community and family enforcement of discipline, entrepreneurial
attitudes, individualism: just as long as no challenge is posed
to the broader market and political system, and just as long as

a supply of willing workers will be provided, and people do not
rely on themselves to such an extent as to refuse to take up arms
to support government foreign policy.
Clearly much that is said by underproductionists makes a lot
of sense. While some contributors to this volume would argue
that increasing productivity in the First World is unnecessary,
or even undesirable, this argument will find little sympathy
in poorer regions; and a case can be made that a truly egalit-
arian, democratic society — one in which people would have
ample time for education and political participation, and in
which the rigid division of labour was largely abolished —
requires high levels of automation, improved communication
systems, and more abundant goods. Likewise, there is often
much force in the wistful underproductionist account of the
erosion of communal values and individual self-reliance. But
this force is entirely misdirected in the associated proposals
to revive such virtues, which typically take the form of authoritarian appeals to reimpose traditional WOL, with no consideration of the changing conditions which have led people to
abandon these traditions, nor any explanation of these changes
other than those in terms of external enemies (subversion) or
internal demons (corrupt human nature).
    The underproductionist perspective outlined above is, hope-
fully, not an unrecognizable caricature of an influential viewpoint in contemporary Western societies. If anything, this
perspective is more interested in preserving the basic structure
of the DWL than in promoting AWL. Certainly some reforms in
WOL are proposed, involving shifts in both consumption and production activities. But these seem to be oriented mainly
towards protecting a social system founded on an economic order
in which production is determined by the market, rather than
by social needs,[5] and in which the great majority of the producers are themselves valued (when employment is offered) only
for their ability to labour by the owners and controllers of
productive technology, rather than as active human agents who
deserve to be equally involved in deciding the course of social
and economic development. What does the diametrically opposed
approach of overdevelopmentalism, which has certainly been
associated with many attempts to live AWL in industrial societies, have to offer here?

Overdevelopmentalism

    Overdevelopmentalists believe that blindly continuing to
increase productivity is no solution to the world crisis. Instead, current economic and social difficulties should be wel-

comed as providing an opportunity to scrutinize the general
direction that economic development has taken, for many social
problems are seen as being rooted firmly in the West's ever-
increasing levels of material consumption. In the industrial
societies, problems of overconsumption are apparent (as Poleszynski and Wemegah argue forcefully in earlier chapters), and a
crassly materialistic culture is fostered by advertising and
a commercial system which invents false needs, while other
world regions find their production oriented, and their resources exported, to the voracious First World.

Whereas underproductionists see the economic systems of the
wealthy countries as basically sound, and as facing problems
on account of political (sometimes atavistic) pressures, over-
productionism takes a rather different tack. While these economic systems may have been appropriate in the past, they are no
longer so: the organizations and institutions that developed
historically to provide for material needs have fairly successfully abolished poverty, but are now obsessively continuing to
churn out goods surplus to requirements, and to stimulate expectations and desires through a consumer culture. The activities and attitudes that have taken us to a reasonable level of
development are now driving us beyond, into overdevelopment.
Thus, new organizations, new WOL, new forms of consciousness,
are required. These can help us regain a more fulfilling level
of development, and restore non-material goals to a more
meaningful position in the social fabric. AWL thus imply much
more of a radical disjunction with the dominant trends in our
society, although some would argue (e.g. Kato in this volume,
or the work of Inglehart, 1971, 1977, and Reich, 1970, on value-
change among youth) that these trends are in any case spontaneously exhausting themselves, and being displaced.

What is required, then, according to overdevelopmentalists,
is a struggle against the DWL, explicitly posing AWL as real
alternatives. In the face of overconsumption and massive
centralization, of excessive dependence upon supplies of materials and food from around the world, and upon experts and
bureaucrats to solve local problems, the goal is to promote
less wasteful, resource-saving, smaller-scale and self-reliant
forms of social organization and WOL. The key to achieving
these is typically seen by overdevelopmentalists as likely to
be found in changing consciousness, to stimulate what might
almost be called a 'moral crusade' for AWL. While the establishment will resist the changes that this new consciousness
embodies, the increasing social, psychological and physical
pathologies associated with the DWL, and the escalating risks
to the future it embodies (for example, in technologies like
nuclear power), already provide fertile soil for new values to

germinate in.

What such groups advocate is change in those aspects of the socioeconomic system that are wreaking environmental and human destruction. Such change involves much more than a temporary period of austerity while the most productive new technologies are introduced. Instead, both production and consumption must be reoriented around AWL so that they are set on a course of development quite contrary to existing trends. Although craft and cottage industry traditions and the spirit of the small community and village may be invoked, AWL here mean much more than a restoration of traditional values and institutions. Indeed, it is vital to experiment with new types of institutions, such as the commune, and to strive for creativity and self-expression, rather than unthinking discipline.

That people should seek to lead AWL within, but in contrast to, the DWL is seen as particularly necessary by overdevelopmentalists. First, this can offer a demonstration of the viability of different WOL, providing both visions for the future and answers to accusations that resistance to continued growth is merely nihilism. Thus, as well as attempts to establish self-sufficient communities or to demonstrate the effectiveness of alternative technologies such as wind power, we find research groups active in drawing up alternative strategies for energy, transport, urban development, agriculture and health care. These can enter general public debate and form arguments in public hearings or court cases involving particular policy decisions. Second, experiments in innovative AWL may provide nuclei from which an alternative society may grow. As more people are attracted to such activities, so their legitimacy and political influence will develop. Furthermore, in the worse possible scenarios — world war or other catastrophes — there is the 'survivalist' prospect of using these as bases on which to build a new society from the ruins.

Figure 11.2 seeks to set out the main elements of the overdevelopmentalist perspective on changing the DWL in a schematic form.[6] We here outline the ways in which it is felt that world development could be better served by establishing AWL in the industrial countries. Permanently changed consumption goals, rather than a temporary deferment of gratification in order to consume more in the future, are seen as reorienting both industrial and Third World countries in desirable directions.

Which people currently support overdevelopmentalist ideas? What role do different sorts of AWL play in their thought and action? The most striking manifestation of the overdevelopmentalist perspective is in environmentalist and anti-nuclear power movements. So-called 'green parties' in the late 1970s have been particularly significant in Northern Europe, but have

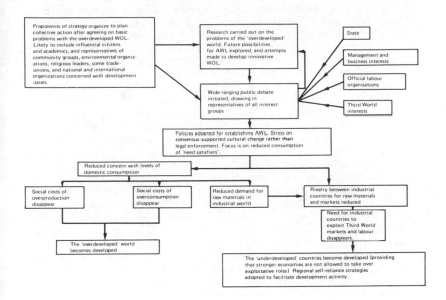

*Fig. 11.2   The overdevelopmentalist view of
changes required in the DWL*

found their echo throughout the West.   As with other AWL movements, and, indeed, with most of the new crop of political
activists (many neoconservatives included) the main protagonists
here have been young, highly educated people, often already
embarked on a career in one of the newer professions or human
services.   A vocal minority, they have often been able to work
together with local interests threatened by, say, the construction of an airport or power station.   But they do not, in
themselves, constitute a particularly powerful electoral or
economic force.

Overdevelopmentalism nevertheless has been a significant intellectual and political influence in the West since the late
1960s.   (As we might expect, it is more rarely employed as an
approach to world or national problems in the poorer parts of
the world, or in those countries that are most severely
suffering in the present economic crisis.)   Its focus on the
hidden costs of gratifying the burgeoning material needs of
industrial societies, its sharp challenge to professional-
ization and bureaucratization, its initiatives towards
decentralization and self-management, have enriched the

thought and action of the less fossilized elements of the political left and right alike. One of the main problems for strategy here (given the weak socioeconomic basis of overdevelopmentalist movements), and thus for the development of a realizable vision of AWL, may actually be the question of alliance with established political groups and the more enduring social forces they represent. Related to this, a few critical points may be made concerning the overdevelopmentalist perspective.

First, we should note that the critique of DWL from this perspective often sounds distinctly puritanical — which may be both consequence and cause of its strength in Northern Europe! The production and consumption of goods in abundance, delight in novelty, spectacle, and excitement, often seem to offend overdevelopmentalists on moral grounds alone. It is by no means unlikely that populist critics of 'anti-growth' and environmentalist positions have a point when they argue that one component of such opinions is a middle class backlash against the 'invasion' of 'their' beaches, the mass consumption of 'their' status symbols, and the tailoring of media towards 'popular' rather than elite tastes. Such views are unlikely to gain much support among less privileged sections of society.

Another problem with overdevelopmentalism involves the apparently powerful thesis that material needs are oversatisfied, and non-material needs undersatisfied, in industrial countries. This does not quite correspond to employment trends in these countries: by far the largest expansion of the labour force has been in the service sector. While many services (transport, retail) go into the production and distribution of material goods, many do not. Education and other human services have been among the leading areas of employment growth. So the problem seems less likely to be one of overprovision of material, and underprovision of non-material, products, as one of the *sort* of goods and services produced.

The expansion of service employment, and especially its professional components, does appear to have provided much of the political base in the population for many overdevelopmentalist movements. But recent years have witnessed threats to many jobs here, either of deskilling or of complete displacement altogether. This, with the decline of sections of the 'old' middle classes, too, has been reflected in alarmist threats of imminent social collapse or ecological disaster, which rather tend to overshadow the very real and immediate problems of resource and wildlife depletion and technological hazards, and the political and economic underpinnings of the undoubted threat of annihilation in nuclear war.

Associated with these problems is a tendency to focus rather one-sidedly on consumption, rather than on production and

consumption together. This appears, for example, in the
abundance of literature on pollution of the natural environment compared with that concerning workplace pollution and its
high human toll. Attacks on the quantity of products, rather
than the quality of production, win limited sympathy among
industrial workers. More generally, the stress on building
new consciousness in the population at large runs into
contradiction with the drive toward continued expansion
built into the very core of the Western industrial system:
enterprises have to play the competitive game to remain viable
in their present form, as underproductionists well recognize.
Even the development of producer-cooperatives and other AWL in
the sphere of work has to confront the 'needs' of economically
and politically powerful firms, national and transnational,
state and privately owned. No major change in the DWL could
be achieved without at least a lengthy transitional period of
reliance on the production of these industries by the great
majority of the population. Thus the question becomes one of
challenging the power relations that give this production its
current form. Our third perspective, maldevelopmentalism, tries
to grapple with the issues we are raising here.

Maldevelopmentalism

   Why are the goods and services produced in the industrial
world — including the quality of work itself — so often antagonistic to the satisfaction of human needs?   The maldevelopmentalist perspective queries not so much the *quantity* of
production and consumption, but their *quality:* how, and under
whose control, are the crucial decisions made? What are the
social relations which govern these spheres of life? It is
argued that the social relations characteristic of the major
economic organizations of Western society themselves structure
the decisions that are made concerning production and consumption: that values and the DWL are conditioned by decisions that
are to a large extent forced upon individuals and institutions
by a structure of unequal social power.
   Maldevelopmentalists point out that the underlying dynamic in
the Western economic system is that of capital accumulation.
Firms and businesses embody, and are constrained by, the search
for profits. Thus the freedom of action of managers is bounded
by the need to maintain the competitiveness of the firms they
make decisions for. Failure to follow this guideline will lead
in a fairly short time to bankruptcy, a withdrawal of loans and
investments, or a managerial reshuffle: in each case the individual will lose income, privileges and status. So an economic
structure is reproduced in which the commodities manufactured

are chosen for their profitability, and the choice of technologies and work organization that is involved corresponds to the associated search for productivity. This results less from individual greed or materialism, then, as from activity being structured by social relations.

The main power relations identified as responsible for this state of affairs rest on a structure of classes. To put it in a decidedly simplistic way, one class owns and controls the major economic organizations; such private ownership of capital is restricted to a small proportion of the population. Rather more people, as managers and other professionals, have some say in the day-to-day control of this capital. But, in contrast, the majority of the population own, as a substantial economic resource, only their ability to work, and this they must sell to owners of capital in order to make a livelihood. Their needs are expressed first and foremost through the purchase of subsistence goods; they can exercise only very limited control of the process of production itself. And, as noted above, the owners and managers of capital are themselves oriented towards ensuring the continued success of their firms, rather than towards representing any other set of social needs. (We put on one side here the existence of other classes — self-employed contractors, small shopkeepers, and peasants do not fit into a two-class scheme — which are by no means insignificant, even in Western society; see Wright (1978).)

But what about public enterprises and the welfare state? Do these not significantly change the picture of *laissez-faire* capitalism outlined above? Some maldevelopmentalists would argue that the growth of popular movements, itself fuelled by the bringing together of workers in urban centres and large workplaces, has managed to set additional limits on the power of private capital. Even so, these limits are themselves quite modest, for too much interference with industry threatens a decline of national wealth, a flight of transnational capital, and the powerful opposition of media and political groups representative of the dominant class. Other maldevelopmentalists argue that the expansion of the state in the twentieth century actually corresponds to the requirements of private industry — for example, the welfare state provides cheap training and maintenance (education and health services) of the workforce, public utilities supply energy and infrastructure, and economic policies moderate dangerous swings in economic affairs as well as provide lucrative subsidies and contracts to privileged firms. The two lines of thought outlined above are actually complementary, and a synthesis of them forms the most sophisticated maldevelopmentalist approach.

On Establishing Alternative Ways of Life   313
Another way of putting this argument is to say that the
relations established between classes in the economic system
are antagonistic. Capital is forced to extract as much as
possible from labour, for as little as possible. In return,
labour will seek to defend its well-being, practising
resistance through methods ranging from deliberate inefficiency at work, to industrial action around wages and working
conditions, and sometimes extending to political organization
in the form of parties and movements. Yet the working class
is a subordinate class, and it remains so in the political
institutions of Western society, even if some measure of
influence has to be conceded to it, in the organizations and
policies of the state itself.

Maldevelopmentalists go on to develop accounts of relations
between other classes and social groups, including those
between the sexes. They outline ways in which these relations
are concretely manifested and reproduced within the social,
cultural and personal life of different Western societies.
Likewise, the circumstances within the 'state socialist'
societies of Eastern Europe and the Soviet Union have been
the subject of much analysis and debate. (These are typically seen as countries in which private ownership of capital
has been abolished, but the mass of workers still remains
isolated from determination of the nature and purposes of
production.) But more to the point at present is to consider
how the current world crisis, and the major problems of DWL
and AWL, are viewed by maldevelopmentalists.

The current problems of the world economy tend to be interpreted as one more manifestation of the necessary tendency of
profit-directed economies to crisis. The exact development of
crisis is multifold, and political changes in the wake of each
major manifestation will inevitably change the form of the next
one. (Thus Keynesian state intervention may have moderated the
business cycle in the wake of the Second World War, but has in
turn laid the seeds of the current round of inflation). Among
the central features, however, are those related to the dynamic
of accumulation, which replaces labour with technology, exacerbating tendencies for the rate of profit to fall; and to the
failure of firms in an unplanned economy to anticipate and produce the mix of commodities demanded by consumer and industrial
markets.[7] There is an overproduction of commodities relative
to market demand; competition intensifies, firms go out of
business, protectionist pressures increase, and so on — all the
costs of a major recession have to be borne before the restructuring of the economy is complete, and a new cycle of accumulation can begin. These costs can be immense: the Great Depression eventuated in world war, on top of the misery of mass unemployment and the emergence of political monstrosities like

fascism.

Crisis has the effect of shattering the political consensus —
witness the decline of social democracy and the polarization of
major parties in Europe, neoconservatism in the United States,
and the new military tensions. This provides opportunities and
dangers for maldevelopmentalists: on the one hand they can gain
new audiences for their critique of private ownership in the
West and bureaucratic planning in the East; but, on the other
hand, the power of the state is thrown into ideological and
coercive defence of the old order and the restructuring necessary to preserve its fundamental relations of power.

Criticism of the DWL is an important activity for maldevelopmentalists, although often preoccupation with workplace issues
tends to overwhelm the broader implications of their analyses.
Also, a healthy doubt concerning the expression of middle-class
privileges in the search for AWL, and a reaction against underproductionist moralizing about social problems reflecting an
erosion of traditional virtues, often leads maldevelopmentalists
to argue that nothing, or very little, can be done within the
existing social order. Some even argue that any improvement
that may be achieved will inevitably weaken people's commitment
to more fundamental change. But despite such uncompromising
and self-isolating positions, maldevelopmentalist analyses of
the DWL and AWL have been gaining in depth and popularity.

Problems with the DWL are typically related in the first instance to the unequal relations of power embodied in the class
structure, and, secondarily, to those further relations (seen
as crucially supported by the former) between sexes, ethnic
groups, age groups, and along other lines of cleavage. These
relations, together with the impersonal demands of profit-
maximization and bureaucratic order, have significant implications for production and the direction of development. What is
produced is what is expected to yield a profit in a market in
which the demands of different groups are vastly unequal and
some collective interests (e.g. many health and ecological
issues) remain totally unrepresented; and the way it is produced
reflects demands for productivity rather than aiming at creative, safe work that is stimulating without being stressful.
The conditions of life do not correspond to any conscious
evaluation of social needs, and uneven development is the rule —
across time (booms and slumps), space (pockets of poverty and
affluence), social groups (benefits and costs being concentrated
in different classes) and social needs (those that can be
reliably satisfied by the produce of alienated labour, and
which do not threaten the social order, being abundantly grati-
fied, with others poorly so).

What approach, then, do maldevelopmentalists take to AWL?
And what forms of AWL are seen as most appropriate? It must
first be pointed out that nothing short of radical change in
the mode of production, and the cultural and political institutions which support it, is seen as ensuring the establishment
and maintenance of a full range of AWL. Social ownership and
control of the economy, participatory democracy, and opportunities for everyone to gain an understanding of social processes
and the ability to express their experience, are seen as the
necessary conditions for social needs to be fully represented
in the organization of production and consumption. Thus nothing
less ambitious than the transformation of the existing economic,
political and cultural system is demanded. Maldevelopmentalists
identify the working classes as the only social agent with both
the power and the interest (even if not consciously articulated)
in this necessary, and necessarily creative, change.
This does not rule out the vital contribution of other social
groups, nor the need for independent action around the oppression
of women, ethnic groups, etc. For a schematic representation of
this framework of change, see Fig. 11.3.[8]
   As noted above, some maldevelopmentalists argue that most
effort needs to be put into securing *the* revolutionary transformation, and that it is premature to speculate about the
kinds of AWL people would establish given the removal of current
constraints. But the consciousness and organization necessary
to achieve change cannot be built by exhortation alone and
others thus argue that action around AWL is part of the struggle
to build such momentum. This may sometimes run into conflict
with attempts to protect the rather mixed blessings of a DWL
which offers some rewards to poorer groups, though these may
well be under erosion in the current economic situation: for
example, there is action to maintain employment levels (and
thus workers' living standards and security in the automobile
and even the armaments industries). At a time when health
services, for instance, are under attack, it can be difficult
to mobilize support for major reforms in health policy — or
such support may come from unwelcome allies in pursuit of quite
contradictory ends. Nevertheless, effort put into reforms of
the DWL can bring benefits to political activism as well as
directly affecting WOL.
   Attitudes to attempts to realize AWL in the here-and-now are
rather sharply divided. While there is little support for the
overdevelopmentalist idea that these might form the nuclei for
the growth of new society within the old — the dominant institutions are seen as too powerful to permit this to happen —
there is some support for demonstrating the feasibility of

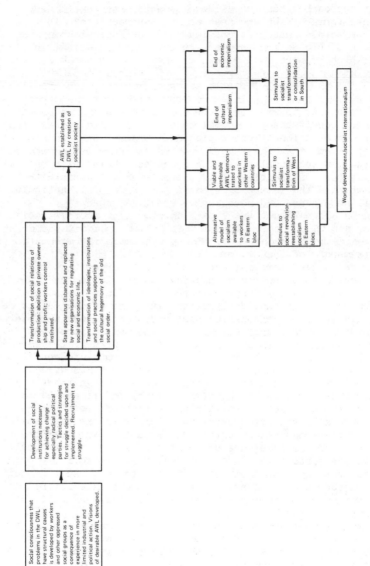

Fig. 11.3 The maldevelopmentalist view of changing the DWL.

alternative production, for new working and living conditions, as a means of raising consciousness that change is possible. Experience in 'prefigurative' actions, too, may yield organizational structure and solidarity to support new WOL. Likewise, AWL may play a therapeutic or supportive function for those engaged in political struggles. Balanced against this is the problem that practitioners of AWL may become isolated from ordinary people, developing concern with their own particular problems, and not with broader issues.

Maldevelopmentalism, as sketched here, will be recognized as the practice of many leftist groups, socialists and libertarians. As such it is adopted by working class and New Left movements in the West, although with considerable national differences. Some socialists, however, take the rigid attitude that all that is required is to place industry under state control: with central planning a reality, problems will fall away. In this they have more in common with underproductionists than over-developmentalists, although, unlike the former, they may have found it possible to hail the growth of the state during the postwar boom as marking significant progress toward socialism. The so-called 'crisis of the Left' reflects the collapse of such gradualist politics of trade-union bureaucrats and social democratic party functionairies, as much as it does the development of radical oppositional currents in allegedly socialist states.

Nevertheless, whether they identify themselves as socialists or not, many of those who would currently adhere to most of our outline of maldevelopmentalism are organized, if at all, into movements, parties and unions whose record with respect to AWL is decidedly patchy. Dismissing social experiments as middle class evasion of industrial action, they have often failed to offer any alternative vision of the future to that represented by the centralized bureaucracies of the East. This is, of course, not the only reason for their failure to gain mass support in many Western countries, and for their accommodation to the status quo in those cases when they have seemed on the verge of gaining it. But this factor cannot be ruled out, either. And in the face of the 'new' movements of women, blacks, and national minorities, there has often been little response other than to mumble the economistic catechism. It has been hard for many left-wing organizations to accept the new opportunities and challenges for theory and practice that are presented here — perhaps because these organizations, too, have developed their own internal structures of power divorced from their purported goals.

GOALS AND STRATEGIES

The three perspectives on the DWL, which we have labelled underproductionism, overdevelopmentalism, and maldevelopmentalism, have different conceptions of the goals and strategies for AWL. In addition to theoretical differences, the access one has to power and resources of given kinds will naturally affect the strategies one advocates or implements. For example, those with more intimate ties to media or policy-making institutions will tend to be more inclined towards strategies in which such institutions play prominent roles. While each of these perspectives does locate the problems of the DWL as stemming from a different set of features of modern society than do the others, the development of strategies around each will therefore also reflect the differential location of their proponents in the political and economic systems.

Some of the points of convergence and divergence between the three perspectives have been indicated above: now we shall discuss the choice of strategies rather more systematically. In order to do so, we shall first distinguish between a number of strategies, and then turn to consider how strategies may be combined in pursuit of specific goals. For a start, we can distinguish *individualist* from *structuralist* strategies. The former involve attempting to create some form of AWL in the lives of individuals or groups, while the latter, in contrast, seek to change features of society that maintain aspects of the DWL, so that particular AWL can emerge on a large scale. We can further identify two variants of these broad approaches.[9] Both individualist and structuralist strategies may be applied within the framework of the DWL and its institutions, or by stepping outside of these to some extent, and the two variants correspond to these alternatives.

Thus, within individualist approaches, *social responsibility* and *counter-culture* represent, respectively, more and less accommodating strategies. The practice of social responsibility involves the adoption of more enlightened and critical patterns of behaviour within the DWL. There is an effort to exercise discrimination in work, consumer choice, and voting, so as to discourage production or consumption that clearly involves oppression or environmental damage. Refusing to buy goods produced under apartheid or factory-farming conditions; 'whistle-blowing' to expose the dumping of toxic wastes or the secret lobbying of politicians by business or bureaucratic interests; supporting political parties which offer programmes congruent with one's critique of the DWL, and generally leading a life characterized by none of its worse excesses: these are all aspects of social responsibility. The counter-culture approach

may seem rather more drastic: the intention is to achieve as
much as possible of AWL without necessarily waiting for wider
social change. The aim is to establish new systems of production and consumption, even if the area or number of people
involved is rather limited. Working in cooperatives, setting
up free schools, producing one's own food in a self-sufficient
manner, living in communes: these are typical manifestations of
the counter-culture strategy.
     The two corresponding variants of structuralist approaches
may be labelled *reformism* and *contestation*. The reformist
strategy aims at influencing political and economic organizations to take on different priorities, so as to promote gradual
shifts in the DWL. Pressure groups seeking environmental conservation or consumer interests; campaigns and action within
major political parties for new forms of health and improved
safety conditions at work; and attempts to bring the problems
of the DWL and the possibilities of shifts toward AWL into
debates about local and national planning: such are characteristic reformist activities. Contestation, in contrast, regards
the existing distribution of power in society as itself part of
the problem, and posits major shifts here as necessary for the
flowering of AWL. Seeking to establish new political organizations whose mass support will not be confined to action within
existing political institutions; support of militant action of
oppressed groups to achieve more control over their lives; opposition to consensus strategies in industry, with attempts to
move toward workers control; contestation involves such
tactics.
     Fig. 11.4 (from Miles, 1980c) expands upon this outline of
the four different strategies by indicating some of their major
manifestations around three major areas of social life in the
West — private industry, the state, and the family. (These
three 'sectors' have been chosen for their significance in the
production of material goods and the reproduction of social
relations, but the list could have been extended to include
the cultural sphere, local community, small business sector,
etc.) We have attempted to sketch in aspects of the DWL in each
'sector' that are criticized, so as to demonstrate the range of
attempts that may be made to overcome such problems. For
reasons of space and clarity (and following the original source),
the emphasis here is largely on maldevelopmentalist views and
action.
     We see here that even people identifying problems in the DWL
in similar ways may take different routes to achieving AWL.
For example, overdevelopmentalist perspectives in the area of
food and nutrition typically focus on a number of different
strategies: social responsibility (change in one's diet, for

Figure 11.4
Strategies for Social Change

Strategy:	Social responsibility	Counter-culture	Reformist	Contestatory
Main features of Strategy	Involves the exercise of individual discrimination, consumer choice, 'whistle-blowing'. Can be costly to adopt different WOL, so most viable for those with most resources. Expose work involves dangers to career, legal position etc. Can have demonstration effect if publicized; those in influential positions may exercise more influence. Demands individual commitment, and, unless reformist-style organization established, liable to wane with individual's fortunes. But has often been successful in stopping abuses and wakening public conscience.	Involves living AWL through new institutions, through becoming part of a (hopefully vanguard) minority. Demands resources to the extent that continued viability does not rest on manifold dependency on DWL. By virtue of minority, and relatively affluent constituency, effects likely to be limited: demonstration may be effective, but innovation may be siphoned off for commercial exploitation. In more repressive climates, may be victimization. Dangers of ghettoisation, or of internal pressures due to felt need to present impossibly good public image. But important in creating exemplars illustrating feasibility, and problems, of AWL.	Involves organized activity seeking to influence dominant institutions in progressive ways, either through mobilizing public opinion. Requires channels of access to wide public (media) or to technical experts and bureaucrats. Liable to be confined within limits of reform, to be bureaucratised, incorporated, to foster illusions in evolutionary progress of DWL. But may also gain real improvements (if always open to erosion), tactical advantages and increased sense of efficiency and commitment of members.	Involves attempt to build oppositional institutions based on shift in social power. This requires mass support if not to become hopelessly purist and fanatical. Runs risk of losing internal democracy in face of isolation and repression, or physical danger through conflict with authority. Also liable to opportunist seizing of issues and fragmentations of struggles. But a vital component in moments of upsurge, offering possibilities for establishing new bases of power, for exposing structural roots of problems, etc.
Social sector — Aspects of sector criticized as exploitative, oppressive, etc.				

1. Private capital	Private ownership of means of production. Profit-guided via market allocation. Workers just one 'factor' of production. Large-scale monopoly organization of leading industries, poor conditions in backward ones.	Support small firms and shops, products designed as ecologically sound and healthy, socially responsible organizations. Join consumer associations and pressure groups. 'Do-it-yourself'.	Seek work in cooperatives, communal production, etc. Establish 'alternative' shops, consume 'alternative' products. Strive for self-sufficiency.	Seek legal controls over work conditions and product safety and environmental impact. Nationalization of vital industries and those failing to serve social needs. Education of consumers.	Organize for alternative planning of major industries based on workers' plans, seizure of control away from monopolists.
2. State sector	Large bureaucracies, restricted access to decisions, hierarchical patterns of control, operate with notions of welfare geared to requirements of sector 1 for trained, healthy but docile labour force and willing consumers.	Exercise choice to favour more responsive smaller organizations, to preserve services that are in decline.	Establish alternative or new services: set up 'free schools', 'people's clinics', 'crash pads', new information services, etc.	Attempt to integrate counter-culture alternatives into mainstream. Press for more participation of community groups in governing bodies. Seek democratic reform of state agencies.	Mobilize groups at the 'receiving end' (schoolchildren, tenants, claimants, invalids, etc.) together with more proletarianized state employees to demand new priorities, new controls.
3. Family sector	Privatized production, often tied to petit bourgeois 'community' informal economy or patriarchal family production. Restricted to 'marginal' needs, and slow to respond to changes in family structures and social relations.	Attempt to make our family relations more open, more equitable. Discuss problems widely, use counselling services, confront problems in own and others' families.	Live in new family forms: communes, etc. Encourage new forms of social encounter – personal growth movement, etc.	Press for socialized childcare, recognition of value of domestic labour. Support campaigns against parental assault on children, for shelters for runaway children and battered wives.	Support militant groups seeking to erode patriarchal system (womens' movements, men against sexism), or to gain more power for children and old people.

example) counter-cultural activity (organic farming, food
cooperatives), reformism (pressure for legislation controlling
the use of fertilizer and pesticides) or contestation (such
as working with trade unionists in trying to impose 'green
bans' on projects threatening agricultural land). A perspective on the DWL does not dictate the use of only one strategy
for AWL: the relationship between perspectives and strategies
will be affected by the ongoing political and economic
situation; and it will usually be the case that people active
around one strategy will also use others, so that combinations
of strategies are the typical approach of individuals and
groups.

Nevertheless, it is also true that each of our three perspectives tends to suggest one or another strategy as the fundamental
means of achieving change. Fig. 11.5 sets out the relationship
between perspectives and strategies, and seeks to pinpoint the
dominant strategy for each perspective in the Western world at
the current time.[10] The relationships between theory and practice, and between the resources available for change and the
choice of strategy, are, hopefully, brought out here. Different
means tend to accompany different ends. The details will differ
from country to country, but the main point is clear: not only
are there different perspectives on the DWL and visions of AWL
but there are also substantially different strategies advocated
and adopted for achieving change. How can we choose between
strategies, then?

ACHIEVING CHANGE IN WAYS OF LIFE

It is clearly not possible to endorse any one strategy as the
route to AWL. Individuals, as we have seen, differ in their
opportunities and resources and in their experience of problems
in the DWL; and they hold different views on the nature and
resolution of issues around WOL. The articulation of different
strategies, too, is contingent upon the perspective that is
brought to bear. With this in mind, can we evaluate the extent
to which underproductionism, overdevelopmentalism, and maldevelopmentalism are useful guides to effecting change? And,
in this case, can we draw any conclusions concerning what role
different strategies, followed by whom, might play?

To provide any answer to these questions requires that we
make our own sympathies explicit. Unlike many contributors to
this volume, the authors of this chapter find maldevelopmentalism to offer the most incisive and convincing account to problems in the DWL and strategies for surmounting them. This is
not to say that the other perspectives fail to make any sig-

Fig. 11.5

Three Perspectives and the Main Strategies Each Adopts for AWL in the West: An Impressionistic Picture

Perspective	Social responsibility	Counter-culture	Reformist	Contestatory
Underproduction	Adopted by individuals in positions of power to draw attention to problems in DWL, or by those with resources to stimulate change — e.g. use of shares in companies and disposal of income (e.g. to private health and education services); such action is fairly well integrated into DWL.	Not made very much use of, since little incentive to form alternative organizations because proponents regard structure of DWL as basically satisfactory.	*Dominant strategy* Adoption based on proponents' interests in economic system and political hegemony. Frequent use since the widespread recognition by elites of prolonged economic crisis.	Only adopted where power base of DWL threatened, or by extreme right-wing organizations believing danger imminent.
Overdevelopment	Adopted by many individuals making moral stand on own consumption, or in influencing their work organization away from wastage, pollution, or malpractices, etc.	*Dominant strategy* Often adopted given the privatized but fairly affluent nature of individuals involved. Centres around detachment from DWL and practicing AWL in alternative communities, businesses, etc.	Adopted when opportunities made available within DWL for questions about AWL to be raised and debated — e.g. to inject questions of ecological and community damage into political systems, through pressure groups, public hearings, parliamentary support, etc.	Adopted where immediate need to intervene in DWL apparent — e.g. in cases where large-scale **waste** or degradation threatened.
Maldevelopment	Valued only insofar as experts can 'expose' underlying causes of problems with DWL. Often an expression of personal rejection of oppression and exploitation.	Generally valued only insofar as demonstrates possibility of viable AWL, and that failure in using this strategy may recruit disillusioned individuals to contestatory strategy.	Adopted on those issues in DWL where limited gains can easily be made without fundamental changes in DWL, and public debate initiated over class basis to DWL.	*Dominant strategy* Adoption based on recognition that class basis to DWL can only be changed by radical transformation of society. Links up different struggles for AWL on class basis.

nificant points, nor that maldevelopmentalists have in the past
paid sufficient attention to the AWL problematic. In particular,
both overdevelopmentalists and maldevelopmentalists could gain
from each other's experiences, and both would benefit, furthermore, from paying more heed to the analyses developed by femin-
ists and some of the other 'new' social movements.

Maldevelopmentalism possesses the great virtue (as we see it)
of locating the problems it identifies squarely in the material
world. The problems of the DWL are seen as most markedly derived from the social relations of production of the modern
world. The historical origin and thus the impermanence of these
relations is understood in terms of the interaction of social
classes. Ideologies, world views, cosmologies, may play an
important role in this course of events, but they have to be
seen as themselves deriving from and existing in this material
world, not as descending from the astral plane or ascending
from a transcendental mind. They are ways of thought and overt
action, social practices whose own development and reproduction
take place within a context heavily conditioned by relations
of ownership and control. It is not surprising that many
leaders of business are underproductionists, given the day-to-
day decisions they have to make as part of a search for corporate profit; a search that has developed its own sciences (economics, management science) and arts (design, advertising). But
then this search derives not from the 'innate' greed or hunger
for power of individuals, nor from achievement-oriented values
that have supposedly evolved from their own accord, but from
the imperatives of survival faced by firms in a competitive
world, and from the conflict with labour that is inherent in
the social relations of capital itself.

In the West, then, we would argue that this profit-oriented
logic shapes both the ideological sphere — there is 'mass production' of ideas, news stories, and theories which define
problems in its terms — and the world of technology and economics. This has implications for AWL. Modern technology, for
example, has been given a characteristic form which fails to
represent concerns about social well-being and environmental
conditions at the points of production and consumption alike.
It cannot simply be re-used uncritically, as some maldevelopmentalists who argue the 'neutrality' of science and technology
believe (see Griffiths et al., 1979). The introduction of
Western techniques of Taylorist industrial organization into
the Soviet Union in the 1920s, for example, may have been
justified by the need to restore production in a war-torn
economy, but surely contributed to the growing stratification
of power and consolidation of elite interests (Claudin-Orondo,
1977). Western maldevelopmentalists have begun to consider the

effects of the direction of technical development on the worker
and workplace relations (in particular since Braverman's work,
1974), but some continue to neglect environmental and community
relations such as are stressed by overdevelopmentalists.
A related issue here is that while some maldevelopmentalists
assume that technology is in itself unproblematic, and all that
is needed is to take its control out of private hands, many
overdevelopmentalists take a rather romantic position with
respect to modern technology as a whole. They claim that some
threshold of productivity has been passed beyond which degener-
ation of humanity and nature (though overconsumption, laziness,
resource depletion, etc) is inevitable. But, as we see it,
technology does not exist, waiting to be discovered; it is a
social product, and one, furthermore, that has yet to be adequately applied to the realization of human needs. The assumption of a single predetermined course of technological development is a metaphysical notion. Technologies are invented by
human beings, working within social structures, and using the
results of previous work. Equally unrealistic is the view that
societies whose class relations propel them along a given
direction of technological development can simply halt this
process without challenge to those structural features. The
capitalist market economy, in particular, only halts its growth
in a period of crisis, after which, if unchecked, it resumes
its work with new vigour.

Underproductionism is in tune with efforts to resolve economic
crisis by means that, in essence, involve increased burdens on
the Western working class (and especially on its more vulnerable fractions like the old and sick, like women and minorities)
and attempts to restore Western dominance over the Third World.
Overdevelopmentalists point to the paradox of affluence creating
destructive DWL, and have helped make AWL more visible than
heretofore. But their individualistic strategies and moral
critiques neither meet the needs of dominant classes (except
insofar as they can use them to support austerity drives) nor
those of the great mass of the subordinated classes (who are
typically unable to spare their scarce resources in following
AWL). Maldevelopmentalists should have more flexibility in
terms of strategy. However, failing to always understand, or
make headway in the face of the seeming passivity of the Western
working classes, they have often fallen into the twin traps of
isolation around a puristic, apocalyptic vision of revolutionary contestation, or of reformism divorced from longer-term
visions. The challenge of drawing together different struggles
against exploitation and oppression, without imposing new hierarchies
and bureaucratic structures upon them, is a major one.

Nevertheless, this challenge must be faced. For there are many signs that the West is drifting toward a more repressive climate of social control in which attempts to establish significant AWL will be ever more marginalized. Likewise, there is a new escalation of the apparatus that threatens us with thermonuclear war. Under these circumstances, the most fundamental opposition to such tendencies, perhaps the only one which can function effectively over the long term, is the organization of the working class around democratic objectives. The labour of this class is, after all, the precondition for any WOL to develop and be sustained. The threat of labour being withdrawn can convince the dominant interests in the DWL that to allow some development of AWL, and the associated civil and political liberties, is their only option. Without the self-activity of the working class there can be no end to the exploitation on which the DWL is founded, for only that class has both the potential capacity and the potential interest required for establishing a new social order.

Of course, the working classes of the West have not yet succeeded in structurally transforming their societies; and for most of the past few decades they have in general made few attempts to do so. This in part accounts for the tendency, so common in the early 1970s, to look for new agents of change, in students and youth, community groups and environmentalists, and in the margins of Western society and its global periphery. Certainly, while the working class is a necessary agent of change, it is not necessarily the sole, nor even the sufficient, agent. Previous generations of radical activists could make confident predictions concerning the growing consciousness and exercise of power on the part of the working classes. These look rather pale in the face of Stalinism and the long drift of labour movements in the West toward containable reformist objectives. Occupational, ethnic and sexual cleavages have fragmented workers' movements, which have often restricted themselves to working within the given state system with its stultifying forms of law and lawmaking. Indeed, these movements may need to divest themselves of many of their existing organizations, whose internal structures and processes of forming leadership often function to support the DWL.

And will change be forthcoming? This is a question of practice rather than prediction. The end of the post-war boom, growing problems in the DWL, and a weakening of the hegemonic political consensus make the future very uncertain, in East and West alike. Individualistic strategies are likely to depend increasingly upon the support of parallel structuralist strategies merely to survive, while the limits of reformism probably

will become increasingly apparent with any attempt at large-
scale change in the DWL.
An overnight transformation to AWL seems beyond the bounds of
possibility, as we write at the beginning of the 1980s. Few
mass movements engage in more than a very limited range of
actions for a limited set of goals. Most of these, too, have
developed their own undemocratic internal structures which
effectively limit the self-activity and emotional life of their
members. At the very least these will have to be revitalized
to effect change; often totally new organizations must be built.
Likewise, consciousness concerning the possibility of AWL has
to be developed. The 'realism' that masks deference to the
existing social order must be replaced by a grasp of the possibilities for a new society. Here examples of AWL can be important, but also vital, again, are 'alternative' channels of
communication — mass media, political organizations — which can
relate together and diffuse information and action critical of
the DWL and constructive of AWL. To achieve such goals may
well require pressing for reforms which can both broaden
people's horizons and permit them to increase their collective
strength. Steps towards establishing AWL can be made within
the present social framework: the task of strategy is to relate
these limited advances to the pressures for structural change
that will make a wider transformation of the DWL possible.
With the growing crises of economics and militarism, with human
and environmental degradation, the issue of structural change
is placed firmly on the agenda again. Perhaps it is the only
hope for human WOL at all.

NOTES

1. A first draft of this paper was presented to a meeting of
the Alternative Ways of Life Project in Trappeto, Sicily, April
1979. We would like to thank the participants at this meeting
for useful feedback (including that provided by the children
who organized their parallel meeting), together with the numerous voluntary associations and pressure groups in Britain and
elsewhere who spared us time to discuss their work, and our
colleagues at the Science Policy Research Unit for providing a
stimulating work environment.

2. An earlier study in which three distinctive world views
were outlined in order to construct scenarios and images of the
future is reported in Freeman and Jahoda (1978). The account
presented here draws in part from these, but is more directly
indebted to Irvine (1980), on which the Figures 11.1, 11.2 and

11.3, are based, and which deals in more detail with First World-Third World links than we are able to do here.

3. While underproductionist views are found in a wide variety of sources, including many standard textbooks and newspaper articles, it may be helpful to identify a few texts that effectively crystallize particular aspects of this perspective on strategies and future developments. Studies that particularly draw on the British experience of social democracy, holding it responsible for poor economic performance and declining personal liberties, include Seldon (1978) and Tyrrel (1977). More general views of the future include Kahn and Bruce-Biggs (1972) and, for the United States in particular, Vermilyen (1979).

4. See here Miles (1980a,b), Tomlinson (1980/1981) and the August 1980 issue of *Undercurrents* (No. 41) devoted to issues around cooperatives.

5. It may be argued that the market is a perfectly adequate method of determining social needs. Against this we would point out that the market weights individual requirements in terms of individual purchasing powers — thus the needs of the poor count for less than those of the rich. Likewise, it can take little account of collective needs, and, rather than ensure economic liberty, will effectively constrain many future choices in the light of past decisions.

6. Overdevelopmentalist views were first forcefully expressed in the environmentalist movement and in the critique of economic growth: *viz.* Hodson (1972), Meadows *et al.* (1972), Miles (1976), Mishan (1978), Olson and Landsberg (1975) and Perelman (1976). More recently, the perspective has been infused by a variety of critiques of the momentum of dominant institutions in the sphere of health, education and work, with Illich's ideas (e.g. 1973) being particularly influential; cf. also Henderson (1978), Roszak (1972) and Stavrianos (1976). For a surprising assessment — especially in terms of Irvine and Miles' chapter in this book — of Britain as progressively moving *away* from overdevelopment, see Nossiter (1978).

7. For reviews of current thinking about different crisis tendencies and their interaction, see URPE Economics Education Project (1978); Mandel (1975); Wright (1978).

8. General accounts of the maldevelopmentalist perspective on the world economic situation and its likely development include, in addition to those in note 7, Frank (1981), Gamble and

Walton (1976) and Mandel (1978). For studies of technological
change and choice see Dickson (1974) and Elliot and Elliot
(1976). An interpretative account of many aspects of U.S.
society is provided by Edwards et al. (1972); Gorz (1967) was
one of the first maldevelopmentalists to relate contemporary
environmental and consumption issues to the general paradigm.
On community versus class conflict, see Cowley et al. (1977),
and on the role of the state, see CSE (1979), and London-
Edinburgh Weekend Return Group (1980).

9. Here we draw on ideas developed by Griffiths et al. (1979)
in assessing different approaches to the problems of science
and technology.

10. As noted, major changes in circumstances will provoke
major shifts in strategy. For example, underproductionists may
use contestatory strategies in the event of accession to power
of a committed socialist regime.

BIBLIOGRAPHY

Braverman, H. (1974) *Labour and Monopoly Capital*. New York,
    Monthly Review Press.
Claudin-Orondo, C. (1977) *Lenin and the Cultural Revolution*.
    Hassocks, Sussex, Harvester.
Cowley, J. et al. (Editors) (1979) *Community or Class Struggle?*
    London, Stage 1.
CSE State Expenditure Group (1979) *Struggle over the State*.
    London, CSE Books.
Dickson, D. (1974) *Alternative Technology and the Politics of
    Technical Change*. London, Fontana.
Edwards, R. C., Reich, M. and Weisskopf, T. E. (Editors) (1972)
    The Capitalist System. Englewood Cliffs, N.J., Prentice-
    Hall.
Elliot, D. and Elliot, R. (1976) *The Control of Technology*.
    London, Wykeham.
Frank, A. G. (1981) *Reflections on the World Economic Crisis*.
    New York, Monthly Review Press.
Freeman, C. and Jahoda, M. (Editors) (1978) *World Futures:
    the Great Debate*. London, Martin Robertson.
Gamble, G. and Walton, P. (1976) *Capitalism in Crisis*. London,
    Macmillan.
Gorz, A. (1967) *A Strategy for Labour*. Boston, Beacon Books.
Griffiths, D., Irvine, J. and Miles, I. (1979) Social statistics:
    political perspectives, in *Demystifying Social Statistics*
    (Edited by Irvine, J., Miles, I. and Evans, J.). London,
    Pluto Press.

Henderson, H. (1979) *Creating Alternative Futures.* Berkeley, University of California Press.
Hodson, H. V. (1977) *The Diseconomics of Growth.* London, Earth Island.
Illich, I. (1973) *Tools for Conviviality.* New York, Harper & Row.
Inglehart, R. (1977) *The Silent Revolution.* Princeton, N.J., Princeton University Press.
Irvine, J. The choice of ways of life in the North. *Development/ International Development Review* 22 (2-3), 55-66.
Kahn, H. and Bruce-Biggs, B. (1972) *Things to Come.* New York, Macmillan.
London-Edinburgh Weekend Return Group (1980) *In and Against the State.* London, Pluto.
Mandel, E. (1975) *Late Capitalism.* London, New Left Books.
Mandel, E. (1978) *The Second Slump.* London, New Left Books.
Meadows, D., Meadows, D., Randers, J. and Behrens, W. W. (1972) *The Limits to Growth.* New York, Universe Books.
Miles, I. (1980a) New Technologies, Old Orders, in *Visions of Desirable Societies - II* (Edited by Masini, E.). Oxford, Pergamon Press (forthcoming).
Miles, I. (1980b) Social choice and ways of life in industrial societies. *Development/International Development Review,* 22 (2-3), 66-71.
Miles, I. (1980c) Notes on Typologies of Alternative Ways of Life. Paper presented at Gregorzewicze SID/GPID meeting.
Miles, I. (1980d) Effacing the political future. *Futures* 12 (6), 436-52.
Miles, R. E. (1976) *Awakening from the American Dream.* New York, Universe Books.
Mishan, E. J. (1978) *The Economic Growth Debate.* London, Alan & Unwin.
Nossiter, B. (1978) *Britain: A Future that Works.* London, André Deutsch.
Olson, M. and Landsberg, M. H. (Editors) (1975) *The No-Growth Society.* London, Woburn Press.
Perelman, L. J. (1976) *The Global Mind.* New York, Mawson/ Charter.
Reich, C. (1970) *The Greening of America.* New York, Random House.
Roszak, T. (1972) *Where the Wasteland Ends.* New York, Anchor.
Seldon, A. (Editor) (1978) *The Coming Confrontation.* London, Institute of Economic Affairs.
Stavrianos, L. S. (1976) *The Promise of the Coming Dark Age.* San Francisco, W. H. Freeman.
Tyrrel, R. E. Jr. (1977) *The Future that Doesn't Work.* New York, Doubleday.

URPE Economics Education Project (1978) *U.S. Capitalism in Crisis*. New York, Union of Radical Political Economics/ Monthly Review Press.
Vermilyen, D. A. (1979) *Social Change and Future Economic Growth*. New York, General Electric Company, Technical Information series, Corporate R & D Distribution.
Tomlinson, J. (1980/1981) British politics and co-operatives. *Capital and Class*, No. 12, 58-65.
Wright, E. O. (1978) *Class, Crisis and the State*. London, New Left Books.

Appendix

Papers presented at GPID/SID Meetings on Alternative Ways of Life

The present volume draws upon only a few of the large number of papers prepared for the three GPID/SID meetings on AWL, held at Cartigny (1978), Trappeto (1979) and Gregorzewicze (1980). Considerable selection has obviously been necessary to overcome the risk of a repetitive or overlong book, and it should be stressed, therefore, that many of the papers not included contain extremely useful material on changing ways of life across a wide range of countries.

A complete list of papers presented follows. We mark those papers that have been revised for publication in this volume by one asterisk (*). A number of papers have also appeared in the 'red cover series' of working papers of the United Nations University Centre in Tokyo, Japan; these are identified by two asterisks (**) and by the publication number in that series. A few papers are identified as being present both in this book and in the 'red cover series', but casual inspection will be sufficient to reveal that revisions have been made in quite different directions. So far, few of the Gregorzewicze papers have been published, although A. Siciński and M. Wemegah are editing most of them into a volume on 'Alternative Ways of Life in Contemporary Europe'.

The address of the UNU Centre, from which working papers may be obtained, is: 29th Floor, Toho Seimei Building, 15-1, Shibuya 2-chome, Shibuya-Ku, Tokyo 150, Japan.

PAPERS PRESENTED AT CARTIGNY MEETING

1. S. Arnold and D. Goulet, 'The 'Abundant Society' Reconsidered: US Life Styles and their Alternatives'.*
2. G. Bonani, 'Alternative Ways of Life: The Italian Case'**
   (HSDRGPID-43, with 11 below).

3. P. Ester, 'Attitudes of the Dutch Population on Alternative Life Styles and Environmental Deterioration'.** (HSDRGPID-27).

4. J. Galtung and M. Wemegah, 'Overdevelopment and Alternative Ways of Life in High-Income Countries'.*

5. M. Gronemeyer with H-E. Bahr and R. Gronemeyer, 'The Prevailing Life Styles in the German Federal Republic'.

6. P. d'Iribarne, 'What Alternatives to the Dominant Way of Life in France?'** (HSDRGPID-42).

7. J. Irvine and I. Miles 'The 'British Way of Life' and Alternatives to It'.*

8. H. Kato, 'From Things to Experiences: Changing Values in Contemporary Japan'.*

9. K. Lemberg, S. Juhler, P. Løvetand, J. Falkentorp and D. Hansen, 'Dominant Ways of Life in Denmark/Alternative Ways of Life in Denmark'.* ** (HSDRGPID-29).

10. T. G. Lim, 'Alternative Ways of Life in Malaysia: What Prospects for the Masses?'** (HSDRGPID-44).

11. E. Masini and A. Coen, 'Italy: Alternative Life Styles in the Future'.** (HSDRGPID-43, with 2 above).

12. D. Poleszynski, 'Negative and Positive Sides of Norwegian Life Styles: An Empirical Assessment of Overdevelopment'.*** (HSDRGPID-26).

13. B. and J. P. Roos, 'Ways of Life in Finland: A Preliminary Investigation'.** (HSDRGPID-31).

14. R. Roy, 'India: Alternative Ways of Life: Poverty of Pollution or Bane of Affluence'.** (HSDRGPID-45).

15. L. Scheer, 'The Dominant Way of Life in Austria'.** (HSDRGPID-30, together with 28 below).

16. A. Siciński, 'Dominant and Alternative Life Styles in Poland: An Outline'.* ** (HSDRGPID-28).

17. K. Valaskakis and I. Martin, 'The Big Rock Candy Mountain: A Paradigm of the Values of the Mass-Consumption Society'.** (HSDRGPID-40).

18. M. Wemegah, 'The Dominant Way of Life in Switzerland: A
    Study of Symptoms of Overdevelopment'.*

19. H. C. Zetterberg, 'Dominant and Alternative Life Styles:
    Some Observations from the Swedish Scene'.

PAPERS PRESENTED AT TRAPPETO MEETING

20. P. Arnopoulous, 'The Conserver Society as an Alternative
    Way of Life'.

21. A. Coen, 'Historical Perspectives of Alternative Ways of
    Life'.

22. J. Galtung, 'Overdevelopment and Alternative Ways of Life'.*

23. G. Hedlund and C-R. Julander, 'Lifestyle-Environment-
    Society'.

24. P. d'Iribarne, 'A New Kind of Married Life'.

25. I. Miles and J. Irvine, 'Establishing Alternative Ways of
    Life in Britain'.*

26. D. Poleszynski, 'Overdevelopment and Alternative Ways of
    Life in Norway: Obstacles on the Road to Development'.

27. D. and J. P. Roos, 'The Upper Class Way of Life — An Alter-
    native for What?'

28. L. Scheer and F. Prager, 'Austria in the Year 1979'.**
    (HSDRGPID-30, together with 15 above).

29. A. H. S.-Van Otterloo and P. Ester, 'Some Notes on Alter-
    native Ways of Life in the Netherlands'.*

30. M. Wemegah, 'Alternative Ways of Life: A Theoretical
    Approach'.*

PAPERS PRESENTED AT GREGORZEWICZE MEETING

31. J. Bomann-Larsen and D. Poleszynski, 'On the 'Green Wave'
    in Norway'.

32. J. Galtung, 'Alternative Ways of Life: Towards a Typology'.

33. J. Galtung, 'On the Strategy of Development of Developed Countries: The Red-Green Alliance and its Problems'.

34. J. Huber, 'Help Yourself the German Way'.

35. P. d'Iribarne, 'L'Articulation entre l'Individuel et le Social dans les Progrès d'une "Société Alternative"'.

36. J. Irvine and I. Miles, 'Science, Technology and Alternative Ways of Life: Green and Red Perspectives in Britain'.

37. I. Miles, 'Notes on Typologies of Alternative Ways of Life'.*

38. C. Pfister, 'You Don't Write About Theatre — You Make It!'.

39. D. Poleszynski, 'Networking Scientists to Strengthen the AWL Movement: One Case from Norway'.

40. D. Poleszynski, 'Typologies for Alternative Ways of Life Movements'.

41. O. Soinivaarn, 'An Economic Strategy towards a Dual Economy'.

42. O. Soinivaarn, 'The Alternative Movements in Finland'.

43. M. Wemegah, 'Alternative Networks'.

44. M. Wemegah, 'AWL — Emergence of a Multi-front Strategy'.

Finally , we would like to draw attention to a number of recently-published articles by participants in the project, dealing with themes closely related to those of this book. A number are published in the *IFDA Dossier*, which may be obtained from the International Foundation for Development Alternatives, 2 Place du Marche, 1260 Nyon, Switzerland.

Galtung, J. (1979) What is a Strategy?, *IFDA Dossier*, No. 6 (Interactions), 13-22.
Galtung, J. (1980) Crisis in the West, *Development/International Development Review*, 22 (2/3), 51-55.
Goulet, D. (1979) Development as Liberation: Policy Lessons from Case Studies, *IFDA Dossier*, 3, 1-17 (Building blocks).
Huber, J. (1980) Social Ecology and Dual Economy, *IFDA Dossier*, 18, 108-113.
d'Iribarne, P. (1980) Reduire la Surconsommation, *IFDA Dossier*,

15, 22-30.
Irvine, J. (1980) The Choice of Ways of Life in the North,
  Development/International Development Review, 22, (2/3)
  67-71.
Miles, I. (1980) Social Choices and Life Styles in Industrial
  Countries, *Development/International Development Review*,
  22 (2/3), 67-71.
Miles, I. and Irvine, J. (1982) Changing Ways of Life, *Futures*,
  14, (1) 11-23.
Schiray, M. (1979) Amenagement Social du Temps, *TFDA Dossier*,
  3 (Interactions) 11-12.
Schiray, M. and Sigal, S. (1979) Demain Aujourd'hui: Experiment-
  ations Sociales et Changements de Styles de Vie, *IFDA
  Dossier*, 14, 67-78.
Wemegah, M. (1979) Une Suisse Moins Tranquille: Les Mefaits de
  l'Abondance, *Futuribles*, 26, 59-73.

Index